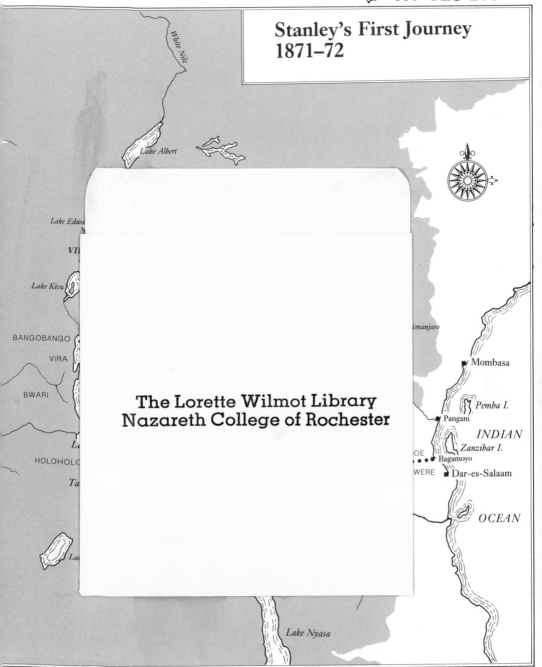

Stanley's First Journey
1871–72

White Nile

Lake Albert

Lake Edwa

VI

Lake Kivu

BANGOBANGO

VIRA

BWARI

HOLOHOLO

Ta

imanjaro

Mombasa

Pemba I.

Pangani

INDIAN

Zanzibar I.

OE

Bagamoyo

WERE — Dar-es-Salaam

OCEAN

Lake Nyasa

STANLEY

Also by Frank McLynn

Charles Edward Stuart
Invasion: from the Armada to Hitler
The Jacobites
The Jacobite army in England
France and the Jacobite rising of 1745

· STANLEY ·

*The making of an
African explorer*

Frank McLynn

Scarborough House/*Publishers*

TO JEFFREY SPAULDING

Scarborough House/*Publishers*
Chelsea, MI 48118

FIRST AMERICAN EDITION 1990

Library of Congress Cataloging-in-Publication Data

McLynn, F. J.
  Stanley, the making of an African explorer / Frank McLynn.
    p.   cm.
  Includes bibliographical references and index.
  ISBN 0-8128-4008-9
  1. Stanley, Henry M.(Henry Morton), 1841-1904. 2. Explorers—
Africa, Sub-Saharan—Biography. 3. Explorers—Great Britain—
Biography. 4. Africa, Sub-Saharan—Discovery and exploration.
I. Title.
DT351.S6M35   1990
916.704'312'092—dc20   90-42151
[B]   CIP

916.704
Sto
McC

· CONTENTS ·

· ILLUSTRATIONS ·

Henry M. Stanley aged twenty (*by permission of the Royal Geographical Society*)
Stanley relaxing near Brighton, August 1872 (*by permission of the Royal Geographical Society*)
Stanley, 1874 (*by permission of the Royal Geographical Society*)
Stanley with Kalulu (*by permission of the Royal Geographical Society*)
Stanley's party on the lower Congo, 1877 (*courtesy of the Stanley family's private collection*)
Mutesa, kabaka of Buganda (*courtesy of the Stanley family's private collection*)
Stanley entering Bagamoyo, May 1872
'Image-making' with Kalulu in London (*by permission of the Royal Geographical Society*)
James Gordon Bennett
David Livingstone, 1864
'Dr Livingstone, I presume' (*by permission of the Royal Geographical Society*)
Livingstone and Stanley going from Ujiji to Rusizi River (*by permission of the Hulton-Deutsch Collection*)
Stanley's 1874 expedition (*by permission of the Hulton-Deutsch Collection*)
Stanley and his men at Zanzibar, 1877
Through the Makata swamp (*by permission of the Hulton-Deutsch Collection*)
Mount Kiboué and the Mkondokwa Valley (*by permission of the Hulton-Deutsch Collection*)
Hauling canoes up Inkisi Falls (*by permission of the Hulton-Deutsch Collection*)
The village of Manyema (*by permission of the Hulton-Deutsch Collection*)
Stanley with admirers in Paris, 1878 (*by permission of the Royal Geographical Society*)

• PREFACE •

Sir Henry Morton Stanley, greatest of the African explorers and one of the most fascinating of the late Victorian adventurers, has never received full biographical treatment. Neither Richard Hall's *Stanley* (1974) nor Frank Hird's *H. M. Stanley. The Authorised Life* (1935), the best of the biographies so far and the only ones to make use of Stanley's private papers, contains footnotes enabling the reader to check their treatment of the sources. Nor has any but a half-hearted attempt been made to probe the enigma of Stanley's psyche. Yet Stanley is surely a key figure in any history of European penetration of Africa. His impact on indigenous societies was profound and widespread: his travels took him over virtually the whole of Central Africa, for good or ill he founded the Belgian Congo as Leopold's servant in 1879–84, and he lives on in general folk memory as the man who found Livingstone and spoke the immortal words, 'Dr Livingstone, I presume?'

This biographical gap must be my excuse for dealing at length with the explorer. The years 1841–77 saw Stanley's most colourful exploits and although history may regard the foundation of the Congo Free State as his most important monument, his greatest feats as an *explorer* had been achieved by the age of thirty-six.

My list of acknowledgements must be headed by HM the Queen, for allowing me to examine the relevant documents in the Royal Archives. Mrs Stanley showed me round the Stanley mansion at Pirbright, and very kindly put a number of illustrations and other valuable material at my disposal. I owe a special debt of gratitude to the Warden and Fellows of St Antony's College, Oxford, for electing me to the Alistair Horne Research Fellowship in 1987, thus providing me with the resources to produce a more meticulous work than I could have done otherwise. Alas, the disinterested scholarly integrity of St Antony's was not in evidence in all quarters where I pursued my researches. About ten years ago the Stanley family papers were sold to the Musee Royal de l'Afrique Centrale at Tervuren in Belgium, and the museum's administrators pursue a policy of turning away all parties interested in inspecting the original documentation. Not even the intervention of the Belgian ambassador in London had any impact on the 'closed-door' policy. So much for the international community of scholars! It was fortunate indeed that the British Library possessed an almost complete microfilm copy of the exported manuscripts.

On a personal level I would like to thank my editor at Constable, Robin Baird-Smith, and especially, my wife Pauline, who read the original script and made many helpful suggestions.

Twickenham, February 1989

1

WHEN Henry Morton Stanley landed at Dover on 1 August 1872, in triumph after his famous meeting with Livingstone on the shores of Lake Tanganyika nine months earlier, he was appalled to find that his cousin and a half-brother from Wales were there to meet him at the dockside. The two relatives were already in an advanced stage of intoxication and mortified Stanley by drawing attention to themselves and to him. Bitterly he recorded in his diary:

> What a welcome! Had these stupid newspapers not mentioned my name, the vanity of my poor relations would not have been kindled. Thus has my presentiment been realised on my first setting foot in England. They had already of course gained considerable *éclat* on the pier by their revelation of their relationship with me and a large crowd of quidnuncs, railway porters and others assembled to witness our meeting. I never felt so ashamed, and would have given all I was worth to have been back in Central Africa. What little Kalulu [Stanley's black servant] must have thought of my drunken relatives I do not know. There is no reason in the world why I should recognise them in public. They only bring to my mind too vividly my treatment, when I deserved something else than the scorn they gave me as a child, and any charity that they might have shown me then, might today have been remembered and returned with interest.[1]

Yet Stanley's negative feelings did not end with bitterness, shame and disgust towards his family. The very mention of his Welshness was anathema to him, and this was not just because he was at the time claiming to be American bred and born. When Francis Galton asked him, in front of 3,000 people at Brighton on 18 August, to confirm that he was Welsh, Stanley confided to his diary his resentment at such curiosity in a British Empire that claimed to be a product of all races:

A person like myself with such a miserable, unfortunate past cannot possibly find pleasure in speaking before people who have wined, and rather to the full, about his poverty-stricken childhood and indulge in maudlin grief over circumstances that were utterly beyond his control . . . What had I to do with my birth in Wales? It was only an accident that my mother did not prefer to stay in London when her pains informed her of the approaching event. Denbigh is only a day's journey for a pedestrian from the English border, and here these people are perpetually talking about Welshmen and Scotchmen and Irishmen as though these nationalities were foreigners to the English.[2]

Repudiation of race and family comes close to a denial of one's real identity. It is no surprise to find that 'Henry Morton Stanley' is a pseudonym. What is more surprising is the discovery that all Stanley's legendary toughness came from a single impulse: a desire for revenge on life and mankind for his unhappy childhood.[3] It was at once Stanley's strength and weakness that he surmounted early miseries that would have overwhelmed most mortals.

Our sources for Stanley's childhood are meagre. The problem for the biographer is particularly acute since the principal 'source', the *Autobiography* published by Dorothy Stanley in 1909, is largely a work of neurotic fantasy. Yet this has its compensations. While we must look elsewhere for the *facts* of Stanley's early life, the *Autobiography* is an extraordinarily rich seam to work for the inner Stanley and provides vital clues to his unconscious demons.[4] To pin down the early years we must establish a 'dialectic' between the few facts at our disposal and the claims Stanley makes in the *Autobiography*.

The man history knows as Henry Morton Stanley was born on 28 January 1841 in Denbigh, Wales and was christened on 19 February in the parish church of St Hilary's. The name given to him at baptism was John Rowlands, after his presumed father. Rowlands was an Anglicised version of the Welsh 'Rollant'.[5] For a long time this simple fact was unknown to the world. The plaque on his coffin at the memorial service in Westminster Abbey in 1904 gave 10 June 1840 as his date of birth and this was the date reproduced by the explorer Sir Harry Johnston in his panegyric.[6] Johnston felt confident of his facts, since Stanley had spoken at length, and apparently freely, of his boyhood when he met Johnston on the Congo in 1883.[7] The confusion over Stanley's exact date of birth was caused partly by Stanley's deliberate obfuscation and partly by the fact that he himself genuinely believed, until confronted with hard evidence in the 1880s, that he had been born in 1843.[8]

The baptismal register records that the infant Rowlands was born out of wedlock to a twenty-six-year-old farmer called John Rowlands and a woman named Elizabeth Parry, born 1822, and thus aged either eighteen or nineteen. Little is known of the father's family but the little that is shows Stanley in the *Autobiography* as a first-rate fantasist. Despite his statement that his father died shortly after his birth, it is now known that John Rowlands actually died in May 1854, aged thirty-nine, of alcoholism. His life appears to have been an utter failure and he possessed none of the energies that had made *his* father a successful farmer. Stanley's paternal grandfather, another John Rowlands, died at seventy-four in 1856.[9]

Since the bibulous John Rowlands has always seemed an unlikely father for the future great explorer, a local legend soon grew up that Rowlands had merely agreed to claim paternity to mask the true father, allegedly one James Vaughan Horne, solicitor, town clerk and Denbigh's deputy recorder. There is considerable irony here, for Horne's own marriage was childless and he died at forty-six from alcohol-related causes (dropsy and liver failure).[10]

We are on more solid ground in more senses than one with Stanley's mother. Stanley's maternal grandmother was the daughter of Andrew Roberts, who died in 1822 aged seventy-four. Roberts had five children: two sons and three daughters. One of his daughters, Mary, stayed on in North Wales to marry a Mr Davies when the Roberts family 'emigrated' to South Wales. When Davies died, she married Moses Parry, then a prosperous butcher and grazier. With her Moses Parry had two sons (Moses junior and Thomas) and three daughters (Mary, Maria and Elizabeth). Elizabeth Parry was the mother of the man who would become H. M. Stanley.[11]

By 1841, Moses Parry was in his late seventies and his family was dispersed. His wife was dead; Maria had married a man named Morris in Liverpool, Mary was already Mrs Owen. Moses junior remains a shadowy figure but it is clear that he was making some success in the paternal trade of butchery. Thomas had become the landlord of the Golden Lion inn. Elizabeth appears to have worked both in domestic service and in a bakery. But by the time of Stanley's birth Moses Parry himself had fallen on hard times. It was his proud boast that in his time he had provided dinners for a household of forty people, including servants and labourers. Whatever the truth of that, by January 1841 he was living in a small cottage in the grounds of Denbigh Castle. It was there that Elizabeth Parry came for her confinement, post-haste from London, as Stanley records.[12]

Stanley was Elizabeth Parry's first child. She was to have four more children, all out of wedlock, two of them with a man she later married.[13] This was exceptional even by the fairly relaxed standards of 1840s Wales and argues either for high libido or a degree of promiscuity bordering on amateur prostitution. There can be little doubt that this aspect of his mother compounded Stanley's shame at his illegitimacy and led to his later notorious difficulty in coming to terms with sexuality. His own portrait of his mother is far from flattering: 'a tall woman with an oval face and a great coil of dark hair'.[14]

Immediately after Stanley's birth Elizabeth Parry departed for London and domestic service. Pregnant again in 1842, she returned to Wales to give birth to her daughter Emma. The young John Rowlands was left largely in his grandfather's care. They lived in the upstairs part of the primitive cottage on the green of Denbigh Castle; Parry's two sons lived below. Most of Stanley's early bonding was with the elderly male. There is no reason to doubt this part of Stanley's reminiscences: 'My grandfather appears to me as a stout old gentleman, clad in corduroy breeches, dark stockings and long Melton coat, with a clean-shaven face, rather round and lit up by humorous grey eyes.'[15] Without question the child was a great favourite with the old man. Prophetically Moses Parry dubbed him 'Fy Nhyn dy Fodol I' – 'my man of the future'.[16]

When he was four, Stanley began to attend school in the crypt of St Hilary's Church where he had been christened. But already the clouds were beginning to gather around him. Moses junior took a wife called Kitty, 'a flaxen-haired fair girl of uncertain temper'. Kitty made it clear that she had her eye on the upper apartments and could not wait for Moses senior to die. She began by forbidding the old man and the child to wander at will in the lower part of the cottage; they were only to descend on express invitation.[17] Her opportunity to evict the unwanted tenants came when grandfather Moses dropped dead one day in June 1846 while working in the fields. At once she persuaded the boy's two uncles (her own husband Moses and Thomas the publican) to board him out. For the rest of 1846 Stanley was placed in the care of Richard and Jenny Price of Bowling Green Cottage near Denbigh Castle. Richard Price combined the offices of sexton, verger and gamekeeper. The Prices were paid 2/6 (12½p) a week for his board and lodging.[18]

What Stanley remembered most about his time with the Prices was the dreadful bespectacled harridan who ruled the village infant school with a birch rod, the somnolent Sundays at the local Wesleyan chapel and the abnormal religiosity and superstition of Mrs Price.[19] A particular trial was the Prices' daughter, Sarah, who inculcated her own morbid fear of demons and ghosts into her young charge.[20] Fortunately or unfortunately, Stanley's osmosis with the supernatural was cut brutally short. The Price interlude came to an end in February 1847, but not before the Prices had dealt him a psychic blow greater than any fear of spectres or phantoms. By this time Moses Parry's other son, Thomas, had married. His new wife was of her sister-in-law Kitty's opinion that 2/6 a week paid for the upkeep of this unwanted bastard was money ill spent. It was decided to consign the young John Rowlands to the workhouse.[21]

As is often the case with people who cannot bear the unpleasant reality of what they are doing, the Prices dealt with the matter in an oblique and underhand way. They did not inform Stanley of his changed situation. Instead, they told him he was going to live with his Aunt Mary (Mrs Owen) at her farm at Ffynnon Beuno. Richard Price, their son, took the boy on his shoulders and told him they were going to walk all the way. When the boy began to protest at the length of the journey, Richard used honeyed cajolery on him. After a long trek his treacherous guide set him down at an immense stone building. They passed through a set of iron gates. Richard pulled at a bell which the boy heard clanking noisily inside. When a hatchet-faced beadle appeared and pulled Stanley roughly inside, Richard turned the knife in the wound by telling the boy his aunt would be with him in a minute. The door clanged shut. Within minutes Stanley realised he was in the St Asaph Union Workhouse. In a paroxysm of tears he finally appreciated the depth of the deception. As he later remarked bitterly: 'It would have been better for me if Dick, being stronger than I, had employed compulsion, instead of shattering my confidence and planting the first seeds of distrust in a child's heart.'[22]

It is difficult to overplay the role of this 'betrayal' in Stanley's psychic development. Saturday, 20 February 1847 remained a black day etched on his memory for ever.[23] The generalised misanthropism and particular suspicion of all strangers has its origin in this shoddy episode of moral cowardice by the Prices and Parrys. To the end of his life this wound rankled. The poison was hot enough twenty-two years later for Stanley to record this impression in the 'autobiography' he wrote to his putative fiancée Katie Gough-Roberts:

This waif now became a burden, an annual expense (the amount of which is just one-tenth of the sum I yearly expend in choice

Havannahs); the waif must be got rid of, but how? What a pity he did not die! Were murder a crime unpunished the waif would have been summarily disposed of . . . the moment the child Rowland (for so he was named) entered the workhouse he was estranged from the rest of the world; Cain's hellish mark was stamped on his forehead; a portion of Adam's sin and shame clung to him. For nine years the waif lived within the workhouse, uncared for by all relations, by all humanity, but cared for by providence and benign law. While in the workhouse the child Rowland was beaten, kicked, cuffed, sneered, jeered at and handcuffed as a workhouse brat – an illegitimate child. At an early age he became imbued with man's feelings.[24]

There can be no doubting the trauma of entry into the workhouse. But was life there quite the living hell Stanley depicts in the *Autobiography*? There are grounds for thinking that Stanley, ever the obfuscator, shifted the focus from the ways in which the workhouse *was* a nightmare – ways not easily absorbed by his prospective Edwardian audience – to the areas where it was not. The real indictment of the workhouse system was that it was a breeding ground of promiscuity, vice and perversion, as the Commissioners of Enquiry into the State of Education in Wales pointed out. St Asaph's workhouse had been visited by the Commissioners a few weeks before Stanley had been deposited on its doorstep. They found it a nursery of female prostitution and male obscenity.[25] Among the workhouse 'clientele' were prostitutes giving birth or recovering from venereal disease, young girls learning the tricks of the trade from their elder sisters, sodomites and other perverts. The children slept two to a bed, invariably an older with the younger, so that the already depraved corrupted the young. Because of their proximity to the adults, children saw them copulating and picked up their bawdy *patois*. The walls were paper-thin, so that a formal separation of adults from children achieved little. We may therefore conjecture that Stanley was at the very least sexually assaulted and manhandled even if he was probably not (for reasons that will later appear) the victim of actual homosexual rape.

A recital of all the evils of the workhouse would have been meat too strong for his Edwardian readers. Stanley in his *Autobiography* therefore concentrates on the kind of brutality they could accept: floggings and beatings of the 'character-forming' public-school type.[26] In this recital the brutal 'heavy' is the workhouse teacher James Francis. Whether the few facts known about Francis altogether square with Stanley's portrait of him is, however, another matter.

18

If we for a moment place a bracket around the sexual area where the workhouse truly was an evil place, then it seems that Stanley's objective experience in the workhouse was not quite so black for him personally as he paints it. This is of course to say nothing of the way in which such a place would have been *perceived* by a boy of Stanley's sensitivity. Nor is it to suggest that St Asaph's was in any way a bed of roses. The monotonous diet of bread, potatoes, gruel and porridge (with meat just once a week), the shaven heads and 'hodden grey' of the boys and the striped cotton dresses of the girls, the fixed routine of bed at eight and reveille at six, everlasting unctuous Sunday sermons: all this was real enough. The crucial question was whether Francis was the sadistic monster Stanley portrays.

All the collateral evidence, and even some circumstantial pointers from Stanley himself, show that young John Rowlands very soon established himself as one of Francis's favourites. Francis soon discovered that the boy was good at arithmetic and geography, had a natural flair for music and a pronounced talent for drawing. It was related of young Rowlands that he loved wandering over a map of the world with a pointer and had the latitude and longitude of all principal cities in the world off pat. His excellent penmanship was early recognised. He was often selected by the porter to enter names in the visitors' book and to help the clerk's office with accounts.[27] Thomas Mumford, a fellow inmate at St Asaph's and later a mechanic, remembered that when Stanley became head boy in the school, Francis would put him in charge of discipline during his absence; Stanley was quite equal to the task and would thrash enthusiastically any pupil who stepped out of line. Moreover, the wife of John Jones, the local painter, testified to Francis's special partiality for Stanley. Mrs Jones kept a cake shop in St Asaph in the 1840s. Whenever Francis received a shilling to spend on the workhouse boys, he used to visit her shop and bring young Rowlands (Stanley) with him to help carry the cakes back. Again and again he used to remark to Mrs Jones that he was sure the boy would be a great man some day.[28]

Francis was at pains to promote Stanley's career at all points. It is likely that he condoned the boy's occasional truancies, as when the restless youngster stole away to his uncle Moses' house in Vale St Denbigh, only to be returned on the coach the next day.[29] It has even been suggested that Francis might have encouraged Stanley to get out of the workhouse at the earliest possible moment and hinted at the career of schoolteacher instead of the likely manual work that loomed.[30] One mark of Francis's efforts was the presentation to the boy of a Bible for 'diligent application to his studies and for general good conduct' made by Dr Vowler Short, Bishop of St Asaph's on 5 January 1855. The story goes that the Bishop was much taken with young Rowlands' quick-wittedness and asked him what he wanted to be when he grew up. 'A bishop, sir,' Stanley is said to have replied.[31]

Another hint that Francis was not the brute Stanley chooses to portray in the famous purple passages of the *Autobiography* was the fact, as Stanley himself concedes, that the schoolmaster tried to bring the boy and his mother closer together. For by 1851 Elizabeth Parry and her two illegitimate children Robert and Emma were themselves committed to the care of the St Asaph Board of Guardians.[32] Elizabeth Parry and Robert were very soon discharged, but Emma stayed on until 1857 when she left to enter domestic service. In the brief time Stanley's mother was in the workhouse, Francis tried in vain to get her to evince some maternal feelings towards her first-born. First he pointed her out to Stanley who, hardly surprisingly, did not know her. 'What, do you not know your own mother?' Francis exclaimed. The sequel is described with great bitterness by Stanley:

> I started with a burning face and directed a shy glance at her and perceived she was regarding me with a look of cool, critical scrutiny. I had expected to feel a gush of tenderness towards her, but her expression was so chilling that the valves of my heart closed as with a snap. 'Honour thy father and mother' had been repeated by me a thousand times, but this loveless parent required no honour from me.[33]

All the evidence, then, shows Francis to have had Stanley's interests at heart. We need not conclude that the schoolmaster *never* beat the boy. Although the incident described in the *Autobiography* when Stanley was soundly whipped for pronouncing 'Joseph' as 'Jophes' has an apocryphal ring about it, there is good reason to think that the beating the boy received for illicitly feasting on blackberries is an authentic occurrence.[34] Stanley speaks of 'a punishment so dreadful that black-berries suggested birching ever afterwards.' This is borne out in his later private diaries. During the Emin Pasha expedition in 1889 he records the following: 'Along yesterday's route ... we found several masses of blackberry bushes, and the luscious fruit recalled to my memory many an incident, some pleasant, others decidedly unpleasant, connected with blackberry picking.'[35]

What do we know of Francis? He was a former collier from Mold who had lost his left hand in a pit accident and then been appointed school-master at the workhouse. Schoolmasters in the 1840s were not required to have high academic attainments. When Stanley arrived at St Asaph's, Francis, then aged thirty-two, had been teaching for seven years. In 1863, i.e. seven years after Stanley left the workhouse, Francis was committed to the Denbigh Lunatic Asylum (North Wales Hospital for Nervous Dis-eases), where he died in January 1866. Francis's main qualification as schoolmaster was that he knew more English than other eligible can-didates, even though the investigating Commissioners spoke of his 'very broken English'. Nevertheless, they praised his general pedagogic abilities; in 1856 he was granted an efficiency award and a wage increase. Local folklore also insists that when Stanley left St Asaph's in May 1856 Francis gave him a sixpenny piece as a parting gift.[36]

This background knowledge is essential when we come to consider the most famous story about Stanley's childhood, the great purple passage of the *Autobiography*. According to this, in May 1856 Francis flew into a tempestuous rage because a deal table had been marked and no one would own up to the damage. He decided to birch the entire class, including Rowlands, the head boy.

The beatings commenced, 'How is this?' he shouted furiously as he came to Stanley. 'Not ready yet? Strip, sir, this minute. I mean to stop this abominable barefaced lying.'

'I did not lie, sir. I know nothing of it.'

'Silence, sir. Down with your clothes.'

'Never again,' shouted Stanley. What follows is his own verbatim account.

The words had scarcely escaped me ere I found myself swung upward into the air by the collar of my jacket, and flung into a nerveless heap on the bench. Then the passionate brute pummelled me in the stomach until I fell backward, gasping for breath. Again I was lifted, and dashed on the bench with a shock that almost broke my spine. What little sense was left in me after these repeated shocks made me aware that I was smitten on the cheeks, right and left, and that soon nothing would be left of me but a mass of shattered nerves and bruised muscles.

Recovering my breath, finally, from the pounding in the stomach, I aimed a vigorous kick at the cruel Master as he stooped to me, and, by chance, the booted foot smashed his glasses, and almost blinded him with their splinters. Starting backward with the excruciating pain, he contrived to stumble over a bench, and the back of his head struck the stone floor; but, as he was in the act of falling, I had bounded to my feet, and possessed myself of his blackthorn. Armed with this, I rushed at the prostrate form and struck him at random over his body, until I was called to a sense of what I was doing by the stirless way he received the thrashing.[37]

The sequel, according to Stanley, was that he fled the workhouse with his 'friend Mose' in terror at the likely repercussions of what he had done. Despite its palpable similarity to Nicholas's famous thrashing of Wackford Squeers in Chapter 13 of *Nicholas Nickleby*, this tall story was, until very recently, accepted as the literal truth concerning Stanley's departure from St Asaph's in 1856.[38]

It is of course an elaborate fantasy, as we can establish from independent evidence. Before 1851 no list of inmates at St Asaph's had been made out, merely lists of admissions and discharges. But from 1851 to 1856 detailed records were kept on the inmates and the name 'John Rowlands' occurs eight times. The last entry is dated 13 May 1856 and records against Rowlands' name 'gone to his uncle at the National School, Holywell'.[39] Had Stanley in fact absconded following a fracas with Francis, this would have been recorded. Moreover, the 'Willie Roberts' whom Stanley earlier accuses Francis of having beaten to death seems to be a figment; there is no sign of any such person in the workhouse records.[40]

A close chronological examination of Stanley shows how he eventually worked up this fantasy, which did not make its appearance until all principal eyewitnesses were dead. In conversations with his servant William Hoffman in the late 1880s, Stanley produced a story of a struggle with Francis in which the schoolmaster had slipped and struck his head against a table.[41] The full-blooded thrashing has not yet made its appearance. It is also possible to appreciate the elements Stanley used in the concoction of this fantasy. His 'friend Mose' (Moses Roberts) was a real person who genuinely did run away from the workhouse, as the St Asaph's records show. But this event occurred on 24 July 1855, almost a year before the fictitious Stanley 'breakout'. Roberts had 'run away' entered against his name on the ledger – a very clear contrast with the entry against 'John Rowlands'. Knowing this enables us to discount the reality of the subsequent wanderings of the pair as recounted in the *Autobiography*, the visit to Moses Roberts' mother and young Stanley's application for help to his paternal grandfather John Rowlands.[42]

The question then arises: why did Stanley find it necessary to make up such a story? In part it was the kind of tale beloved by Victorian audiences, in which innocence triumphs over evil. With his shrewd journalistic instinct Stanley would have realised that such a story was 'good copy'. In part it was an obvious fantasy of the powerless, transmogrifying impotence into control. But there are grounds for believing that the story was also a necessary outlet for the intense guilt and ambivalence Stanley entertained towards his grandfather Moses Parry. From Moses Parry and James Francis Stanley had received almost his only experience of kindness and compassion. Now Moses Parry was a one-armed man and Francis was similarly maimed, having lost his left hand. The loss of his grandfather in 1846 was for Stanley the 'end of Eden', marking a brutal transition to the reality principle. Yet the circumstances of Parry's death, *as perceived by the young Stanley*, were peculiarly calculated to instil a sense of guilt. Stanley describes them as follows:

> There came an afternoon when, to my dismay and fright, a pitcher with which I was sent for water fell from my hands and was broken. My grandfather came to the garden door on hearing the crash, and, viewing what had happened, lifted his forefinger menacingly and said, 'Very well, Shonin, my lad, when I return, thou shalt have a sound whipping. You naughty boy!'[43]

That very afternoon Moses Parry dropped dead in the fields. It is entirely plausible that the boy would have felt that he was in some sense the cause of his grandfather's death. In fact, unconsciously Stanley reveals his unease by the odd verbal usage he employs. Instead of saying that he dropped the pitcher, he says it 'fell from my hands' – a clear attempt to exculpate himself from the accident.[44]

The sober truth, then, is that Stanley left the workhouse at the age of fifteen when he had come to the end of his natural term at St Asaph's. The discharge record is in error on only one point: the school at Brynford, half an hour's walk from Holywell, was run by his *cousin* Moses Owen. Elizabeth Parry's elder sister Mary was now widowed, having produced four sons. The eldest, Edward, was a railway official at Morley; the second son, Moses Owen, twenty-three, was the schoolmaster at the National School at Brynford. John, eighteen, was on the point of taking up a post as a railway clerk. David Owen, thirteen, helped his mother on the farm. Stanley's aunt Mary combined small-scale farming with shopkeeping in the farmhouse called Ffynnon Beuno (St Beuno's Spring or Well) on the hill beyond Brynford hamlet.

Stanley's arrival at Brynford was not welcomed by his aunt Mary. Moses Owen had agreed to take the young Rowlands on as a pupil-teacher after an interview showed him to be a lad of exceptional intellectual promise. But his mother thought his decision unwise. In her opinion, Stanley's pedagogic apprenticeship would tie Moses down financially so that he would be unable to marry. The agreement was that Stanley would work for a month on Aunt Mary's farm until he had earned enough to equip himself with suitable clothes for schoolmastering. When the boy arrived at Ffynnon Beuno, his aunt received him coldly. Apart from thinking her son's action rash, Mary regarded her sister Elizabeth as the 'bad seed' of the family. She frowned on her numerous peccadilloes and regarded Stanley as the fruit of sinfulness. Mary's disapproval of her sister was especially acute at this moment. In the very month of Stanley's discharge from St Asaph's (May 1856) Elizabeth Parry gave birth to James, her fourth illegitimate child.[45] Aunt Mary thought Elizabeth a dreadful example. She was a dedicated penny-pincher, obsessed with the idea that any departure from frugality would lead her to the workhouse like her younger sister.

With such views, not surprisingly she treated Stanley with glacial reserve. She displayed open favouritism to her own children. Her obsessive financial economies usually had Stanley as their overt target. In one area alone she was prodigal: the food she set before the household was always plentiful and of superior quality. Yet the sensitive boy yearned to break through the reserve and acquire the maternal love his own mother had denied him. When he failed to move Aunt Mary, Stanley came to think that he had merely exchanged one form of misery for another:

> A young boy cannot be expected to penetrate into the secret motives of his elders, but though his understanding may be dull, the constant iteration of hints will not fail in the end to sharpen his intelligence. Thus it was that I came to perceive that my condition had not been bettered much by my abrupt exit from St Asaph. If in one I had suffered physical slavery, I was now about to suffer moral slavery.[46]

After a month of mowing, ploughing, milking and churning Stanley had earned enough to buy his school clothes. He proceeded to Moses Owen's school, where he was to be monitor of the second class. From 8 a.m. to 4 p.m. Stanley instructed the boys in the subjects where he was their superior: English, history and geography. From 4 p.m. to supper-time he learned geometry, algebra and Latin, subjects in which the other boys had an edge, partly from Moses but mainly from his cousin's extensive library. A frugal supper of porridge and milk brought the day to an end. Then Stanley would read in bed. Since Moses questioned him about his studies during meals, Stanley estimated that he spent eighteen hours out of every twenty-four in the world of learning. A particular literary favourite at this time was Johnson's *Rasselas*.[47] From this experience grew not just a love of books but a realisation that with books he could hold the harsh realities of the world at bay.

After a few months Stanley had easily established himself as the academic superior of the head boys. But his passage was not an easy one: on the one hand he was unpopular with his peers; on the other, he was beginning to arouse Moses Owen's envy and resentment. The boys sensed Stanley's intellectual distinction and his general difference and hated him for it. They were irreligious, loutish, bawdy, much given to crudity and obscene language.[48] Worst of all, they had discovered the secret of Stanley's illegitimacy and used the knowledge to silence any remonstration on his part:

> They all appeared to have become acquainted with my antecedents and their general behaviour towards me was not dissimilar to that which the unconvicted show towards 'ticket-of-leave'. The gentlest retort was followed by expressions which reminded me of my ignoble origin. Often they did not wait to be provoked, but indulged their natural malice as from divine privilege. The effect of this was to drive me within my own shell, and to impress the lesson on me that I was forever banned by having been an inmate of the Workhouse.[49]

On the other hand, once Moses Owen saw that his protégé might soon outstrip his own intellectual attainments, he began to undermine the boy's confidence by exaggerating his shortcomings and playing down his achievements. Aunt Mary, sensing that her son was beginning to turn against the unwelcome cuckoo in her nest, heaped coals on the fire. She continued to sap Moses' confidence in his own judgement. She was a much stronger person than her son and her campaign began to pay off. Yet instead of admitting that he had been wrong in his original decision to take on the financial burden of the young Stanley, Owen pretended that he had been right but that it was Stanley's subsequent performance at the school which was disappointing. The insincerity and bad faith involved in this increased Stanley's sense of the duplicity and treachery of the adult world, a sense first inculcated by the Prices' 'betrayal'.

After a nine-month 'cold war' in which Owen unceasingly sniped at Stanley's abilities, it was agreed that the boy should abandon his pedagogic apprenticeship and return to Ffynnon Beuno to work on Aunt Mary's farm. We know that the final breach was sudden: local folklore maintained that it came about when Owen peremptorily demanded that his pupil-teacher clean his (Owen's) boots and Stanley refused.[50] But even at Ffynnon Beuno he continued to be a thorn in the family's side. Stanley got on well with the village locals and began to emerge tentatively from his shell. This irritated the members of the Owen household, even their maid Jane, and they at once proceeded to put the boy in his place:

> My aunt was nothing loth to subdue any ebullience of spirit with the mention of the fact that I was only a temporary visitor, and my cousin David was quick, as boys generally are, to point out how ill it became me to forget it, while Jane used it as an effective weapon to crush any symptom of manliness.[51]

For more than a year Stanley endured this second-class status. His tasks at Ffynnon Beuno now centred on shepherding the flocks and serving behind the bar of the primitive inn his aunt kept in addition to her shop. Saturday night was a rowdy, carousing night, but even the most hardened drinker quailed at the thought of a tongue-lashing from the village termagant. When the cacophony in the bar became too great, the dark-eyed virago would appear from the back parlour and silence the revellers with an imperious glance. As he marked time, Stanley withdrew more and more to an inner life. He liked to walk in secluded spots where he could be alone with his thoughts. A favourite eyrie was the summit of the Craig, commanding a view over the Vale of Clywd.[52]

Behind the scenes Aunt Mary manoeuvred to rid herself of the incubus on her family. A visit from her sister Maria, married to Thomas Morris in Liverpool, seemed to hold out a solution. The Morrises had a contact – or thought they had – in a Liverpool insurance office. It was decided that they would place young Stanley in a clerkship there. Once again there was a delay while the boy worked on the farm to earn suitable clothes for the interview. When no word came from Liverpool, Stanley wrote a desperate appeal to his uncle to save him from the anathema into which he had been cast by Aunt Mary's dislike. This is the only surviving letter in which Stanley signs himself 'John Rowlands'. The letter reveals that Mary Owen had accused Stanley of having botched his chances for employment in Liverpool by alienating his uncle Tom Morris:

Dear Uncle, I sincerely hope I have not displeased you in anything, as my Aunt thinks I have done . . . They have not succeeded in finding me a situation at Mold Railway Station as the master was a very bad scholar and his health was very imperfect, and he was very unlikely to stay there long. Hoping sincerely you will return me an answer by return of post. I shall feel extremely obliged to you, so I remain,

Your very Humble nephew,
John Rowlands.[53]

The simultaneous reference to railways and schools is at once mysterious and interesting, as combining the two occupational ambits of the Owen family. Perhaps here we see some influence of John Owen, the only member of the family for whom Stanley had any time and whom he visited in Shrewsbury in late 1866.[54]

Confirmation of the Morrises' willingness to take Stanley into their home soon followed. In August 1858 the seventeen-year-old journeyed to the Mersey from Mostyn Docks on a packet-steamer. Stanley records vividly the culture shock experienced by one who had never seen any town larger than Denbigh, and who was used to green, open spaces, when he confronted the noise and bustle and sheer size of Liverpool. Most of all it was the din and racket of city life that appalled him.[55] He made his way to the Morrises' house at 22 Sheriff Street.[56]

Stanley took to his uncle Tom; 'corpulent, rubicund, genial . . . he had the heartiness and rollicking of the traditional "sea-dog"'[57] Tom began by getting his twelve-year-old son Teddy to familiarise Stanley with the city. Then came the day when Mr Morris had to make good his boast by securing the youth the longed-for insurance clerkship. Unfortunately this venture ended in disaster. When Uncle Tom's 'friend' Mr Winter put them off with a vague promise yet again, after twenty-one visits to his office, Morris exploded in anger, calling Winter a humbug and hypocrite.[58]

Stanley was jobless and prospectless. When his interview suit and, shortly afterwards, his overcoat were taken to the pawnbrokers he got a very clear light on the finances of the Morris household. He began to tramp the streets of Liverpool, looking for work. He found a position in a haberdasher's in London Road at a wage of 5 shillings a week. He worked from 7 a.m. to 9 p.m. at shop-sweeping, lamp-trimming and window-polishing. But after two months of this, he fell ill. After a week he returned to work, only to find that he had been dismissed in his absence and his place taken by a more robust youth. It was back to tramping the streets, all the way from Everton to the Docks.[59] At Bramley Moore Dock he was taken on as a butcher's boy, with the task of delivering fresh meat to the ships berthed on the Mersey. He lasted just a fortnight at this, but learned enough to realise that it was possible to ship out for exotic parts as a cabin-boy. Meanwhile he was being overwhelmed by the hostility of the butcher's foreman by day and the spite of young Teddy Morris by night. The situation in the Morris household seemed to be the Owen scenario all over again:

> Here also, as at Ffynnon Beuno, there was a wide distinction between children who had parents and those who were orphaned. For if ever a discussion rose between my cousin and myself, my uncle and aunt were invariably partial to their own, when called to arbitrate between us.[60]

Faced with these twin evils. Stanley took the opportunity when delivering meat to the packet-ship *Windermere*, whose captain was David Hardinge, to propose himself as cabin-boy for a voyage to New Orleans. He was signed on at a wage of $5 a month. The resistance to his departure at Sheriff Street was token only. On 20 December 1858, a month before his eighteenth birthday, Stanley watched as the *Windermere* was warped out of dock, then towed to mid-river by a tug. The sailors hoisted topsails and by nightfall they were on the open sea, America-bound.

What kind of general assessment can we make of the young Stanley as he departs for the USA aged seventeen? He was a youth obsessed with the different ways in which the world deemed him inadequate, fearfully ashamed of his own illegitimacy, his mother and much of the rest of his extended family, paranoid about divers aspects of his 'betrayal', with a partial, Old Testament, view of Christianity, and a pronounced tendency to seek refuge from his ills in fantasy.

There can be no doubting the agony suffered by Stanley when he contemplated his 'low birth', illegitimacy and poverty. In the brief private journal he composed later to cover the first twenty-five years of his life, he was unable to write about his childhood experiences in English, but employed Swahili so as to distance the events from himself.[61] Quite apart from his illegitimacy, Stanley had no proper experience of parenting. As he ruefully admits: 'I must have been twelve ere I knew that a mother was indispensable to every child.'[62] His mother was cold and detached even when near him in the workhouse. Nor did his experiences with the Owens and Morrises provide him with a surrogate mother, for both Aunt Mary Owen and Aunt Maria Morris seem to have been as cold in their own way as Elizabeth Parry. Stanley was driven to use his imagination to reconstruct the likely affection existing between a mother and son, as in the fictitious embrace between Moses Roberts and his mother after the St Asaph 'breakout'.[63]

The profound horrified recoil from his natural parents can be observed in a number of ways. Whichever man, John Rowlands or James Vaughan Horne, was Stanley's true father, it is significant that both were alcoholics and that Stanley remained abstemious and near-teetotal all his life. Likewise, the promiscuous sexuality of his mother contrasts with Stanley's own neuter-like abstinence from normal manifestations of erotic feeling. A certain misogynistic strain in contemporary Welsh culture did not help matters.[64] We have already noticed, too, Stanley's desire to 'destroy' any actual person who might stand in a paternal relationship with him: John Rowlands, Moses Parry, James Francis. All this makes Stanley a prime candidate for the 'Family Romance' syndrome – the neurotic fantasy that one's parents are an unknown, lost couple, usually kings and queens or other celebrities, quite different from the people purporting to be one's parents.[65]

We have already seen that unconscious guilt figures largely in Stanley's psychological profile: guilt about Moses Parry and a profound shame about his mother's sexual promiscuity and his own sexual experiences in the workhouse. This feeling is likely to have been reinforced by the peculiar brand of Christianity the boy absorbed; Stanley himself explicitly links the notion of guilt with his early religious socialisation.[66] The cloying religiosity of the close world of the workhouse made it peculiarly difficult to test the reality of a stark world of Heaven and Hell against the 'normal' world. What impressed itself on Stanley's mind was the Calvinistic sense of doom. Stanley throughout his life paid lip-service to the New Testament providential God.[67] But his true deity was never Jesus Christ and the law of love; it was the wrathful smiting Yahweh of the Old Testament. Stanley always retained a powerful sense of Evil; what was hard for him was to see the operation of Good.

Stanley records that he had the most vivid nightmares involving ghosts and demons until he left St Asaph's at the age of fifteen.[68] This was partly the damage done by the hyper-superstitious Sarah Price. It was also partly the fire-and-brimstone narrow Calvinism of workhouse dogma. One of the impulses drawing Stanley in later life to the conquest of the Dark Continent may well have been a desire to transcend the darkness within and to exorcise the (literal) demons whose images had been inculcated in childhood.

All of this psychic damage was bad enough. In addition, Stanley had to deal with feelings of inadequacy about his own physical appearance. The young Stanley was short-legged and short of stature and had a tendency to run to fat. During his time at St Asaph's he had to endure a deal of chaffing about this from adults. One suggested he should be put under a garden-roller; another stated that he would be in prime condition for eating after a month's stuffing on raisins.[69] The young Stanley was not to know that the short-legged man is, in folklore, like Odysseus, traditionally gifted with cunning in recompense. It merely increased his sense of humiliation and his conviction that only power could change his destiny. The brutality later evident in Stanley's behaviour has *one* of its roots in the pain he experienced as a man of less than average height. But he is not alone in this. Similar over-compensation by small men has produced some of the worst authoritarian excesses in the history of the world: Caesar, Napoleon, Hitler, Stalin, Mussolini and Franco are well-known examples.[70]

The result of all this was to produce a wounded, paranoid, hyper-suspicious personality, obsessed with notions of betrayal and with a tendency to self-pity. A contemporary description neatly encapsulates the physical and psychical aspects: 'full-faced, stubborn, self-willed, round-headed, uncompromising, deep . . . in conversation with you, his large, dark eyes would roll away from you as if he was really in deep meditation about half a dozen things besides the subject of conversation . . . his temperament was unusually sensitive; he could stand no chaff, nor the least bit of humour.'[71]

The self-pity and acute sense of having been betrayed at every turn could be exhaustively documented. Two citations from the *Autobiography* will suffice: 'Those to whom in my trustful age I ventured to consign the secret hopes and interests of my heart, invariably betrayed me.' And again: 'I regarded myself as the most miserable being in existence, deprived of even a right to love the land that I was born in. I said to myself: "I have done no harm to any living soul, yet if I but get attached to a field, all conspire to tear me away from it, and send me wandering like a vagabond over the unknown." '[72]

The early years left Stanley permanently scarred, bottling up a volcanic rage against the world. The outward signs of this rage were neurotic symptoms like his fetishistic regard for books and his fanatical neatness.[73] Suspicion of everyone in the world led to compulsive secretiveness. It is from this combination of deliberate obfuscation and his own genuine ignorance of his origins that much of the confusion surrounding Stanley during his career derived. One of the astonishing aspects of Stanley's story is how little solid intelligence the public possessed about his early years during his lifetime. When Stanley returned from finding Livingstone in 1872, a veritable cataclysm of ill-informed rumour burst on the public. One author asserted categorically that Stanley's real name was Howell Jones and that he had been born on 16 November 1840.[74] Despite the accuracy of Cadwalader Rowlands' 1872 account, Stanley successfully fought his corner and persuaded the public that he had been born and bred in the USA. The next upsurge in speculation was in the late 1880s during the Emin Pasha Expedition. An anonymous letter in *The Times* confidently asserted that Stanley's real name was Owen and that he was born at Mold, Flintshire.[75] Complacently signed 'One who knows', this farrago of nonsense was refuted a week later by one signing himself 'One who knows better.'[76] Only in the 1890s did the main outline of Stanley's life become clear.[77] But Stanley was successful in keeping much hidden. Yet it is hardly surprising that the identity of the man should so long remain obscure to the public, when its possessor remained fundamentally uncertain of it himself. The existentialist cliché about man constantly recreating his own identity has never seemed so apt as it does in the case of 'H. M. Stanley'.

2

ANY idea that young Stanley had escaped from the determinism of life with his relatives into a new realm of freedom was dispelled within days on the *Windermere*. He learned he was not to be a cabin-boy but merely one more unit of sweated labour aloft. Giving him just enough time to find his sea-legs, the brutal mate soon had him swabbing the decks in heaving seas, Boston, the *Windermere*'s home port, was legendary at the time for its 'death ships' and brutal officers. Moreover, Stanley learned from his fellow victims that the voyage to New Orleans was certain to be a one-way trip. Now at last he realised why Captain Hardinge had been so ready to sign him on. Hardinge and his officers ran a racket which involved pocketing the wages of their deck-hands. Their method was simple. They made their young charges' lives such hell on board that the boys would jump ship at the first port rather than endure further brutality.

The routine savagery on board the *Windermere* was compounded by a conditioned reflex usage of oaths and obscenity. This was St Asaph's raised to a new power. The second mate, Nelson, really was the brute Stanley later accused Francis of being. Ever the survivor, Stanley set about finding protective cover. He ingratiated himself with the cook, Long Hart, who enthralled him with tales of storm-tossed roundings of Cape Horn and voyages to Africa. He received less of the rope's end than three young Irish stowaways who were uncovered on the fifth day out and who lacked the wit to deflect the mate's worst excesses of brutish violence.[1]

Gradually Stanley inured himself to the hardships of life at sea. He found a violent storm in the Bay of Biscay exhilarating rather than frightening. But he failed to establish any rapport with his peers – the below-decks seamen. This increased his sense of paranoia and his conviction that suspicion and mistrust should be his watchword:

From this date began, I think, the noting of a strange coincidence, which has been so common with me that I accept it as a rule. When I pray for a man, it happens that at that moment he is cursing me; when I praise, I am slandered; if I commend, I am reviled; if I feel affectionate or sympathetic towards one, it is my fate to be detested or scorned by him. I first noticed this curious coincidence on board the *Windermere*. I bore no grudge, and thought no evil of any person, but prayed for all, morning and evening, extolled the courage, strength and energy of my ship-mates, likened them to sea-lions, and felt it an honour to be in the company of such brave men; but, invariably, they damned my eyes, my face, my heart, my soul, my person, my nationality; I was damned aft, and damned forward. I was wholly obnoxious to everyone aboard, and the only service they asked of God towards me was that He should damn me to all eternity.[2]

This sounds very like humbug. If true, it argues for a naïvety astonishing in one who had been through the workhouse experience. More likely, it suggests that Stanley had not mastered the art of charm without sycophancy.

On the fifty-second day out from Liverpool, the *Windermere* dropped anchor off the mouth of the Mississippi. A tug took the vessel 100 miles up the river to New Orleans. From the wharves drifted the smell of green coffee, fermenting molasses, Stockholm tar, brine, rum and whisky drippings. Hundreds of ships lay alongside the quays. Multitudes of men of all races were busy sifting the barrels, hogsheads and bales. There was a chaos of horses, mules, drays and wagons. In places the freight lay in mountainous heaps.[3]

Within minutes of docking, Stanley and a cabin-boy called Harry were the only crew members left aboard the *Windermere*. The rest had all dispersed to the crimp-houses, clip-joints and stews of New Orleans. At sunset the two boys finally got shore leave. Stanley and his companion reeled through the streets in a state of sensuous intoxication. After a while the street-wise Harry suggested that they enter a 'bar' for some refreshment. The naïve Stanley agreed. When four young girls entered the room in their underwear, he realised he was in a brothel and fled in terror.[4] Already the legacy of St Asaph's was such as to leave Stanley quaking in terror at any overt demonstration of sexuality.

Next day, finding to their surprise and anger that the 'Welsh monkey' was still aboard, Hardinge and Nelson tightened the screws to achieve their desired effect. They set Stanley to cleaning brasswork, then found fault with his efforts and kicked and clouted him. It became clear that this was a war of attrition that the eighteen-year-old could not win. That night he emptied his sea-bag, put on his best clothes and, armed with just the Bible that Bishop Short had given him, stole ashore. He spent the night in a mound of cotton bales.

Next morning he set out to find employment for, as he remarked, 'the absolutely penniless has a choice of two things, work or starve'.[5] On Tchapitoulas Street the sun was already hot at 6.30 a.m. Half an hour later he came to a warehouse billed as the property of Speake and McCreary, wholesale merchants. Lolling outside, reading a newspaper, was a bearded, middle-aged man in a dark alpaca suit. Taken with his air of distinction Stanley tried on him the Dickensian line, 'Do you want a boy, sir?'

The upshot was that after a quick literacy test the man took the 'boy' to his manager Mr Speake and Stanley was given a week's trial at $5 a week.[6] Ensconced in an attic room in a respectable boarding house, Stanley exerted all his efforts during the week's probation. At the end of the week Speake told him that he was now permanently engaged as a junior clerk at $25 a month. After paying for board and lodging, Stanley was left with a monthly surplus of $15. To a former workhouse boy this was the wealth of Croesus.

By this time Stanley was learning something of his original benefactor. He was rather more than the 'agent' he had humbly described himself as; he was in fact a wealthy cotton broker with an established reputation in New Orleans. Dazzled by the reputation of his benefactor and by his many kindnesses, the youth decided to jettison his given name of John Rowlands in favour of that of his protector: Stanley. From 1859 onwards Rowlands was Henry Stanley, though the name 'Morton' took longer to be fixed.[7]

As his protégé continued to make impressive progress as a clerk, Stanley senior increasingly took him under his wing. He began by inviting him to his house for Sunday breakfast. He introduced the young man to his wife; the couple were childless. Stanley was bowled over by the refinement and elegance of the first 'lady' he had ever known. But although husband and wife treated the young man as a son, ultimately the impact of Mrs Stanley was baneful. By putting her on a pedestal Stanley set up an impossible feminine ideal for actual women to match. He was in danger of falling into the trap of the madonna/whore syndrome: there were 'women' like his mother and the other fallen creatures of St Asaph's and the New Orleans brothels; and there were 'ladies' like the wife of his benefactor. In this respect his own testimony is eloquent:

It was at this hour I made the discovery of the immense distance between a lady and a mere woman; and while I gazed at her clear, lustrous eyes, and noted the charms which played about her features, I was thinking that, if a lady could be so superior to an ordinary housewife, with her careless manner of speech, and matter-of-fact ways, what a beautiful thing an angel must be![8]

Gradually Stanley learned the true story of his protector, though he suppressed this in the *Autobiography* for his own self-serving ends. Henry Hope Stanley had been born in Stockport, Cheshire, which was why the Welsh lilt of the young vagabond had initially so intrigued him. His business career in New Orleans spanned the years 1838–78. He first came to the United States in 1836. After a short period in Charleston, South Carolina, he left for Texas where he married the first Mrs Stanley. Moving to New Orleans, they began by opening a boarding house on Dorsiere near Canal Street. His first wife died in 1843 without issue, but shortly before that the couple had adopted a three-year-old girl, Joanne.[9]

Meanwhile Stanley senior's business career was thriving. He began in the cedar trade but soon diversified into sugar, cotton and iron foundries. By 1846 he was wealthy enough to make a trip back to his native England, where he met and married the fifteen-year-old Frances Meller. The woman who so entranced the young Stanley was thus twenty-eight at the time of the Sunday breakfasts. The entire Meller clan then followed Stanley back to New Orleans where they lived on Live Oak (Constance) Street in Old Lafayette (now the Fourth district).

Contemporary accounts describe Stanley senior as having a 'roast-beef' complexion and side whiskers with no moustache. He was said to give generously to charity but to have a tendency to switch business partners more often than was considered sound. His restlessness led him to move from cedar into cotton in a big way. In 1858 he operated a cotton-weighing business (the Mississippi Cotton Press) together with partners named Wright and Eager from offices at Exchange Place and Iberville (132–4 Exchange Place). By the mid-1850s he moved to a house at 904 Orange Street in Annunciation Square. In addition, he owned a huge plantation called Jefferson Hall in Tangipa Hoa parish near Arcola. It was at Orange Street and Arcola that young Stanley was to spend much of 1859.[10]

The women in the life of Henry Hope Stanley seemed to have been singularly ill-starred. His second wife was also childless. When they adopted a girl, Annie, the experiment did not prove a success. Annie eloped with a suitor violently opposed by her foster-father. Meanwhile Joanne married and died young.

Given the fondness of both Stanleys for their young protégé, it was not surprising that Stanley was soon a son in all but name. Henry Hope taught him the business and gave him a responsible position on the Arcola plantation. He also encouraged his self-education. Under his mentor's tutelage Stanley devoured Shakespeare, Byron, Irving, Goldsmith, Ben Jonson, Cowper. But, as with Stanley's admiration for his adopted 'mother', a pathological element began to creep in. His obsession with books as the perfect barrier between himself and the physical world, especially the world of sexuality, became almost fetishistic: 'without them [his adopted parents], probably my love of books would have proved sufficient safeguard against the baser kinds of temptations; but with them, I was rendered almost impregnable to vice.'[11] The other neurotic symptom in evidence in New Orleans was an obsessive tidiness, which first manifested itself in the months at the Speake store, before Stanley senior moved him on to Arcola.[12]

We can infer that sexuality gnawed away at Stanley in this period from a revealing story he relates in the *Autobiography* which, while unconvincing naturalistically, is of great symbolic importance. He tells us that in his early period in New Orleans, while still at Mrs Williams' boarding house, he shared his room and his large four-poster bed with 'Dick Heaton', ostensibly a Liverpool cabin-boy who had experienced the same sort of shipboard brutality as himself. Stanley noticed that 'Dick' never undressed at night and always shrank from touching him in the four-poster. Eventually the secret came out: 'Dick' was really a girl in boy's clothes and her name was Alice.[13] We may conjecture that the proximate source for this fantasy was the Shakespearian comedies Stanley was reading at the time. But there is a more profound meaning for the fantasy. It is utterly implausible for a former inmate of St Asaph's to tell us, as Stanley does, that he knew nothing of female anatomy and had never seen a girl's breasts before. The true significance of the tale is Stanley's uncertainty about *his own* sexual identity.

Stanley was soon at home in the country of his adoption. He liked the cosmopolitan atmosphere of New Orleans and the absence of rigid social stratification based on externals of class like name, accent and education. The American myth of 'log-cabin to White House' had an obvious appeal for a workhouse brat. But he was less happy with his adopted father. At first all went well. Stanley senior helped the young man to overcome his more obvious feelings of inferiority: 'I don't know', he said, 'what the customs of the Welsh people may be, but here we regard personal character and worth, not pedigree. With us, people are advanced not for what their parentage may have been, but for what they are themselves.'[14] So far so good. But there were from the earliest days signs that Stanley *père et fils* were too alike in temperament to be really comfortable with each other. The taciturn Henry Hope reprimanded his 'son' for too much idle talk. He reinforced Stanley's feeling that books were to be used as an artificial barrier against 'low company' and the conversation of idlers. He was moody, and young Stanley found this hard to deal with. Most of all, he was short-tempered, like his charge, and this caused a lot of friction. 'A choleric disposition on his part would have been as a flame to my nature, and the result might have been guessed,' writes Stanley in the conditional, hinting at what actually happened.[15]

Some time around the end of 1859 or early 1860 a decisive rupture took place. The causes of the quarrel remain obscure, but the result was that Stanley senior sent his refractory protégé to work on a friend's plantation in Arkansas.[16] Stanley's answer to this development was of a piece with his treatment of earlier father-figures: he simply 'killed off' his protector. At this point the *Autobiography* becomes a heady brew of deliberately confusing chronology and out-and-out fantasy. After paying a fulsome tribute to his adopted father, Stanley announces that his own departure for Arkansas followed the death of the second Mrs Stanley by fever and the subsequent voyage to Cuba by the grief-stricken Henry Hope. While he was in Arkansas, Stanley continues, he heard the dreadful news that his protector and father had died.[17] In this tragic way ended his connection with the Stanley family from whom he had taken his name.

All of this is a tissue of lies. Henry Hope Stanley's wife did *not* die in 1859 but on 9 April 1878, aged forty-six, in New Orleans. Henry Hope Stanley himself dropped dead six months later (November 1878) at sixty-seven, at Foley Plantation, in Assumption parish on Bayou Lafourche. He left an estate of $130,000 but not a penny of it went to his adopted son. Henry Hope gave instructions after the quarrel in 1859–60 that Stanley's name was never again to be mentioned in his presence.[18]

Even more astonishing than the pack of lies in the *Autobiography* is the fantasy Stanley concocted for his own amusement in his private diaries. Here he records a scene, as if it were actuality, in which he tearfully views his protector's corpse:

For the first time I understood the sharpness of the pang which pierces the soul when a loved one lies with folded hands icy cold in the eternal sleep. As I contemplated the body I vexed myself with asking. Had my conduct been as perfect as I then wished it had been? Had I failed in aught? Had I esteemed him as he deserved? Then a craving wish to hear him speak but one word of consolation, to utter one word of blessing made me address him as though he might hear. But no answer ever came, and I experienced a shiver of sadness, and then wished I could join him.[19]

There are many curious aspects of the 'death' of Henry Stanley senior. To lie to the world is one thing; to lie to oneself in the privacy of one's diary argues for serious neurosis. But there is more. Some unconscious guilt about this 'parricide' led Stanley to leave clues in the *Autobiography* that might suggest to the perceptive reader that his story of Henry Hope's death is false and that it was a quarrel that severed the relationship.[20] Not for the last time the carapace of 'character-armour' with which Stanley shielded himself was betrayed by unconscious manifestations of self-disgust and worthlessness.

Stanley's life in 1860–61 presents a tangled, deliberately obfuscated skein, of which only the main outlines are visible. He roamed the Mississippi and its lower tributaries: the Washita, Saline and Arkansas rivers. At various times he visited St Louis, Cairo, Memphis, Vicksburg, Natchez. He learned the arts of the bargees and flat-boatmen. Later he ventured farther afield, to Cincinnati and Louisville: 'at one time I was profound in the statistics relating to population, commerce, and navigation of the Southern and South-Western states.'[21] The *Autobiography* is full of stories of derring-do on the Mississippi, armed robberies, knife fights, duels between gamblers, some of which Stanley may have witnessed but which assuredly lost nothing in the telling. It is not easy to determine whether these journeys were part of his duties on the Arkansas river or (more likely) periods of self-assigned furlough during which Stanley picked up odd jobs as he went.

The Arkansas episode itself is obscure both in provenance and in chronology. Stanley tells us that he went to 'Major Ingham's plantation in Arkansas partly as a result of Stanley senior's precipitate departure to Cuba', partly as a result of his patron's desire to expand the business up-country – Stanley cannot quite decide which story he wants us to believe. The sober truth is that he was sent there in disgrace as a form of 'internal exile'. Within weeks he had quarrelled bitterly with the plantation owner – in Stanley's version because he objected to the brutality of an overseer.[22] Bearing a letter of introduction, Stanley then moved on to a store at Cypress Bend on the Arkansas river, owned by a German-Jewish trader named Altschul. Altschul took him on as a clerk and junior salesman. This formed the basis for another Stanley fantasy, when he later claimed to have worked for a salary of £200 p.a. at this time.[23]

There was one major problem about Cypress Bends. It was in Arkansas's swamplands. Malaria and ague were everyday hazards. Stanley quickly succumbed to fever. The attack began with a violent shaking, followed by a congealed feeling as though his blood was iced. After a couple of hours' shivering, clutching at hot-water bottles and swathed in blankets, Stanley was overtaken by twelve hours of delirium and a coda in the form of exhausting perspiration. After one bout he found that his weight had sunk to 95 pounds.[24] It was here that he first learned to take quinine in a dosage of five grains every other hour from dawn to noon. Even so, Stanley later admitted that these Arkansas fevers had done nothing to prepare him for the far greater ravages of African disease.[25]

The prickly and mercurial poor whites of Arkansas took some adjusting too, but Stanley was helped through his swamp baptism by the geniality of the senior salesman Cronin. Cronin, a New York Irishman, very soon attenuated the prejudices against the Irish that Stanley had learned from his workhouse mates.[26] A heavy drinker, accomplished ladies' man and born salesman, Cronin possessed all the extrovert charm that Stanley lacked and envied. His larger-than-life personality swept all before it and overpowered the dour and hostile swamp folk. Eventually Cronin fell foul of Altschul when his employer discovered the extent of his informal harem among the black slaves.[27]

The attack on Fort Sumter in April 1861 opened four years of bloody conflict in which more than 600,000 were to lose their lives. Feeling himself aloof from the Civil War, Stanley saw no reason to do anything but continue in his comfortable niche at Altschul's store. He felt contemptuous of the southerners who were hoist on the petard of their own code of honour and chivalry and smirked at those who enlisted in the southern armies simply because they could not endure the scorn of Dixie womanhood. He remained on the sidelines as the locals organised themselves into a company called 'the Greys'. He might well have brazened out his failure to volunteer to bear arms, even in face of a white feather. Then a female cousin of his friends the Gorees hit on a lucky idea.

She sent Stanley a parcel containing a petticoat of the kind a black lady's maid might wear.[28] This was meant to be a simple symbol of cowardice. But its powerful effect on Stanley was precisely that it tapped into fears and uncertainties about his own sexual identity. He hesitated no longer. That very afternoon he signed on for the 'Dixie Greys'.

It did not take him long to regret his hasty decision. 'Enlisting in the Confederate service, because I received a packet of female clothes, was certainly a grave blunder,' he recalled.[29] In July 1861 the Greys were ordered up to Little Rock, where they were sworn to the service of the Confederate States for twelve months and issued with knapsacks and heavy flint-lock muskets. The swearing ceremony was presided over by General Burgevine, later to serve with 'Chinese' Gordon in the Taiping rebellion.

What Stanley found hard to come to terms with was not military discipline but anomie: what he calls 'this curious volte-face in morality', whereby what was illicit in civilian life was now permitted and encouraged, where the murderer became the hero. Rigorous physical exercise on forced marches had the effect on Stanley that his African explorations were later to have: he lost weight rapidly. In a 'state of nature' Stanley always had a tendency to run to fat; but the spartan regime and diet of Little Rock soon slimmed down the sleek young men of Cypress Bends: Stanley records that by the end of 1861 he possessed a waspish waist, which measured a little more than two hands.[30]

By the end of August basic training was completed. The Dixie Greys were shipped across the Arkansas river. Immediately a typhus epidemic invaded the camp and carried off large numbers of his comrades. Stanley blamed the loss of life on incompetent generalship. Southern generals, he found, were very good at strategy and organising commissariat, but were indifferent to the health and well-being of their men. No preventive measures or prophylactic diets were prescribed, so that disease in the army camps was rampant. Stanley remained unaffected and toughened his constitution by bouts of underwater swimming and diving in the Arkansas river. Then the Greys were ordered to the western front on the other side of the Mississippi. It took them until the beginning of November to reach the theatre of war.

On 7 November they observed, but did not participate in, the battle of Belmont, in which the Federal General Grant defeated the Confederate General Polk.[31] Then the Greys were entrained at Columbus for Cave City, Kentucky, where they arrived on 25 November 1861. Here they remained quietly until February 1862, still without a taste of active combat. Doubtless because of his fear of contact with young women, Stanley boasted of his appeal for the older female and how, using the skills he had acquired when dealing with the difficult Aunt Mary, he was able to wheedle eggs and other delicacies out of farmers' wives. During the long winter Stanley won the plaudits of his peers by his skills as a forager. A daring raid on a Unionist farm secured his company a dinner of roast pork for Christmas. More tedious, however, was the resolute philistinism of his peers. Stanley had to read his Bible in secret for fear of taunts from his fellow troopers: 'and I was as ready to deny that I prayed, as Peter was to deny Christ.'[32]

The period of 'phoney war' came to an end in mid-February. 350 miles of forced marches took the Confederates to Pittsburgh Landing where, on 6–7 April 1862, the dreadful battle of Shiloh was fought. Stanley witnessed the appalling carnage at close quarters on the first day and probably owed his survival to being taken prisoner early on the second morning of the blood-letting. There are some grounds for thinking that Stanley might deliberately have got himself taken prisoner by advancing too far too fast and thus blundering into the Federal lines. He himself explained the curious circumstances of his departure from the battlefield as an over-reaction to an imputation of cowardice from his officer.

'With my musket on the trail I found myself in active motion, more active than otherwise I should have been, perhaps, because Captain Smith had said "Now, Mr Stanley, if you please, step briskly forward!" This singling out of me wounded my amour propre and sent me forward like a rocket.'[33] He found himself surrounded by blue uniforms and was roughly ordered to drop his gun. To his intense chagrin he was a prisoner.

After Shiloh we enter a period of obscurity in Stanley's life, where verification of his own account becomes impossible. There is a discrepancy between the *Autobiography* and the unofficial 'autobiography' he wrote to Katie Gough-Roberts in 1869. However, both versions agree that he served time as a prisoner of war at Camp Douglas near Chicago. It is in the sequel that the accounts diverge.

From Shiloh Stanley and several hundred other Confederate prisoners were taken by steamer to St Louis, where they arrived on 13 April 1862 and were sympathetically received by the Missourian locals, who had come within an ace of declaring for the Confederacy the year before.[34] But the 'rebels' were soon removed from this friendly ambit to the heartland of the industrial North. The railway took them to a converted cattle-yard in the Chicago suburbs which masqueraded under the formal title of Camp Douglas. Within the square enclosure hundreds of prisoners were herded. There were sentry-boxes every 60 yards along the walls. The guards had orders to shoot to kill anyone crossing the 'dead-line' – a perimeter denoted by a line of lime-wash. The prisoners were housed in barn-like structures of planking, each about 250 feet by 40 and accommodating between two and three hundred men. The total prisoner muster in the camp was about 3,000.[35]

Restricted to just 30 inches of space in their bunks, with nothing to do, nothing to read and no scope for physical exercise, the prisoners began to waste away and drop like flies. Dysentery, typhus and vermin were endemic. The iron rations compounded the problem. The death-toll began to mount. Sick men could be heard at night, praying for death to take them and relieve their suffering. Many of the invalids were so debilitated that they fell into the primitive latrines while answering calls of nature and lay there for hours, moaning and inhaling the miasmata, until they were hauled out. Every morning wagons came to collect the carcasses of the deceased, much as if they had been joints of 'New Zealand frozen mutton'.[36] In Stanley's recollection, the horrors of Camp Douglas equalled the more-trumpeted atrocities visited on Federal prisoners at Andersonville.

The only human rapport Stanley established in the camp was, first, with a fellow Confederate named W. H. Wilkes, nephew of a US Navy admiral, and, more importantly for his own survival, with the camp commissary Shipman. Stanley's tenacity as a survivor allied to his 'driven' determination to surmount all obstacles led to Shipman's appointing him a camp trusty, with responsibility for issuing rations and taking roll calls.[37] It was Shipman who suggested to Stanley that the only way for him to avoid joining the daily swelling throng of the dead was to volunteer for the Union armies. According to Stanley, he wrestled heroically with his conscience for six weeks before falling in with the suggestion. This period of agonising is implausible, for it would mean that Shipman uniquely singled out Stanley for rescue immediately on arrival at Camp Douglas. The plain truth is that Stanley almost certainly accepted with alacrity an offer that released him from his living hell. That there is guilt about the way he evaded the fate of so many of his comrades can be inferred from the 'autobiography' he provided for Katie Gough-Roberts. Here he provides an heroic version of his escape from Camp Douglas. According to this, after *three* months, he broke out on a dreadful rainy night. Dodging the bullets of a dozen sentries that whined around him, he escaped by plunging into a river and swimming to liberty 'once more a free man and for the fourth time on the world'.[38]

On 4 June 1862 Stanley took the oath of allegiance to the North and was drafted into the 1st Regiment, Illinois Light Artillery. The real Stanley, as opposed to the mythical persona portrayed in the *Autobiography*, would have felt no moral scruple about such apostasy. Ruthlessness and lack of integrity were to be hallmarks of the future great explorer. But neither Shipman nor the Union gained much from persuading Stanley to change sides. The pent-up virulence of Camp David dysentery almost immediately overwhelmed him. No sooner was he back in the war zone, at Harper's Ferry, than he collapsed and was rushed to an army hospital where he was pronounced unfit for active duties. On 22 June the Union army discharged him. He was weak and penniless, but this was not an age of sentiment, above all not in wartime.

The sick man staggered off into the wilderness, clothed only in a pair of blue military trousers, a dark serge coat and a 'mongrel hat'. He could not walk 300 yards without pausing for breath. As he lay in the open under the stars, Stanley could perceive the sensation of internal bleeding. It took him a week to stagger 12 miles, half-way from Harper's Ferry to Hagerstown. Near to death, he collapsed at the Baker farm, 3 miles from Sharpsburg. He was unconscious for three days.[39]

He awoke to find that he had fallen among Good Samaritans. He was in a clean bed, with fresh clothes on his back. The family nursed him back to health with a careful diet and allowed him to convalesce by sitting in their orchard. When he had recovered, Stanley helped the farmer gather in his harvest. He stayed with the Bakers until mid-August, building up his strength for the ordeals ahead. Stanley's mind had now concentrated on the thought that his four years in the United States had been an unmitigated disaster. Perhaps it was time to return to the land of his birth and try his luck there. He accepted the farmer's offer of his rail fare to Baltimore, where he could find a ship. Baker drove him to Hagerstown and put him on the slow train to Baltimore via Harrisburg.

On arrival in Baltimore Stanley sought out the fiancée of his fellow-prisoner W. H. Wilkes, possibly with a view to financial assistance. Nothing came of the interview. Stanley then found a temporary job on an oyster schooner. The accidental drowning of the captain brought that episode to an end. A few weeks later Stanley found what he was looking for: the opportunity to work his passage across the Atlantic. He signed on with the sailing-ship *E. Sherman* for a month's voyage to Liverpool.[40]

Once in Liverpool, in November 1862, Stanley set out to walk the 40 miles to Denbigh. He was very poor, his clothes were shabby and a recrudescence of Camp David fever left him in poor health. But he was buoyed up by the thought that he was now a man, with battle honours. Surely this time his mother would welcome him with open arms and the memory of their workhouse encounter would be expunged. There was, too, the thought that her material circumstances had improved. Stanley had learned from the Morrises in Liverpool that his mother, now forty, had married Robert Jones, father of two of her children, on 20 August 1860 at St Asaph.[41] Jones had given up his job as a plasterer to take up the tenancy of the Cross Foxes Inn at Glascoed near Abergale.[42]

What followed was one of the searing experiences of Stanley's life. His mother received him coldly, grudgingly provided him with a single night's lodging and gave him a shilling next morning to take him back to Liverpool. There is some suggestion that Elizabeth Parry (now Jones) was suffering from depression because of the recent death from meningitis of her son James. At any rate she told Stanley that his arrival in such clothes and without means disgraced her and her husband in the eyes of the neighbours. She added this warning: 'Never come back to me unless you come better dressed and in better circumstances than you seem to be in now.'[43]

Stanley was so choked with emotions of rejection and rage that he could not bring himself to record in his diary anything more than the bare fact of his rebuff; only in the *Autobiography* did his wife reveal some of the trauma he experienced.[44] Such a profound wound cut the ground from under his aspirations for a new life in Wales. He decided to return to the New World. He obtained new clothes and £16 from 'relations of his second father' (this presumably refers to Henry Hope Stanley rather than his stepfather Robert Jones).[45]

From November 1862 to August 1864 the Stanley trail goes cold. Just a few cryptic diary entries enable us to track his progress. 'December 1862. Ship Ernestine. New York.' is followed by the occasional jotting indicating service as an able seaman in the Merchant Navy, generally on voyages between Boston and Mediterranean ports: Mentone, Palermo, Cette. That he got a close look at Barcelona during 1863 is demonstrated by two separate entries from two different diaries. 'May 1863, Barcelona, Barque *Jehu*, naked night. Barracks of carabiniers.' And again: 'Wrecked off Barcelona, crew lost, in the night. Stripped naked and swam to shore. Barrack of carabiniers . . . demanded my papers!' It has been convincingly demonstrated that these two accounts blend faulty memory and deliberate fantasy (we have already noted that Stanley had no problem about lying to himself). In the first place the *Jehu*, a 250-ton Boston vessel, arrived in Barcelona in June, not May. Secondly, and more importantly, it was not shipwrecked.[46] The truth is that Stanley deserted his ship in Barcelona harbour by diving into the sea with a pack. While swimming to land he lost this bundle, containing his clothes.[47] A sentry found him on the shore and locked him in the castle for the night. He was then released and made his way through Catalonia as a vagabond. Once across the French frontier he was arrested at Narbonne, freed shortly after, thence worked his passage back to the USA.[48]

In October 1863 Stanley gave up seafaring for a time and tried his hand as a lawyer's clerk. His employer was Judge Thomas Irwin Hughes of Brooklyn, a notary public who lived at 313 Ryerson Street. Once again Stanley's talent for finding employment that ended with a melodramatic flourish was in evidence. One night the judge, in a rare state of intoxi-cation, tried to murder his wife with a hatchet; Stanley had to restrain him. The reward for an outsider's intervention in a marital quarrel was the usual one: the next morning the judge's wife turned on Stanley and raved at him for smoking in her house.[49]

The record for early 1864 is equally vague. The diary entries hint at another Merchant Navy voyage, this time to the West Indies; but confusingly other accounts place Stanley in Hughes' offices at Cedar Street, Lower Manhattan. It seems to have been under the influence of an acquaintance (possibly a former employee) of Judge Hughes, who met Stanley first at Cedar Street, that he took the momentous decision to re-enter the Civil War for the third time. Louis R. Stegman was on leave from Sherman's army and argued the federal cause eloquently, as well as the possible rich pickings to be made in journalism.[50] When Stegman returned to active service in Georgia, Stanley decided to put his service in the merchant marine to good use by enlisting for three years in the Federal Navy. Ironically, immediately on joining up on 19 July 1864, he was entered as a 'landsman' (non-sailor).[51]

Exhortations and cajolery from Stegman (who was the same age as Stanley) notwithstanding, the decision to re-enter the arena of fratricidal blood-letting seems odd in the light of Stanley's earlier experiences. The reason he gave to journalists later – that he was in danger of arrest by the Federal authorities as an escaped prisoner[52] – is pure nonsense and depends for its effect on the suppression of the true story of his departure from Camp David. The explanation almost certainly lies deeper and has to do with the imperatives of a man of action. As Wassermann has postulated, Stanley was driven by a constant need for momentum in his

45

life: 'his thoughts are relevant to actions and not to other thoughts.'[53] The catch is that the more one lives for action alone, the less is one capable of discrimination about *which* actions are valuable; hence the near-mania of the Alexanders, Napoleons, Caesars and Cromwells.[54] So although Stanley's apparent reasons for re-enlistment seem tenuous, at a deeper level they make psychological sense.

Stanley's first ship in the US Navy was the *North Carolina*. The rank of 'landsman' was an inferior grade to sailor so that there is a certain mystery about how Stanley was entered under this heading.[55] Even more surprisingly, Stanley's first work aboard ship was as a cook; Stanley apparently took pride in his alleged prowess as a short-order cook.[56] After three weeks, Stanley was transferred to the *Minnesota* at Hampton Roads, Commodore Joseph Lanman commanding. Here his superior handwriting was noticed and he was made ship's clerk. It was while he was discharging this duty that he made the acquaintance of a fifteen-year-old youth, Lewis Noe, who had recently enlisted in a fit of bravado and was employed as ship's messenger. Noe is a key figure in Stanley's life in more ways than one. Although Stanley and his powerful friends later went to great lengths to blacken his character, Noe was a truthful witness whose testimony always emerges well from any testing against unimpeachable sources.[57]

As messenger Noe was in daily contact with the ship's clerk and was able to observe Stanley closely. All his observations tally closely with other recorded impressions. Stanley was always very tactful when dealing with the powerful, but was cold and aloof with his peers. He scarcely spoke to anyone in a social way and sat by himself and read whenever he had the chance. He was an excellent penman, could write a dozen different kinds of hands, and could forge anyone's signature within seconds of seeing it.[58]

From Noe's evidence we can appreciate the nature and extent of the fantasies Stanley wove out of his basically unadventurous period of service on the *Minnesota*. Some of his exaggerations are harmless enough, as when he expands being ship's clerk under a commodore into being the private secretary of an admiral and securing promotion as an ensign at a salary of £350 p.a.[59] But some of his lies are more serious. Stanley claimed that after four months he was transferred to the USS *Ticonderoga*. Noe denied that such a transfer ever took place; the US Navy records bear him out.[60] Not content with this fictitious 'promotion', Stanley proceeded to turn himself into the hero of the late naval battles of the Civil War. Here it is important to be meticulous in the separation of fact from fantasy. On 20 December the combined naval armour of the Federal fleet bombarded

Fort Fisher, North Carolina, which guarded the entrances to the blockade-running Confederate port of Wilmington. After a desperate struggle, the Federal Navy was beaten off. Stanley observed the action from the *Minnesota* which was engaged on the outer fringes of the action and wrote up his perceptions in colourful prose – his first sustained act as a writer.[61]

In January 1865 the US Navy returned to the assault. By this time, according to himself, Stanley had been transferred to the *Ticonderoga*. But Stanley was neither on the *Ticonderoga* nor in any way involved in this second battle. This did not prevent him from concocting his most elaborate fantasy yet, in which he becomes the hero of the entire engagement. In Stanley's version, he swam 500 yards under fire and tied a rope to a Confederate ship, so that the *Ticonderoga* was able to secure her as a prize.[62]

It was in fact precisely the *inaction* on board the *Minnesota* and the lack of a proper stage on which to parade his talents that led Stanley to desert in February 1865. By this time Stanley had taken the young Noe under his wing. He bestowed on the youth the signal favour of showing him a photograph of Elizabeth Parry; he told Noe he was the only person in the world to whom he had shown it.[63] Stanley outlined his plans for getting free from the irksome three-year naval indentures. The two of them would make all ready and dress in their civilian clothes. Then they would put on their sailor suits over the 'civvies' and simply walk through the dockyard gate with a pass signed by the commodore, which Stanley would forge.

The opportunity came when the *Minnesota* put in for repairs at Portsmouth, New Hampshire. On 10 February 1865 Stanley and Noe walked blithely out of the gates of the naval yard, flourishing the 'commodore's pass'.[64]

3

T HE sequel to the desertion was not quite what Stanley had hoped. He had confided to Noe his ambition to acquire enough money for passage to the Middle East where they would surely make their fortunes. He proposed to raise the passage money by 'bounty jumping': he would 'persuade' Noe to enlist, then collect the bounty payable to anyone raising recruits for the Union army; Noe would then desert, Stanley would re-enlist him under another name at another recruiting centre, collect a fresh tranche of bounty, and so on, until they had raised the necessary sum.[1] But when Noe visited his parents at Sayville, Long Island, and told them he had deserted, they were appalled and filled his head with the terrors of hanging if he was caught. In a panic Noe went out and joined the Eighth New York Mounted Volunteers under Colonel Pope. He used the assumed name Lewis Morton that Stanley had earlier suggested as the first of his bounty-jumping aliases.[2]

Stanley was furious at seeing his plans lying in ruins. After vainly trying to persuade Noe to desert again (offering to meet him at a rendezvous with civilian clothes), he reluctantly concluded that the money he needed for his Eastern enterprise would have to be earned in some other way. For a short time he worked in the office of a lawyer called Lyon (or Lyons).[3] While he was there, the Civil War ended, on Palm Sunday 1865. The following Friday was one of the most traumatic days in American history. Stanley noted in his diary in a typical juxtaposition of the sublime and the ridiculous: 'New York. Assassination of Lincoln. Great Excitement. Office of Evening Post.'[4] The subtext of the last cryptic sentence was that Stanley was already making the rounds of newspaper offices, hawking the pieces he had written on the Fort Fisher battles. Evidently the advice proffered was that it was a mistake to try to start at the top, that he should try to work his way up from the provincial press. Some time shortly after 9

May 1865, Stanley took the advice and set out for St Louis, where he had contacts from his Southern days.[5]

In St Louis in June the editor of the *Missouri Democrat* was sufficiently impressed by Stanley's Civil War writing to accept him as an 'occasional' – someone whose freelance material would at least be considered and not consigned to the 'slush-pile'. He suggested that Stanley's best chance of obtaining 'good copy' was in the West. Stanley moved on. By late June he was in St Joseph, Missouri and in July had got as far as Salt Lake City.[6] In early August he reached San Francisco after travelling over the high Sierras through the Donner pass.

We know little of Stanley's sojourn in California beyond the fact that he, like most nineteenth-century travellers, found the scenery bewitching.[7] But he did not tarry there long. He doubled back to Colorado, spent a short while roughing it at Pike's Peak mining camp, and made a brief stopover at Denver City. 4 September 1865 saw him in Black Hawk City, Colorado, which remained his base until January 1866.[8]

In Black Hawk City Stanley began as a day-labourer at $5 a day in the Lyons & Co. smelting works. He opened a bank account and began to save in earnest for his projected trip, now taking shape more clearly in his mind as 'Asia Minor'. Meanwhile he continued to bombard the Colorado newspaper with letters drawing attention to his literary abilities. Free-masonry was beginning to make strides in the Colorado mining communities; ever the opportunist, Stanley quickly set himself up as the head of a Templar's lodge.[9]

Taking orders from an overseer was not, however, something that a man of Stanley's authoritarian personality could stomach long. His natural pugnacity soon surfaced. Fortunately for him, it won the attention of the Lyons management. A new quartz crusher had just been installed at the smelting works. The owner and his new superintendent, a man named Johnson, watched as the men shovelled quartz into the crusher. Aware of their presence, a burly foreman tried to impress them with his leadership qualities. He bawled at Stanley to shovel the quartz in faster. When the shift ended, Stanley challenged the foreman to a fight for the insult and offered him the choice of fists, knives or pistols. There was always something deeply frightening about Stanley when he was in this mood. The foreman evidently intuited that if he fought he would have to kill or be killed. He settled for an apology. When Johnson heard of the incident, he was so impressed that he invited Stanley to share his bachelor quarters with him. The arrangement lasted until Stanley left Black Hawk City.[10]

Some time around the end of January 1866 Stanley threw up his job at the smelting works and decided to try his luck in Central City. The Lyons contact secured him a job as a bookkeeper. He got on well with everyone in the business community, but already the itch for constant action was plaguing him. He was not getting on fast enough. He fantasised about going gold-prospecting in Alaska once he had learned the rudiments of mining and panning. According to one story, Stanley passed up an opportunity to join an Alaskan expedition because he was besotted by a Mormon's black-haired daughter, who rode into town occasionally for provisions. This seems to be another of Stanley's madonnas that he worshipped from afar, for the story continues that the infatuation fizzled out when the Mormon family left for Omaha.[11]

Feeling frustrated, Stanley abandoned bookkeeping when he got the offer of an apprenticeship as a printer with the *Miner's Daily Register*. This opportunity certainly seemed to take him closer to the journalistic fame for which he already hungered. But the editor did not pay his apprentice printers very much. Stanley was forced to alternate his printing with periods of prospecting. He began to work the Huff Lode in Central City. This was the time when he burnt his arm in an open fire as he was cooking a meal for his comrades. Nothing daunted, Stanley used the resultant scar as the raw material for a new fantasy: ever afterwards he told enquirers that the scar was the wound from an Indian arrow.[12]

Stanley needed quick results, which his gold-prospecting was not providing. Printing, too, required sustained application for many years to yield fruit. Ever impatient and greedy for success *now*, Stanley conceived an audacious plan for a financial breakthrough, which he did not dare reveal even to his closest associates. But to achieve his end, he needed at least the passage money to 'Asia Minor'.

It was at this point that William Harlow Cook entered Stanley's life in a big way. Stanley had known Cook since his Black Hawk days, ever since Cook sent him a congratulatory piece on an article published in a Central City sheet. Cook, like Stanley, was an aspiring freelance journalist, but he utterly lacked Stanley's toughness, willpower and ruthlessness. Cook comes across in his reminiscences as an essentially negative personality, absurdly deferential to Stanley and credulous to a degree. Unlike Noe's testimony, Cook's 'evidence' is largely a rehash of Stanley fantasies or an endorsement of his lies.[13] Such a companion, who automatically accepted Stanley's leadership and showed no independent spirit, was exactly what Stanley relished. He decided that he would take Cook with him on his daring 'Asia Minor' adventure. But first the two of them had to reach a standard of physical fitness necessary for the rigours Stanley saw ahead. He suggested, and Cook acquiesced in, a boat journey down the Missouri.

The first stage was to float down the Platte River in a flat-bottomed boat. The two men left Central City on 6 May 1866 and proceeded by stage to Denver. There Stanley supervised the construction of a boat for the 700-mile voyage down the Platte to Omaha.[14] The timid Cook was aware that he was involved in a perilous project, since the melting spring snow from the mountains made the Platte a raging torrent at this time of the year.

They were both raw amateurs at navigating a flat-bottom in a river. They began the voyage by striking a tree in midstream but recovered and soon began to learn valuable lessons about currents and other aspects of river navigation – lessons that were to be put to good use many years later on the Congo. But on the seventh night out, they hit a large tree in midstream, which capsized the boat, spilling Cook and Stanley into the icy waters of the Platte. Here Stanley's abilities as a swimmer proved their worth. Even though the empty boat had been carried over the tree and downstream by the raging flood, Stanley managed to outrun it along the shore. At a suitable point he plunged into the waters and pulled the boat to the shore. The two of them then turned the boat upside down and slept under it, shivering in wet blankets.[15]

Next morning Stanley again entered the swirling waters of the Platte, diving deep in hopes of recovering a prized rifle and revolver, but in vain. They trekked on wearily to Fort Laramie, in hopes of succour, but the military commandant took one look at their ragged and dishevelled state and put them under restraint as suspected army deserters. He did not actually arrest them but warned them not to leave the settlement until he had completed his enquiries.

Stanley was determined that all his plans would not be baulked by this pipsqueak captain commanding the garrison. He was not prepared to waste his hard-earned money on subsistence in Fort Laramie while the captain put the slow-grinding wheels of army bureaucracy into action. To a man of Stanley's aggressiveness, an army officer was no more formidable than the foreman at Black Hawk. Calmly he ate dinner in a small hotel in town, loaded up with provisions for the onward journey.

The captain had Stanley and Cook under surveillance and watched their preparations for departure. The two men returned to the hotel to pay their bill and depart. When they turned to leave they found the way barred by the captain. He glared at them. 'Do you want me to put you under arrest?' he challenged. Stanley fixed him with the look that so terrified

Noe and Cook and replied, hand ostentatiously on revolver: 'Yes, if you have men enough to do it.' The captain knew this was no bluff and that blood would have to be shed. If the two men were not deserters, a full-blown scandal might erupt and his army career could be ruined. Like the foreman before him, he decided that discretion was the better part of valour. After a momentary hesitation, he stood aside and let the men walk out.[16]

Stanley relaunched the boat and they continued downriver to Plattsmouth and Nebraska. Eleven days brought them to Omaha, reached on 27 May 1866.[17] From there they took a steamer to St Louis, then carried on to New York by train via Chicago and Niagara Falls.[18]

In New York they stayed for four days at the Richmond Hotel.[19] Stanley visited Noe, with whom he had corresponded regularly from Colorado. He persuaded Noe's parents to allow the seventeen-year-old to accompany him on his proposed trip to Turkey. He smoothed over the parents' anxieties and convinced them that the desertion from the *Minnesota* had been no more than a youthful indiscretion.[20] Wisely, Noe had not mentioned the 'bounty-jumping' proposal at home. To simple folk, Stanley's Asia Minor project seemed plausible. He argued that precious stones, diamonds and rubies, plus shawls and fabrics, could be picked up in Central Asia for next to nothing, then resold in the USA for huge profits.[21] Noe's mother and father – and his influential sister – gave the scheme their blessing.

Next Stanley introduced Cook to Noe. The two did not get on. Cook had been Stanley's *fidus Achates* in Colorado, but he immediately sensed that Noe was more important to Stanley. From that moment Cook's antipathy to Noe was to be marked. But the trio at once set off for Boston, where they booked passage for Smyrna on a fruit ship, the *E. H. Yarington*, under Captain Mayo. They waited nearly a month in Boston (from 16 June on).[22] The ship cleared from Boston on 10 July 1866.[23]

The first shock for Noe on what was to be a deeply traumatic expedition was to find that Stanley expected him to work his passage across the Atlantic.[24] The youth found this all the more galling since Stanley himself shipped out as a passenger and spent much of his time reading. Cook recalled that Stanley tried to improve his marksmanship by shooting at sea birds from the poop deck, but without any success. He also showed Cook some verses he had written. Cook's verdict was: 'If it did not reveal poetic genius, it showed at any rate that he had read history to some advantage.'[25] When the ship passed Trafalgar just before entering the Straits of Gibraltar, Stanley composed a poem on Nelson's victory, based on his own *Minnesota* experiences; to Cook this seemed slightly odd, as Stanley was forever dinning into him his admiration for Alexander the Great and Napoleon.

After fifty-one uneventful days they arrived at Smyrna (modern Izmir) on 28 August.[26] Stanley entered in his diary his plans for a crossing of Asia that would take the three of them to China.[27] But first he accompanied the captain on a visit to the US Consul. The consul was less than taken with Stanley's smart-alec riposte when he (the consul) asked Captain Mayo for details of his cargo. 'Missionaries and whisky,' quipped Stanley. On a more serious note, Stanley soon settled down with maps and charts and began to learn phrasebook Turkish. He appeared to have the flair of a linguist. Cook relates: 'He was soon able to speak it sufficiently well and this combined with his extraordinary intuitive perception made it possible to travel through the country without the aid of guides or dragomen, who are only so many leeches on the traveller.'[28]

Stanley and his two companions left Smyrna singularly ill-equipped for a journey to China. After the purchase of two inferior horses and some cheap cooking utensils, the total Stanley war-chest amounted to no more than $5 gold; the entire stock was worth no more than $100. Noe was again reminded of his inferior status on the expedition by having to trudge along on foot while the other two rode.[29]

Stanley wrote a detailed narrative of his Turkish adventure, in addition to his diary entries. The narrative conveys an admiration for the antiquities of Asia Minor combined with a lip-curling contempt for modern Turkey: 'the Turks are a degraded, semi-barbarous nation, ignorant and extremely superstitious.'[30] The narrative abounds with admiring references to Alexander the Great, Croesus and Cyrus; Stanley confesses himself bowled over by the acropolis at Sardis. But whenever modern Turkey puts in an appearance, the sour note is evident: even Turkish women, Stanley remarks, are 'not as prepossessing as our American women'.[31] At the town of Cassaba, reached on 6 September, Stanley was more interested in the way his horses munched the grass than in the everyday life of the locals.

Perhaps out of boredom Stanley indulged Noe in his tendency towards juvenile delinquency and even joined in himself. This disposition led to trouble with the Turks as early as the second day out. There was bad blood between Noe and Cook; Noe, encouraged surreptitiously by Stanley, decided to have a good laugh at Cook's expense. He set fire to some bushes near where they were camped and thoroughly alarmed the timid and circumspect Cook. When Cook saw Stanley laughing at his alarm, it deepened his feelings of hostility towards Noe. Stanley was cleverly playing off one of his minions against the other, ensuring that when he came to deal with Noe in his own way, he would have no trouble from Cook.

The trouble on this occasion came from the locals. The fire spread into a briar hedge and threatened to damage peasant property. The village police took Stanley and Cook into custody but Noe angered his mentor by decamping back towards Smyrna. The glib-tongued Stanley soon talked his way out of trouble in the village and browbeat the locals by brandishing his American papers. Then he and Cook doubled back to find Noe.[32]

The fact that Noe had deserted them deeply angered Stanley. It gave him the pretext to work out his erotic fantasies on the seventeen-year-old. For by now even Cook had sensed something of the truth – that Stanley's attachment for this unprepossessing youth he called his 'half-brother' contained a repressed homosexual element. Unable to find an outlet for his erotic energies through heterosexual contact – because of his deep fear of women – and too deeply imprinted by the sense of sin he had acquired in a Calvinistic childhood to become an active homosexual, Stanley rationalised his problems by sado-masochism. The obtaining of sexual satisfaction by cruelty alone contained too large a ballast of guilt; it had therefore to be balanced in Stanley's psyche by a compensating masochistic element: redemption through suffering.

In his dealings with Noe it was the sadistic element that predominated. Stanley began his campaign to crush Noe's will by impressing on him that he was a servant pure and simple. To test his mettle, he sent Noe on some minor thieving excursions in the neighbouring villages. He told him ominously, 'Remember, you are here to do my bidding. If I tell you to cut a man's throat, you do it.'[33]

It was shortly after the visit to Sardis that Stanley revealed his sexual hand. He and Noe were passing through a pomegranate forest; Cook was riding some way ahead, for Stanley habitually used him in this way as a scout. Suddenly Stanley got down from his horse, bound Noe's hands and then lashed him to a tree. 'I am going to give you the damnedest thrashing you ever had,' he told him. He ripped the shirt from Noe's back, then cut a switch from the grove, taking care to leave the knots in the wood exposed. Then he scourged Noe with the primitive whip until the blood ran. It seemed to Noe that the whipping went on for hours. As Stanley rested between strokes of the switch, he rehearsed the many occasions when Noe had angered him, some of them dating back to their service on the *Minnesota*. But the particular source of his anger seemed to be Noe's enlistment in New York without his consent. When the whipping ended,

Stanley 'comforted' his victim by telling him that he had shown his mettle by taking it so well. Noe, with scabs from the wounds that did not heal for another five days, understandably found this scant consolation.[34]

Why did Noe tolerate this behaviour? In part the answer is that he did not, for he tried to escape, was caught and scourged again. Stanley warned him that if he attempted to make off again, he would be shot down like a dog. But he also felt himself, at seventeen, in an alien land, whose language he did not speak and without weapons, to be powerless. Clearly he suffered from some kind of personality weakness, for he later confessed that with Stanley he was like the bird with the snake; the older man had absolute power over him as if he were hypnotised.

But Noe's ordeal was just beginning. The plan Stanley had evolved in his mind in faraway Colorado was now about to take shape, and the effeminate-looking Noe was to play a key role in it. In essence Stanley's plan amounted to provoking some kind of armed confrontation with the locals, so that he could claim afterwards to have been robbed of a large sum of money. He would then report the robbery in Erzurum, the largest city on Turkey's eastern border, adding the embellishment that his letters of credit on a merchant in Tiflis, Georgia, had also been stolen. He further hoped to produce fictitious credentials enabling him to raise a loan for the onward journey to Tiflis. By the time the Turkish bankers discovered the fraud, Stanley would be too far into Persia for it to be worthwhile for the bank to chase him.[35]

After surviving so many perils in the United States, Stanley had grown over-confident of his ability to manipulate events and did not fully appreciate how dangerous his strategy was. On 18 September 1866 he was to learn about unintended consequences with a vengeance.

That afternoon as they plodded through the mountains in the autumn heat, Stanley thought he saw his chance and took it. They were near a dismal hamlet called Chi-Hissar, about 300 miles inland from Smyrna. Their horses were near to expiring from exhaustion. Cook was riding about a mile in their rear as his horse was faltering. Stanley told Noe that he had a plan for procuring fresh mounts but it would require his full co-operation and unquestioning obedience. After the recent flagellation experience, Noe was not disposed to cavil.

Very soon they came in sight of a Turk, riding one horse and leading another. He introduced himself as Achmet. Stanley said something to him in broken Turkish that Noe did not understand. Achmet motioned to a hollow basin nearby surrounded by hills. The three of them rode into the hollow and dismounted. Achmet strode up to Noe and began fondling his genitals. At this Stanley suddenly seized his sabre and smote the Turk a buffet across the head that made him stagger. The blow would have killed him but for the protection afforded his head by the pasteboard stiffening inside his fez.

Achmet struck back at his would-be assassin. Drawing his knife, he closed with Stanley, who soon found himself outclassed in this kind of combat and called out to Noe to shoot his assailant dead. There was some desperation in his voice: 'Shoot him, Lewis, shoot him or he'll kill me!'[36] Mindful of Stanley's earlier words, Noe took aim and pulled the trigger, but the chamber was empty. Stanley had been using the rifle that morning for target practice and had neglected to reload it. Since Stanley was still yelling, 'Kill him!', Noe waded in and clubbed Achmet with the rifle butt. Again the Turk staggered but did not fall.

By this time Stanley's hands were ripped and bleeding from the struggle to keep the Turk's knife away from his heart. He rushed to his saddle bags to get his revolver. By the time he retrieved it, Achmet was at the top of the hollow and running for his life. Despite his marksmanship, Stanley failed to hit him with a couple of shots. Within seconds Achmet had made good his escape.[37]

The sequence of events in the hollow from the entry of the trio to Achmet's escape is related almost identically in the two utterly independent extant accounts of the incident, Noe's to the *New York Sun*, and Stanley's in the unpublished 'Adventures of an American Traveller in Turkey'. The two accounts differ only in their interpretation. Stanley says he entered the hollow in all innocence; the next thing he knew, Achmet was making sodomitical overtures to Noe. Noe says that Stanley lured the Turk into the hollow with the promise that if he inspected Noe's person, he would find a girl in boy's clothing.[38] According to Noe, it was Stanley's purpose to murder the Turk, gain possession of his horses, plead self-defence and then carry to Erzurum a story about how the Turk's comrades had robbed them of their money, which was how the shooting began in the first place.

There can be little question which version is more plausible. Can we seriously believe that a lone Turk would have asked two well-armed foreigners to turn aside into a hollow for some unstated purpose, that Stanley would have agreed, and that the said Turk would then make sodomitical overtures spontaneously? We must remember too that he had many companions nearby, as we shall see in a moment. The account Stanley provides in his 'Adventures' has the same whiff of fantasy as his many other 'true stories'.

As soon as Achmet had made good his escape, Stanley realised the deadly peril they were in. At this moment Cook trooped wearily in and Stanley put his astonished comrade in the picture. They turned back in the direction they had come from. But very soon whooping sounds and a cloud of dust at their backs told them that Achmet had brought reinforcements. A mounted chase commenced.

For four hours they careered wildly over the mountains. The exhausted horses frequently butted into each other in the attempt to keep their footing. They raced through dense woods and deep mountain gorges. At last they paused for rest in a 'deep dell enclosed on all sides by high mountains, whose summits everlastingly kissed the clouds'.[39] In the clear mountain air the only sound they could hear was the distant tinkling of cowbells. Yet Stanley's instincts told him they were not yet safe. He urged his two comrades to one last effort; once over the almost perpendicular mountain wall ahead of them they would be truly secure.

The climb proved too much for the emaciated horses. One of them stumbled and rolled back down the slope, almost crushing Noe. They abandoned the horses and pressed on to the summit on foot. Triumphantly they sat on a grassy ridge, confident that the danger was behind them. Suddenly, as if from nowhere, Achmet and his companions rushed them, pinioned their arms, then trussed and blindfolded them.

Their captors led them down the slopes to a Turcoman encampment. At its outskirts Stanley began to feel real fear for the first time. Achmet and his men were joined by 'three hideous, ragged ruffians' who cocked their guns and swore by Allah that they would shoot the infidels. Just in time an old man waving a sword interposed himself and the three desperadoes moved sullenly to the rear. Then Achmet and the others tied their prisoners to a post and began shooting around them. The bullets whined dangerously near their heads. Just when Stanley was giving himself up for dead, the old man again intervened:

At one time he hovered around us like a guardian angel with his drawn sword, again he energetically harangued them on the cruel, foolish course which they wished to adopt. Gradually his eloquence seemed to tell and we breathed free when hearing the word 'Hayde, Hayde' – 'Go ahead'. Although uttered harshly, they were none the less welcome.[40]

The Turks ceased their 'target practice', untethered their victims and took them on to a village, which they reached at dusk. Their arrival caused the greatest excitement. A babel of yelling and halloing was counterpointed by the firing of guns and the barking of dogs. Women and young boys came out of the houses and pelted the prisoners with stones and mud. One old man approached them with tottering steps and dealt Noe a number of energetic cuffs around the head. Piteously Noe asked Stanley whether they were to be killed. Stanley shrugged.

Next the prisoners were dragged to an open portico that seemed to double as a court. A sea of scowling faces confronted them. The old man who had cuffed Noe took the place of honour; Stanley observed cynically that the villagers deferred to him and called him 'Emir'. This patriarch and his council then proceeded to try the miscreants. Achmet was called to give evidence and pointed Stanley out with a show of great indignation. The council debated inconclusively what to do with the prisoners, then at midnight announced an adjournment until the next morning. The three Westerners were left in the hands of their captors.

The situation of Stanley and his two comrades was parlous. They were haltered with ropes around their necks, and thus in a state of semi-strangulation, half-sitting, half-lying on the ground, out in the open, exposed to the cold night air and without any shelter or covering. But there was worse to come. The three ruffians who had caused Stanley such a *frisson* earlier in the day put in an appearance in the small hours, once the village had settled down to sleep. While two of them held a knife to Noe's throat and warned him not to make a noise, the third raped him. The others then took their turn at buggery, 'a crime common in Turkey but not fit to be mentioned to polite ears'. Stanley was not at first aware of the full horror of what was going on but 'I was awakened out of a fitful doze by deep, agonised, though stifled groans. They had no pity or remorse but one by one they committed their diabolical crime which is, I think, or I hope, unknown to civilised nations, especially Christian America.'[41]

Stanley's mental turmoil was real enough. His graphic evidence suggests that he himself had not actually been sodomised in the workhouse, but the rape would doubtless have conjured memories of many lewd acts he *had* witnessed in St Asaph's. Even more poignantly, the Turks' actions brought home forcibly to Stanley the reality of the instincts towards Noe which he was suppressing and which had found their outlet in the bloody beating. The three ruffians were acting out a possibility he could not face.

Stanley's contempt for Islam was never so great as when, at sunrise, the three rapists turned towards Mecca to pray. Evidently the village council at this stage washed its hands of the whole affair, for Achmet and his men set about searching them and their effects roughly for money. They found none but offered to set them free for 1,400 piastres. Then their captors hauled them back to the Turcoman encampment. They were given coffee while Achmet again harangued bystanders on the dreadful treatment Stanley had meted out to him. One old woman was so incensed by the tale that she broke through the ranks of the men and fetched Stanley a blow on the head that momentarily stunned him. One of the elders rebuked her for overstepping her social bounds, whereat she slunk away like a whipped cur.

Still undecided what to do with them, Achmet and his henchmen took them on, still bound, to a larger village. Here the three prisoners were released from their bonds and grilled on where they had hidden the money. All three swore there was no money. Achmet lost his temper, waved a sword menacingly over their heads and then hit Stanley hard on the hand with the flat of his sword in an effort to make him talk. This was another critical moment for Stanley. 'I now resigned myself to my fate and refused to answer any question whatever.'[42]

Noe and Cook were more co-operative. After both had sworn a solemn oath to Allah that they were penniless, Achmet saw that he had but two choices: cold-blooded murder or a formal indictment before a magistrate. Once more he tied up his prisoners and set out with them for the town of Rashakeni.

This was a bad mistake on Achmet's part. Rashakeni happened to possess an intelligent governor who knew something of Western ways. In a dialectical contest a simple peasant like Achmet was no match for the educated, quick-witted Stanley. When both sides were called on to make their depositions, Stanley made verbal mincemeat of the opposition. He convinced the governor that the violence had started when Achmet and his comrades tried to rob them. For all that, the governor took a dim view of what he saw as Stanley's attempt to take the law into his own hands. He ordered that all parties to the dispute be chained and taken to the prison at Karahisar, five hours' ride distant.

At Karahisar Noe was again the butt of Turkish violence. When they arrived at the prison gates, there was a conversation between their escort and the prison porter, following which the porter struck Noe a blow that almost doubled him up. Noe appealed piteously to Stanley: 'Oh, Henry, I have been hit.' Stanley's response was typical. By his own admission, he could scarcely refrain from laughing.[43]

The laughter was stilled when the three of them were thrown into a dungeon reeking with an intolerable stench and full of local riff-raff who surrounded them and began to take liberties with their private parts: 'You can imagine our feelings when surrounded by these people, who were too ready to induct us into their sodomitical practices. I really pitied the poor boy Louis, as he was mentally marked by these ruffians as that night's victim.'[44]

Providence intervened, for at that very moment they were taken to be interviewed by the prison commandant. He immediately saw that these were Westerners of higher status than had previously been represented to him. He rehoused them on their own in a better part of the jail. Next morning they were taken to see Raouf Bey, the governor. He was dressed in European clothes and for the first time Stanley was able to establish some true intellectual rapport. Raouf at once realised that there was an international dimension to the case. He decided to send Stanley and his companions to Bursa, where there were Turkish-speaking Americans who could represent them. Accordingly on 27 September 1866 the three men left Karahisar. Achmet and his minions were to be sent up to Bursa in chains when the trial started.[45]

On 30 September they halted at Actumtael. Stanley recorded: 'We are all in excellent spirits, Louis especially. Entirely forgotten their dastardly barbarity committed on him.'[46] On 2 October they were at Klutrial, where they were well treated by a sept of Armenian Christians. On 8 October they arrived at Bursa and lodged at the home of an American missionary called Richardson. Richardson and his wife invited them to treat their home as their own.[47]

On 11 October Achmet and his men arrived in chains and a preliminary hearing commenced. Since Stanley claimed that he and his companions had been robbed of 80,000 piastres, yet only 40 piastres had been found on the robbers, the Bursa magistrate decided that Stanley should swear a formal affidavit with the American consul in Constantinople.[48] Stanley and his friends arrived there on the evening of 14 October, put up in the Hotel d'Orient and spent the next week drawing up a statement of their grievances.[49]

The US Minister in Turkey at the time was the fifty-one-year-old Edward Jay Morris, who had been in post since 1861. He confessed then and later to finding Stanley's allegations puzzling on a number of counts. Stanley claimed to have had a large sum of money in gold and banknotes hidden in cartridge boxes plus a letter of credit on a Tiflis merchant for 200,000 piastres (about $1,500). The gold alone was said to amount to $300. Morris thought it strange that his three compatriots should be travelling in Turkey with American coin, and even odder that Stanley should have had a draft on Tiflis drawn on a merchant in Maiden Lane, New York, since in his five years in Turkey Morris had never heard of any commercial intercourse between New York and Tiflis.[50] Nor did Stanley increase the plausibility of his story by having a handbill printed in which he claimed to have been robbed of $4,000 in cash.[51] He seemed as unable to decide exactly how much money had been 'robbed' as Senator McCarthy was later uncertain about how many Communists there were in the Eisenhower administration.

Stanley explained to Morris that as a result of the 'robbery' they were penniless. He asked Morris for a loan of £150 against a draft for that amount on his father, whom Stanley claimed was a rich lawyer at 20 Liberty Street, New York.[52] Morris accepted the draft and paid Stanley the £150. Stanley then divided it among the three of them, but further alienated Noe by giving himself and Cook £59 each while Noe received just £32.[53]

On 26 October the trio had to return from Constantinople to Bursa for the formal trial of Achmet and his comrades.[54] Morris, who after some hesitation decided to back Stanley to the hilt, made a formal complaint to the Turkish government. The newspapers were full of the story of a 'barbarous attack on American travellers'.[55] The affair threatened to become a *cause célèbre*. The Turks, who in the prevailing international climate needed all the friends they could get, decided to conciliate the USA by indicting Achmet and the others for aggravated robbery and assault. The government accepted implicitly that if they found the 'robbers' guilty, they would have to pay compensation to the victims.

By 9 November Stanley, Cook and Noe had made their detailed depositions in Bursa and were free to leave. By this time they had overstayed their welcome with the missionaries and Mr Richardson had in any case requested them to leave his household.[56] Stanley took Noe with him to Constantinople, leaving Cook to await the outcome of the trial and to send on any compensation payable. Once in Constantinople he did not bother to call on Minister Morris who had so trustingly helped him out, but immediately booked passage to Marseilles.[57]

On 14 November 1866 Stanley and Noe embarked for Marseilles. There was a terrific storm in the Aegean, during which a man was lost overboard, then another violent gale after they passed Messina and entered the Tyrrhenian Sea. Sailing under the lee of Sardinia and Corsica, they arrived at Marseilles on the 23rd but were detained in quarantine for twelve hours before being permitted to land.[58] They caught the 10.45 p.m. train to Paris, arrived at Lyons next morning and reached the French capital after twenty-four hours 'on the cars'. After resting for three days at the Hotel de Dieppe, they caught the Newhaven packet and arrived in London late on 27 November. They at once took the night train to Liverpool.[59]

During the fortnight's journey from Constantinople to Liverpool, the final breach between Stanley and Noe took place. Once back in 'civilisation' Noe complained bitterly about Stanley's treatment of him, about the beatings and the way Stanley's recklessness had led to the rape.[60] The quarrel simmered on when they reached Liverpool. Stanley prevailed on Uncle Tom Morris and Aunt Maria to take Noe in while he went visiting his other relations in Wales; this time the Morrises had moved to 18 Davies Street.[61]

Stanley had learned nothing from his experiences in Turkey. Undaunted by the fact that his fantasy world had brought him inches away from violent death, he uncoiled a further lariat of lies once in North Wales. After visiting his cousin John Owen in Shrewsbury, he called on his mother at the Cross Foxes in Glascoed to present her with a portrait of himself and impress her with the news that he was now an ensign in the US Navy.[62] He developed the fantasy in an entry in the visitors' book at Denbigh Castle on 14 December: 'John Rowlands, formerly of this Castle now Ensign in the United States Navy in North America, belonging to the US ship *Ticonderoga*, now at Constantinople, Turkey; absent on furlough.'[63] It was typical of Stanley's guile to interweave a truth (that he had recently been in Constantinople) with an egregious lie.

With the balance of the money he had inveigled out of Minister Morris, Stanley was able to cut a dash in Denbigh and sustain his fantasy of being a well-paid naval officer. The rest of his family were regaled with the same story. His cousin Henry Parry actually received a photograph of Stanley in naval uniform (presumably from his *Minnesota* days), signed 'Your loving cousin John Rowlands, 22 December, 1866'.[64] It is noteworthy that in Wales Stanley was still 'John Rowlands'. He gave a tea party at St Asaph's for the children as a sort of informal quid pro quo for a reference from the chairman, Captain Leigh Thomas.[65] Quite what he was supposed to be doing soliciting for references at St Asaph's (and from Bishop Vowler Short and Squire Pennant at Tremerchion) if he had risen so high in the world is unclear. But it may be that some doubts crept in and that Stanley tried to get Noe to come down to corroborate his story, for Noe conferred with Uncle Tom Morris on the advisability of the trip, only to receive the chilling admonition by no means to venture there since 'if John got me in the mountains there, with his present feelings against me, I should never get out alive.'[66] If ever Noe had thought that his morbid fear of Stanley and his capacity to commit any crime was some form of paranoid delusion,

Uncle Tom Morris's words alerted him that others perceived Stanley in exactly the same way. Ever afterwards Noe and his family combined insensate hatred of Stanley with a genuine fear of assassination.[67]

The one positive thing Stanley brought back from his trip to North Wales was a further reinforcement of his contacts with the *Missouri Democrat*. When Stanley happened to mention to the Bishop's coachman at the Palace Lodge that he had contributed occasional pieces to that newspaper, the coachman gave him the names of two relations named Ebbells who lived in Missouri and knew the editor well.[68] Stanley had already decided that his future once more lay in the New World. On 7 January 1867 he returned to Liverpool and put up at the Commercial Hotel. Next day he went with Noe to visit the municipal museum and library, then on 14 January sailed for New York in the *Denmark*.[69]

The Turkish adventure merits further consideration, since it provides vital clues to Stanley's character and personality. Hitherto we have been able to convict Stanley as a liar, but arguably before 1866 his lies were 'inner-directed' rather than 'other-directed'. In Turkey for the first time Stanley gave unmistakable evidence that his lies were truly pathological, that he would bend the truth in all directions to secure his own ends, no matter who was hurt in the process. Moreover, although his ambiguous sexuality had clearly been a problem to him since adolescence. Turkey provided the first clear evidence of a 'solution' via sado-masochism.

First, the lies and the breathtaking criminality of the way in which Stanley proposed providing himself with money. It was the very audacity of his plan that guaranteed ultimate success, for although his story of the 'robbery' did not stand up to detailed scrutiny, the alternative scenario for men like Morris if they rejected it was too horrifying to contemplate. It was essentially the technique of the 'big lie': psychologically Morris was almost bound to believe that Stanley's story was in essence correct, even if it was ragged at the edges. It was simply inconceivable that there could be *no truth at all in it*.[70]

Yet in his dark moments Morris must have allowed this possibility to surface. His own Secretary of Legation, Brown, told him bluntly that he had been a fool to trust Stanley, and Morris self-confessedly was hurt when Stanley left Constantinople without any further contact with him once he had paid over the £150.[71] The sequel confirmed his worst fears. Morris sent Stanley's draft to his agent in Philadelphia, who reported back that no such person as 'Stanley senior' lived on Liberty Street. Morris would have been defrauded of the £150 had not the Achmet case turned out satisfactorily. Part of the affidavit Stanley had sworn to in Turkey contained an accusation of sodomy, which was proved against two of the rapists.[72] The fact that the charge of buggery was sustained had a 'knock-on' effect on the rest of the indictment. Morris modified Stanley's compensation claim from $4,000 to the more believable $2,000 and accepted $1,200 the Turkish authorities actually offered. Out of the compensation money he repaid himself his £150.

Having taken no material loss, Morris, in retirement in Atlantic City, was not disposed to get involved in a nasty wrangle in 1872 when Noe's accusations first surfaced in the American press. Noe correctly accused Stanley of a complicated larceny and of having defrauded Morris of £150. Since Stanley was by this time famous as the man who had found Livingstone, Morris naturally did not want to get into a bare-knuckle fight with Stanley and his protectors at the *New York Herald*. He therefore concocted the plausible story that he had advanced Stanley the £150 against the expected compensation money, though how he can have been *sure* the Turkish court would find in his compatriots' favour is not explained.[73] More skilful cross-questioning from the rival *Sun*'s reporter a few days later dug out the true story for anyone who cared to see it. Morris was forced to retract the categorical assurances he had made a few days earlier and admitted that he *had* sent the draft to Philadelphia for encashment.[74]

Since we have established that Noe's allegations about Stanley's naval career in the Civil War and his larceny in Turkey are accurate, there are strong prima-facie grounds for presuming that his story of the thrashing Stanley gave him in the pomegranate grove is also true. In fact, Stanley himself admitted that he had given Noe a 'few strokes of a switch' allegedly for starting the fire in a 'valuable grove'.[75] Noe successfully refuted the story by demonstrating that the ignited bushes were not a valuable grove and that Stanley had encouraged him to set them alight as part of the horseplay to tease Cook.[76] Stanley's defence against Noe was twofold. First, there was vulgar abuse of a personal kind written by his acolytes but in no way answering the specific charges Noe made.[77] Secondly, there was the 'corroborating' testimony of Harlow Cook. Cook's evidence is vitiated by the fact that he hated Noe and hero-worshipped Stanley and was not present at either the thrashing or the Achmet incident; furthermore, anyone reading the 'affidavit' he provided to enquiring journalists in 1872 will find it merely risible.[78] The very speech and body-language described by the interviewer provide a virtual polygraph test of their own: 'A look of surprise but no quick answer'; 'Musingly "Yes, a considerable time"'; '"Well, I must think it over now"'; '"I do not want to tell what I can at this time for more reasons than one."'[79] The only surprise is that Cook did not plead the Fifth Amendment!

There would be many more beatings of servants and underlings in the future to lend credence to Noe's story. The true significance of the Turkey experience is the way it conflates the themes of lying and fantasy with those of sexual ambiguity and sado-masochism. Both strands were organically linked in the Stanley personality.

The deeper the neurosis, the more difficulty there is in distinguishing fantasy from reality. In part Stanley's lies were a product of his refusal to accept the facts about his childhood and early life. The denial of his Welshness, of his true identity as John Rowlands, his commitment to a 'Family Romance' were all part of this. Another aspect of the departure from reality is concerned with the need for constant action. A man in a frenzy of activity will be led increasingly into the realms of the preposterous.[80] At a certain point the boundary between fantasy and actuality will begin to blur even in the perceiving subject. Another outstandingly gifted man of Africa spotted this aspect of Stanley: 'I never knew a European or any other creature who could lie like him. How can he tell truth from falsehood?'[81]

Just as Stanley perilously straddled the twilight area between fantasy and reality, so did he inhabit the limbo between homosexuality and heterosexuality. Stanley was attracted to women, to their beauty and their compassionate qualities, but he could not integrate sexuality into his perception of them, except by the rigid madonna/whore bifurcation. His relations with women therefore remained at the superficial level of idealisation and courtly love. Since he could only either worship or despise a woman, he could not have a female as a partner. The rough comradeship of men held out more hope of easy contact. There was no occasion to be shy or awkward with those who inhabited the same masculine world of action and violent adventure. At the same time, true equality with a man was also impossible, since a genuine equal would also be a potential rival for the esteem of the world.[82] So Stanley chose men who were inferior to him in one way or another, in age, social status or, if it came to it, in will-power. Lewis Noe was the first of a long line that included Edwin Balch, Edward King, Frank Pocock, Albert Christopherson and Mounteney-Jephson, to say nothing of Stanley's black or Arab servants: Selim, Kalulu, Baruti and the others. His homosexual feelings towards them remained at a passive level. If we are to dub Stanley 'bisexual' we must be clear that we are not talking about the active bisexuality of, say, the Ancient World. One obvious way to sublimate these contradictory sexual impulses is through the dominant/submissive polarity of sado-masochism.

Ambiguity, then, was the key to Stanley's personality. Mounteney-Jephson perceived something of this when he wrote of Stanley in the late 1880s: 'Half a white man, half an Arab . . . describes Stanley very well. All the falseness and doubledealing, the indifference to breaking his word, the meanness, brutality and greediness, are the Arab side. The wonderful dogged determination to carry through to a successful issue all that he takes in hand, his cleverness in mapping, writing, conversation etc. all belong to the European side. He has two distinct personalities, one cannot be too much admired and praised, the other is contemptible in the extreme.'[83]

There is much irony here. Stanley denied his own Welshness, yet in pointing up the duality of the Welsh, he unwittingly provided a portrait of himself: 'A compound of opposites – exclusive as Spaniards, vindictive as Corsicans, conservative as Osmanlis, sensible in business, but not enterprising; quarrelsome, but law-abiding; devout but litigious; industrious and thrifty, but not rich; loyal but discontented.'[84]

4

1867 was the year Stanley won his spurs as war correspondent. Originally hired by the *Missouri Democrat* as an 'occasional' on the strength of his unpublished Civil War jottings, he impressed them sufficiently to be taken on as a regular correspondent. His first assignment was to cover General Hancock's military expedition against the Southern Cheyenne. Later he reported on the peace conferences between the plains Indians and General Sherman and the other Peace Commissioners appointed by Washington: at North Platte (with the Sioux and Cheyenne) and at Medicine Lodge (with the Kiowas, Arapahoes, Comanches and Apache). During this colourful year on the plains Stanley made the acquaintance of many legendary figures in the history of the West: Generals Sherman, Terry and Hancock; Wild Bill Hickock and Custer; and the Indian chiefs Spotted Tail, Satank and Satanta. So successful was Stanley as a war correspondent that by the end of 1867 his pieces were in demand not just by the *Missouri Democrat* but by the big eastern newspapers, especially the *New York Tribune* and *New York Herald*.[1]

In December 1867 Stanley presented himself at the New York offices of the *Herald*. By great good fortune (Stanley was always a lucky person), he found the proprietor James Gordon Bennett junior on one of his rare visits to his paper's headquarters. Bennett knew of, and was impressed by, Stanley's coverage of events in the West, but when Stanley proposed himself as a war correspondent in Abyssinia, Bennett scornfully replied that British imperial wars were of no great interest to an American readership. This despite the fact that the campaign promised to be a unique and sensational one. Ethiopia's emperor Theodore had taken a number of British subjects hostage in his mountain fortress of Magdala. When all diplomatic measures to secure the hostages had failed, the British reluctantly put General Sir Robert Napier, a hero of the Indian mutiny, in command of a powerful punitive expedition.

When Stanley insisted that there was 'good copy' in the war, Bennett, intrigued, asked what his terms were. Stanley replied that he would accept an assignment either as a *Herald* special correspondent, on salary and expenses, or as a freelance, payable by letter, in which case he reserved the option to send material to other newspapers. At that Bennett's face clouded over; the *Herald* shared with nobody, he said testily. But he suggested a compromise: he would be prepared to pay a very high rate per letter for exclusive rights to Stanley's reports, but Stanley had to pay his own passage and all his expenses. As an afterthought he asked what Stanley's experience was outside the United States. Stanley rattled off a long list of Mediterranean place-names which satisfied the dour proprietor.[2]

Bennett then wrote to his agent, Colonel Finlay Anderson, head of the *Herald*'s London bureau. Stanley made preparations for an immediate sailing to Europe, but first he took the precaution of securing letters of introduction by telegraph from Generals Grant and Sherman. With £300 in his pocket Stanley took the first available steamer from New York to Liverpool.[3]

After crossing the Atlantic and making the necessary arrangements in London, Stanley sped to Suez, via Paris and Marseilles. The preparations of the British commander General Napier were already well advanced for the march on Theodore's capital of Magdala. At Suez Stanley took a momentous decision. He bribed the telegraph operator heavily to ensure that his copy was forwarded to London ahead of that of his journalistic rivals.[4] Then he sped on to the Red Sea port of Annesley Bay in the Horn of Africa, where Napier was assembling his assault forces for the long inland march on Theodore's mountain stronghold.

Stanley arrived at Annesley Bay at the end of January 1868. For two months he marched with the British forces into the mountains and jungles of Abyssinia. On Good Friday, 10 April, Napier scored a spectacular victory over Theodore's forces in the plains below Magdala. The fortress was stormed, the emperor committed suicide. The British sacked Magdala before putting it to the torch.[5]

There followed a gruelling march back to the coast in the height of the rainy season. By the end of May, having taken appalling risks and cut his safety margin to the bone and beyond, a lone-travelling Stanley was approaching journey's end, ahead of his fellow journalists. At Suez on 6 June his first stop was the telegraph office, where he rewarded his accomplice and sent off fresh material. He was conscious of having scooped the field, but it was only when he travelled up to Alexandria on 26

June that he first realised what a sensation his despatches from Abyssinia had created. He had expected, after his bribery, to be first in the field. What he had not counted on was that his scoop would be such a sensation.

Immediately after Stanley's first batch of copy had been relayed from the Suez telegraph office the cable between Malta and Alexandria broke and was out of action for days. The consequences was that Stanley's copy was the first detailed news of the Magdala triumph and was the sole authoritative source for almost a week. So completely had Stanley slipped the field that his feat was regarded with incredulity. It seemed inconceivable that the first comprehensive intelligence from Abyssinia should be coming from a 'Yankee' journalist. He was dubbed charlatan and impostor. When, a week later, the despatches from the correspondents of *The Times*, *Telegraph* and *Standard* came in and confirmed Stanley's story, something very like a howl of indignation went up in London.[6]

Stanley had now well and truly arrived as a war correspondent. He was immediately put on the *Herald*'s permanent payroll. So great was the pleasure of Gordon Bennett junior at the discomfiture of his British rivals that he printed all Stanley's despatches at great length without cuts and taunted other newspapers with the superiority of its 'special' H. M. Stanley: 'Our readers will not fail to perceive the vast superiority in style of writing, minuteness of detail and graphic portrayal of event which the *Herald* correspondence possesses over the written accounts of the same matter printed in the London journals, of which we furnished specimens in the shape of extracts a few days ago.'[7] As Bennett later admitted, it was Stanley's Abyssinian triumph that led eventually to his being chosen as the right man to 'find' Dr Livingstone.[8]

In the balmy days of triumph in Alexandria, when the full scale of his achievement was gradually dawning on him, Stanley struck up an acquaintance with Douglas Gibbs, local manager of the *Daily Telegraph*. Gibbs was kind to Stanley, frequently entertained him to dinner, and praised lavishly his achievements in Abyssinia. Yet he was not without his eccentricities. Stanley arrived in Alexandria virtually broke, yet owed £200 from Finlay Anderson. When he approached Gibbs for a loan of £5, Gibbs turned him down, even though Stanley expostulated that he was good for a hundred times that sum and even though, as Stanley pointed out, Gibbs spent more than that on every one of the sumptuous dinners he treated him to.[9]

Stanley now had to await word from his new employers as to his next assignment, so had time on his hands. He began by shipping 'Fayed' (the Arab horse he had bought from an aristocratic officer) and the groom to

Liverpool.[10] Then he went up to Ismailia for a week to report on the progress of the canal being dug at Suez.[11] His report on this, though not commissioned, was published eagerly by the *Herald*.[12] Another important contact Stanley made at this time was the Egyptian diplomat Hekekyan Bey, whom he met in Cairo, and to whom he introduced consul Cameron, one of the captives of Magdala.[13]

On his return to Alexandria, on 17 July 1868, he fell ill and was in bed for several days with a fever. Men like Stanley are always impatient with illness, and will not accept the limitations to their actions placed on them by an ailing body. Barely recuperated, Stanley took himself off to a Mediterranean bay and decided to get back into shape by swimming. Since Stanley was an excellent swimmer, this would normally have presented no risk, but he reckoned without his weakened constitution. At first all went well: he plunged into the bay, felt invigorated and struck out strongly towards the sea. But after about 50 yards, he began to feel weak, then suddenly realised to his horror that he lacked the strength to return to the shore and so was in imminent danger of drowning. It so happened that the Reuter's correspondent, one Edward Viruard, was swimming nearby. Seeing Stanley in distress, he managed to life-save him back to the beach.[14] Years later, when Stanley was famous, Viruard claimed a financial 'reward' for saving his life.

The shock temporarily brought Stanley to his senses. This time he convalesced properly. It was just as well, for the orders that arrived from London on 7 August consigned him to another theatre of war. This time it was Crete, where the indigenous inhabitants had raised the standard of revolt against the Turks, seeking to emulate the 1828 example of the Greek mother-country.[15] The Russians, always ready to discomfit the Turks in the 'Near East', had already sent aid to the rebels; American sentiment, too, was overwhelmingly pro-Cretan, and the *Herald* had been watching the build-up in hostilities with concern and interest ever since March.[16] Reports that Turkish regulars had been decisively worsted on the island by Cretan guerrillas were the particular trigger for the sending of Stanley.[17]

On 13 August Stanley left Alexandria for Crete, after a long rest capped by exhaustive sightseeing among the Alexandrine ruins. Turkish shipping embargoes plus the lack of any direct route from Egypt meant a round-about itinerary, passing first by the lee of Rhodes. His first stop was Scio, a small seaport on the Turkish coast, in the Izmir area. While there he revived unpleasant memories by visiting the spot where Noe started the fire in the grove in 1866. Back at the Hotel Europe, he booked passage on a steamer bound for the island of Siros (Sira), on which he, an American and a Hong Kong lawyer were the only non-Greek passengers. Before he left, a contact named Alexandroff gave him a letter of introduction to one of the Siros bigwigs, one Christos Evangelides ('What a name!' Stanley recorded in his diary), a naturalised American.[18]

On arrival at Siros at noon on 19 August, Stanley sought out Evangelides, a middle-aged man with a snowy white beard, and handed him the letter of introduction. Evangelides turned out to be another romancer of the Levison stamp, 'a Greek of Greeks', as Stanley put it, so the *Herald* reporter determined on keeping his sceptical distance.[19] But Evangelides overwhelmed him with charm and offered to be his guide on the islands. He took Stanley first to visit Julia Ward Howe, author of the 'Battle Hymn of the Republic', not knowing that Stanley had had first-hand experience of the Civil War's 'terrible swift sword'. Then they went on to a seminary where Stanley made the mistake of commenting favourably on the good looks of young Greeks. Immediately Evangelides pounced and suggested that Stanley marry a Greek girl. The twenty-seven-year-old reporter's reactions, as confided to his diary, were of a piece with his combined uncertain sexuality and pedestal worship of the female:

> Up to this moment it had never entered my mind that it must be some day my fate to select a wife . . . yet the suggestion was delicious from other points of view. A wife! My wife! How grand the proprietorship of a fair woman appeared! To be loved with heart and soul above all else, forever united in thought and sympathy with a fair and virtuous being, whose very touch gave strength and courage and confidence! Oh dear! how my warm imagination glows at the strange idea![20]

Seeing the effect his words had had, Evangelides tried to press home his advantage and urged a Greek marriage all the more strongly. Stanley demurred on the grounds that he was a rover of the world and in any case had no money. Evangelides refused to take no for an answer and offered to be Stanley's proxy and to find him a nubile girl of unmatched beauty and character. Unfortunately the Greek's idea of what constituted these qualities was not Stanley's, for that very evening Evangelides proposed his unprepossessing daughter Calliope as candidate. Calliope's homeliness was such that it was difficult for Stanley not to burst out laughing in the paternal face.[21]

Stanley returned to his hotel to bone up on the Cretan rebellion. There was plenty of evidence on Siros of the plight of the Cretan refugees, who were existing on food doles and hand-outs of clothes; an American missionary told him the story was the same on Naxos and Tenedos.[22] But even while Stanley was revolving all this in his mind, the irrepressible Evangelides returned to the attack next morning by again proposing his daughter as Stanley's wife. The puritanical Welsh-American was deeply shocked: 'It is scarcely credible that a father would be so indifferent to his daughter's happiness as to cast her upon the first stranger he meets.'[23] He made his excuses again, and spent the day of 22 August on a horseback excursion into the interior of Siros, reeling at the impact of a stainless sky and the 'wine-dark' sea: 'When I returned to the town, I quite understood Byron's passion for Hellas.' But Evangelides had not finished with him yet. That evening, while Stanley was taking his evening walk around the main square in Ermoupolis (Hermopolis), Evangelides again collared him and took him to visit a respectable middle-aged couple named Ambella in the residential quarter of the town. After some inconsequential banter 'in glided a young lady who came as near as possible to the realisation of the ideal which my fancy had portrayed . . . demure . . . wrapped in virgin modesty. Her name was Virginia and well it befitted her. She is about sixteen, and, if she can speak English, who knows?'[24]

Stanley's way of thinking and talking about Virginia Ambella reveals his limitations as a serious suitor, even by Victorian standards. But there was nothing frivolous about the Ambella family's attitude. To his great uneasiness, Virginia's mother then cross-questioned him about his attitude to marriage in general and Virginia's suitability as wife in particular. Stanley was shocked at this matter-of-factness and lack of reserve. His embarrassed blushes rivalled those of the maidenly Virginia. But no amount of winking and nodding could shake Evangelides' 'astonishing effrontery'.[25] Stanley was glad to get out of the house and back to his hotel.

Yet clearly he was left with mixed feelings, corresponding to his deeply ambivalent psyche. On the one hand he was profoundly attracted by Virginia's physical beauty. On the other, he must have known that, in terms of a serious relationship with a woman, he was merely shadow-boxing. Yet he allowed Evangelides to lure him back to the Ambella household next morning, when further verbal fencing went on between Stanley and the determined matron. The mother accused him of excessive shyness. When they left the house, Stanley complained to Evangelides that he felt he was being 'bounced' into a marriage; why all the rush? Evangelides shrugged and said it was the Greek way. Stanley countered that he knew no Greek and little French, while Virginia knew no English and little French too; what sort of a basis was that for partnership? Evangelides responded by declaring that the Ambella family was well off. They parted, and Stanley noticed him going back to the Ambella house: 'What an extraordinary people!' he confided to his diary.[26]

Evangelides came back later that day to say that the Ambella parents had agreed to a marriage with their daughter provided Stanley made a formal proposal for Virginia's hand. Stanley replied that, since he was setting off for Crete next day, that hardly seemed a sensible procedure. But eventually Evangelides wore him down. He composed a formal letter of proposal. The jubilant Greek bore it away and returned in the evening with news that the Ambellas would give him a formal answer when he returned from Crete.

The sheer artificiality of this 'romance' emerges most clearly in Stanley's diary for the 24th, when he was at sea, heading for Crete. Although Virginia was in his thoughts, his affections were under control and he was disposed to leave matters in the lap of the gods. The calmness of the sea and his position as the only non-Greek passenger aided his detachment. He had, in any case, other things on his mind, for the war zone was looming. That afternoon the ship anchored in the bay of Iraklion, dominated by the Venetian fort lost to the Turks in 1569. After three hours there, the ship ran along the coast to Rethimnon, reached at 9.30 that evening. It was after midnight before the final stretch of the journey, to Khania, was accomplished.[27]

At Khania they encountered a rigorous customs search, so that it was about 7 a.m. before Stanley got clear of the port. He pressed on immediately to the nearby village of Kalippa, where he was to introduce himself to Mr Stillman, the US consul. Stillman proved to be a tall, thin, nervous man of about forty. He had literary ambitions and wrote articles for journals and was out of his depth in the Cretan rebellion, though constrained to continue in post in order to support his large family; as Stanley remarked, 'I fear he will be fit only for a madhouse if he lives here much longer.'[28]

Evidently Stillman took to Stanley – perhaps it was the common interest in literature – for he stayed with them for a week, compiling data on the rebellion. But he showed no hurry to venture near the war zone; the diaries are full of entries on sea-bathing, sightseeing and overnight stays at ancient convents.[29] Part of the problem was that Stanley was in the wrong part of Crete. After the success of Omar Pasha's 'blockhouse' system, the Cretans under Gogoneus decided to abandon the western provinces of Crete. On 31 August Stanley decided that the Cretan rebellion was a bore, that there was probably better 'copy' on the Greek mainland. The Stillmans saw him off on a ship bound for Siros.

The vessel ploughed through a ferocious Aegean gale that left Stanley unconcerned. He stayed in the ship's library and read Marryat's *Percival Keene*.[30] After retracing the exact outward journey, Stanley arrived back in Siros at 3 a.m. on 2 September. He made his way to Evangelides' house for an early breakfast, but on learning that there was no news yet from the Ambella family, at once embarked on the *Eunomia* bound for Athens. After stops at Kithnos and Kea, the *Eunomia* arrived at Piraeus at 9 p.m. Stanley hired a carriage for the drive to Athens and by midnight was ensconced in the Hotel de L'Angleterre.[31]

He slept late next morning but was still in time to report a great day for Athens: the baptism of Prince Constantine, heir-apparent to the throne. A lavish banquet was laid on for the poor of Athens on the plain of Zeus the Olympian and before the temple of Theseus. The particular interest for *Herald* readers was the participation of US Admiral Farragut in the celebrations. He had arrived two days earlier at Piraeus with the *Franklin* and the *Frolic* and kindled Cretan aspirations with a rousing speech to 3,000 of their exiled fighters.[32]

After writing his despatch for the *Herald*, Stanley was in no particular mood to move on. He spent five days sightseeing the classical antiquities before departing for Siros.[33] On arrival there on the morning of 9 September he was greeted effusively by Evangelides, who informed him that his suit for Virginia's hand was successful and the marriage as good as concluded. A visit to the Ambella household confirmed this. This time two of Virginia's brothers and a sister were present, and it was obvious that Stanley was being scrutinised as a prospective brother-in-law. A tentative date for the marriage was fixed for the following Sunday. It was arranged that Stanley would have his first meeting with Virginia alone that very evening.[34]

At last Stanley came to his senses and realised the enormity of the step he was about to take. Thoroughly frightened, he hinted to Evangelides that there were things in his past life that would not bear close examination. The hint worked. When Stanley returned to the Ambellas that evening, he was allowed to talk to Virginia alone; he recorded that his misgivings were temporarily dispelled by the touch of her hand and the moistness of her eyes. But Mrs Ambella was now setting new conditions:

after all, she told Stanley, they knew nothing about him and before surrendering their cherished daughter to him they ought to know something of his background; she hoped that he would not be offended if the marriage was put off while she took up references. Stanley's reply clearly hints at his own divided emotions: 'Well so be it,' I said, 'though I am sorry and perhaps you may be sorry, but I cannot deny that you are just and wise.'[35] His ambivalence comes through even more strongly when he reflects on the dinner he gave the Ambella family at the hotel de l'Amerique in Siros on 11 September: 'It is as well that I go away shortly, for I feel that she is a treasure; and my admiration, if encouraged, would soon be coverted into love, and if once I love, I am lost! However, the possibility of losing her serves to restrain me.'[36]

Stanley's initial actions certainly suggest the ardent suitor. He suggested to Mrs Ambella that she take up references from the *Missouri Democrat* in St Louis and from the Egyptian authorities in Cairo. He himself wrote to Hekekyan Bey to put him in the picture. The letter is revealing as its lifts a corner on his true feelings towards the Ambellas. After describing Virginia as 'a Greek girl steeped in poverty but famous for her beauty', he goes on, 'She is cursed with rather obnoxious parents but I risk all to marry her . . . I have offered to settle on the poor girl the sum of $50 per month as long as she lives, but those parents are avaricious and want more.'[37] So far as one can tell, the statement about Virginia's parents is utter nonsense, but the significance of the letter is that Stanley is already preparing an escape route for himself and a 'justification' for the marriage's failure.

12 September 1868 was the last full day Stanley ever spent with his Greek calf-love. He dined with the family again and enjoyed Virginia's demure company and her lady-like talents on the piano: 'We are convinced that we could be happy together, if it is our destiny to be united.'[38] Next day he left for Izmir on the *Menzaleh*. He found his regrets at parting keener than he expected but 'what must be, must be'.

There was a day's stopover in Izmir, during which Stanley again rode out over part of his 1866 route. On the 16th he put to sea once more. Passing Samos, Rhodes, the ship hugged the coast of southern Turkey, then headed down the coasts of modern Syria, Lebanon and Israel. Stanley managed shore excursions at Mersin, Iskenderun, Latakia, Tripoli (Syria), Beirut and Haifa.[39] At Port Said he was able to report good progress on the Suez Canal, before coming to journey's end at Alexandria. There he found a cablegram from Finlay Anderson ordering him to Spain to cover the recent revolution. To buy some time in

Alexandria while he sorted out the Virginia affair, he wired Anderson for further instructions.[40]

On 26 September, the day after his arrival in Alexandria, Stanley wrote to Hekekyan Bey to thank him: 'I hope you gave me a good character to my *inamorata*, otherwise I gravely affirm that there is but the slightest chance that I will succeed.'[41] That afternoon he received a cable from Anderson to proceed to Barcelona via Marseilles and to wire London for precise instructions from the French port. Next day Stanley wrote to Evangelides and Mrs Ambella that he could not now return to Siros without a definite unequivocal 'yes' to his marriage proposal.[42] On 28 September he left Alexandria for Marseilles on the *Said*. He never saw Virginia Ambella again.

The 'romance' with this young Greek girl may seem an insignificant affair, half typical Stanley insincerity, half a case of his not knowing his own mind (or heart). But there is more to it than that. The Virginia Ambella episode is deeply revealing of the inner Stanley, both of his sexuality and morbid fear of women and of his neurotic compulsion towards lies and fantasy. The real reason the affair petered out was that Stanley wished to act out a psychic fantasy of suffering, wherein it was always his fate to be rejected by women. This was to mask the fact that, for him, a total loving relationship with a woman, including sexual intercourse, was the ultimate horror. In a word, Stanley had to set up situations where he would be rejected so that he could console himself with a martyrology of suffering. He tried various ploys to get himself turned down by the Ambellas: he had no money, he had a lurid past, he was too shy to court a wife, and so on. But the crafty Ambella matron called his bluff. She insisted on sending for references. Stanley correctly foresaw that his reputation was not of the pearliest in the American West and that this was the place to direct Mrs Ambella. Unfortunately for him, though he was correct in thinking that the people of Omaha were not especially disposed to give him a 'character', he did not foresee that they might deal with an enquiry from the Ambellas by simply ignoring it, which is what they did.[43] As the Hekekyan Bey, he did what Stanley asked him to. The consequence was that the Ambellas received one very satisfactory reply on their prospective son-in-law and 'no reply', suggesting that their letter had gone astray in the wilds of the American West. Now quite satisfied, they wrote to Stanley to set a definite date for the wedding.

Stanley then tried a different tack. In Siros the Ambellas had countered his objection that he had to rove the world to make a living by pointing out that, in addition to the large dowry Virginia would bring with her, they would find Stanley a comfortable well-paid sinecure in Greece. Stanley now wrote to say that he found this proposition offensive to his honour as a man and that it would be necessary for Virginia to live with him in the USA; the dowry arrangement left an unpleasant taste in his mouth, as it suggested that in Greece it was the practice to sell off their girls. As expected, this drew an angry response from the Ambellas. A letter in halting English, signed 'The Brothers' and 'The Parents', rebuked Stanley for his animadversions on the 'venal' Greek culture and reiterated that there was no question of Virginia's being allowed to go to live in the USA; if Stanley wanted her as a wife, he would have to settle down in Greece.[44]

This provided Stanley with the excuse for inaction he needed. And the discussion about money provided him with further ammunition for his later self-justifying 'reason' why he had not married Virginia Ambella. In 1890 he produced a wild fantasy that it was *he* who had been expected to provide a 'dowry'. According to this tall tale, Stanley was actually in church on the day of the marriage ceremony, fully intending to take Virginia as his wife, when her father asked through an interpreter for the 'bride price'. What was that, Stanley asked. The interpreter explained that it was the custom in Greece for the bridegroom to hand over a large sum to the bride's father as compensation for the loss of her services and the expenses of bringing her up. When he heard this, Stanley left Virginia standing at the altar, drew aside with the father and the interpreter and said indignantly, 'Sir, I came here to marry, not to buy, your daughter!'[45] It was typical of Stanley's inattention to detail that he was completely unworried that the most superficial research into Greek customs would expose the story as bogus.

That the Virginia Ambella episode had a profound importance in Stanley's inner world can be gauged from the way he allowed it to affect his outer life and career. The arrangement for reporting the Cretan insurrection had been that Stanley would sniff the air for a month before reporting back to Anderson from Alexandria. Because of his absorption with the Ambella affair and the cul-de-sac he ran into in western Crete, Stanley's copy during August-September had seemed remarkably lack-lustre after the purple passages from Abyssinia. Aware of the anticlimactic effect this was having, Stanley set out to remedy the situation with an entirely imaginary slice of war correspondence. According to this, he left Siros on a Greek blockade runner on 7 September and proceeded to Aghia Rumeli on the south coast of Crete. After dodging Turkish cruisers, Stanley landed on the Cretan coast, then made his way up into the mountains of the interior. Gruelling route marches took him to the guerrilla camp at Askyfo, whence he accompanied the Cretan irregulars on an assault on a Turkish column. Superior mobility won the day for the Greeks, and twenty-five Turks were killed in an hour's bitter fighting near Rethimnon. After this battle Stanley made his way back over the mountains to Aghia Rumeli, from where he took ship directly to Alexandria. The *Herald* gladly published the thrilling tale of derring-do witnessed by its own 'special'.[46]

The trouble is that Stanley was nowhere near Crete on the dates (7–18 September) when he was supposed to be accompanying the gallant guerrillas. On these days he was either in Athens or Siros or on board ship in the Aegean. Moreover, he claimed to have taken a direct service from the south of Crete to Alexandria, when everyone knew there was no such service. The entire exciting episode is a fiction, expertly cobbled together with copious circumstantial detail from the mass of information Stanley had acquired on his passage through the islands. This was Stanley's most audacious application of the facility for 'bilocation' he had already employed in the American West. But it was typical of Stanley's near-inability to distinguish fantasy from reality that his private accounts (on which he based his claims for expenses to the *Herald*) told the same story as his bogus despatch.[47] Once again, we observe Stanley as a devotee of the 'coherence' theory of truth.

The fact that Stanley played such a dangerous game means that he was neglecting his professional duties because of his conflicting feelings over Virginia Ambella. A close reading of the diaries during the Siros period reveals not just a profound ambivalence over Virginia – who seemed the avatar of purity, virginity, modesty etc. (therefore Stanley could allow himself to idolise her) – but an 'overdetermined' impulse pushing him in her direction. It is of great significance that Stanley twice visited the scenes of 1866, and that Greece was at war with Turkey. Since the association of Turkey would be with Noe's homosexual rape, which in turn confronted Stanley with the reality of his homoerotic feelings, what more natural than that he should turn to a *Greek female*, virtually the polar opposite of Turkish sodomy, to expunge these feelings?

At any rate, by October 1868 Virginia Ambella was already in effect a closed book. Stanley now looked ahead to Spain, where the nymphomaniac Queen Isabella II had just been expelled by a coalition of liberal military officers in a convulsion compared by *The Times* in London to the French Revolution.[48] General Prim and Admiral Topete, the ringleaders, landed at Cadiz on 19 September and then set up a provisional junta under Francisco Serrano, Duke de la Torre, before proceeding to Madrid on 7 October.[49] Events in Spain had a particular interest for the *New York Herald*, since the USA was at loggerheads with the Spanish over the rebellion in Cuba.[50] Spanish attempts to suppress the Cuban insurgents were perceived as a breach of the Monroe doctrine.

On 6 October Stanley reached Marseilles, after being delayed two days in the Straits of Messina when the ship broke its steamer shaft.[51] After receiving confirmation from London, he boarded the *Estremadura* for Barcelona, which he reached on 8 October: 'The city has not changed since I saw it five years ago,' he noted.[52] On the 10th he travelled to Madrid via Zaragoza to begin his assignment in earnest. He put up at the Hotel los Principes in Puerta del Sol and renewed acquaintance with many old press faces from Abyssinia, including Henty of the *Standard*.[53] Next day he secured an interview with General Juan Prim y Prats, architect of Queen Isabella's overthrow.

Stanley found Prim grave, reserved, meditative and unimpulsive. A Catalan, he had the high cheekbones and broad space between the temples that Stanley claimed were typical of the Celts. Prim was in civilian dress, as he had been a few days before when he arrived in Madrid.[54] He received Stanley with great cordiality and freedom and spoke of his mission to regenerate the nation. Stanley ventured to remark that the new Spanish government could count on the friendship and sympathy of the USA as evidenced by Washington's swift recognition of the new regime in Madrid. Prim expressed his pleasure at this and said that the bad old days when the Spanish military took the law into their own hands were over. He had already suppressed the Jesuits, abolished the Moral Guard, the feudal police force, and was reforming the Army with a view to cutting down costs and surplus numbers. He had already called a municipal election under universal suffrage.[55]

They proceeded to speak of Cuba. Stanley had already taken it as a good omen that Washington's portrait had replaced Isabella's in Barcelona's town hall. Prim agreed that the Spanish people felt very warmly towards the United States and he was well aware that the reactionary regimes of Europe (especially the France of Louis Napoleon) were trying to inveigle Madrid and Washington into conflict over Cuba. He hoped the appointment of the liberal Admiral Topete would be read as a reassuring sign.[56] Stanley came away convinced that Prim was a true patriot and libertarian. His programme of universal suffrage, freedom of worship and association and the press, plus decentralisation plans consti- tuted for the *Herald* reporter 'a bill of rights that if enforced will give to

79

Spain a degree of liberty to the person and to the world generally such as few nations in the world possess', would lead to emergence from the seventeenth to the nineteenth centuries, and in general make Spain great again.[57]

Stanley prepared to interview other Spanish notables. Suddenly he received a message of recall to London.[58] In some perturbation he hastened away. Was Bennett displeased with him? It was true that there was another senior *Herald* reporter in Spain, but the degree of interest in Spanish affairs entertained by the US press surely meant there was scope for him as well.[59] What was the explanation? Anxiety gave him wings. Travelling via San Sebastian and Bordeaux, he was in Paris early on the morning on 15 October and in London the same evening.[60]

An interview with Anderson next morning did nothing to clear up the mystery. He was very fulsome about Abyssinia, but otherwise acted in an enigmatic way that Stanley found sinister, especially when the Colonel suggested they should defer their discussion until tomorrow.[61] However, next day all became clear. Bennett had heard that the famous Dr Livingstone, who had disappeared years ago into the heart of Africa, was now approaching the Zanzibar coast; he wanted his star 'special' to go out and interview him.[62] Stanley consented, but requested a few days' leave first, which Anderson granted.

Stanley sped to Denbigh, to give his mother the good news that he had made good and was therefore a fit person to receive at the Cross Foxes. Once again we can perceive how deep was the trauma of his rejection in 1862.[63] There is something poignant in the way he deluged her with photos and presents: a head of the Emperor Theodore and other trinkets from Abyssinia that he had saved from the flood in the Sooroo pass.[64] In North Wales, too, Stanley made two other important female contacts. He struck up a rapport with his half-sister Emma, who had left the workhouse to enter domestic service a year after Stanley's own departure from St Asaph's. She was particularly taken with John Rowlands' metamorphosis as H. M. Stanley. Emma later married a tanner, Llewellyn Hughes (on 1 August 1872). When she bore a second daughter (on 26 January 1875) she called her Emma Stanley Hughes.[65] This kind of hero-worship was already foreshadowed in the autumn of 1868. To the irritation of the Parry aunts (the same who had forced the child Stanley from the Denbigh Castle cottage into the workhouse), Emma insisted on calling herself 'Emma Stanley'.[66]

The other female contact was even more significant. During his time at the Cross Foxes Stanley spent most of his time writing and did not mix with the locals. For relaxation he went walking in the woods. But one day he was persuaded to accompany his mother into Denbigh. There they ran into the wife of a local retired barrister named Gough-Roberts, for whom Elizabeth Parry had sometimes done domestic work. On the mother's arm was her daughter Catherine, then aged nineteen.[67] From this casual meeting much future heartache would come.

Always with Stanley, contact with the female called forth an opposite and countervailing response. Doubtless feeling some of the Virginia Ambella sort of stirrings after the casual encounter with Katie Gough-Roberts, Stanley at once went to Mumford's corner shop and suggested to the Mumford parents that their seventeen-year-old son might want to accompany him on his global travels; this would 'make a man of him'.[68] But young Mumford was too comfortable where he was, so Stanley made enquiries at St Asaph's itself. He identified an outgoing workhouse boy for whom he proposed the same future, but when the Board contacted his mother, she became alarmed at Stanley's intentions and refused permission.[69]

It was characteristic of all Stanley's travels that he needed a young male as companion, protégé and amanuensis. But for the moment he was thwarted and had to return to London to make the journey out to Africa alone. On 23 October he left London for Alexandria, travelling via Paris and Marseilles. By the end of the month he was in Alexandria, but switched his base to Suez to be in touch via his old friends at the cable office with all the latest news on Livingstone.[70] On the 10th Bennett sent him further instructions: use your own judgement but on no account send despatches on the Indian telegraph as this would alert the opposition.[71]

On 12 November Stanley, who hoped to interview Livingstone, had a foretaste of Scotsmen when he met John MacGregor, then forty-three, already famous as the pioneer and populariser of canoeing in Britain and designer of the 'Rob Roy' canoe. It was scarcely a meeting of minds or spirits. MacGregor scornfully referred to Stanley as 'this active little Yankee'.[72] Stanley's contempt was as amused, though privately recorded: 'His fondness for canoeing reminds me of my youthful passion for aquatics when at New Orleans, but it seems strange to me that a mature man should still retain his boyish love.'[73] Interestingly, when Stanley did eventually meet Livingstone, the subject of MacGregor, whom Livingstone knew, came up again.[74]

By 17 November, still with absolutely no news of Livingstone, Stanley decided to travel to the other end of the Red Sea and take up station at Aden, ready, if the occasion arose, to cross the Indian Ocean to Zanzibar.

Four days later he arrived at Aden, which he found a depressing hole: 'a strange place this, fit only for a coal depot'.[75] Although he did not share Anderson's belief that Livingstone would emerge on the coast, he wrote a confidential letter to Francis R. Webb, US consul at Zanzibar, explaining his mission and asking for a cablegram if Livingstone was reported.[76] Meanwhile, finding that the local British officials and bureaucrats seemed to have no other interest than getting drunk, Stanley kept himself to himself and started to complete his self-education. Apart from scores of geographical guides, he devoured mainly the classical authors: Josephus, Herodotus, Plutarch, Homer and Virgil; 'without them the time would be tedious in this extremely warm place.'[77]

In December Stanley crossed to Berbera on the Somali coast. He amused himself by donning Arab dress then, having had himself photographed as 'Khan Bahadoor', he sent the photo and a covering letter to Lewis Noe, thus breaking a silence of nearly two years.[78] He also sent a despatch to the *Herald*, recounting all the various Livingstone rumours. This fitted quite well into Bennett's plans as he had already begun insidiously to fan the flames of interest in the great explorer among his American readers.[79] However, to give the despatch more cogency and 'news value', Bennett changed the dateline from Aden to Zanzibar and held up its publication until Stanley was well and truly launched on the 'find Livingstone' exploit.[80]

Back in Aden Stanley whiled away the dull days with an extraordinarily ambitious programme of reading: Tickell, Cowper, Fletcher, Dryden, Pope, Murphy, Milton, Ben Jonson, Massinger, Spenser and, always, Shakespeare. Helvétius also took his fancy, and for lighter reading there was the copy of *A Christmas Carol* given him by a friendly sea-captain *en route* from Aden to Rangoon.[81] He also began compiling a biographical dictionary, mainly of early Church fathers and other figures from the Ancient World. His notes on history prefigure the discoverer to come: 'Hengist, Horsa, Alaric, Attila and Captain Smith were doing the same tasks of leading men from overcrowded countries to strange ones where plenty was to be had.'[82] In his commonplace book, under 2 January 1869, he writes of the agonies of trying to give up smoking. Since the Civil War days Stanley was seldom seen without a cigar or cheroot in his mouth.

January 1869 was another month in the doldrums. The diary entry on New Year's Day is that of a sour and depressed man: 'What is happiness ... happiness is not to be secured in this world except for brief periods.'[83] Stanley finished his book on the Abyssinian campaign (which was to wait another five years before publication), and explored Aden and its environs with a view to the future implications of the Suez Canal.[84] The sheer boredom of his life and the continuing absence of news from Zanzibar soon cracked his New Year's resolution; by 7 January he was smoking again.[85] At length a letter arrived from Consul Webb, scouting the idea that there was any chance of Livingstone's coming to Zanzibar. Finally on 1 February his recall came through: 'I am relieved at last,' he notes joyfully.[86]

On 2 February he embarked on the auspiciously named *Magdala* for Suez. The pent-up stress of the preceding three months – inactivity was a peculiar torture for a man like Stanley, who lived for action and action alone – found expression in a virulent fever that kept him confined to his cabin for three days. When he ventured forth on the 6th, his reactions to shipboard life were those of a crusty old colonel; he found fault with everything, and particularly resented the extras in tips and 'contributions' levied by ship's officers and crew on any and every pretext. But this sensibility did not enable him to make common cause with the testy veterans of India, who were interested only in alcohol: 'at lunch the most usual topic is beer . . . the subject is also a weariness to me. Why cannot they take their drinks in silence? What does it matter to me which one is their favourite.' Then he adds archly: 'At dinner the topics are more varied. They range from brandy and soda to champagne.'[87]

After a slow seven-day passage up the Red Sea, the *Magdala* reached Suez. Stanley immediately made for Alexandria, where he dined with Douglas Gibbs and intuited that Mrs Gibbs was in love with another man.[88] But, finding nothing else of interest there, after five days he doubled back to Cairo. He capped a six-hour afternoon journey with a, for Stanley, rare binge on Irish whiskey.[89] In Cairo he visited the circus, went sightseeing and waited for further orders from London, depressed and dispirited. Cairo was not his kind of town: 'I always feel out of place in any town or country that has in it the least of anything approaching to French tastes.' In addition, he found the food and rooms at the Shepheard's Hotel execrable. He further punished himself by reliving in his mind his three-month exile in Aden and rehearsing all the likely reasons why his book on Abyssinia would not be published. Once again the stress of inactivity brought on another dose of Aden fever, which even Stanley by this time recognised as partly psychosomatic in its triggering: 'Heavens, what a punishment it would be to have no object or aim in life!' he exclaims.[90]

On 17 February his prayers were answered and he was recalled to London by a cable whose curtness upset him: 'It is so brief that I fancy the

Herald is disappointed with me.'[91] Typically, Stanley then confided to his diary that he was hardly to blame just because Livingstone had not revealed himself to the world; he railed at the injustice of being in disgrace when he could not alter events or change destinies. The residue of unconscious guilt in Stanley shows itself clearly in the need to exculpate himself not only against charges that had not yet been made nor would be made, but even against those it had never occurred to anyone to make.

On 19 February Stanley made another long journey from Cairo to Alexandria and embarked on the *Pelusi* for Marseilles. Despite his strictures on life at Cairo, he felt a pang of regret as he saw the palm-tufted strand fade from view and he realised that it would probably be many years before he saw Egypt again (as with so many things, Stanley was wrong on this score too).[92] There was little to interest him on the Mediterranean voyage, except the curious fact that many young Abyssinians were, in the wake of Theodore's defeat, being taken to London to be 're-educated' as missionaries (they were already Coptic Christians).[93] On 22 February the *Pelusi* anchored for two hours in the Bay of Messina; Stanley went ashore and had a coffee.[94] Then it was Marseilles, Paris and London, where he arrived on 26 February.

There were changes at the *Herald* bureau. It turned out that it was Finlay Anderson, not Stanley, who was being recalled in disgrace to the USA. Anderson was extremely bitter about Bennett's arbitrary behaviour, but Stanley cynically observed that there was no smoke without fire. Though at one level sorry to see Anderson go, he still harboured a grudge that, because of Anderson's negligence, he had arrived in Egypt from Ethiopia to find himself penniless.[95] At the beginning of March he learned that he himself was still in high favour. Anderson's replacement, Douglas Levien, told him that he was to go to Spain to report the revolution there on an extended stint at £400 a year.[96]

1869 was to be a crucial year for Stanley in many years, both in his inner and outer life. He himself had some intimation of this, for when on the *Pelusi* he reflected on some very different rites of passage:

There is a period which marks the transition from boy to man, when the boy discards his errors and his awkwardness, and puts on the man's mask, and adopts his ways. The duration of the period depends upon circumstances, and not upon any defined time. With me it lasted some months; and though I feel in ideas more manly than when I left the States, I am often reminded that I am still a boy in many things. In impulse I am boy-like, but in reflection a man; and then I condemn the

boy-like action and make a new resolve . . . I am still a boy when I obey
my first thought; the man takes that thought and views it from many
sides before action . . . I want work, close, absorbing and congenial
work, only so that there will be no time for regrets, and vain desires, and
morbid thoughts. In the interval, books come handy . . . though there is
much wisdom in them, they are ill-suited to young men with a craze for
action.[97]

But in these reflections perhaps Stanley was overdoing the discontinuity
between man and boy. In all essentials, including physical appearance,
John Rowlands was father to H. M. Stanley. All the mature attributes –
high intelligence, great ambition, physical courage, administrative flair,
dauntless willpower – were discernible in the alumnus of St Asaph's. At
fifteen he was the height (5 feet, 5 inches) he would remain. As to the rest
the continuity is best established by a comparison of two descriptions,
respectively of the fifteen-year-old Rowlands and the Stanley of the
1880s:

Full-faced, stubborn, self-willed, round-headed, uncompromising,
deep . . . in conversation with you, his large dark eyes would roll away
from you as if he was really in deep meditation about half a dozen things
besides the subject of conversation . . . his temperament was unusually
sensitive . . . he could stand no chaff nor the least bit of humour.[98]

The second description, having established his height and weight (180
pounds), goes on: 'but he was far from being fat. His flesh was all solid
flesh, evenly distributed, and, I fancy, his muscles weighed nearly as much
as the fleshy covering. Anybody could see at a glance that he was a man of
wonderful muscular power. His chest was broad and deep and his legs
made one think of a couple of short posts, so solid did they look. His face
was – and of course is – a face marked in every line with determination.
His eyes are small, near together, and have – or, at least, had – the look of a
tiger's . . . he always struck me as being a rather moody sort of fellow, who
disliked crowds, lived largely within himself, and didn't care to talk much,
except with his intimates. He is not exactly what you'd call a vain man, and
yet, when I last saw him, he apparently had a pretty good opinion of
himself. No doubt he had good reasons for his opinions, but he was rather
fond of using the personal pronoun and was inclined to be a little dramatic
whenever opportunity offered.'[99]

All physical descriptions of Stanley emphasise the short stature, the stocky, barrel-chested frame, and the piercing basilisk eyes (*pace* the second description, they were certainly not small). But the good opinion Stanley undoubtedly did hold of himself was in conflict with a countervailing feeling of being inferior and worthless. Stanley credited the world with a kind of X-ray vision, whereby it could penetrate the carapace of cosmopolitan urbanity he had armoured himself with, to perceive the workhouse brat within. His abnormal sensitivity on this score often threatened to topple over into outright paranoia. The English upper classes were a particular focus for his suspicion, and an incident at Suez in 1868 reinforced his worst fears. On a sightseeing trip Stanley took two young English aristocrats under his wing, entertained them and massaged their gaucherie and culture shock. To his utmost mortification, in the hotel at Suez, through the paper-thin walls that separated his room from theirs, Stanley heard himself being mocked and ridiculed in a way that seemed to him wildly incompatible with the kindness he had showered on them.[100] Not only did this incident breed a morbid fear of and distaste for the English oligarchy; it also weakened his self-esteem and, at the unconscious level, reinforced his determination to punish himself the next time he met a woman to whom he was attracted. The opportunity came sooner than he expected.

5

ON 3 March 1869 at the Queen's Hotel on the Strand, Stanley had an unexpected visitor. Catherine Gough-Roberts, the girl he had met the previous autumn in Denbigh, appeared with her lawyer father. It seems that Thomas Gough-Roberts, the father, had spotted a future 'winner'. When Katie remarked at home on Stanley's air of distinction and quiet confidence, her parents discussed the possibility of an alliance between their money and the fame of the *Herald*'s star 'special'. The upshot was the visit to London.[1]

Gough-Roberts *père* did not beat about the bush but came straight to the point. Having ascertained that Stanley did indeed entertain a high opinion of his daughter ('plump and good-looking' was Stanley's private estimate), he proposed a dowry of £1,000 if he took Katie to wife; naturally, Stanley would first have to propose and be accepted. Stanley explained that he was due in Spain at the end of the month, so this would have to be a whirlwind courtship. Roberts, who had been drinking heavily, agreed to let matters take their course.

Having nearly been caught in the net of the Ambella family, Stanley was much more cautious this time. Though attracted by the idea of the marriage, he bore himself coolly. To his diary he confided his real thoughts on the matter, which show him far from encoiled by obvious passions:

> When a well-to-do solicitor of our native town is so frank and so good-natured as to be oblivious of St Asaph, it must be that he thinks more highly of me than I can persuade myself to do. One of my secret aspirations has been to be able to wed some fair-haired girl of a silent and amiable disposition, whose affection for me would enable me to forget the ills of life and live up to that ideal we must all have at one time or another thought to be blessedness.

He dilates on the advantages of the promised money: 'Any other way is immaterial and not likely to call up the rapture of love. However, it will be no harm to let the affair proceed . . . it may be that Fate had chosen this singular way of conquering my reserve, for I know no man less forward than I in the presence of a woman.'[2]

For a few days Stanley got to know Katie while he made preparations for his Spanish assignment. With typical thoroughness he armed himself with books on Spain and its history.[3] His commonplace book shows the shift of interest. Notes on Helvétius, Virgil's *Georgics*, Mecca, the Koran, men who murdered their relations and the difference between the Ancient Greeks and Old Testament Jews give way to entries on Spain of which the following (13 March) is typical: 'Spanish Republicans from being Catholics became atheists.'[4] But the same commonplace book shows a rival interest, perhaps best signified by the following entries: 'faithful wives', 'vengeful women', 'what has been done for love of woman' plus a list of 'heroic women' including Joan of Arc and Emma, daughter of Charlemagne.[5]

While he pondered what to do about Katie Gough-Roberts, Stanley switched his attention to two other women, his mother and half-sister Emma. At last he was in a position to show his mother what a figure he now cut in the world and to wipe out the memory of the 1862 humiliation. He sent for the two women, lodged them in his hotel overnight, then took them to Paris for two days of sightseeing. This was the Paris of Offenbach and the *gaîté parisienne*, basking in the false light of the penultimate year of the Second Empire. The two simple Welshwomen were bowled over by it: 'Mother is in raptures with Paris – the life in the boulevards, the Bois and the imperial palaces. Emma, I observe, is too full of thoughts for much talk.'[6] We can infer what some of those thoughts might have been, for it is clear from later events that Emma decided, now that her beloved half-brother had come into money, that no other daughter of Denbigh was going to be allowed to enjoy it.

Typically of Stanley, he does not appear to have mentioned Katie Gough-Roberts to his mother, but only Virginia Ambella, safely in the past, for he records the following: 'I gathered from the old lady that she has been cherishing the thought of being able to mate me to one of my own countrywomen, with the view to saving me from being snatched by some "vile foreigner". She does not scruple to exaggerate the virtues of British girls nor, though she is not acquainted with a single "foreigner", does she hesitate to express her opinion that foreign women "though pretty enough, goodness knows and perhaps rich and all that" do not come up to her standard of what wives should be according to her.'[7]

On the second day in Paris Stanley took his two women to the Louvre before going on to dine at the Café Vefour. The idea of Elizabeth Parry and Emma in the Louvre conjures memories of the wedding party in Zola's *L'Assommoir*. On the 11th they returned to London, and next day Stanley put them on a train for Wales, but not before, in his usual manner, making a meticulous note of what the entire excursion had cost him.[8]

Back in London Stanley continued his preparations for Spain. He also kept the Livingstone business on the boil with another letter to Consul Webb in Zanzibar.[9] But most of all his thoughts ran on Katie Gough-Roberts. His emotions tightened to the point where he was prepared to tell all about his early Welsh experiences. The way his mind was working can be inferred from the entries in the commonplace book: 'filial affection' (18 March), 'the sins of the fathers visited upon the children' (21 March). Finally, on 22 March he took the plunge. In an immensely long letter he begins by declaring his love for her, then admits his illegitimacy, the horror of his early life in North Wales, and the searing experience of St Asaph's workhouse.[10] In this section of the letter Stanley is careful to tell the truth, as it could easily be verified by the Roberts family. But when he comes to his public life, Stanley at once lurches into lurid fantasy. The *Ticonderoga* story is resurrected, this time with the embellishment that after the Civil War Stanley served on her on a round-the-world cruise; he finally obtained a furlough at Constantinople in December 1866, whence he came to Wales.

But the lies get worse. First Stanley claimed to have been on a salary of £350 a year while on the *Ticonderoga*. Then this was supposed to have risen to £600 p.a. with the *Missouri Democrat*. 1868, in turn, was allegedly packed with travel. There was no dreary sojourn in Aden, no absurd love affair with Virginia Ambella. Instead Stanley ran together past and future travels by claiming to have visited Arabia, Zanzibar, Egypt, Crete, Greece, Turkey, Syria and Persia and to have dined with three kings: the Sultan of Turkey, the Viceroy of Egypt and the King of Greece; 'he is known over all America as a traveller, a gentleman and an author.'[11]

Doubtless this absurdly mendacious boasting might just have passed muster with a young, ingenuous girl from North Wales; there was always method in Stanley's madness, as he made a point of lying about his private life to the public (who could verify his public life) and about his public life to private individuals who lacked the intellectual sophistication to falsify his tall tales. But his absurd claim to have £5,000 in the bank *plus* a

140-acre farm in Omaha argues for his poor estimate of Katie's intelligence, since simple arithmetic would have exposed the hollowness of this hyperbole within minutes. The searing, conflicting emotions he entertained about Katie, which we shall examine later, must have made him careless.

Affecting insouciance about the £1,000 dowry, Stanley ended his long epistle by stating that what he wanted was 'not a pretty doll-faced wife but a woman educated, possessed of energy.'[12] He then peremptorily asked for a definite answer to his proposal before the following Wednesday when he was due to set out for Spain. But the Roberts parents felt they were being rushed into the marriage; they suggested that it would be better to wait until after Stanley finished his stint in Spain, when a proper wedding could be arranged. Stanley affected to be disgruntled by this reply, but at an unconscious level it was the answer he wanted to hear.

On receiving this reply, Stanley left London for Paris, to meet Gordon Bennett for the first time since December 1867. Bennett confirmed his Spanish appointment and spoke very flatteringly not just about the Abyssinian coup but also of his letters from Crete and Suez.[13] It was therefore in good spirits that Stanley arrived in Madrid, on the last day of March 1869, ready to report the new order in Spain.

He spent just over six months in Spain, reporting the birth-pangs of the new republic, threatened by fissiparous elements within its ruling élite and from Right and Left by, respectively, the Carlists and the Radicals. Until the final month Stanley's duties were far from arduous. He had the leisure to read omnivorously; he taught himself rudimentary Spanish (Stanley was never a great linguist, his phrase book Turkish not withstanding); and he sent back competent, but prosaic political reports. He came into his own only with the great Radical insurrection of October 1869 which convulsed southern Spain. There was particularly bloody hand-to-hand fighting between the Army and leftist irregulars in the cities of Zaragoza and Valencia, and Stanley's exciting eyewitness copy showed that he had lost none of his skill as a war reporter.

On his return to Madrid in late October he found a cable from Bennett summoning him to Paris on 'important business'. He spent the next six days putting his affairs in order, then on 27 October took the train to Paris.[14]

The story of how James Gordon Bennett junior commissioned Stanley for the famous journey to 'find' Livingstone is one of the best-known items of Stanleyana. According to Stanley's own published account, he made his way to the Grand Hotel in Paris, located Bennett's room, knocked on the door and identified himself as H. M. Stanley. There then ensued the following celebrated conversation.

'Where do you think Livingstone is?'

'I really do not know, sir!'

'Do you think he is alive?'

'He may be and he may not be,' I answered.

'Well, I think he is alive and that he can be found and I am going to send you to find him.'

'What!' said I. 'Do you really think I can find Dr Livingstone? Do you mean me to go to Central Africa?'

'Yes; I mean that you shall go and find him wherever you may hear that he is, and to get what news you can of him and perhaps "delivering himself thoughtfully and deliberately," the old man may be in want; take enough with you to help him should he require it. Of course you will act according to your own plans, and do what you think best – but find Livingstone!'

Stanley then mentioned that the expenses of such an expedition could top £5,000 – the cost of the 1857 Burton-Speke endeavour. Bennett was not a bit abashed.

'Well, I will tell you what you will do. Draw a thousand pounds now; and when you have gone through that, draw another thousand, and when this is spent draw another thousand, and so on but FIND LIVINGSTONE!'[15]

Whether the conversation actually took place exactly like this is doubtful. It was natural for Stanley to dramatise everything, and from the early 1870s, even in his private diary notes, he went in for the recording of 'verbatim' conversations. Some of these accounts have the ring of authenticity; more often, though, they seem designed to show off the wit, wisdom and infallible judgement of H. M. Stanley. What *is* certain is that Bennett gave his star 'special' a roving commission to find Livingstone. In order to make sense of this singular assignment, we must look more closely at the career of both seeker and sought.

David Livingstone was born into poverty at Blantyre, Scotland, in 1813. By great moral strength he secured himself an education as a medical missionary, and it was with the London Missionary Society in the late

1830s that he became 'Dr Livingstone'. He went out to South Africa in 1840 as a missionary, but his passion for exploration (self-aggrandisement, his enemies said) gradually led him to become impatient with the slow, tedious life of a saver of souls. His 'missionary travels' of the late 1840s, when he discovered Lake Ngami, were really disguised explorations but, although Livingstone never made a single clear convert, he continued to assert that his journeys were necessary for the propagation of the Gospel. Whatever his true motivations, he gradually established himself as the most powerful European propagandist yet for the 'civilising' of Africa.[16]

Livingstone lacked both the financial resources and the human qualities needed to lead large expeditions but, ironically, it was the very small scale of his travels that struck a chord in British hearts, since he seemed to be a latter-day Pilgrim battling against the Apollyons and Vanity Fairs of the 'Dark Continent'. His crossing of Africa in 1854–6 from Luande on the west coast to Quelimane (in modern Mozambique), accompanied by a mere handful of devoted African servants, fired the imagination of Europe. He returned to England as a famous man. His *Missionary Travels* became a best-seller. He was the lion of Victorian England.[17]

But Livingstone's very success led him into débâcle. After severing his connection with the London Missionary Society, he led a large expedition to the Zambezi, which opened up Lake Nyasa and the Shire River (modern Malawi). On this expedition were the supposed advance forces of a huge missionary effort in southern Africa. But Livingstone's own psychological problems led him into violent conflict with his European subordinates. The expedition was a colossal failure, and when it was recalled in 1863, Livingstone vowed to travel no more with white men.[18]

Under the auspices of the Royal Geographical Society, Livingstone set out on his last African journey in 1866. His mission was to settle the dispute over the true sources of the Nile that had led to the famous controversy between John Speke and Richard Burton. He started from Zanzibar in March 1866, pressed westward as far as Ujiji on the shore of Lake Tanganyika, then penetrated the Manyema country as far as the River Lualaba, which he thought was probably the headwaters of the Nile. Mutinies among his men and his own illness compelled him to abandon the exploration of the Lualaba and return to Ujiji. Livingstone, then, was at Ujiji in 1869, then away on the journey to the Lualaba until 1871.[19] This fact is of crucial importance in understanding Gordon Bennett's remarkable hunch that the 'finding' of Livingstone could well turn out to be the journalistic scoop of the century.

What of Bennett himself? Born in 1841 (the same year as Stanley), he was the son of a Scottish journalist from Banffshire, who emigrated to the USA and in 1835 brought out the first number of the *New York Herald*.[20] In 1866 Bennett senior turned over the management of the *Herald* to his son. 'Jamie' shared both his father's dislike of England and his Irish mother's distaste for the USA. His upbringing had been a disastrous mixture of pampering and instability, since as soon as his father made his first million, his mother decamped for Paris. 'Jamie' spent his young years in an ambience of fantastic wealth, surrounded by sycophants, but without adequate parenting. Forever commuting across the Atlantic between Paris and New York, and by 1869 enjoying an income of a million dollars a year, James Gordon Bennett junior oscillated between alcoholism and a fanatical desire to outdo his father by making the *Herald* an even greater sensation in the world.[21]

'Jamie's' was a severely fractured personality, and at this level there was an affinity between him and Stanley. When in his cups, Bennett was impossible. He would go on stupendous alcoholic binges, pick fights with strangers in bars, drive his carriage through the streets of Paris like a maniac, shedding his clothes as he went, so that he arrived home naked. Usually Bennett silenced all protesters by buying them off, but sometimes he went too far even for his millions to protect him. On New Year's Day 1877 he capped all his wild exploits by urinating in the fireplace at his fiancée's home in New York. This brought him a horsewhipping from the (at once former) fiancée's male cousin, and banishment from the few segments of polite New York society from which he was not already ostracised.

But as a businessman 'Jamie' was peerless. He pioneered the 'New Journalism' (soon to be known as the 'yellow press'): celebrity interviews, lavish illustrations, society gossip, salacious news. Much of the *Herald*'s success was based on its 'Personal Column' advertisements – a guide to every prostitute in New York able to publicise her wares and in particular to the brothels of Bleecker Street and Sixth Avenue. To scoop his rivals it was 'money no object' to Bennett. He thought nothing of transmitting long despatches across the Atlantic by expensive cablegram and had a fleet of yachts permanently cruising the sea lanes on the New York approaches, ready to intercept steamers and send on the latest eye-witness interviews from European travellers.

The dark side of Bennett was less well known. He had all the capricious cruelty of the tyrannical child of arrested development. He was not above sacking his entire senior staff on a whim or putting his best reporters through the most agonising hoops just to test their loyalty. When Stanley knocked on the door of the Paris hotel in late October and a dressing-gowned Bennett invited him inside, Stanley had good reason for trepidation.

On the face of it, Bennett's interest in Livingstone and Africa was decidedly odd. To Bennett the blacks were 'niggers', as a column heading describing Grant's New Year's Day reception in 1870 made clear: describing the arrival of the sumptuously dressed Alexander Tate, Haitian ambassador to the USA, the headline ran 'A Gorgeous Nigger'.[22] Bennett was much too cynical a man to have any real interest in what Livingstone was trying to do in Africa. Yet Bennett was a journalist of genius. Not only did he have an uncanny understanding of the kinds of stories a mass public would go for, but he also knew the precise optimal moment to break those stories. 'Jamie' had been following the agonised 1869 correspondence in *The Times* on the whereabouts of the 'lost' Livingstone.[23] His famous intuition told him that here were banner headlines in the making. The hour of the 'Dark Continent' in news value seemed about to strike, especially as international news was in a doldrum period.[24]

Yet if Bennett had decided to throw all the resources of the *Herald* into an expedition to search for Livingstone, it still remains to explain why he had chosen Stanley. Tall, angular, dark, with a long face and drooping moustache, 'Jamie' was the physical opposite of Stanley. Moreover, Stanley loved literature, art and history, and made this plain in his copy. The philistine 'Jamie' hated and detested aesthetes and intellectuals. Furthermore, Stanley's Abyssinian triumph and his rise to fame had been the work of the now disgraced Finlay Anderson, and it was Anderson who had originally suggested Stanley for the Livingstone assignment.[25]

The plain truth was that Bennett had wanted to give the assignment to another reporter, Randolph Keim, but could not contact him immediately in the USA and was too impatient to wait for him to cross the Atlantic.[26] And there was something to be said for Stanley. His rugged individualism and lack of any aristocratic polish appealed to Bennett; doubtless he could see in Stanley's gimlet eyes the same suspicious ruthlessness that stared back at him from his own mirror. And he *had* already proved himself on an African assignment. So Stanley, then, it was. Bennett ordered him to go to London and make his detailed plans with Levien, the head of the bureau there.

But first he made a stipulation that most clearly evinced his journalistic flair. In order to screw the tension from the missing Livingstone up to its highest notch, he told Stanley to delay his search for Livingstone for a year. Bennett guessed that the current debate about the famous explorer would die down for a while, only to burst out later with even greater strength. When that happened he wanted the *Herald* correspondent to be on hand to shake the world. 'If the Grand Lama of Tibet "shuffles off this mortal coil", a reporter of the *Herald* is present in the death chamber to feel the pulse of the dying sovereign,' one of Bennett's competitors remarked sneeringly.[27] But to Bennett that kind of scoop was a source of pride.

Bennett took a well-calculated gamble. He would send Stanley on a long trip through Asia as far as India. If by that time Livingstone was still missing, Stanley should launch an all-out effort to find him. If Livingstone meanwhile emerged at the African coast or was discovered by some other European, Stanley would abandon the Livingstone mission and proceed to China.[28]

The first port of call on the Asian trip would be the Suez Canal, due to be formally opened on 17 November; the *Herald* had 'trailed' this event in August.[29] Stanley had little time left if he was to be in Suez on schedule. On 29 October he crossed to London to confer with Levien. The bureau chief promised him a £600 letter of credit, plus further supplies of money in the future, and spoke rapturously if sycophantically about Bennett's 'positively Napoleonic' conception. He also advised Stanley not to conceal from *Herald* readers the failure of the Suez Canal, if indeed it turned out to be the flop predicted by its detractors. Levien later sent Stanley a written summary of their conversation.[30]

The next day, 30 October, saw the decisive resolution of the 'romance' with Katie Gough-Roberts. From Paris Stanley had wired father and daughter Roberts to meet him in London. On a cold autumn Saturday the three of them met and tried to make sense of the tangled relationship. Stanley, knowing such an offer must surely be refused, proposed an immediate marriage by special licence followed by an Egyptian honeymoon while he reported the opening of the Suez Canal.[31] Katie's father demurred at such precipitate action. Either Stanley stayed in England and allowed a decent interval to elapse, with banns called and a proper wedding planned, or the marriage would have to be postponed until he completed this latest peripatetic phase of his career. Stanley remonstrated that he had no choice. The canal opened on 17 November and unless he was there to report it he would very soon be jobless; you did not trifle with a man like Bennett. Stanley tried to explain Egyptian affairs and found Katie utterly ignorant on the subject. More worryingly for his immediate and ostensible project, she seemed cold and aloof, hardly surprisingly in view of the violent mood-swings evinced in Stanley's letters of 'courtship'.[32]

It was left that the situation would be reviewed when Stanley returned. He continued to write to her spasmodically during his Asian travels and in April 1870 was still talking of imminent marriage, possibly in India.[33] His final letter was dated 7 October 1870 at Bombay. But by this time the saboteur in his own unconscious had done its work well. Stanley finally secured the rejection he had unconsciously sought. Tired of his indecision and sensing that she was out of her depth with this particular psychological cripple, Katie accepted a proposal from one Urban Rufus Bradshaw and married him on 22 September 1870, before Stanley wrote his last letter to her in Bombay.[34] She bore a son in August 1871 and a daughter in February 1873. There is evidence, too, that Stanley's own unconscious masochistic urges had a conscious ally. His half-sister Emma was madly jealous of Katie Gough-Roberts, both because Emma's identity was now bound up in Stanley's and she feared the coming severance, and because she saw the supply of money and fringe benefits from Stanley about to dry up. She managed to get herself taken on as a servant in the Gough-Roberts household and set about an insidious destruction of the relationship. First she hinted that Stanley was already secretly married. When this ploy did not work, she intercepted Stanley's letters to Katie. One of them was later found floating in a water butt where Emma had thrown it.[35]

The fact that Stanley had unconsciously willed his own rejection did not prevent him from being bitter and outraged at the conscious level. After his death, when Lady Stanley was trying to threaten, cajole or bamboozle his love letters out of Katie, her agent wrote to Mrs Bradshaw (née Gough-Roberts) as follows: 'You are aware that up to his last hour he regarded your long past act as an unspeakable betrayal at a time when he was daily passing through the valley of the shadow of death.'[36]

Stanley also ran true to form in his bisexual rebounding. Immediately after the unsatisfactory interview with the Robertses, he took the night train to Paris, then spent Sunday and Monday trying to persuade the Balch family to allow young Edwin to accompany him on his Asian travels.[37] When this request was, predictably, refused (the boy was still only fourteen), Stanley subtly began to transfer his affections to another young man, Edward King, a fledgeling journalist who saw him off on the Marseilles express at the Gare de Lyon.[38] As with Noe, Stanley did not discard his displaced favourite all at once; he wrote to Balch from

Malta, but swiftly thereafter his correspondence and sentiment petered out.

From Marseilles Stanley crossed to Alexandria, covered the opening of the Suez Canal, sailed up the Nile as a guest of the Khedive, then explored the Holy Land. Thereafter he visited Odessa, the Crimean battlefields, Constantinople and Trabzon (Trebizond). He proceeded through Russian Georgia to Baku on the Caspian.[39] Entering Persia at Rasht, he made a 1000-mile sweep through Tehran, Isfahan, Shiraz and Persepolis, where he slept in the ruins and carved his initials on a temple pillar. He debouched at the Indian Ocean at Bushehr, then took a steamer to Bombay, where he arrived on the first day of August 1870.[40] Nine months of continuous travelling had yielded some colourful travel writing but to what ultimate purpose? It was as well for Stanley's mental equanimity that when he arrived in Bombay he found that the hunt for Livingstone was still on and that he would not be condemned to journey to China or seek out the High Lama in his Tibetan fastness.

$$6$$

S TANLEY himself once noted the Duke of Wellington's remark that he never knew a good-tempered man in India.[1] The hero of Waterloo's apophthegm would not have been refuted by a scrutiny of Stanley in Bombay in August–October 1870. After he had completed the first half of Bennett's 'budget of instructions which I look upon even to this day with dismay'[2] Stanley's frustration was at a high point as he alternated the writing of seventeen letters on his travels with the assembling of rifles, revolvers and ammunition for the plunge into the Dark Continent ahead. While he spent his days at the Bycalla Hotel with furious scribbling, he also kept an ear open for the unlikely chance that a ship might call at Bombay which was sailing to Zanzibar direct. He was, as he expected, disappointed. When his preparations were complete and the epistles to the *Herald* all written, he was obliged to book berths for himself and Selim on the *Polly*, under Captain Petherick, bound for Mauritius, where he hoped to secure onward passage on a vessel making for Zanzibar from the Far East.[3]

The *Polly* left Bombay on 12 October. For thirty-seven days it rolled, pitched and yawed on the vast Indian Ocean, making very heavy weather until it picked up the south-east trades on 3 November. Stanley alleviated the boredom by overeating and reading: Fenimore Cooper was a favourite on this voyage.[4] There were just two noteworthy incidents on the way to Mauritius. William Farquahar, the first mate, drew himself to Stanley's attention by thrashing a young deck-hand called Charlie on the starboard watch. The incident recalled Stanley's own treatment when a boy on the *Windermere*; it helps to account for his later treatment of Farquahar.[5] Secondly, Stanley left a rare record of one of his dreams – a vital clue to the elusive inner man. He dreamed that he had entered Purgatory from above through a large aperture in 'the skyey dome' and that a male companion of 'beautiful face, form and figure' had touched him while he sleepwalked.[6] The content and symbolism is too obvious to need interpretation.

The news of Katie Gough-Roberts' 'betrayal', which caught up with him a little later, reinforced Stanley's sexual anxieties and brought on one of his bitterest attacks yet of sado-masochistic reviling of the sins of the flesh. The early days in Zanzibar are full of fulminations against sexual intercourse in general and miscegenation in particular.[7]

On 18 November, wafted by a spanking breeze, they passed Round Island and anchored at Bell Buoy in sight of the main harbour of Mauritius. Next day they spent a day in the island's principal town, Mahebourg, and on the 20th inspected the Pamplemousse botanical gardens with their black and white swans imported from Madagascar. On 21 November Stanley engaged first mate William Lawrence Farquahar from the *Polly* to be his chief of porters in Africa, but on condition that his pay would commence only on departure from Zanzibar.[8]

On the morning of 22 November they set sail for the north in the brigantine *Romp*, bound for the Seychelles, 1,200 miles due north. Sharing the captain's table was an ordeal for Stanley, since the master, 'a fidgety . . . superstitious and most selfish fellow', was a Creole with a chip on his shoulder, who thought that Creoles spoke better French than Parisians and that all Englishmen and Yankees were desperadoes.[9] The combination of his company and the impotent lolling of the *Romp* in the doldrums was calculated to reduce a man like Stanley to despair. His lamentations sound like Captain Ahab on the *Pequod* in pursuit of Moby Dick: 'Oh insufferable ennui! Ah, torment of an impatient soul! Whatever is the value of a sailing vessel in the tropics! My back aches with pain, my mind becomes old and tends to dotage with these dispiriting calms.'[10]

On 7 December they sighted Silhouette Island 50 miles away to the north, then Make Island next day. But it was the evening of the 9th, 'a fine moonlit night', before they made landfall at St Anne's Island.[11] And still Zanzibar was 1,000 miles away due west. Stanley's urgent enquiries revealed that the only vessel going to Zanzibar was an American whaler, the *Falcon*, whose captain was Isaiah Richmond of New Bedford. The problem was that Richmond was adamant that he wanted no passengers on his ship. Stanley spent all day on the 11th, pleading and blustering with Richmond to no avail. He finally won over the dour New Englander by revealing in desperation what his true mission was, and selling it as an opportunity for Yankees to steal a march on the 'limeys'. But Stanley's ordeal was not quite over. Next day was spent haggling over the passage price. It was a battle of the giants between two penny-pinchers. Richmond agreed to take Stanley's party for $150, provided Selim helped the steward in the galley. When Stanley tried to beat him down to $125, Richmond shut off the bidding with the unanswerable retort that Bennett was rich enough to pay the going price.[12]

On 14 December Stanley, Farquahar and Selim went on board and learned that the *Falcon* had already been twenty-eight months away from her home port. A further day was spent waiting for the calm to die away. They then made very slow progress out through the islands of the Seychelles group before running due west on latitude 5, cruising for whales.[13] On 23 December Richmond took Stanley with him when he visited a fellow whaling captain on the *Hecla*.[14] That was the sole incident that alleviated the tedium apart from a false alarm of 'Thar she blows' as they were eating their Christmas turkey.[15] Once again Stanley became fretful and fractious with the boredom, especially when rough squally weather began to retard their already slow progress: 'Am unwell from sheer inactivity and overindulgence in smoking,' he recorded the day after Christmas.

Stanley found a focus for his frustrated rage in Farquahar. In his diary he railed at the Scotsman's laziness. When he asked him to make an oilskin coat for him, Farquahar demurred, on the perfectly reasonable grounds that his salary had not yet commenced. Stanley riposted by bringing up the advance he had paid him at the Seychelles.[16] Soon Stanley became angry that Farquahar was not showing him due deference: 'Mr Farquahar's conduct became so unbearable that I spoke to him about it, at which he gave signs of being considerably astonished. Apparently he had forgotten the position in which we stood towards each other. Had I permitted his unwarrantable conduct to proceed further without comment, it would have spoiled him completely and rendered him unfit to be my companion.'[17]

Stanley's feud with Farquahar continued into the New Year. On 2 January he ordered the ex-mate to make Selim a pair of Turkish trousers. After much grumbling about having to indulge the absurd tastes of a 'damned barbarous nation' the Scotsman reluctantly made one pair. When Stanley asked him to make another, Farquahar indignantly threw down his needle and thread and said he had done enough for one day. Stanley privately vowed to settle the score.[18]

On 4 January Captain Richmond promised them they would see land next day. As the reality of Zanzibar loomed, Stanley began to fret about the viability of his assignment. If Livingstone had already found the source of the Nile and proceeded to follow its course, there would be nothing left for his would-be 'finder' but to return to China, as ordered by Bennett. That was unthinkable, for already Stanley had had enough of maritime existence to last a lifetime: 'My long imprisonment at sea on shipboard I shall not readily forget.'[19]

Zanzibar came as a relief and a revelation. After standing off the island on the evening of 5–6 January, not daring to approach the sound in darkness, Richmond landed his passengers next morning. Stanley was enchanted: 'one of the fairest gems of Nature's creation . . . of all the islands I have seen it is the most perfect for the comfort of man.'[20]

The next two days, when Consul Webb, his only contact, was too busy to see him, enabled Stanley to put his initial reactions to the test. The island of Zanzibar, 46 miles long and between 9 and 19 miles in width, was a low-lying, green and naturally fragrant land: as Stanley sailed along its coast prior to landfall his nostrils were assailed by natural scents and his eyes ravished by the variegated greens of mango, tamarind, bombax and cocoa palm. But the sweet sensuousness of nature soon yielded to man-made pollution. Anchorage at Zanzibar was a mere 400 yards from the town, and the harbour area was a forest of masts and sails: the (as yet) occasional European ship mingled with Arab dhows and a variety of small craft, slaving vessels and wood carriers.[21]

The town of Zanzibar rose from the beach in a crescent form, 'white, glaring and unsymmetrical'. In the centre of the first line of buildings was the tall, whitewashed house of Zanzibar's sultan, Prince Barghash bin Said. Then there were the shore batteries and, to the right of them, the houses of the foreign diplomats and residents. To the left of the batteries were a number of sheds roofed with palm fronds – the Zanzibar Customs House. To the left of this again was the unfinished wooden palace of the Sultan and his harem, and the residence of his Prime Minister. Beyond this began the suburb of Melinde – the residential area for Europeans – which abutted the unhealthy Malagash inlet.[22] Back from the shore, the indigenous quarters of the town were dominated by white light and blazing heat – the plentiful shade of the European suburb was absent. Everywhere was the amber-coloured dust of copal and the orchilla seed, the sweet fragrance of cloves and the stale sweat of hordes of slaves. The smell of decay was pervasive: festering sugar-cane debris, rotting orange and banana peelings, human refuse. In the business sector spicy smells and the odours of fruit, oils, peppers and cloth were counterpointed by swarms of flies. The pullulating population was supported by agriculture in the fields around. Here was an abundance of manioc, cassava, Indian corn, millet, sesame, plantains, mangoes, oranges, limes, pomegranates and jack fruit trees.[23]

Commercially Zanzibar was both an entrepreneur's paradise and the cockpit for intense Anglo-American rivalry. A shrewd businessman had no particular difficulty in quadrupling his capital, especially in the ivory trade, since prices increased exponentially between the interior and Zanzibar. Until the close of the Civil War it was mainly the Americans who benefited from this unique investment opportunity. In a trade conducted mainly from New York and Salem, Yankee businessmen brought in annually some $3,500,000 worth of brandy, gunpowder, muskets, beads, cottons, brass-wire, chinaware, and especially 'Merikani' sheeting cloth, and departed with some $3,000,000 of ivory, gum-copal, cloves, hides, cowries, sesamum, pepper and coconut oil.[24] But in the late 1860s the Americans' near-monopoly began to be challenged by the British and Germans; by the time the Suez Canal opened in 1869, the US share of trading tonnage dipped alarmingly.[25]

Added to this commercial rivalry was a political antagonism between the British and Americans. The Americans suspected that the British drive against the African slave trade masked a desire to absorb the independent principality of Zanzibar into an African empire and that the anti-slavery crusade itself camouflaged much more mundane economic interests. The two consular representatives on the island reflected the different styles and official aspirations of the two English-speaking nations. The US consul was the thirty-eight-year-old Francis Ropes Webb, also director of the Boston firm John Bertram & Co., and now in the third year of his Zanzibar consulate.[26] The British political agent was Dr John (later Sir John) Kirk, vice-consul since 1866 and soon (1873) to be consul-general, in which post he remained (except for leaves) in Zanzibar until 1887. Kirk was primarily a diplomat, not a trader; he had served with Livingstone on the Zambezi expedition in the 1850s[27]

These two men were to be key players in the drama of Stanley's search for Livingstone. When Stanley arrived in Zanzibar, it was bad enough that he found no news at all of Livingstone. But he was stupefied to find that, with just $8 in gold left after fourteen months' travel, there was no letter from Bennett awaiting him to confirm the verbal orders in Paris and hence no money.[28] In desperation, on 8 January he threw himself on Webb's mercy and asked him to pledge his personal credit of between $20,000 and $40,000 to the Livingstone expedition. It was fortunate for Stanley that he had already on several occasions established his credentials by letter and that Webb knew Gordon Bennett's interest in Livingstone was a long-standing one. Although Stanley's petition was, on the face of it, a very tall order financially, Webb agreed, on two conditions: Stanley would stay at the US consulate until his departure for the mainland so that Webb could protect his investment: and he would allow Webb to make all the preparations for the expedition with Sultan Barghash; Webb in turn would 'sell' the expedition to the Sultan as a way in which the Zanzibaris and Americans could turn the flank on encroaching British imperialism.[29]

With the agreement secured, the two of them made their way to the Sultan's palace for a formal audience. Webb was fussily anxious that Stanley should not breach any of the rules of court etiquette and kept whispering instructions to him, reminding him that at no time should he turn his back on Barghash.[30] Stanley was contemptuous of all this protocol, and also of the banality of the Sultan's conversation, but he played along with Webb, and was well rewarded at the outcome. Barghash gave him letters of introduction to Said Bin Salim, governor of Unyanyembe and a veteran of the two Speke expeditions.[31] Another important letter of introduction was to the influential sheikh of the interior, Bin Nasib.[32]

Next, without revealing what his true intentions were – only Webb of all the people in Zanzibar ever knew their true scope – Stanley made friends with the American mercantile community and began to amass a combined arsenal and warehouse at Webb's house: cloth, beads, wire, tar, canvas, tents, utensils, even two boats (one 25 feet by 6 feet, the other 10 feet long by 4½ feet wide), which he stripped of their boards and then dismantled into sections that could be screwed together.[33]

One of the necessary preparatory tasks was to cut up cloth for tents and canvas for saddles. Inevitably, Farquahar soon began to complain of the magnitude of the task, so Stanley looked around for another sailor with relevant experience. His choice fell on John W. Shaw, recently discharged mate of the USS *Nevada*. Shaw was a British sailor who had arrived in Zanzibar with charges of mutinous conduct hanging over him. The captain of the *Nevada* insisted on imprisoning Shaw and three other men in the Zanzibar Fort, saying he would neither pay them nor take them back to the USA. Webb investigated the charges and found them groundless; clearly the captain was merely trying to avoid paying the 'mutineers'. Forced to take them on to the USA the *Nevada*'s master 'solved' his problem dropping the four men overboard in a longboat 7 miles off the coast. Now although the mutiny charges had been shown to be false – and on Webb's advice the captain was arrested on arrival in the USA – in terms of mercantile marine service there was a question mark against anyone who had been involved in such an incident. It was Shaw's knowledge that another ship would be hard to find that induced him to sign up with Stanley as Farquhar's Number Two.[34]

With two white lieutenants in his employment, Stanley next had to engage porters, soldiers, bearers and their overseers from among the racially mixed *wangwana* or 'Zanzibaris' – the devoutly Muslim products of Arabo-African 'miscegenation.'[35] The two principal 'captains'engaged – at $80 a year and with a coveted uniform thrown in – were Bombay, a Yao former slave and veteran of the Speke expeditions, and Mabruki.[36] Others of the 'old faithfuls' from the Burton, Speke and Grant ventures signed on at $40 a year apiece: Uledi, Ulimengo, Baruti, Ambari. The expedition gradually began to take shape: men, donkeys, provisions, barter goods, all increased in number throughout January.

But if Stanley enjoyed the best possible relations with the Sultan and his officials, and with the American community, he found the British on the island hard to take. The English missionaries were a particular irritant, especially their nominal overlord, Bishop William G. Tozer, who had achieved the singular distinction of *withdrawing* the Universities Mission to Central Africa from the mainland. Tozer, a High Church man, liked to go around Zanzibar dressed in priestly purple and fine linen and the sight of him for Stanley 'acted upon the Yankee as a red cloth on an insane bull'.[37] But Stanley was not alone in his distaste for Tozer; Livingstone felt it too, and it was their common antipathy to Tozer and his High Church posturings that was to forge yet another bond between the Welsh reporter and the Scottish explorer.

Stanley's attitude to Tozer and his acolytes was one of mild contempt. Kirk was another matter. The 'Zambezi doctor' evoked in Stanley an immediate visceral antipathy. Each man seemed immediately to recognise the enemy in the other. Both were larger-than-life figures with a will of iron, arrogant and autocratic. Dr Kirk seldom inspired middle-range emotions. Those who came into contact with him either fell under his spell or detested him cordially.[38] So on top of the coolness existing between the British and American communities, and between Kirk and Webb, there was placed a fresh layer of personal animosity between Kirk and Stanley. The full extent of his was not yet manifest, but the latent tensions were evident at their very first meeting on 9 January when Stanley caught Kirk directing a 'broad stare' in his direction. Later in the evening Kirk drew Stanley aside, ostensibly to show him a gun but really to talk to him about Livingstone, for Stanley had made it known that as a *Herald* reporter he was interested in any titbits of gossip about the great Victorian hero; he did not of course reveal to Kirk that his mission was to 'find' Livingstone. Kirk told him that Livingstone was a difficult man to get along with. Stanley, trying to be casual, asked what would happen if he accidentally 'stumbled' across him in Africa. Kirk replied: 'To tell you the truth, I do not think he would like it very much. I know, if Burton or Grant or Baker, or any of those fellows were going after him and he heard of their coming, Livingstone would put a hundred miles of swamp in a very short time between himself and them.'[39] The idea that he was in search of a misanthrope did nothing to lift Stanley's spirits.

Moreover, what Kirk had to say about Livingstone at the second meeting was not encouraging: 'He [Kirk] gives me a very bad impression of Livingstone. I am told he is a hard man to get along with, is very narrow minded. Has had no personal quarrel with him but he has always had trouble with his companions. He thinks he ought to come home now and permit a younger man to go in his place.'[40] These words, when later reported to Livingstone (for naturally Stanley made a point of repeating the conversation as part of his campaign to discredit the British consul), would whip him up into a frenzy against Kirk.

For the rest of January Stanley laboured away at the difficult task of assembling a credible African expedition. He had a number of meetings with Ladha Damji, the Sultan's customs master, in order to expedite Barghash's orders. He made the acquaintance of a man who was later to be important in his African work, an American bureaucrat, Augustus Sparhawk. He chafed at the suspected dishonesty of his agent, the nineteen-year-old local entrepreneurial talent Sewa Haji Paru. He had further meetings with the Sultan. He arranged how his porters would carry their loads (68 pounds per man). He learned about local currencies and the *per diem* payments of *dhoti* or cloth: how many yards of the various cloths to take, and how many beads (the currency preferred by some tribes) and of what colour. Most of all he learned from Sheikh Hashid about the most prized currency of all: wire, the thickness of telegraph wire.[41]

By 5 February 1871 he was ready to cross to the mainland. As a parting gift he received two horses: one from the Sultan, the other from William Goodhue, a Salem merchant.[42] But on the morning he was due to sail the *dhows* across the straits to Bagamoyo, Stanley found both Shaw and Farquahar missing. He tracked them down to a bar where they were both hopelessly drunk and insisting they did not want to cross to the mainland. Stanley threatened them with imprisonment for breach of contract and defalcation (they had already spent their advance of salary) if they did not immediately embark. Reluctantly the two went aboard.[43]

As his flotilla crossed with bellying sails to the expedition's starting point at Bagamoyo, Stanley felt grounds for guarded confidence in the progress he had made so far. In a single month he had spent $8,000 of the advance extended by Webb against Bennett's wealth.[44] On the first night in Bagamoyo his spirits were still further lifted by a noble dinner given him by the priests of the Catholic Holy Ghost Mission. This French order had been engaged in evangelical work in Zanzibar since 1860, and Bagamoyo since 1868.[45] Its father superior Anton Horner decided to open the prize vintages in the missionaries' cellars for this special occasion when the *Herald* correspondent, Dr Kirk and Captain Tucker of the anti-slavery cruiser HMS *Columbine* would all be present.[46] Kirk had come over to the mainland on a shooting expedition with the French consul Charles de Vienne, and Tucker had seized the opportunity to request that he be included in a few days' 'sport'.[47]

The dinner that evening was a truly splendid affair. But Stanley spoiled the fathers' generous gesture by his later cynical references to the occasion and by insinuating that the missionaries did a little too well for themselves, overlooking the fact that they were merely trying to impress their distinguished guests and that the array of fine wines did not represent their usual fare: 'The champagne – think of champagne Cliquot in East Africa! La Fitte, La Rose, Burgundy and Bordeaux were of first rate quality, and the meek and lowly eyes of the fathers were not a little brightened under the vinous influence.'[48]

The 'vinous influence' also enabled Stanley and Kirk to get along well enough that evening. But next day Stanley found further evidence to fuel the animus he felt towards the British consul. For years Livingstone had been dependent for survival in Central Africa on supplies sent from Zanzibar by his erstwhile comrade Kirk. Yet Kirk's attitude to getting these supplies through to Unyanyembe, the great entrepôt in western Tanzania, was dilatory to say the least. In November 1870 Kirk had despatched to the mainland £1,000 worth of goods supplied by the British government in a fit of anxiety and guilt about Livingstone. Instead of crossing to the mainland and making sure this vital convoy got under way for the interior, Kirk sent it across with a seven-man escort, five of them slaves. For onward transportation to Unyanyembe, at least thirty-five porters were needed, yet Kirk did nothing about recruiting them. The almost inevitable upshot was that when Kirk and Stanley came over to Bagamoyo in February 1871, Livingstone's relief caravan was still loitering on the coast. To save face Kirk then had to improvise hurriedly to get at least part of the supplies despatched inland.[49]

The tension between Stanley and Kirk increased when Stanley remonstrated about the inept administration of Livingstone's supplies. Kirk coldly informed Stanley that he would change his tune when he experienced African conditions at first hand and prophesied that his two horses would not last a week in the African bush. Stanley got his revenge by a derogatory report about Kirk's marksmanship during the mainland 'shoot'.[50]

Since Livingstone was later to accuse Kirk of gross dereliction of his official and moral duties towards him, it is worth establishing at this stage that Stanley's accusations had substance. Kirk's many later defenders asserted that Stanley's secrecy was largely to blame: had he revealed his true intentions, Kirk could have sent the caravan to Ujiji under his aegis.[51] But this argument will not hold, since it ignores the political realities of Anglo-American rivalry discussed above. Even had Kirk suspected Stanley's true designs, he would not have entrusted goods funded by the *British* government to an American and an overt ally of consul Webb. Nor can naïvety be pleaded in Kirk's defence: he, of all people, knew Africa and its delays – indeed he boasted of this knowledge to Stanley. We are left with the inescapable conclusion that, for reasons unexplained, he did not exert himself on Livingstone's behalf. Livingstone's later fulminations against Kirk are usually dismissed as the semi-paranoid ravings of a disappointed old man, who was being egged on by Stanley. But there was rather more substance to his criticisms than that. One explanation is that Livingstone was actually right, that Kirk bore an obscure, possibly unconscious, grudge towards him from the Zambezi days. Kirk had often got the sharp edge of Livingstone's tongue in those disastrous days and had parted from him on bad terms. One Kirk diary entry, dated 18 September 1862, is particularly significant: 'I can come to no other conclusion than that Dr Livingstone is out of his mind.'[52]

Yet in Bagamoyo the issue of Kirk was a deferred item, not an immediately pressing one. All Stanley's time was taken up with the problem of finding sufficient *pagazis* or porters for his great exploit. The great cholera epidemic of 1870 had claimed so many lives that potential bearers were avoiding Zanzibar and the coast.[53] For two months Stanley wrestled with an obstacle that threatened to wreck his expedition before it even got started. 'My life at Zanzibar I thought hard, but my two months at Bagamoyo a convict at Sing Sing would not have envied. It was work all day, thinking all night; not an hour could I call my own.'[54]

In these two dead months at Bagamoyo Stanley also received his first education in the complex realities of African politics. At the level of technology reached in Africa in the early 1870s the porter was 'the camel, the horse, the mule, the train, the waggon and the cart of East and Central Africa. Without him Salem would not obtain her ivory, Boston and New York their African ebony, their frankincense, myrrh and gum copal.'[55] Yet these crucial carriers, the Nyamwezi of what is now central Tanzania, were themselves divided politically into numerous small states. Overlaying the economic problem of short-term shortage of *pagazis* were political problems deriving from kinship, suzerainty and territoriality.[56] Yet at the very time Stanley was being held back by a mesh of delaying factors, his anxieties were rising daily. These were twofold, that the rainy season was approaching, and that, in the light of Kirk's remarks, Livingstone might decamp if he heard a white man was looking for him.[57]

Stanley's frustration and anger over the long delay found a focus in the hated nineteen-year-old Sewa Haji. Stanley itched to take the dazzling young entrepreneur down a peg or two by a thrashing (preferably a flogging) for the many suspected peculations and financial irregularities, but Sewa was just too good at recruiting *pagazis*, who were hard to find even when paid well above market rate – Stanley's hiring bills in February–March 1871 came to $2,000 worth of cloth.[58] And the young agent did give him one piece of invaluable advice: to send out his caravan in detachments, both because the chiefs of the interior were more likely to attack a large 'threatening' body and because, even if pacific, they would demand larger tribute or *hongo*.

Accordingly Stanley sent out his first two detachments, the second under Farquahar. He particularly wanted Farquahar out of the way, as the ex-mate had spent his time in Bagamoyo drinking heavily, whoring, and quarrelling with Shaw. Finally, by the end of March, Stanley was ready to leave himself.[59] In all his detachments Stanley could count 192 men but in his own column, far the largest, he had (apart from himself, Shaw, Selim and Bombay) twenty-two soldiers and eighty-two *pagazis*. With them they took twenty-seven donkeys, two horses (including the bay which Stanley rode out of Bagamoyo), fifty-two bales of cloth, a boat, seven man-loads of wire, sixteen man-loads of beads, three loads of tents, four loads of clothes and baggage, two loads of cooking utensils, three of powder, five of bullets and cartridges, three of instruments and luxury items, and twenty loads of boat fixtures. The armaments of the expedition were also impressive. They comprised one double-barrelled smooth-bore No. 12, two American Winchesters ('sixteen shooters'), two Starr's breech-loading carbines, one Jocelyn breech-loader, one elephant rifle, two breech-loading revolvers, twenty-four flintlock muskets, six single-barrelled pistols, plus a quantity of axes, swords, daggers, hatchets and other weapons.[60]

Altogether Stanley and his men took 116 loads, or 8½ tons, of material into the interior of the Dark Continent. Stanley's very first expedition was already the largest ever to set out on a journey of African exploration. This fact was often underscored uncritically by later writers, who saw only the financial resources available to Stanley.[61] They did not see that the very scale of Stanley's expeditions imposed its own logic, so that he could not afford to be as slow, methodical or flexible in his methods as his rivals. The Royal Geographical Society might send out explorers in a spirit of dispassionate discovery, but a hard task-master like James Gordon Bennett wanted fast dramatic results for his huge financial outlay.[62]

As he left the suburbs of Bagamoyo behind, Stanley noticed that his expedition was already the object of much excited attention. Africans left the fields where they were planting and sowing to see the parade of soldiers and *pagazis* pass by. Stanley pretended, for the benefit of his Victorian readers, to be scandalised by their absolute nudity: 'compared to which Adam and Eve in their fig-leaf apparel must have been *en grande tenue*.'[63] The expedition defiled up the narrow shaded lane, flanked by two parallel hedges of mimosa, that led inland from Bagamoyo. But soon they were clear of populated areas and approaching their first obstacle, the Kingani River. Here, after cutting down trees with axes to make a bridge over the feeder tributaries, Stanley's men ferried themselves across the main Kingani without difficulty.

Next day at dawn the *kudu* horn sounded and they breakfasted in the half-light. Stanley waited until the last straggler had left camp, then galloped to the head of the column, leaving Shaw to bring up the rear. On the western side of the Kingani, the terrain improved. No longer muddy jungle, it resembled the sward surrounding an English mansion. The trail led smoothly upwards towards a forest-clad plain, topped with occasional ridges from which panoramic views could be obtained. There was wild life in abundance: pigeons, jays, ibises, turtledoves, golden pheasants, quails, moorhens, crows, hawks, pelicans, eagles, as well as monkeys, antelope, steinbok, kudu, giraffe and zebra. Stanley tried out his .44 calibre Winchester rifle on the swarms of basking hippopotami but made no more impression on their hide than if he had used sling-shot. But since Stanley hated any kind of failure as if it were evil itself, he had to satisfy himself by killing one of the pachyderms with the No. 12 smooth-bore; as he himself admitted, this was purely a matter of 'sport', since his party was not in need of meat.[64]

Stanley's prodigality was soon punished. On 27 March they were at Rosako, still in parkland, but now the supply of game was drying up. Already the sixth detachment was lagging behind, so he called a halt while Bombay went back to energise Maganga, the captain of the rearguard. It was four days before Bombay returned and a further four days before Maganga arrived.[65] During the enforced rest, the expedition came close to collapse. Stanley's men began to sicken with fever and to desert. Stanley himself played with fire by allowing the tsetse flies he was examining to bite him, unaware that they carried elephantiasis and sleeping sickness.[66] This incident is illustrative both of the primitive state of tropical medicine then prevailing, and, more particularly, of the appalling ignorance regarding the tsetse fly.[67] But while Stanley experimented with flies, it was his horses that succumbed, not himself. The Sultan's horse dropped dead, and Stanley, in his present state of 'scientific' curiosity, carried out an autopsy. Despite the evidence, he remained adamant that it was some rare worm, not a horse fly that had killed the horse. Next day the bay that Goodhue had given him also died. Again Stanley evinced a certain morbidity by insisting on cutting up this carcass too.[68] On top of these disasters, the heavens opened and the rainy season proper began. When Stanley was troubled with the nauseous stench of an anteater, which he had to dispatch with the Winchester, it seemed that his cup was running over.[69]

At Rosako Stanley went through the first, and in many ways most serious, mental crisis of the Livingstone expedition. His two horses were dead, donkeys were starting to die, his sick list lengthened daily, and already the caravans he was not personally directing were falling behind. Worst of all was the realisation that the detested Kirk was right, that Stanley had severely underrated the risks and pitfalls ahead.[70] Kirk had jeered that only a professional explorer could find Livingstone, and here was Stanley, not yet a week out from Bagamoyo, having to confront his own serious misjudgements and inadequacies. If he was so clearly wrong about the viability of horses in Africa, might he not also be wrong about the feasibility of the entire Livingstone expedition? It was symptomatic of his state of uncertainty that while hunting in the bush, Stanley himself got lost and retraced his steps back to camp only with great difficulty.[71]

As with many people like Stanley, who habitually inhabit the twilight area between sanity and madness, the possibility of failure imparted renewed strength. Rage fuelled his determination to succeed; with the dedication of fanaticism, he decided to divest himself of all human weaknesses and become a man of iron. The change in Stanley's attitude was evinced in two ways. Normally, his propensity to beat and flog manifested itself towards those who were potential or putative rivals in one sphere or another (Noe, Sewa Haji); towards those who did not purport to be his equals he was complaisant. But now he decided to beat and flog *all* who did not meet his standards. And he decided (albeit unconsciously) to make Shaw the particular butt for his anger. Since Stanley's personality was being stretched to the limits of its capabilities, it is not surprising that many normally latent dark impulses began to surface. In this particular case it was a sadism directed primarily at an exponent of heterosexual promiscuity, for Shaw's various dalliances had long troubled Stanley and excited his wrathful contempt.[72]

Moreover, Shaw was already a marked man in Stanley's conscious mind, for two reasons. In the first place Stanley found him humourless and inordinately vain and a bad influence on Farquahar. Secondly, Shaw had alienated Stanley by referring to the Zanzibar Arabs as 'niggers': 'he fully showed the uneducated Anglo-Saxon's ineptitude for travel and intercourse with other races.'[73] As they began to climb up on to the East African highlands through the monsoon rains, and Shaw's complaints grew more vociferous, Stanley subtly increased the pressure on him and gradually edged him towards breaking point. He put Shaw in charge of the baggage cart during a trek through a fetid jungle on the way to Msuwa. For three days Stanley railed at him when he arrived late.[74]: 'Shaw was in charge in the cart, and his experiences were most bitter, as he informed me he had expended a whole vocabulary of stormy abuse known to sailors, and a new one which he had invented extempore. He did not arrive until two o'clock next morning, and was completely worn out.'[75] When Stanley had been mounted on his bay, Shaw rode a donkey. Now he walked while Stanley rode the donkey. Stanley's donkey-riding can be seen both as part of a new realism and as a desire to put Shaw in his place: he would never allow him to do exactly what he did.

At Msuwa, on the plateau, they halted for a day while Uledi and Ferrajji were sent in pursuit of Khamisi, who had deserted with two goats and Uledi's personal possessions.[76] It was part of Stanley's plan to stop at the regular caravan stations, situated on the outskirts of villages, where goats, chickens and other food could be obtained. The usual pattern, as at Msuwa, was that the village and encampment would be surrounded by a protecting palisade. The drawback about these stations was that they were insanitary and fever-ridden, crawling with fleas, tsetse flies and malarial mosquitoes. The net consequence was that Stanley unwittingly further debilitated his manpower, since whereas in the bush his porters would certainly have been bitten, they would not have been constantly rein-fected, nor would there have been so many noxious bacteria from human filth.

At Msuwa too Stanley had his first real taste of the tribute or *hongo* system, when he gave the chief two *doti*. But he salved the 'humiliation' he felt over this – for Stanley had not yet reconciled himself to African realities – by impressing the villagers with the firepower of his Winchester and breech-loading revolvers.[77] On 10 April the expedition quit Msuwa and pursued the road to Kisemo, passing a chained slave-gang heading east as they went. At Kisemo Uledi and Ferrajji returned with the runaway Khamisi. His recapture provided a suitable cautionary tale for the other men. Uledi and Ferrajji related that they had rescued him in the nick of time from the Washensi people who were just about to kill him. Stanley summoned a court of eight bearers and four soldiers to decide what to do about the deserting Khamisi. Since the prestige of the Wanyamezi was diminished by his absconding, the court ordered a flogging; as presiding judge Stanley decided that the twelve jurors and Shaw should administer one stroke of the birch each.[78]

Stanley involved Shaw in the administration of 'justice' as a way of reprimanding him for not preventing straggling. He tightened the screw on the luckless sailor in another way. Since Stanley had been accused by local tribes of 'bad medicine' in reading printed words from a book, he manoeuvred Shaw into lifting a 'sacred stone' out of the caravan's path to insinuate to his Zanzibari followers that the real Jonah on the expedition was Shaw.[79]

On 12 April they reached the western edge of Ukwere at Mussoudi. Beyond lay the territory of the Wakami. Here they halted one day to replenish supplies before beginning the descent from the plateau into a valley of changing scenery and sable loam soil where plentiful sugar-cane, Indian corn, egg-plant and cucumber were grown. So far they had met only peaceful tribes, and the rumour was that the people Stanley called Wakami were no exception; any warlike propensities had been hammered out of them by the impact of the slave trade.[80]

On 14 April they crossed the Ungerengeri River and began climbing out of the valley through a forest of tamarind, tamarisk, acacia, mimosa and *mparamusi*. Thence they ascended the southern face of the Kira peak and proceeded into the valley of Kiwrima. Stanley's hard driving meant they again overtook the fourth caravan at Mullaleh. To his chagrin it was full of sick men, hardly surprisingly since Stanley's detachment was the only one that carried modern medicines.[81] More importantly to him,

Stanley met a man who claimed to have seen Livingstone at Ujiji a year ago. This was Salid bin Rashid al Manzuri, who had helped Burton greatly during the 1856–8 expedition.[82]

Encouraged by this definite news of Livingstone, Stanley prepared for the four marches that would take him to the great stone city of Simbawenni. But during a two-day halt he confronted two problems that would plague him to the 'city of the lions' and beyond. One was that the Luguru peoples he was now meeting were much more 'insolent and aggressive' than any tribes encountered hitherto. The other was Shaw. When Stanley took him to task for driving the donkeys across gulleys breast-deep in water, when prudence dictated unloading them first, Shaw exploded and called Stanley an overfastidious ingrate, a slave driver whom it was impossible to please. Shaw capped his remarks by stating that he would resign as soon as he met a caravan going back east. Stanley replied that he was free to do so, but he (Stanley) would retain all his effects against the advance money paid in Zanzibar. At this Shaw relapsed into a sullen silence.[83]

18 April saw them outside the great stone fortress of Simbawenni (the site of modern Morogoro), whose population Stanley estimated at 3–5,000. Here Stanley was obliged by torrential rains to halt another four days, while he pondered in alarm the great mortality among the donkeys in the caravans.[84] Simbawenni had been founded by Kisabengo, a Spartacus-like leader of runaway slaves, who died in 1867. His daughter was named for the fortress itself ('lion-like') and had established herself as a power in the land.[85] She now sent to Stanley for tribute, which he refused on the ground that Farquahar had already paid it. For the moment she bided her time and contented herself with sending her people to stare at Stanley's caravan.[86]

The four days outside Simbawenni were a nightmare. There was a constant downpour: 'a real London rain – an eternal drizzle accompanied with mist and fog.'[87] Selim broke the trigger of Stanley's gun and nearly blew his own head off. Stanley himself was attacked by a fever that recalled the 'ague' of Arkansas and he was forced to dose himself experimentally with medicines.[88] Worst of all, the caravan camp itself was a hotbed of malaria. Then filth of generations of *pagazis* had produced a plague of insects: red ants, centipedes, wasps, beetles; 'in short the richest entomological collection could not vie in variety and numbers with the species which the four walls of my tent enclosed from morning until night.'[89]

On the fifth day the rain ceased long enough to allow them to wade through the Stygian mire to the flooded river-bank. They then crossed the river by a very unsteady suspension bridge and found a comfortable camp at the foot of the Usagara mountains, 5 miles to the north-west of the river crossing.[90] On the morning of 24 April Stanley caught his cook pilfering for the sixth time and ordered Shaw to flog him as an exemplary punishment. Unfortunately, the cook's comrades saw the flogging as grotesquely unfitting for such a petty crime and helped him to decamp to Simbawenni. Stanley then sent three soldiers to bring the runaway back, but they were captured by the Sultana of Simbawenni, who took away their guns and chained them, then repeated her demand to Stanley for tribute. This presented him with a ticklish problem of credibility. Fortunately, some Arabs under Sheik Thani who had visited the *Herald* caravan passed on to the Sultana the canard that Stanley had guns with an effective range of a half a mile. At this she changed her tune and released her prisoners, retaining just two guns as a face-saver. The cook who had precipitated all the trouble was later found murdered.[91]

The incident with the cook outside Simbawenni heightened tensions in the caravan. Bombay, who had earlier been reduced to the ranks for failing to get the stragglers into camp before midnight, now regarded Stanley as a madman, unlike Burton or even Speke, who had knocked his front teeth out in 1862. Shaw, too, who had been involved both in the initial flogging and then the retrieval mission to Simbawenni, started to realise just how dangerous was this man with whom he had signed a contract.

Between Simbawenni and Rehenneko, their next major objective, loomed the dreadful Makata swamp.[92] There was an easier circuitous track that would have taken them to their destination, but Stanley was obsessed with the need to make sure the first three detachments were already well ahead of them, and not festering at Rehenneko. His methods had been unusual from the very first. Normally explorers did not travel in the rainy season – and it had rained every day since Stanley left Bagamoyo – but his impatient fanaticism would brook no delay.[93]

So into the Mataka swamp they plunged. They marched 45 miles in five days, knee-deep in water and black mud. Fever, smallpox and dysentery assailed them. Shaw, Selim, the soldiers, the dog Omar all went down to one strain or another, the dog fatally so. Stanley suffered from fever, *then* from dysentery; including his spell in bed at Rehenneko he had lost 40 pounds in little more than a week (reducing from 170 pounds to 130).[94] The men trekked on because they were more afraid of Stanley and his whip than of the swamp and floods ahead. Stanley here first showed clearly a trait that was later to become notorious: his habit of abandoning the ailing and sick. He left behind one man dying of smallpox then had the pharisaical effrontery to justify his action by claiming that he did so 'lest they commit the barbarism of leaving him unburied when he was dead'. He topped this mouth-stopping arrogance by likening the situation to that of a man falling overboard during a hurricane, forgetting that a hurricane is a natural force and that the only force driving these particular men was his own demoniacal will.[95]

That was not his only moral blemish during these agonising days in Makata. Although Stanley would always call a halt if he was dangerously ill, as he demonstrated later on the expedition, he showed no such consideration for anyone else. If another white man fell ill, Stanley immediately rationalised the inconvenience as 'malingering'. When, therefore, Shaw appeared at the point of death with fever in the swamp, Stanley simply pressed on faster. His grotesque injustice to his two white comrades can be seen from an example of unconscious irony when he simultaneously castigates Farquahar for his performance so far on the expedition *and* boasts about his own 'Sisyphean labours' in the Makata swamp, failing to see that those same labours had already been performed by Farquahar ahead of him.[96] Stanley's published account of the passage from Simbawenni to Rehenneko is singularly revealing; it must be one of the few occasions when a public figure reveals himself more clearly in his published writings than in his private journal:

The first of May found us struggling through the mire and water of the Makata with a caravan bodily sick . . . Shaw was still suffering from his first *munkunguru* (fever), exhibiting himself under a new phase – a phase none of the pleasantest. Besides delivering himself of certain desires not at all complimentary to the Expedition within our hearing, he seemed to assume by degrees the character of a chronic hypochondriac, which, at all times an unlovely character, is positively hateful to the *mtongi* (leader) of an African expedition battling with swamp and rain, with a sickened caravan . . . Mabruk Saleem, a youth of lusty frame . . . laid himself down on the marshy ground, professing, while imitating a man who vomits, his total inability to breast the Makata swamp, but a plaited thong vigorously laid across his naked shoulders expunged the seeming nausea from the stomach; Abdul Kader, the Hindi tailor and adventurer . . . was ever ailing . . . but ever hungry. 'Oh God!' was the cry of my tired soul, 'were all the men of my expedition like this man I should be compelled to return, but not before taking summary vengeance upon the whole of them.' The virtue of a good whip was well tested by me on this day . . . and I was compelled to observe that when mud and wet sapped the physical energy of the lazily-inclined, a dog-whip became their backs, restoring them to a sound – sometimes to an extravagant activity.[97]

At Rehenneko (near modern Kilosa), Stanley halted for four days to recover from his own fever, a luxury he would never allow to others in his expedition. At last the rainy season came to an end, so that the worst seemed over. But now came news from ahead that Farquahar was seriously ill. Stanley was angry with Farquahar both for this 'malingering' and (unconsciously) because Farquahar too had conquered the 'incomparable sufferings' of the Makata swamp, so that Stanley was not 'first'. Since he was too ill to write himself, he ordered Shaw to compose a letter.

Shaw composed an illiterate screed, to which Farquahar, now seriously ill, was only able to scribble a few incoherent lines in reply. Stanley later reproduced both letters, to show the 'impossibility' of his two white assistants, without explaining the desperate pass to which Farquahar's health had come. 'Callous' is a mild word to characterise Stanley's observations:

> However ungrammatical and misspelt the above note [from Shaw] is, it is far more intelligible to me . . . than the reply which was received from the third caravan . . . this was the precious response I received to an anxious inquiry as to the condition of himself and his caravan. Had the man been stark crazy he could scarcely have indited anything better calculated to confuse one . . . in short the letter is incomprehensible to me unless the man Farquahar is hydrophobically insane.[98]

We may note in passing a typical Stanley ploy: condemn person X, then condemn person Y even more vehemently by giving faint praise to the already damned person X.[99]

When Stanley recovered from his fever, he went on ahead to Kiora to learn the true situation with Farquahar. He found him grievously ill from dropsy and elephantiasis. But what concerned Stanley more was Farquahar's overgenerous payments to his porters (six bales of cloth) and the fact that all his donkeys were dead: 'An Arab proprietor would have slaughtered him for his extravagance and imbecility, but I had no other course but to relieve him of all charge of such goods.'[100] As for Farquahar's ghastly illness, that merely elicited from Stanley a prime example of the sadistic mentality: 'As he heard my voice, Farquahar staggered out of his tent, as changed from my spruce mate who started from Bagamoyo as if he had been expressly fattened by the Wabembe of the Tanganyika, as we do geese and turkeys for the Christmas dinner – as interesting a case of hypertrophy as Barnum's fat woman.'[101]

Stanley's attitude to Farquahar was despicable on just about every count. There was no word of either gratitude for the sterling job the Scot had done in such dreadful conditions, or compassion for his tsetse-induced state. Instead Stanley coldly quoted the proverb 'Set a beggar on horseback and he will ride to the devil'. Nor can Stanley be absolved on the grounds of being a mere psychopath, for he was capable of extreme compassion for his 'dark companions' and for animals, as the following stricture on Farquahar shows: 'I had given him a capital Zanzibar riding-ass . . . which he had ridden to death. He had never condescended to dismount from the moment he left one camp until he arrived at another, and, not knowing how to ride, he had see-sawed from side to side until the poor animal's back was so chafed that it soon died.'[102]

Both Shaw and Farquahar were now in need of a sustained rest, but Stanley insisted on pressing on at once. They began to ascend the Usagara mountains.[103] From Kiora the united caravans wound along the banks of the Mkondoa River, compelled constantly to cross and recross the stream because mountain spurs blocked the way. Since Farquahar and Shaw were only just able to sit on their donkeys and had no energies left for anything else, the column began to get strung out. Eventually Shaw was left far behind. Stanley sent him word to catch up, then sent a stiff written note. When no answer was received after four hours, Stanley's patience snapped and he rode back along the trail, to find Shaw and the rearguard 2 miles from camp.[104]

For two days and nights Shaw had been grabbing what sleep he could in the open, since his tent and equipment were at the front of the column with Stanley. None of this weighed with Stanley who was simply enraged that he found 'Mr Shaw was riding at a gait which seemed to leave it doubtful whether he or the animal felt most sleepy.'[105] Stanley at once ordered him to dismount, ill though he was, and walk the rest of the way to the camp, on the grounds that the donkey needed to be taken back at a brisk pace to be loaded.[106]

But the alleged need for intemperate haste was waived next day when Stanley called a halt while his 'police' went in search of a deserter. The hapless Shaw and Farquahar were able to sleep undisturbed while Stanley took himself off on an exploration of Lake Gombo.[107] But the retrieval of the deserter precipitated the three white men into a new phase of their running personal crisis, for the runaway, a Hindu handyman, was a personal friend of Shaw and Farquahar. From the surliness of their attitude at mealtime that night, Stanley knew a storm was imminent, but he was perhaps unprepared for its violence. Immediately on seating himself at the supper table, Shaw launched into a vituperative attack on his leader. He started by claiming that their food was not fit for a dog, then broadened the indictment by saying that Stanley had systematically breached the terms of their agreement, the latest instance being his insistence that Shaw walk to camp instead of riding the donkey. He ended with a flourish: 'I feel as if I would rather be in hell than in this damned expedition!'[108]

Stanley hit back angrily. The two men had had exactly the same food as he had; as for the donkeys, it was very clear that in a few days they would all be dead. 'Have you considered well your position? Do you realise where you are? Do you know that you are my servant, sir, and not my companion?'

This was too much for Shaw. 'Servant, be damned!' he exclaimed. At this Stanley sprang up and knocked him down. Shaw staggered to his feet and faced his tormentor. 'I tell you what it is, sir,' he muttered, 'I think I had better go back. I have had enough and I do not want to go any farther with you. I ask my discharge from you.'[109]

This was playing into Stanley's hands. At once he ordered Bombay to strike Shaw's tent and carry it and his baggage 200 yards from the camp. When Bombay had completed the task, Stanley told him to put Shaw's gun and pistol in the same place. When Shaw calmed down, he realised he had made a bad mistake, for he could not survive in the wilds alone in his present debilitated condition. He had to play for time and obtain food, water and shelter while he decided what to do next. At sunrise he went to Stanley and made a grovelling apology. Knowing he had the whiphand, Stanley made a show of gracious acceptance.[110]

The desertions, sickness, and terrible rains made Stanley decide to wait another day before moving on to Mpapwa. He therefore returned to Lake Gombo to shoot grouse.[111] While he was gone, Shaw and Farquahar conferred on the most effectual way to rid themselves of their tormentor. They decided on a desperate expedient. They would murder Stanley, proceed to Mpapwa to buy food and spread the word that their leader had been killed by hostile tribesmen, then return to Zanzibar and safety. It was a hare-brained scheme. Had the two men been in full possession of their mental faculties, they would have realised that the *wangwana* were too loyal to Stanley for their assassination bid to succeed. There was the further snag that Farquahar, an excellent shot, was too ill to do the shooting and it would have to be performed by Shaw, an inferior gunman.

That night when Stanley returned from the lake, the two men put their scheme into operation. The minute Stanley had finished writing his notes and extinguished his lamp, there was a loud report and a bullet tore through his tent, missing him by inches. He snatched up his revolver and rushed out of the tent. He found Shaw pretending to be asleep but with the tell-tale weapon lying alongside him. Shaw sat up and rubbed his eyes drowsily, but Stanley bent down, picked up the gun and found that the barrel was still warm. He thrust his finger into the barrel and withdrew it black with gunpowder. Grimly Stanley asked Shaw if he had recently fired it. Shaw hastily improvised a story of having seen a thief pass his door. Stanley fixed him with his withering basilisk stare and said coldly: 'I would advise you in future, in order to avoid all suspicion, not to fire into my tent or at least so near me. I might get hurt, you know, in which case, ugly reports would get about, and this perhaps would be disagreeable, as you are probably aware. Goodnight.'[112]

Stanley knew very well that there had been a murder attempt, but violence did not appal him as it would most men. He was content that he had a hold over Shaw, for he now had witnesses to an attempted homicide. Shaw, by contrast, was likely to have been in the deepest despair after bungling the assassination. If he attempted to desert now, Stanley could send word to the authorities in Zanzibar to have him hanged. As for Farquahar, Stanley knew perfectly well that he had been an accomplice in the plot, so decided to take his revenge by abandoning him at Mpapwa. Although he promised to pay a headman to look after him, in Farquahar's state abandonment was tantamount to a death sentence. Farquahar was far too ill to care, and was overjoyed at the prospect of rest when Stanley sent him ahead on a donkey, surrounded by solicitous porters, to Mpapwa.

On 17 May the expedition marched up a dry river bed to the foot of green mountains, where lay the great caravan town of Mpapwa. Already many caravans were strung across the welcome shade of forest covering the slope of the foothills.[113] Stanley ascertained that Farquahar was ensconced in a nearby village and that his fourth detachment in the van was well on the way to Tabora. He retired to his tent for his first full refreshing sleep for a month.

Next day he ran into Sheikh Thani, the Arab leader who had aided him at Simbawenni. Thani had overtaken him by the simple expedient of travelling by the direct route. He believed in travelling with long rests and recuperations and exhorted Stanley to feast on the produce of the caravanserai: fresh milk, sweet potatoes, beef, mutton, honey, beans, sorghum, grain and nuts. After fifty-seven days on a diet of tough goat and *matama* porridge, Stanley needed no second bidding.[114]

Thani also introduced him to a man with even more recent news of Livingstone: Sheikh Abdulla bin Nasibu.[115] Nasibu painted a picture of a portly disciplinarian, a 'heavy grubber' feared by his men. A few days later another Arab, Amir bin Sultan al Harthi, one of Barghash's favourites, asserted that Livingstone was still at Ujiji.

This was exciting news, and Stanley made fervid preparations to move on as soon as possible. But Thani counselled caution and urged at least three days' solid preparation. Ahead of them lay forced marches, necessary to avoid the bleaching sun of the waterless plains of Ugogo and the notoriously belligerent Wagogo. Only the very largest caravans or those too small to be worth plundering risked crossing their tribal areas; all others went in convoy. Thani suggested that Stanley join a caravan under Sheikh Hamed.

Stanley deferred a definite decision, but spent two days collecting supplies, mending broken equipment, buying livestock, repacking loads. He spent the days while his men worked climbing the mountains behind Mpapwa.[116] Then he told Thani he could wait no longer. At night in his tent he was being plagued by white ants and earwigs, a special source of terror to African travellers, ever since Speke had an eardrum pierced when one of them burrowed into his auditory canal. Faced with thousands of earwigs as companions at night, Stanley felt that henceforth locusts, fleas and lice would hold no terrors for him. Speke's fate was uppermost in his mind: 'My intense, nervous watchfulness alone, I believe, saved me from a like calamity.'[117]

So Stanley dashed off ahead of the Arabs, exhorting them to catch up with him at the camp at Chunyu. But his haste was costly. Within four hours twelve donkeys died from drinking the brackish water at the camp — water so notoriously bad that the Arabs never allowed their baggage animals near it. The men too suffered nausea, bellyache and 'an unconscionable irritability' from imbibing the noxious fluid: 'The water had the flavour of warm horse urine and mud.'[118]

Stanley's departure from Mpapwa effectively sealed Farquahar's fate. Stanley went through the motions of believing that the Scotsman's chances of recovery were good. When the headman at the village where Farquahar was 'convalescing' requested that an interpreter be present, Stanley sent him Jako, the Hindu whose desertion at Lake Gombo had precipitated the confrontation between Stanley and his two white lieuten-ants. He also handed over enough cloth and beads to pay for Farquahar's keep, plus a special issue of cloth to be made over by Jako as a present to the headman if Farquahar recovered. But Stanley must have known that without medicine Farquahar could not hope to survive, and he later revealed his true sentiments by describing his doomed comrade as an incubus: 'Farquahar had become the laughing stock of the caravan from his utter helplessness to do anything at all for himself.'[119]

Too ill to realise fully what was happening to him, Farquahar lingered just five days after the big convoy left Chunyu before succumbing.[120] Farquahar was the first of many victims of Stanley's hard-driving, callous brutality. Although Stanley had never divulged to him the true object of the expedition, Farquahar had actually performed manfully in blazing the trail past Simbawenni, through the Makata swamp and up into the mountains before falling to the infection-aggravated diseases of the tsetse. Naturally, it was beyond Stanley ever to admit that any of his lieutenants had done well.[121]

The question arises, why did Stanley think it necessary to take on Shaw and Farquahar in the first place? Doubtless he was misled by the example of other African explorers (Livingstone excepted) who never travelled into the interior without white companions. But he should have reflected that these were always *handpicked* comrades. Rather than picking up men from the bars of Zanzibar or the forecastles of 'hell ships', Stanley would have done better to employ an experienced African guide. Yet Farquahar's death was more than a mistake. It was a harbinger of things to come. The death rate among whites who accompanied Stanley to Africa would always be terrific. Farquahar in the vanguard blazed a trail for those coming after him in more senses than one.

D ESPITE the many travails encountered so far, Stanley's descriptions of Usagara were sufficiently enticing to stimulate German would-be empire builders to look favourably on this part of East Africa, with its relatively docile Sagara people.[1] Nobody ever made the same claim for Ugogo, the land through which the expedition conducted its next nine marches. The Wagogo were 'the Irish of Africa, clannish and full of fight'.[2] All caravans passing through their territory had the simple choice: pay or fight. The Wagogo controlled the scarce water supplies that alone made travel across their barren plains feasible; strategically situated between the Masai and the Hehe, they were for a time a major force in East African politics.[3] Most caravans were content to be mulcted rather than face ferocious armed opposition; it therefore cost Stanley $170 to get through to Unyanyembe.

Stanley was in no position to argue with the Wagogo. Desertions and deaths among his *pagazis* and the loss of seventeen donkeys had reduced him to an auxiliary position in a mighty caravan led by Sheikh Hamed. Stanley was in the rear of the convoy with Sheikh Thani, providing a powerful screen of riflemen for the travellers. From the Arabs he acquired a further tranche of expertise in African trekking. The route of a caravan, he learned, was not a single track but a number of different divergent roads, and the skill lay in choosing the right one for the prevailing season. During the rainy season a caravan leader would choose the route that avoided low-lying ground. In the dry season he would travel on the most direct route between one waterhole and another.

It was now high dry season, and the first part of the trek was a seventeen-hour slog across 30 miles of waterless terrain – what Stanley called 'the fiery plain'. The country abounded in game but was 'as safe from our rifles as if we had been on the Indian ocean'.[4] The rigours of this journey brought on another attack of fever. Here, as ever, Stanley was lucky. If the Arabs benefited from his riflemen, he gained from being under their tutelage. With an invalid Stanley in his care, Shaw alone would have turned back to Mpapwa; even worse, the cross-grained valetudinarian Stanley might well have lost his temper with the inquisitive, aggressive Wagogo, possibly with fatal results.[5] As it was, Sheikh Thani's men nursed Stanley through a delirium on the first afternoon. His fever dropped during the night and he was at the head of his column when it set out again at 3 a.m. on the second day.[6]

At 8 a.m. on 1 June they crossed an invisible dividing line between thorn-tree desert and fertile crop country and at once tasted the legendary arrogant aggression of the Wagogo. At the village of Mvumi there was almost a riot. The Gogo people had allegedly never seen a white man before and alternated between stupefied staring and embarrassed laughter.[7] Stanley had not yet fully adjusted to the culture shock of Africa that had been partly responsible for the demise of Farquahar; in addition he was only semi-recovered from fever. The staring of the Wagogo infuriated him, but his anger served only to attract larger crowds of onlookers. At last, in fury, Stanley picked out the most 'insolent' bystander and thrashed him with his donkey whip. This intemperate action could well have precipitated a general mêlée. Indignant Wagogo pressed closer to Stanley, taking care, however, to keep out of range of his flailing whip.[8] A very nasty situation was finally contained with the arrival of Thani, who calmed Stanley and pointed out the impracticability of trying to shoot it out with the well-organised locals. Stanley tried to dig in his heels, but a timely recrudescence of fever removed him from the arena.

Thani was not well pleased with his ally's truculence. After all, Stanley's expedition was *sui generis*, but they, the Arabs, had to live and deal with the Wagogo on an ongoing basis. When Stanley recovered again, Thani talked him round to paying the detested tribute. Stanley once more relapsed into fever and doctored himself with heavier and heavier doses of quinine; his one turn of good fortune came when one of his soldiers shot dead a large hyena that had been disturbing his sleep and terrifying Shaw and Selim with its ululations.[9]

On 4 June Stanley felt well enough to travel on, but the 'humiliation' inflicted on him by the Wagogo continued to fester. The sado-masochistic equilibrium in his reactions can be seen in the mixture of an (impossible) desire to wreak vengeance on his oppressors by wholesale bloodshed and a countervailing impulse towards redemption through suffering: 'Ugogo is to the white traveller what Vanity Fair was to

Christian and his friends. It is an ordeal to prove of what stuff he is made of. He will be tempted a score of times each day to draw a bead with his rifle on some of the yelping, taunting savages who prance alongside him.'[10] To salve his violent feelings, Stanley got his own back on Thani for his 'weakness'. He marched to the next village of Kiddimo and promptly paid the *hongo* demanded without demur, thus disturbing the fragile barter economy built up so painstakingly by the Arabs and making things more difficult for future travellers.[11]

That was not the end of the Arabs' problems with Stanley. He continued to adopt a confrontational posture with the troublesome Wagogo. At Nyambua he took his lash to them again; at Mukondoku he adopted the tactic of laughing at *them*.[12] Once again, it took a council of tribal elders and Arab sheikhs to pour oil on troubled waters. Another problem arose from the intermittent shivering fever Stanley suffered from all the way to Unyanyembe, which meant that he recorded the journey only intermittently while he dosed himself with quinine, waking from restless tossing to espy the endless herds of elephant, rhino, zebra, antelope and giraffe before succumbing again.[13] Not only did this increase Stanley's short-tempered propensity to solve irritants by force; sometimes, as at Mizinza, it led to the entire convoy's coming to a halt, since Stanley was too ill to continue.[14]

There could scarcely have been a greater clash of temperaments than that between Stanley and the caravan leader, Sheikh Hamed. Stanley was naturally pugnacious and disposed to cut corners, brooking no delays (except when he himself was ill). Hamed was a small, dapper, finicky, nervous man, whose anxiety to avoid trouble seemed only to attract it the more, as at Nyambua when a careless slip led him to pay extra tribute, while Stanley who had physically assaulted the Wagogo got away scot-free. Moreover, Hamed was a Shylock in business and the wearying negotiations with the Wagogo over *hongo* reduced his nerves to tatters.[15]

Stanley's insistence on resting a day at Mizinza pushed Hamed close to breaking point. The reason was that at the previous village his two prize donkeys, valued at $100, had wandered off and been impounded by the local chief. The chief then claimed ransom money of $25 to compensate him for the grass the donkeys had eaten! After protracted negotiations a *hongo* of 36 yards of cloth, on top of the normal tribute of 60 yards, was agreed on. To make up the loss thus sustained, Hamed decided to crack on at a blistering pace, hoping to save on food for men and beasts. But after just one day of Stanley-like progress, Stanley fell ill and demanded a day's halt at Mizinza. Beside himself with frustration, Hamed announced that he was going on alone. Stanley appeared to acquiesce, knowing that Hamed was too timid to advance without the white man's firepower.[16]

Chafing over the enforced delay, Hamed next tried sleight of hand. At Mukonduku, on the western border of the Gogo country, there was a choice of three routes to Unyanyembe. There was a long, rough northern route that skirted settlements and meant reduced *hongo*. There was a short and dangerous track; there was also a middle itinerary known only to Stanley's men. At first Hamed opted for the northern route to save money, but his porters mutinied and he was obliged to promise them he would go by the short route.[17] Stanley, however, was adamant that he would follow only the middle trail. Hamed appeared to accept this and set off along the middle track, intending to branch off on to the short trail desired by his porters. Stanley, who was checking the direction of the column with a compass, spotted the manoeuvre and gave orders that any of his porters following Hamed would be shot. Thani followed Stanley on to his chosen route. After an hour they saw the chastened Hamed plodding along in their rear. Without Stanley he had feared to try conclusions with the Kiwyeh warriors along the 'short' trail.[18]

They started up the escarpment, its sides scored with erosion and covered with thorn trees and bushes. It was a difficult climb: 'The ascent of the ridge was rugged and steep, thorns of the prickliest nature punished us severely, the *acacia horrida* was here more horrid than usual, the gums stretched out their branches and entangled the loads, the mimosa with its umbrella-like top served to shade us from the sun but impeded a rapid advance.'[19] At the summit a road ran straight through the jungle to Munieka. While trekking along it, the humiliated Hamed expunged his wounded feelings by picking a fight with Thani.

As the caravan pressed on beyond Munieka, the plentiful water supply put the column in unusually good spirits. The prospect of a nocturnal halt in the wilds, with no village at hand and in the cold night air of the plateau at 4,000 feet above sea level, did not damp their spirits. They were pleased to be well clear of the Wagogo and had as company only the jungle ruins of a Stonehenge-like set of standing stones. But Hamed had been plotting his own revenge on Stanley. Waiting until all were asleep, at about 1 a.m. he suddenly ordered his herald to sound the *kudu* horn. The entire encampment rose up and rushed to arms, thinking they were under attack. A march commenced in the darkness, which Stanley did not try to interrupt as he was unsure of the true situation. As soon as he ascertained it, he ordered his men to throw themselves down in the first village to resume their interrupted sleep (it was now 3 a.m.).[20]

In the morning they learned that Hamed had moved on to the next village, some 7 miles farther on. Stanley quickly caught him up, to learn that the Arab's fabled ill luck had struck once again. Not only had his favourite girl in the harem died of smallpox but his three body-servants had absconded, taking all his best clothes. In his attempts to find the runaways, Hamed lost further time and ended by falling behind Stanley and Thani.[21]

But now the smallpox epidemic was tearing such swathes through Thani's followers that the Arab had to excuse himself from further hard marching. Stanley paused for a day to revictual, then plunged off into unknown country, but not before he had used the whip on his men, who hated the idea of parting from Thani. During the day's rest, he had been overtaken by Hamed who pressed on without taking on fresh supplies. This was a bad mistake, as ahead of the convoys stretched the Tura forest, uninhabited since the Tabora Arabs had burned down all the local settlements after a revolt. Where the forest merged with the first plains of Unyamwezi Stanley caught up with the Hamed caravan. After beating off an attack by thieves on the encampment, the two parties travelled on together to Tabora.[22]

The ravages of smallpox on his party put Stanley into a rare state of despondency during the march through Tura, and the monotony of the terrain did not improve his temper. His cook tendered his resignation, but asked to accompany them to safety in Tabora. Stanley replied that the man must either work all the way to Tabora or disappear into the forest then and there. When the cook replied that he could go no further because of the incubus of two donkey saddles he had to carry, Stanley took the whip to him for his 'impertinence'.[23] Another man asked permission to retire into the forest to die quietly of smallpox but Stanley insisted that he carry his load until he dropped.[24] This was the wrong moment for the chief porter to suggest that the men be given a bonus for all their forced marching. Stanley rounded on Bombay violently and said that the men would be rewarded in Tabora but not before. To underline the point he laid around him with the donkey lash.[25]

The trail through Tura was criss-crossed by elephant and rhino tracks and they even met the occasional band of local elephant hunters. Such was the received opinion that elephants could be the only business of men in the Tura that when Stanley encountered Hassan, son of the Arab governor of Unyanyembe, it was difficult to persuade him that Livingstone, not a giant tusker, was Stanley's quarry. But Hassan, who had met Livingstone, was able to provide an interesting description (of mixed accuracy) of the great man: 'He is a very old man with a beard nearly quite white, has the left shoulder out of joint by a wild beast' (clearly a reference to Livingstone's famous encounter with the lion in Mabotse).[26]

As they came closer to Tabora, the number of Arabs they met on the trail began to increase. One invited him to eat outside his tent, as his harem was lodged within. Another treated him to an excellent chicken curry and regaled him with a rum story about Lake Victoria: how it was a salt-water lake fed from the sea. [27] Soon Stanley was at Rubuga – a flourishing town in Burton's time, but now gutted and occupied by nomadic squatters. Kigwa too was desolate, with burnt-out houses and overgrown fields, like Rubuga a victim of abortive revolts against the Arabs at Tabora.[28] Only at Shiza, the last camp before Tabora, was life normal; the chief there killed a bullock and gave a feast in Stanley's honour and provided a 5-gallon jar of beer for his men.[29]

Having reached Tabora, Stanley had grounds for cautious self-congratulation. He had marched 525 miles in eighty-four days at 6¼ miles a day, as compared with 134 days for the same distance on the Burton/Speke expedition and 115 days on the later Speke/Grant exploration. But Stanley would undoubtedly have been stupefied if anyone had told him that his progress in the next three months would be precisely nil. Stanley did not realise that he had blundered straight into a war between the Tabora Arabs and the most powerful Nyamwezi chief Mirambo and that the theatre of war barred the way to Ujiji.[30]

In his first three days in Tabora, the Arabs did not see fit to tell him. They wanted his succour in the war but feared to reveal their hand too openly. So to begin with they treated him like a prince. He was assigned a *tembe* in nearby Kwihara: a large, strong mud house, one-storeyed, with a flat roof and a single door, with walls 3 feet thick. Inside the hallway to Stanley's rooms was guarded day and night by men with loaded guns; the detail was under the direction of the giant Mabruki, the veteran of the Speke/Burton and Speke/Grant expeditions.[31] In his early days in the *tembe* Stanley feared natural enemies more than human, for Tabora was a notorious centre for Tanzania's 114 varieties of snake, including the dreaded black mamba.[32]

The Arabs now prepared to gull Stanley into military support. The governor began by laying on a sumptuous banquet, in which course was piled on course over a period of hours: 'Just when I began to feel hungry again, came several slaves in succession, bearing trays full of good things from the Arabs; first an enormous dish of rice, with a bowlful of curried chicken, another with a dozen huge wheaten cakes, another with a plateful of smoking hot crullers, another with pawpaws, another with pomegranates and lemons . . . After these came men driving five fat hump-backed oxen, eight sheep, and ten goats, and another man came with a dozen chickens, and a dozen fresh eggs. This was real, practical, noble courtesy, magnificent hospitality, which quite took my gratitude by storm.'[33]

The Arabs followed this up by laying on lavish spreads for his men, to encourage them to follow their master into any and every venture. While they caroused, Stanley found himself with time on his hands. Strolling around Tabora, he was 'casually' invited in to a council by the Arabs, who had of course planned every step. Here at last they came to the point that was exercising them. Would Stanley participate in an attack on Mirambo? They were confident that they could defeat the Nyamwezi chief within fifteen days, and this was a consummation to be wished by Stanley, since Mirambo's forces at present barred the way to Ujiji. Stanley listened to the arguments adduced by Said bin Majid and his son Soud.[34] They seemed plausible enough. Lacking a detailed knowledge of the complex politics of Tanzania, Stanley was not to know that he was being inveigled into a particularly desperate endeavour. Nor did the Arabs realise that they were pitting themselves against one of the great African warriors, a man who in fourteen years would conquer all lands from Tabora to Lake Victoria to the north, Lake Tanganyika to the south, and Lake Rukwa to the south.[35]

It was left that Stanley would rendezvous with the Arab forces once he had engaged new men and then proceed with them to the battlefront, leaving the *tembe* and its stores under heavy guard. But almost immediately after the conference with the Arab leaders, Stanley was struck down with a virulent fever that came close to killing him. It was five days before he was able to move out of his bed, and he then immediately sustained such a violent relapse that he once more hovered on the threshold of death; in his hallucinated state he passed in review the main events of his life.[36]

It was 29 July before Stanley was fully recovered. In the meantime open warfare had broken out between Mirambo and the Arabs. Sheikh Said bin Salim had already taken the main Arab army out of Tabora. Stanley ordered Shaw to distribute powder, balls and thirty rounds to each of their soldiers, then headed north to Zimbiro, where he made contact with his allies.[37] Three days of stubborn irregular warfare and skirmishing brought the combined Arab/*Herald* army to the outskirts of Mirambo's stronghold at Wilyankuru. There Stanley conferred with Said bin Salim and Soud and suggested firing the long grass around the village to prevent an ambuscade.[38] Salim brushed aside Stanley's suggestion and confidently sent his son Soud and 500 men into Wilyankuru for the *coup de grâce*. Mirambo appeared to flee in terror, departing at one gate as Soud entered by the other. Soud's men looted and sacked the stronghold and staggered out on to the Wilyankuru/Zimbiro road at the other end of the town, laden with ivory. Suddenly Mirambo's 400 men arose from their ambush in the long grass and slaughtered them to a man.[39]

When this news reached Stanley and Said in Zimbiro (a handful of slaves still in the town escaped the slaughter), the panic was almost absolute. The only Arab leader to retain presence of mind was Khamis bin Abdulla al Barwani.[40] Stanley, who had felt his fever returning on the second day of the campaign, was in his sickbed when the chaos and confusion in Zimbiro engulfed him. His men were swept up in the general panic. Both Shaw and Bombay lost their heads, and Stanley would have been abandoned if he had not forced one of his soldiers at gunpoint to fold his tent and accompany him. He came on Shaw in the act of saddling a donkey with Stanley's own saddle, quite prepared to leave his employer to Mirambo's mercies. Selim sprang at Shaw, wrenched the saddle away from him and ordered Bombay to prepare Stanley's donkey. For a moment Bombay stood transfixed with fear, then snapped to and obeyed the order.[41]

Stanley assembled a small party, then set out, ill as he was, for a twenty-four hour forced march. With him were Shaw, Selim, Bombay, Mabruki, Chanda, Sarmean and Uledi.[42] They got to Mfuto, half-way to Unyanyembe, at midnight, before Stanley considered it safe to slacken their pace.[43] Mirambo was in no hurry to follow. It was ten days before his forces appeared at Tabora. In the meantime his 1,500 Watuta or Negroni under Mtambalika with 1,000 guns, assisted by the *ruga-ruga* or professional mercenaries of Unyamwezi, spread havoc and destruction on the road to the Arab capital and picked up an arsenal of discarded ammunition and abandoned tents left behind by the fleeing Arabs.[44]

Meanwhile most of the Arabs in Tabora opted for abandoning the settlement completely. Even though it contained some opulent houses, like that of Amrani bin Masudi, the town was really a glorified collection of *tembes*, each surrounded by a fence.[45] Stanley had no choice but to stay and fight it out if he was ever to get to Ujiji. He fortified his *tembe* at Kwihara, distributed his 150 defenders around embrasures in the walls and laid in five days' supply of water. He estimated that he had enough ammunition and food to withstand a month's siege, so ran up the American flag and waited.[46]

When Mirambo's hordes arrived at Tabora, they carried away vast quantities of cattle, ivory and slaves and put the town to the torch. Fully one quarter of it caught fire and was gutted. There was little resistance. One of the few to display personal courage was Khamis bin Abdallah, who sallied out with his son, five Arab followers and eighty slaves to do battle with the *ruga-rugas*. But the slaves immediately deserted and the seven Arabs were cut down in a hail of bullets.[47] Mirambo's men skinned them, cut off their genitals, then boiled skin and genitals up into a gruel which they used as a kind of gravy with their dish of goat and rice.[48] Panic-stricken refugees began to stream out of Tabora to refuge at Stanley's *tembe* at Kwihara. At their ditches and embrasures the defenders stood ready; Stanley was determined on a kind of last-ditch Rorke's Drift *avant la lettre*. Professing quiet confidence, he wrote on the evening of 23 August: 'We have passed a very anxious day all in the valley of Kwihara. Our eyes were constantly directed over the saddle which connected the two hills separating Kwihara from the plain of Tabora.'[49]

But the attack did not come. On the morning of 24 August Mirambo and his followers departed as suddenly as they had arrived. Mirambo was thought to have withdrawn because he feared a counterattack on the return to Urambo. Besides, with another victory under their belts, his men were so laden with booty that they would have been as vulnerable to an Arab backlash as Soud's men had been outside Wilyankuru. Also, Mirambo realised that his men did not have the equipment for a long siege of Stanley's heavily fortified *tembe*; the longer the siege and the shorter their provisions grew, the more they would be exposed to the likelihood of a successful Arab sortie.[50]

As soon as Mirambo had withdrawn, Stanley went up to Tabora and tried to rally the Arab survivors. He found them confused and broken in spirit, fearful that Mirambo would return to attack them once he had secured his booty. On 26 and 27 August he attended Councils of War with the Arabs, at which their lack of ability or desire to open the Ujiji road was evident; indeed many of them talked of withdrawing permanently to Zanzibar.[51] Stanley railed at their indecisiveness and lack of resolution:

Alas! all my fine spun ideas of proceeding by boat over Victoria Nyanza, thence down the Nile, have been totally demolished and scattered by this war with the black Napoleon. Already I have been here over two months and there is every prospect that I shall be two months longer because the Arabs take such a long time to make up their minds, to arrive at a decisive conclusion.[52]

Once again Stanley had miscalculated badly. Not only had he backed the wrong horse in assisting the Arabs in their war for the control of the Ujiji caravan route, but he had placed all future European travellers in potential danger from Mirambo, who now regarded them as the Sultan's allies.[53] His decision was widely thought to have ended all hope of finding Livingstone; Mirambo now stood like an angel with a fiery sword between the doctor and his would-be rescuers.[54] The other consideration was that the news of the Mirambo war, and Stanley's participation in it, alerted all intelligent observers to the fact that Stanley's mission was to find Livingstone, not to explore the Lufiji River as he had claimed.[55]

Stanley returned to his *tembe* and began the task of hiring extra porters. Whatever his critics said, he was determined to press on to Ujiji, even if it meant going it alone without the Arabs. One consolation he derived from his frustrating last month in Tabora was the company of Kalulu, a seven-year-old Lunda slave given him as a present by one of the Arabs. Stanley made him his personal servant and chief butler. Kalulu was one of the most important in the long line of young male companions Stanley felt the need to have at his side; very soon he supplanted Selim in his master's affections, and there is much evidence thereafter of a running rivalry between the two boys.[56] Stanley was delighted with the newcomer: 'He understands my ways and mode of life exactly. Some weeks ago he ousted Selim from the post of chief butler by sheer diligence and smartness. Selim, the Arab boy, cannot wait at table. Kalulu – young antelope – is frisky. I have but to express a wish and it is gratified. He is a perfect Mercury, though a marvellously black one.'[57]

But if Kalulu was a source of comfort for Stanley, the boredom of his daily life at Tabora fuelled the impotent rage within. Once more he turned on Shaw as the butt for his frustrated impulses. After Mpapwa Shaw had a respite from Stanley's worst excesses: Stanley was ill most of the time on the road to Tabora and his gamesmanship with Thani and Hamed absorbed the remainder of his destructive energies. Shaw was much more successful in dealing with the aggravation of the Wagogo and Stanley even allowed himself to appreciate Shaw's attempts at humour when dealing with the staring of the Gogo people: 'Shaw said "These must be the genuine Agogians" for they stare – stare! My God there is no end to their staring.'[58] For a time Stanley even tried to establish friendly relations with Shaw and rubbed out many of his diary animadversions on his companion.[59] In response to this new geniality Shaw unfolded a series of tall tales: he had been at four levees of the Queen of England, was the son of a naval captain, had been studying Malay since the age of seven, had been in the Metropolitan Horse Guards and had lost £5,000 when buying himself out, was a devoted admirer of monarchy and aristocracy.[60]

But after the incident at Zimbiro when Shaw tried to escape and leave Stanley to his fate, the earlier hostility returned. Stanley's journals are full of complaints about Shaw's laziness and malingering.[61] Stanley responded by a show of open contempt for Shaw's intellectual powers. 'Shaw is a sentimental driveller with a large share of the principles of Joseph Surface within his nature. He is able at times to kindle into an eloquent rash about the vices of mankind, particularly those of rich people ... he is very angry, though, with me, because I laugh at him, and has just opened a sentimental battery on me which makes me almost cry out with vexation that I encumbered myself with such a fool.'[62]

Soon Shaw's very presence and his physical mannerisms were grating on Stanley and kindled within him sadistic fantasies of beating and flagellation. 'Piff-puff at his nasty pipe. Hear him breathe! You would think he was dying; but he is not even sick. He told me only the other day, that he knew every trick of old sea-salts, when they wished to shirk duty at sea. I am sure he is practising a trick on me. This intermittent fever! I know every stage of it; and I feel convinced he has not got it. Of one thing, I feel sure, that if I took a stick, I could take the nonsense out of him.'[63] And again, on Shaw's 'hypochondria': 'I know it proceeds from nothing else than a sick ennui. If I had recourse to the stick, I could cure him in less than ten minutes of all this annoying by-play.'[64]

On Shaw's side, the more he learned of Stanley, the more he became convinced that he had signed up with a dangerous maniac. This conviction was reinforced when Stanley, in an attempt to establish a true rapport, divulged the true objective of the expedition. So far from reassuring him, this news terrified Shaw and precipitated him into a near mental collapse at the thought of the dangers and hardships to come.[65] Disappointed at Shaw's reactions to the 'good news', Stanley decided to turn the knife in the wound. When news of Farquahar's death came in, Stanley taunted Shaw with weakness. 'There is one of us gone, Shaw, my boy! Who will be the next?'[66] Shaw was out of his depth with this sort of thing and his clumsy attempt at retaliation in kind merely increased Stanley's hatred for him. On the last night at Kwihara, when Stanley was delirious with fever, Shaw made the mistake of creeping into his room and enquiring archly who was Stanley's next of kin since 'even the strongest of us may die'.[67]

The troughs and crests in Stanley's moods while he waited at Kwihara, his alternating exhilaration as he hired *wangwana* for the onward journey at triple the normal rate and depression as he observed the Arabs' inertia, the joy caused by Kalulu on one hand and the anger induced by Shaw on the other, fed into his *Herald* despatches, so that even his geographical descriptions seemed to exhibit a kind of manic-depression. His analysis of Nyamwezi and the Usukuma country to the north of Tabora oscillated between a euphoric celebration of its potential for Europeans and a gloomy deterministic pessimism.

On the one hand, Stanley portrayed Nyamwezi as a paradise, far superior to the jungle plains of Ugogo, the forests of Unyanzi and the plains of Tura and Rubuga. From a vantage point it looked like a succession of blue waves in an ocean of forest; hills of syenite dotted the prospect, like islands in a sea or crenellated fortresses. Around the rocky hills were fields of maize, *holcus sorghum*, millet, vetch, sweet potato, manioc; herds of sheep, goats and hump-backed cattle. Especially in the south, there was an amazing profusion of game: elephants, buffalo, zebra, eland, hartebeeste, zebra, springbok, blackbuck, wild boar, lions, leopards and hippos. But on the other, he asserted that the climate and vast extent of the terrain (it extended over three degrees of latitude) made it deadly for Europeans: 'Supposing it were necessary to send an expedition such as that which boldly entered Abyssinia to Unyamwezi, the results would be worse than the retreat of Napoleon from Moscow.'[68] Yet he was later to state that it was Usukuma which first opened his eyes to the potential of Africa for Europeans![69]

The other aspect of Stanley's ambivalence touched a peculiarly raw nerve. Mirambo had defeated him, so it was necessary subtly to downgrade the fighting qualities of the Nyamwezi warriors. Suddenly we find that his tormentors the Wagogo are the superior fighters: from a despicable rabble they become 'a bumptious full-chested, square-shouldered people'[70] by comparison with whom the Nyamwezi are negligible. 'The Arabs never dream of arming the Wanyamwezi as escorts, as they are utterly unreliable. A Mgogo boy with a spear in his hand would be sufficient to make a legion of Wanyamwezi tremble.'[71]

The truth is that Stanley in his limbo at Tabora and Kwihara was in a state of depression where he was not able to get a clear fix on the reality of his situation and thus jumbled up solid objective observations with illusory subjective perceptions; he admitted that the border-line between illusion and reality was becoming so hazy that he began to think that Livingstone was simply a figment of his imagination.[72] The way out of such a seeming impasse for Stanley was always through the brutal exercise of willpower. He forced himself to transcend the seemingly insurmountable.

By 1 September Stanley had enough porters to travel on without the Arabs. But he noticed that whenever he mentioned his intended departure for Lake Tanganyika, the Arabs always declared adamantly that to go on alone through a war zone was suicidal.[73] Stanley came to see what their real game was when he overheard Sheikh Thani saying farewell to another traveller making for Ujiji. It was quite clear that the Arabs wanted Stanley's firepower to aid their war against Mirambo.[74] The conviction hardened when he heard that Sheikh bin Nasib was extremely angry with local guides who had given him information concerning the Ukononzo road.[75] When Stanley pressed hard for a letter of introduction to the Arab governor of Ujiji, the upshot convinced him that the Arabs might be prepared to go to any lengths to keep him at Tabora. He found himself vomiting and nauseous after a meal the Arabs had given him, and became convinced they had poisoned him, not with the intention of killing him but of keeping him as an invalid at Kwihara. This was the wrong tactic to try on a man like Stanley. He responded by telling the sheikhs that he had no intention of waiting another six months and was about to set out, whether they approved or not.[76]

Sheikh bin Nasib retaliated by spreading a rumour that an attack by Mirambo was imminent and that he would be using the levies of the Bende from the shores of Lake Tanganyika.[77] But Stanley learned from independent sources that Mirambo had in fact been driven off with losses from the town of Mfuto.[78] He was just about to implement his final preparations for departure when his men were stricken with a fresh attack of smallpox. Baruti died at once; the languishing spirits of the others were further cast down by rumours spread by the Arabs of the dreadful state of the roads ahead and the infestation of the country by *ruga-rugas*.[79] The smallpox epidemic threatened to achieve what the Arabs could not: destroy all hope of an onward march to Ujiji. One by one the expedition members succumbed to its onslaught. From 4 September on Selim and Shaw were ill almost continually until the final departure. This time even Stanley was forced to admit that Shaw's illness was real and he dosed him with two grains of morphine.[80]

This fresh blow to the expedition brought Stanley close to breaking point and saw his unconscious sadism at its very worst. Stanley's young male companions were ever the focus for the repressed homosexual side of his personality, and it was just at the time of the smallpox attack that Selim was being replaced as his personal favourite by Kalulu. This is the explanation for a truly revolting demonstration of brutality on 11 September. In a lucid interval on that day, before relapsing into delirium, Selim mixed himself a dish of milk and sugar to sustain himself through the crisis. Now Stanley's standing instructions laid down that he and he alone had access to the sugar. When Stanley learned what Selim had done, he ordered a flogging, smallpox or no, not only for the theft but because Selim lied about it.[81] The humbug about lying from a professional liar is revolting enough. But to beat someone brutally who was already gravely ill with smallpox passes belief if we postulate a man of normal sensitivity and integrated responses. Anyone who doubts the pathological nature of much of Stanley's drive, and the aetiology of that pathology, will need to provide a 'normal' explanation of the dreadful events of 11 September 1871.

By 15 September the worst of the epidemic was over. Stanley announced that he would leave for Ujiji on 20 September and to this end began to distribute the loads for his *pagazis*. He took on another thirty *wangwana* to replace those lost in the war with Mirambo and through smallpox and reduced the impedimenta of the expedition to a bare minimum.[82] Following the announcement, his men spent the night in a funeral celebration, dancing and singing the names of their dead companions and consuming vast quantities of liquor.[83] On 17 September Stanley followed the usual custom before a great journey and gave a feast for his thirty-three soldiers: a roast sheep, fifteen chickens, 45 pounds of beef, 80 pounds of rice, eight large loaves of bread, corn, eggs, butter, sweet milk and a 20-gallon jar of the local brew.[84]

On the eve of his departure Stanley himself went down with fever. His men were delighted. Overcome with trepidation at the dangers ahead, they now consoled themselves that the march to Ujiji would be abandoned. To their horror Stanley insisted on departing anyway. On 20 September the expedition trooped morosely out of Tabora, on a south-westerly track that Stanley reckoned would take them away from the theatre of war. The dispirited *pagazis* consoled themselves with the thought that their master, now delirious from smallpox, would have to return within a couple of days anyway.[85] When the 'man of iron' began to defy their expectations, they started to desert. Stanley thundered that he would use a slave-chain on all deserters. To show that he meant business, he had his soldiers round up a couple of the runaways and placed them in fetters.

If the porters and soldiers were terrified at this leap into the unknown, unsupported by the Arab caravan, Shaw now plunged into terminal mental collapse. The morning of 20 September saw enacted another pitiful scene which Stanley reproduces as follows.

'Now, Mr Shaw, I am waiting, sir. Mount your donkey, if you cannot walk.'

'Please, Mr Stanley, I am afraid I cannot go.'

'Why?'

'I don't know. I am sure I feel very weak.'

'So am I weak. It was but last night, as you know, that the fever left me. Don't back out, man, before these Arabs; remember you are a white man. Selim, Mabruki, Bombay, please help Mr Shaw on his donkey and walk by him.'[86]

After proceeding about 500 yards, Shaw fell off his donkey and pleaded to be allowed to return to Kwihara. Stanley refused. For the next two days he kept Shaw on the go, propped up on his donkey by the soldiers. On the third and fourth day Shaw proved unable either to dismount or to stay on the beast. Stanley was enraged: 'this little by-play of Mr Shaw's was getting too frequent.' When the porters rushed to help him, Stanley ordered them to leave Shaw be. Shaw lay for an hour on the ground in the full sun. Eventually Stanley approached him and asked him if he did not feel rather uncomfortable. At this Shaw sat up and wept like a child. Stanley takes up the story.

'Do you wish to go back, Mr Shaw?'

'If you please. I do not believe I can go any farther . . .'

'Well, Mr Shaw, I have come to the conclusion that it is best you should return. My patience is worn out . . . You are simply suffering from hypochondria. You imagine yourself sick, and nothing, evidently, will persuade you that you are not. Mark my words – to return to Unyanyembe is to die!'

'Ah dear me; I wish I had never ventured to come! I thought life in Africa was different from this. I would rather go back, if you will permit me.'[87]

Why did Stanley acquiesce now, when he had been so adamant throughout that the unwilling Shaw be dragged ever farther into the heart of the Dark Continent? Stanley himself in his diary presented his decision as bowing to the inevitability of Fate, after six months of absolute uselessness on Shaw's part.[88] But more likely, Stanley now felt confident that to reach Ujiji he did not need Shaw and would thus be the sole white man to greet Livingstone. Failure with Shaw no longer implied ultimate failure on the expedition. It is also possible that, for all his bluster, he realised that Shaw was now seriously ill and he wanted him to die away from the expedition, where he would not be an inconvenience. But he made the grand gesture of giving Shaw the keys to the storecupboards at the Kwihara *tembe* and sent him back on a litter, so that he could not later be blamed for his death.[89] Whatever the case, within days of returning to Kwihara Shaw died.[90]

Yet Shaw was not Stanley's only problem. Any slight relapse into fever was the signal for his men to desert in droves. Stanley sent back to Tabora to purchase from Sheikh Nabib the longest slave-chain he possessed. Then he offered Bombay and Chowpereh a new cloth for every deserter recaptured.[91] Fourteen out of twenty were retaken and flogged, then chained around their necks. Stanley swore up and down that whatever the 'bleeding hearts' of Exeter Hall might say, he would always thereafter use the whip and the slave-chain while travelling in Africa.[92] As an added disincentive to desert, he pressed on into the unknown by forced marches. But, as ever with Stanley, he could not resist a final self-justifying flourish to vindicate his treatment of the deserters: 'these men were as much bounty jumpers as our refractory roughs during the war, who pocketed their thousands and then coolly deserted.'[93] When one recalls that it was Stanley himself who in 1865 was encouraging Noe to be a bounty-jumper, this sentence is truly breathtaking for its hypocrisy and, once again, suggests a mind unable genuinely to distinguish truth and falsehood.

The last days of September were disheartening ones for Stanley as he penetrated the forest separating Unyanyembe from Ugunda. Wave after wave of lengthy rectilinear ridges stretched ahead of him: 'Woods, woods, woods, forests, leafy branches, green and sere, yellow and dark red and purple, then an indefinable ocean, bluer than the bluest sky. The horizon all around shows the same scene – a sky dropping into the depths of the endless forest, with but two or three tall giants of the forest, higher than their neighbours, which are conspicuous in their outlines, to break the monotony of the scene.'[94]

After a seven-hour trek through the forest they came to the capital of the new district of Ugunda, ruled by the Nyamwezi chief Muli-Manombe.[95] Ugunda was a strongly-palisaded, turreted and impregnable fortress, but it could provide no fresh porters.[96] Then they made long marches through the territory of Manyara, a region infested by tsetse flies. The chief initially held himself aloof but was induced to trade by the carrot of *doti* and the stick of a demonstration of Winchester power. They proceeded on a long forest march under a hot sun to the Gombe area, the most famous hunting grounds between Bagamoyo and Lake

Tanganyika.[97] The prospect put Stanley in good spirits. Commenting on the giant *myukus* (sycamores) in the forest, he wrote:

> When daylight was dying, and the sun was sinking down rapidly over the western horizon, vividly painting the sky with the colours of gold and silver, saffron and opal, when its rays and gorgeous tints reflected upon the tops of the everlasting forest . . . infusing . . . the exquisite enjoyment of such a life as we were now leading in the depths of a great expanse of forest, the only and sole human occupants of it – this was the time . . . when we all could produce our pipes and could best enjoy the labours which we had performed . . . I am contented and happy, stretched on my carpet under the dome of living foliage, smoking my short meerschaum.[98]

The sensuous euphoria induced by the forest again led Stanley to query the existence of Livingstone, then to accept it and wonder whether he was alive or dead. But the remarks he penned about Livingstone seem to have a deeper resonance, relating to his own psychic drama: 'Why is man so feeble and weak, that he must tramp, tramp hundreds of miles to satisfy the doubts his impatient and uncurbed mind feels?'[99]

Once arrived at Gombe creek, Stanley set about replenishing the expedition's meat supply. The Gombe area teemed with game of all kinds: buffalo, giraffe, zebra, waterbuck, pallah, stembock, wild boar, warthog, springbok, gemsbok, blackbuck, eland, as well as lions and hippo. The first day Stanley brought back two buffalo, a kudu and a wild boar for his men to feast on. On the second day he added four guinea fowl and five quail to his 'bag' of a zebra, two boars and three buffalo.[100] Stanley's only complaint was that the Winchester cartridges supplied by a New York ammunition company were far inferior to the English cartridges provided by Eley of London. Whereas all the cartridges in the English double-barrelled smooth-bore fired, only a fifth of those in the Winchester 15-shooter were effective.[101]

On the third day at Gombe Stanley's men requested a further halt to allow them time to dry the meat for the journey ahead. Stanley consented, on condition the lost time was made up later. After a lunch of antelope steak, hot corn-crake and Mocha coffee, he set out for the chase again with his two gun-bearers Kalulu and Majwara. They passed flocks of honey-birds, *perpusillas*, fish-eagles and bustards, but for Stanley they were small beer. Soon he came on a herd of grazing zebra. Although Stanley claimed that he hunted game out of necessity and not for sport and that he felt sorry for the animals he was obliged to kill, it is hard not to detect a cruel, gloating quality about his thoughts at this moment, at odds with the overt sentiments:

> It was my option to shoot any of them. Mine they were without money and without price, yet, knowing this, twice I dropped my rifle, loth to wound the royal beasts, but, crack! and a royal one was on his back, battling the air with his legs. Ah, it was such a pity! but hasten, draw the keen, sharp-edged knife across the beautiful stripes which fold around the throat and – what an ugly gash! – it is done, and I have a superb animal at my feet. Hurrah! I shall taste of *ukonongo* zebra tonight.[102]

As so often when reading Stanley, the word 'humbug' hovers tantalisingly in the air. Stanley never truly felt sorry for the animals he shot. By pretending pity he makes obeisance to Victorian pieties, but when he is off guard, he reveals his true feelings. Often he wounded an animal, and the sole disappointment recorded is that the beast escaped.

It was perhaps an unconscious intuition that he had given himself away in that passage that makes Stanley go on to develop the theme of nature 'red in tooth and claw', with himself as much a potential victim as the zebra. He claimed that after shooting the zebra he was just about to take a dip in the cool waters of the Gombe and had waded ankle-deep into the water preparatory to diving when suddenly a huge crocodile shot to the surface yards away from him.[103] However, Stanley's diary makes no mention of this incident – surely inconceivable if he had really had such a close brush with death. It seems to be a subsequent extrapolation from the later, genuine crocodile incident on the Malagarazi.[104]

The three days by the Gombe were like an idyll in Lotus-land, but they were rather too enjoyable for Stanley's purposes. When he sounded the *kudu* next morning for a day's march, he found he had a mutiny on his hands. The ringleaders were Mabruki and the giant (6 feet 4 inches) Asmani, his brother.[105] Stanley ordered Asmani at riflepoint to lead his men out on the march. Asmani hesitated and seemed about to cock his own gun at Stanley in an act that would surely have brought his death from the trigger-happy explorer. For a moment the two men faced each other in a Wild West shoot-out posture. Suddenly Mabruki rushed in and knocked his brother's weapon to the ground. Mabruki then pleaded with Stanley to forgive Asmani. Typically, Stanley felt no appreciation for Mabruki's statesmanlike action but merely felt irritated that the guide's diplomacy had removed the pretext for flogging both of them.[106] Baulked of his main prey, and in no way self-critical that it was his own fanatical hard-driving relentlessness that had provoked the mutiny, Stanley looked around for a scapegoat. He decided to whip Bombay on the specious grounds that he was really the secret organiser of the mutiny.

> I at once proceeded about it with such vigour that Bombay's back will for as long a time bear the traces of the punishment which I administered to him as his front teeth do to that which Speke rightfully bestowed on him some eleven years ago. And here I may as well interpolate by way of parenthesis that I am not at all obliged to Captain Burton for a recommendation of a man who so ill deserved it as Bombay.[107]

Again, this is vintage Stanley. First, the self-righteous brutality; then the introduction of another explorer to mitigate his own excesses; then the gratuitous slipping of the knife between the shoulder blades of a third explorer.

After this Stanley got his thoroughly cowed expedition on to the road to Marefu. They marched for five days through the monotonous forest of Ukonongo, through ruined villages, devastated by the *ruga-ruga*. There was plenty of wild fruit along the way and they encountered the largest herds of buffalo yet seen.[108] Stanley admired the way his men could make a fire by rubbing a hard stick in the palm of their hands, but he was even more impressed by the honey-bird (*indicator indicator*), which guided humans to the nests of wild bees so that they could eat the honeycomb and the grubs when the nest was chopped out.[109]

At Marefu they learned that they had edged closer than intended to the war zone and that the road ahead was blocked. Stanley's party fell in with an Arab embassy on its way to the Watuta to try to secure their services in the conflict with Mirambo, but the road to the Watuta lay through the war-torn territory of Chief Nyungu Ya Mawe.[110] The only other road was the scene of a civil war among the Wavira.[111] The head of the Arab embassy, an old man named Hassan, lacked the qualities for his mission. When Stanley suggested joining forces and striking north-west, instead of following the intended track south-west, the elderly Arab was horrified at the thought of a march across uncharted country.[112]

Nothing daunted, Stanley plunged on: 'made a most determined march to avoid sleeping in a jungle infested by the Ruga.'[113] As they crossed the mountainous ridge of Mwaru, the vegetation grew more varied: new types of fruit appeared, including the *mbura* (*parinari curatellaefolium*), the tamarind, the *mtonga* (*nux vomica*), like an orange, the wild plum (*syzigium jambolanum*).[114] This plentiful fruit restored their health. The only serious invalid in the party now was Selim, whom Stanley was treating with Dover's Powders after he had drunk brackish water.[115] However, what Stanley did not reveal in any of his published accounts was that Selim had only imbibed the tainted water after Stanley castigated him for over-drinking his water ration.[116]

But still the trekking itself was gruelling. They survived a forest fire that roared on to them, even though Stanley feared his men would drop their loads and bolt.[117] They passed through many charred and deserted villages, victims of the war between the Wakongo and Wavira. In one of them nine bleached skulls, stuck on top of a pole, told their own lurid story.[118] Despite the war, the area teemed with game: buffalo, rhino, giraffe, ibises, fish-eagles, pelicans, storks, spoonbills, flamingos, ptarmigans, guinea fowl. Stanley shot a nimba antelope for meat, and later caught sight of his first herd of wild elephants – the species that for Stanley truly deserved the title 'king of beasts'.[119]

Ascending a ridge on to a plateau they came out of the forest and into the village of Mrera. Here Stanley called a halt for three days. This was one of his more humane decisions, for Selim by now hovered near death and his men were exhausted.[120] At Mrera, where every tribesman seemed to possess a musket, they learned that they were still heading into the war zone so Stanley once again shifted tack to the north-west. Selim was recovering well – fortunately, since they now faced another long forest march.[121] They camped at nights in ravines near quagmires of mud then continued zigzagging north-westward through the hill country at the base of the Kasera mountains. Sometimes Stanley sank up to his neck in the Stygian ooze of the mud churned up by elephants, rhino and buffalo: 'I had to tramp through the oozy beds of the Rungwa sources with my clothes wet and black with mud and slime. Decency forbade that I should strip and wade through the sedgy marsh naked, and the hot sun would also blister my body.'[122] His sole consolation was a sighting of the rare sable antelope.[123]

At last they emerged on to easier terrain, blessed with plentiful game. On 21 October they camped by the Mpokwa River, whose banks were clothed in sycamores, giant tamarinds and *mvules*.[124] Next day they crossed to the Mtambu River and soon learned from a bitter lesson the truth of the local lore that the dense undergrowth and tall grass around the two rivers housed troops of lions and solitary leopards. At night lions would come prowling and roaring around the perimeter of their encampment, only to retreat at dawn. The leopards were more daring. A herd-keeper was driving a herd of donkeys and goats to water through a kind of tunnel in the brake made by the passage of elephant and rhino. The animals had scarcely entered the conduit to the water's edge when a leopard leaped on to the back of one of the donkeys and fastened its fangs in its neck. Fortunately, it was at once driven off by the massed cacophony of a dozen braying beasts.[125]

The next week was one of the worst on the entire journey. That Stanley's luck was turning, and not for the better, seemed evinced by the failure of his next hunting trip. After disturbing a troop of monkeys, he began to stalk a wild boar, leaving Kalulu behind one tree and his solar helmet behind another. Firing from 40 yards, he pumped several shots into the boar. The stricken beast charged past Stanley then dropped. As Stanley advanced to skin it, the boar seemed suddenly to catch a second wind at sight of Kalulu and the helmet. It rushed off into a thick brake where, since it was now getting dark, Stanley did not dare follow it.[126]

Next morning they made an early start to try to pierce the ring of mountains that barred their way to the Malagarazi River. They progressed through 'increasingly sublime' scenery, including the peak of Makoma that reminded Stanley of Magdala.[127] At night the lions continued to roar. Stanley attempted to fire his Winchester into the darkness at them but gave up when the American cartridges failed him once again.[128] On 26 October he had to suppress another near-mutiny after he rejected the men's plea to spend a day shooting game. To 'encourage the others' he had Selim flogged on the flimsy pretext that he stole a *mbemba* fruit contrary to orders which brought on a second attack of dysentery (again Stanley had no qualms about beating a man while he was already sick).[129]

At the village of Itaga they found no meat but only some grain and vegetables. Once again it was demonstrated that Stanley was wrong and his men right: they should have laid in a supply of game while they had the chance. The supposed two-day journey to the Malagarazi was stretching into a week; meanwhile every shot Stanley took at wild life, be it leopard or buffalo, seemed to miss.[130] On the morning of 28 October an entire herd of buffalo blundered into their camp but realised their error and careered off before they could be shot.[131] By now Stanley's lack of foresight had placed them on starvation rations. Everyone was desperately hungry and keeping going only on the peaches or *mbemba* they had collected in the forest. They were also journeying in the full heat of the sun, out of the shade of the dense woods.[132] Since Stanley still had plentiful supplies of tea and sugar he tried to sustain morale by brewing up and distributing cups of hot sweet tea.[133] On 29 October they camped at night in a valley among rocky plateaux and precipitous ravines. Next morning, as the famished men descended further into the valley, they came on lots of rhino tracks and buffalo droppings and soon after, to their intense joy, reached a village where food could be purchased in exchange for excessive *doti*.[134]

Their ordeal by starvation was now over, for away to the Malagarazi stretched a succession of crop-filled fields. After just one day of rest and recovery, Stanley struck out for the river. But once again Stanley's refusal to take advice and his headstrong determination not to be put off by the locals led them into trouble. Before they got to the Malagarazi they had to negotiate an extensive and treacherous marsh:

> Fancy a river broad as the Hudson at Albany, though not near so deep or swift, covered over by water plants and grasses, which had become so interwoven and netted together as to form a bridge covering its entire length and breadth, under which the river flowed calm and deep below. It was over this natural bridge we were expected to cross. Adding to the terror which one naturally felt at having to cross this frail bridge was the tradition that only a few yards up an Arab and his donkey, thirty-five slaves and sixteen tusks of ivory had suddenly sunk forever out of sight.[135]

As the men got on to this 'bridge' it sank one foot into the water and covered their feet. A donkey came within an ace of crashing through the grassy 'ice' and it required ten men to extricate him. During this struggle the 'bridge' sank another two feet and Stanley fully expected to see all ten men and the donkey disappear into the depths. Finally on the other side, they commenced a series of steep descents to the banks of the Malagarazi itself.[136]

But at the river Stanley found that he had the 'insolence' of the local chief Nzogera and his son Kiala to deal with. Kiala extracted tolls from travellers for ferry rights over the Malagarazi. To square him, Stanley had to part with six *doti* of cloth and a quantity of the precious *sami-sami* beads, the most desirable form of East African currency.[137] This settled both the *hongo* and the hire of canoes for crossing the river.

The second day of November was spent ferrying the men and stores across the 30-yard ferrying point. This was not as easy as it sounded for, as Stanley pointed out: 'I would prefer attempting to cross the Mississippi by swimming rather than the Malagarazi. Such another river for crocodiles, cruel as death, I cannot conceive. Their long tapering heads dotted the river everywhere, and though I amused myself, pelting them with two-inch balls, I made no effect on their numbers.'[138]

At first all went well, except that after two canoe-loads had been landed at the other side Kiala appeared with a request for a further two *doti*. Stanley granted this grudgingly but warned the chief that any further extortion would lead to bloodshed. Eventually all the men except Stanley and Bombay were on the far side of the river. It now remained to get their two remaining donkeys across. Around sunset Stanley's favourite animal, Simba, was driven into the water with a rope attached to his neck. He reached the middle of the river where the water was no more than 15 feet deep when a crocodile seized him by the throat. Chowpereh and the others pulled frantically on the rope and the donkey's struggles were terrific. One crocodile could not have availed against the combined pulling of the *wangwana*, but as Stanley recorded laconically in his diary: 'there must have arrived other crocodiles for the poor animal suddenly sank like lead.'[139]

Stunned at the audacity of the saurians, for Stanley was certain that the very noise of the activity would keep the reptiles at bay, he abandoned work for the night, saddened at the loss of his favourite donkey. Next morning the one remaining donkey swam across without being attacked; Stanley's men attributed this to the charm they placed around the donkey's neck, but he himself, more detachedly, pointed out that in the early morning crocodiles liked to sunbathe on the shore.[140]

At the first village on the other side of the Malagarazi Stanley received the exciting news that a white man had recently arrived at Ujiji from Maniema.[141] Convinced that this was Livingstone, Stanley prepared to make a forced march to Ujiji at once. But there was a snag. The direct route from the village of Isinga ran through the scene of a bitter civil war between two Uvinza pretenders. Stanley decided to risk the two day-march through the Ha territory, although he had been warned by the Arabs that this was the one tribe he should avoid.[142]

The Ha were one of the most powerful and warlike confederations of East Africa. Divided into six chiefdoms, they levied *hongo* well above the going rate on any traveller foolish or intrepid enough to cross their territory.[143] It was into the Ha chiefdom of Luguru that Stanley now plunged, and once again his fanatical determination to press on through unknown terrain, whatever the local lore said of its dangers, brought his expedition inches away from disaster. In two days among the Ha, Stanley was mulcted of half his expedition's goods; if matters had continued thus, there would have been no point in his meeting Livingstone at Ujiji for he would have been denuded of all his effects.[144]

The problem started when Stanley's column was intercepted on the road by the Ha chief Mionvu, who invited the expedition to rest at his kraal. Stanley, suspecting treachery, refused. In an atmosphere of high tension negotiations for the tribute commenced while the column lay drawn up at the ready on the road. Stanley's inclination was to shoot it out but his men argued that this would be suicide; they were just forty-five men against thousands of Ha warriors.[145] Despite hard bargaining from 6 to 10 p.m., Stanley was obliged to agree to the extortionate *hongo* of eighty-three *doti*, in return for a promise that no more tribute would be exacted during the passage through the Ha chiefdoms. Stanley fumed at the humiliation. As he put it in his despatch to Bennett: 'The next time you wish me to enter Africa I only hope you will think it worthwhile to send me a hundred good men from the *Herald* office to punish this audacious Mionvu, who fears neither the *New York Herald* nor the Star Spangled Banner.'[146]

But there was worse to come. Next day, despite Mionvu's assurances, Stanley was again stopped on the road, this time by Mionvu's brother, who insisted on tribute of twenty-six *doti*. When Stanley objected, citing Mionvu's promise, his brother replied witheringly that Mionvu had no right or authority to bind his fellow chiefs in that way. Stanley agreed to the tribute and decided to rest that night in the Ha village while he pondered his next step. Since there were four more chiefs along the line of march, it did not require great arithmetical talent to work out that by the time he had emerged from Ha territory, he would be destitute.[147]

Desperate cases called for desperate remedies. In the village Stanley consulted with his guide about possible ways out of the Ha territory that would avoid population centres. The guide found a friendly slave – formerly the property of his old associate Sheikh Thani – who agreed to show them a way to Ujiji that avoided all human contact. His price for the information was twelve *doti* and he insisted that his stratagem could work only if Stanley had complete control of his party.[148] Brushing aside the possibility that the slave might betray them, Stanley concerted his measures. At dead of night, at 2.30 a.m. on the morning of 7 November, Stanley and his expedition members made their several ways past the huts where the Ha slept and to the village gates. In bright moonlight they struck south, then turned west, parallel to the main road but about 4 miles inland from it.[149]

At dawn they hit the Rusugi River. They were all hungry and the banks of the Rusugi teemed tantalisingly with buffalo, eland and hippo which they dared not shoot. While crossing the Rusugi, one of the women in the party became hysterical and began to scream at the top of her voice. To prevent her alerting the Ha and causing panic among his men, Stanley struck at her with his whip but had to lash her nine times before her voice subsided. His men solved the problem by gagging her with a cloth and tying her hands. Even so, there was some evidence that they had been spotted and that the Ha would even then be raising the alarm.[150]

Crossing the Rusugi, they struck north-west through a jungle of bamboo, leaving no trail. At 1 p.m. they reached Lake Musunya.[151] After ten hours of non-stop marching, Stanley ordered a cooking halt, then they plunged into the bamboo again and spent the night shivering silently without fires perilously close to a Ha settlement. At dawn the next day their guide made a mistake and nearly took them into a Ha village. An alarm was raised, but Stanley dissuaded pursuit by slaughtering all the goats and chickens the expedition had with them and leaving them on the road for the Ha to gorge on.[152]

A long march that day and a further one at night finally took them out of Ha territory, across the Mkuti River and into Ukaranga and the Bende people. They had marched at the rate of about 4 miles an hour (an incredible achievement in Africa), in desperate hunger, forced to trek past amazingly tame herds of eland, buffalo, elephant and rhino without firing on them, lest the shots betray their presence.[153]

At Ukaranga his coming at first caused panic, since the townspeople thought the expedition was Mirambo and his men. But they soon recovered and received their unexpected guests cordially.[154] Next morning Stanley ordered the American flag unfurled; he himself donned his best clothes: 'My helmet was well chalked and new puggeree folded around it, my boots were well oiled and my white flannels put on, and altogether, without joking, I might have paraded the streets of Bombay without attracting any very great attention.'[155]

The expedition set out in good spirits for the final leg of the journey to Ujiji. After two hours, from the summit of a hill, they caught their first glimpse of the breathtaking Lake Tanganyika. From the western base of the hill to Ujiji was a three-hour march but 'no march ever passed so quickly'. They crossed the Luiche River with its tall *matete* or elephant grass. At last they stood on the summit of the final hill in the overlapping folds that ran down to the lapping lake water. Ujiji was directly below them.[156]

They began to enter the town. Where the suburbs started, Stanley ordered his men to commence firing. The guide blew his clangorous horn. The Stars and Stripes fluttered in the breeze. Bende tribesmen and Arabs came rushing up. Suddenly a black man was at Stanley's shoulder, speaking in English.

'How do you do, sir?'

'Hello, who the deuce are you?'

'I am the servant of Dr Livingstone,' the man replied, then rushed off like a madman.[157]

As the throng of Arabs got bigger, Stanley threaded his way from the rear of the column to the front. All at once he was confronted by a knot of Arabs, at the centre of which stood a pale-looking, grey-bearded white man, dressed in a red woollen jacket, wearing a navy cap with a faded gold band around it. The two men raised their hats.

'Dr Livingstone, I presume?'

'Yes.'

'Doctor, I thank God I have been permitted to shake hands with you.'

'I feel thankful that I am here to welcome you.'[158]

8

T HE meeting between Stanley and Livingstone at Ujiji, just after midday on an autumn Friday in 1871, is one of the most celebrated incidents in all modern history.[1] Unfortunately for Stanley, his absurdly stiff 'Dr Livingstone, I presume' caught the popular imagination in the wrong sort of way and became a music-hall joke. We are entitled to ask then, whatever possessed him to produce such a potentially risible greeting at such a moment?

Stanley never denied that he had spoken the famous four words, and usually explained disingenuously that he could not think what else to say.[2] In fact the formula was the result of a good deal of agonising and soul-searching. The man who could brave the terrors of Africa, its fevers, crocodiles, snakes and savage tribesmen, was mortally afraid of rejection. Kirk's words came back to haunt him: that Livingstone would bitterly resent another white man coming to see him. As he later explained it:

> The newspapers described him as worthy of the Christian world's best regard; privately men whispered strange things of him. One that he had married an African princess and was comfortably domiciled in Africa; another that he was something of a misanthrope, and would take care to maintain a discreet distance from any European who might be tempted to visit him. Not knowing whom to believe, I proceeded to him with indifference, ready to take umbrage.[3]

This account is borne out by Stanley's private diaries. He confessed that he originally intended to stay in Ujiji no more than a day, just long enough to get a letter from Livingstone, acknowledging receipt of the stores and confirmation that the *Herald* reporter had 'found' him. He had no intention of risking being slighted or humiliated.[4] After all, apart from Livingstone's reported misanthropic proclivities, he was an 'Englishman'

(Stanley's phrase) and in Abyssinia and after Stanley had had enough of the peculiar foibles of the upper-class Englishman to last him a lifetime.[5] In addition to his fears concerning Livingstone's individual reaction and those of Englishmen in general, Stanley had a third reason for his apparently austere pomposity: the conviction that any display of overt emotion in the presence of Arabs would lessen the prestige of the white man. The myth of the 'superman', increasingly required by the exigencies of imperialism, seemed, on Stanley's fallacious reading, to require the stiffest of stiff upper lips.[6] It is perhaps significant that Stanley misread the situation in all three areas of motivation. Livingstone did not react as he had expected: Englishmen found Stanley's formality ludicrous; the Arabs formed a lesser, not a higher, opinion of European civilisation from the incident.[7]

There is no reason to dissent from the general judgement that 'I presume' resulted from Stanley's basic lack of spontaneity in 'unnatural' situations where he could not be himself.[8] Indeed he admits as much in a diary entry for 10 November: 'What would I not have given for a bit of friendly wilderness wherein I might vent my joy in some mad freaks, such as idiotically biting my hand, twisting a somersault, slashing at trees . . . these exciting feelings before appearing in the presence of Livingstone.'[9] Yet it is also true that the latent content of Stanley's words, as opposed to their manifest content, speaks volumes of his unconscious turmoil.[10]

Ironically, there was no need for Stanley's coiled-up hesitancy and self-doubt. He and Livingstone very soon discovered a natural rapport. After a few moments' general conversation Livingstone led him to his house. The two white men sat with their backs to the wall, while the Arabs took their seats on the left. After a short while, the Arabs, with what Stanley considered commendable delicacy, left them alone.[11]

At once Stanley remembered the famous (or infamous) letter bag, originally dispatched by Kirk in November 1870 – the same which was languishing at Bagamoyo in February 1871, and which Stanley had later overtaken at Tabora and now brought on. At Stanley's invitation to open and read his long-delayed correspondence Livingstone demurred: Africa had taught him patience, he said; he had waited so long that it would not harm him to wait another day. In the meantime he would prefer to hear all the public news from Stanley. So Stanley started in. First there was the Franco-Prussian war, the election of General Grant as US President, the laying of the transatlantic cable and the completion of the Union Pacific railroad; then came the events where Stanley had a more intimate connection: the Cretan insurrection, the opening of the Suez Canal, the flight of Queen Isabella, the Spanish revolution, the recent assassination of General Prim and the election of Amàdeus of Savoy as constitutional monarch in Spain.[12]

Suddenly Stanley remembered the bottle of champagne he had brought all the way from Bagamoyo for this exact occasion. He sent for the bottle, uncorked it and toasted Livingstone. The afternoon that followed Stanley remembered as one of the most pleasant of his life. Livingstone was genial and exuberant. He told anecdotes and jokes about his friends, particularly those who had accompanied him on his African travels, like William Cotton Oswell, William Webb, Gordon Cumming and Frank Vardon. He amazed Stanley by being able to quote huge chunks of Burns, Byron, Tennyson and Longfellow and disconcerted Stanley, who prided himself on his knowledge of literature, by being better informed on Whittier, Lowell and many other writers than the *Herald* correspondent himself, whose job it was to be *au courant* with matters American. So spirited and jovial was Livingstone that afternoon that Stanley suspected him of slight hysteria. 'You have brought me new life,' Livingstone repeated several times to him.[13]

Stanley was not to know that Livingstone was speaking the literal truth. While away in Nyangwe the doctor had left all his trade goods and medical supplies in Ujiji with an Arab named Sherif, thinking they were in good hands. Sherif, a notorious drunkard and speculator, helped himself to Livingstone's cloths and beads to set himself up as a rich wastrel and sybarite in Ujiji, imagining that his 'benefactor' would not survive the rigours to the west of Lake Tanganyika. When Livingstone staggered into Ujiji half-dead in the middle of October, just two weeks or so before Stanley arrived, he found himself destitute. Sherif had wasted his entire substance on riotous living. Fortunately for Livingstone he had laid by an exiguous emergency supply of local currency with an honest Arab trader, but this represented just one month's subsistence. When Stanley arrived, half of the emergency supply was gone and imminent starvation stared the doctor in the face.[14]

This helps to explain the gusto with which Livingstone tucked into the repast Stanley laid before him. Anxiety and shortage of money had combined to produce loss of appetite in the past terrible two weeks in Ujiji, but as Kalulu and Selim combined with Livingstone's cook to produce curried chicken, rice, stewed goat, meat cakes, yoghurt, honey and fruit, the doctor's reputation as a 'trencherman' seemed fully justified. Livingstone ate and drank his way through the afternoon's conversation. The two men talked animatedly until dusk.[15]

Then Livingstone showed Stanley to his quarters in the *tembe*. The hut was a low, rectangular, thatched building with mud walls; it was about 45 feet long and 7 feet wide. There were two large rooms in front, which enjoyed an eastward prospect across Ujiji market-place and to the mountains down which Stanley had just travelled. Stanley had the right-hand room, Livingstone the left; there was a passage between them. To the rear of the *tembe* was Lake Tanganyika and on the front verandah (extended from the eaves and propped up by poles) was a combined office, study and reception room.[16] Near the equator as Ujiji was, it enjoyed twelve hours of daylight from 6 a.m. when both men arose. Stanley enjoyed the unwonted luxury of a few moments' reflection in bed, scarcely able to believe that his quest was at an end and that Livingstone was found. His worry now was that the high spirits and joviality of the first day might simply be a flash in the pan and that Livingstone would revert to the curmudgeon his legend credited him with being.[17] This was a particularly pertinent consideration, since he would have to 'come clean' this morning about his mission. Amazingly, in the euphoria of the first day Livingstone had not only not read his letters but had not bothered to ask Stanley what his business in Ujiji was.

For the first few minutes that morning Stanley's worst forebodings seemed about to be borne out. Over coffee Livingstone told him his news from the letters he had read after retiring last night.[18] Stanley then remarked that Livingstone was probably wondering what he was doing in Ujiji. Livingstone replied that he had thought him an emissary from the French government until he had seen the Stars and Stripes but 'I did not want to ask you yesterday as it was none of my business.'

Stanley then confessed that his 975-mile, 236-day journey from Bagamoyo into the heart of Africa had been made explicitly for the purpose of contacting Livingstone. Livingstone claimed not to understand.

'Well,' said Stanley, 'you have heard of the *New York Herald*?'

'Who has not heard of that despicable newspaper!' Livingstone answered tartly.[19]

Stanley laughed. 'You will not call it despicable after you have heard what I have to say.' He then proceeded to present his mission as one actuated by pure philanthropy, pointedly not referring to 'scoops' or other newspaper practices. He outlined the resources he was prepared to make over to Livingstone to allow his work to continue and stressed that he had no desire to poach on Livingstone's preserves as a famous explorer; all he required was a formal letter of thanks for Gordon Bennett.

At this Livingstone recovered his animation of the day before. They spent a delightful morning swapping anecdotes. Livingstone confided that Stanley's coming had restored his appetite and zest for life.[20] He told him how close to the edge of starvation he had come after Sherif's treachery. Stanley in turn recounted the zigzag progress of his quest for the lost explorer, how Bennett's order to go to Asia first was a signal example of God's providence, since otherwise they would not have been at Ujiji at the same time.[21] Another joyous day closed with prayer; Stanley was having to revive the practices of his pious Welsh youth, for Livingstone insisted on grace before and after each of the three heavy meals he consumed that day.

The close relationship so quickly established never faltered thereafter during the four months the two men were together. Both Stanley and Livingstone were notoriously difficult and prickly individuals. On paper a successful outcome to their meeting would have seemed unlikely. For one thing, Livingstone's opinion of Americans was not high: 'Aye, they have a great population, viz. 21 millions of the greatest bores that the moon ever saw,' he wrote in 1852.[22] For another, Stanley was a journalist and Livingstone had taken a roasting from the press after the death of Bishop Mackenzie on the Zambezi expedition. Stanley was prepared to storm off at the first sign of any affront from Livingstone. Yet the relationship prospered mightily. What, then, were the special factors contributing to this?

In the first place, neither was what the other assumed him to be: Stanley was no more an American than Livingstone was an Englishman. Both men were Celts, both born in poverty, both with a distaste for the upper-class Englishman. If Stanley had vivid memories of monocled aristocratic buffoons in Abyssinia, Livingstone for his part was still smarting under the humiliation of the terms on which the Foreign Office had granted him his consulship which he regarded as 'the most exuberant impertinence that ever issued from the Foreign Office'.[23] The sense of inferiority that pervaded the men who had come a very long way socially, respectively from the Blantyre textile mill and St Asaph's workhouse, led them to make uncritical and unbalanced assessments of oligarchic patrons who took them under their wing; Livingstone's almost childish enjoyment of his lionising by London high society in 1864 was to find a later counterpart in Stanley's rather slavish bedazzlement by royalty in the person of Leopold of Belgium.

The two men also shared many points of similarity in temperament. Both were primarily journalists of genius. Livingstone's status as missionary and explorer was shaky. As a missionary he had made a single (later lapsed) convert and as an explorer his only undisputed discovery was Lake Bangweulu. What he possessed in abundance was a literary talent that made his readers feel that they had actually been in Africa and perceived the same things Livingstone had. In this way he made the Dark Continent the sensation of Victorian England and laid the foundation for his own legend.

On the other hand, both had the toughness and curiosity of the true explorer. Both were deeply religious – even though Stanley's God was primarily the Yahweh of the Old Testament while Livingstone followed Jesus and the law of love. They were brave, stubborn, prodigious in energy and intolerant of other men's weakness. Neither liked criticism or ridicule. Each was deeply sceptical of organised missionary activity; Livingstone especially shared Stanley's distaste for Tozer, whom he despised for basing himself on Zanzibar: 'The Mission in fleeing from Morambala to an island in the Indian Ocean acted as though St Augustine would have done had he located himself on one of the Channel Islands when sent to Christianise the inhabitants of Central England.'[24]

On the debit side, the two men shared many of the same faults. Both had a pathological determination to be 'first' in their explorations and not to share the credit with associates; both habitually demeaned the achievements of other travellers in Africa. One of the causes for the many unexpected obstacles encountered by Stanley on his march from the coast was that he was determined to blaze a new trail to Ujiji and not simply follow in Speke's footsteps. Livingstone's experience on the Zambezi expedition rather uncannily pre-echoed Stanley's later career. They shared an inability to get on with other Europeans. Both were incapable of 'man management' and jealous that any other white man might try to steal their glory. A recent judgement on Livingstone vis-à-vis his European companions could also be predicated of Stanley: 'He was unconcerned for their interests and lacked insight into their problems. He viewed their illnesses as malingering, disagreement as insubordination, and failure as culpable negligence.'[25]

The desire to be the first to discover anything and the refusal to share glory with other Europeans led both men to downgrade the contributions of their companions and, if necessary, to use lies to discredit them. It was bad enough that Livingstone failed to acknowledge the financial and exploration contribution made by the saintly William Cotton Oswell or the discoveries and travels of the Hungarian Lazlo Magyar and the Portuguese Candido Cardoso.[26] But it was even worse that he should lie about the Makololo missions and then traduce Roger Price in order to escape censure for having grossly misrepresented the situation with Sekeletu in Barotseland.[27] At the limit Livingstone was even prepared to be as violent as Stanley. In 1859 he beat an insubordinate Makololo with a cook's ladle. Nine days later he thrashed a troublesome stoker, after telling Kirk he would 'break the heads' of any troublemakers.[28]

Not insignificant, too, as a factor in the Stanley/Livingstone rapport was the fact that both men were below average height, so that there was none of the hatred and dislike that unbalanced men of short stature often feel for tall males.[29] Both men, in fact, shared the compensatory drive often associated with physical smallness. Keltie of the Royal Geographical Society even claimed there was a physical resemblance between Stanley and Livingstone: 'In each the lower part of the face especially is almost identical, the same massive square jaw and firm mouth, indicative of unconquerable will, inexhaustible endurance, unflinching purpose.'[30] But the similarities should not be pushed too far. Recent research establishes Livingstone as a victim of cyclothymia or hereditary manic depression. It was the cyclical nature of this illness that led to his worst acts of persecution against his European assistants, especially Richard Thornton and Thomas Baines.[31] Stanley often felt depressed in the normal sense, but only when he was compelled to remain inactive for long periods. He never suffered from genuine depressive illness the way Livingstone did. Stanley's outbursts of violence, his paranoia and persecution of his colleagues derived more from the 'will to power' than innate depressive tendencies.

Yet the overwhelming element predisposing the two men to forge close bonds was psychological. For Stanley, Livingstone represented the wise and benevolent father he had never known. For Livingstone, Stanley in an eerie way represented the return of the prodigal son. As a parent, Livingstone had not been successful. His eldest son Robert ran away to the USA, fought and was killed in the American Civil War.[32] In the letterbag that Stanley brought on from Unyanyembe Livingstone received the first definite news of Robert's death from battle wounds. Yet the man who brought the news of the death of David's Absalom was himself a Civil War veteran. There were thus powerful impulses on both sides in the construction of a surrogate father/son relationship.

Such an interpretation of the relationship is no mere a priori speculation. Livingstone spent many hours discussing Robert with Stanley, almost as though he were bestowing on him the mantle of eldest son.[33] His remark to Uledi at Ujiji is highly significant: 'I am very happy, you have brought me my child.'[34] Stanley frequently referred to the paternal role

Livingstone played towards him. When he was feverish in December, Livingstone was attentiveness itself: 'In an instant his tone changed and had he been my own father, he could not have been kinder.'[35]

But perhaps the most extensive indication of Livingstone as surrogate father comes in Stanley's diary entry for 16 November, just six days after their meeting:

> His manner suits my nature better than that of any man I can remember of late years. Perhaps I should best describe it as benevolently paternal. It is almost tender, *though I don't know much about tenderness* [italics mine] but it steals an influence on me without any effort on his part. He does not soften his voice or draw back his lips in an affected smile or mince his words or courtesy to my wish or will – but is sincerely natural and courteous with me as if I were his own age or of equal experience. The consequence is that I have come to entertain an immense respect for myself and begin to think myself somebody, though I never suspected it before. If it were other than perfectly natural with him, my conceit tells me I should discover it. It was all right to be acknowledged as someone by my own paid followers but when a man old enough to be my brother manages to convey it to me in every action, I get as proud as can be, as though I had some great honour thrust on me.[36]

Soon Stanley learned to relax with Livingstone and lay aside his earlier fears of rejection. Their relationship gathered momentum. On the third day Livingstone took his new colleague to visit his Arab friends in Ujiji, then they walked along the lake shore, watching the long rollers breaking on the beach as if it were the ocean.[37] Stanley asked the doctor if he did not feel like returning home. Livingstone replied that although he wanted to see his children again, he could not give up his quest for the Nile sources now, when he was just six or seven months away from providing a definitive solution to the problem.[38] At first Stanley could not understand why the doctor had returned to Ujiji if that was his aim. Livingstone then carefully explained the circumstances of his men's mutiny in Manyema. This drew from Stanley a reflection on Livingstone's greatness: that if other men had explored as much as he had, they would be running to and from the coast to announce their discoveries, instead of doggedly persevering as the great Scotsman was doing.[39]

They returned to the hut and Livingstone explained his future plans on a large wall map – drawn on a much bigger scale than anything Stanley had. Since it was a Sunday, Livingstone spent much of the rest of the day on religious services. He expounded a chapter in the Bible to a select group including Susi, Chumah and Selim. In the evening both men retired to write. The following day was spent in a detailed narrative of the Manyema expedition.[40] Next morning Livingstone, in sanguine mood, proposed that Stanley accompany him back to Manyema to complete his work. This was a ticklish situation for Stanley. He did not quite know how to refuse without giving offence. Because he had presented the *Herald* expedition as a philanthropic concern, he could not reveal just how hard a taskmaster Bennett really was: 'from what I know of him, he would even begrudge the few days I must naturally stay here.'[41]

Stanley replied that he was not a free agent: his mission had been to take supplies to Livingstone; now he would have to return to the coast for further orders. Livingstone's face clouded over at this reply. Then he brightened and said: 'I see how it is. You would come if you thought it would be permitted. Well, there is nothing like sticking to duty and I will not be one to tempt you.'[42]

They plunged into a discussion on Africa. Stanley said that he did not think he was cut out to be an African explorer. He found the African native peoples troublesome and ungrateful and confessed himself disillusioned on a number of scores since leaving Zanzibar: then there was novelty and excitement and he still believed in the power of kindness; since then the necessity for hard driving, the toll Africa took on the nerves and the constant need to dose oneself with quinine had turned him sour on the Dark Continent.[43] Livingstone dealt with this gently. He said it was a great pity that few white men who came to Africa could look at it objectively and get beyond their own feelings; he expressed the hope that Stanley would come to look on the continent more kindly before he departed. Had he ever seen such natural beauty, such landscapes? Rather peevishly Stanley replied that he had seen many sights as impressive on his travels, and he was not even sure that parts of the scenery of the United States were not superior. There was an awkward silence until Stanley remarked conciliatingly that he could not dissociate Africa from fever: 'whether the cause is in me myself or the land, I fancy something of sadness in what I see.'

'I know what you mean,' said Livingstone. 'That is the bile. Nothing more than the effect of bile in your own system. As long as you look at Africa with eyes of yellow bile, you cannot help but feel that.'[44]

Overwhelmed by Livingstone's compassion and his own guilt about rejecting the invitation to Manyema, Stanley forced himself into a magnanimous gesture. Whereas he could not afford a year to travel to

Manyema, he did not see how Bennett could object to a month's diversion. He therefore proposed that he and Livingstone make a trip to northern Lake Tanganyika to see if there was a river that flowed out northwards towards Lake Albert and the Nile; the entire trip would be financed by the *New York Herald*.[45] To remove the least scintilla of a patronising role in their relationship, Stanley divided all his effects, clothes, medicines, trade-goods, food, into two heaps and then told Livingstone to choose whichever heap he wished and retain it as his own.[46] He also informed Livingstone that he regarded the older man as the leader of the joint expedition. Stanley would not have deferred like this to any other man in the world.

Their first step was to acquire a suitable canoe for the lake-borne journey. Sayid bin Majid, the Arab '*grand seigneur*' of Ujiji, supplied them with a large craft that would carry twenty-five men and 3,500 pounds of ivory. Stanley's arrival had brought about a remarkable transformation in Majid's attitude towards Livingstone. Where he had previously seen him as a penurious old eccentric, a suitable object for charity and compassion, Stanley's coming had alerted the Arab to Livingstone's real importance in the wider European world.[47]

On 16 November they set off, Livingstone in high hopes that he would find a route that would enable Nile shipping to penetrate as far as Ujiji. Apart from Stanley and Livingstone, the exploration party comprised sixteen rowers, Selim, Ferrajji the cook and two Wajiji guides. They had been warned that the trip could be dangerous and that the Warundi, previously victors over the Arabs in war, might not let them pass.[48] At first the canoe rolled horribly because of overloading. Stanley made his men unload, jettison much of the cargo and then repack to make the boat manoeuvrable.

Once on the lake, whose shores reminded Stanley of the Turkish Black Sea littoral, Livingstone continued to beguile Stanley about the virtues of the African continent, and how the removal of the blight of the slave trade would transform a potential Eden. Stanley listened politely without agreeing. As so often in their four months together he and Livingstone contrasted strongly: it was respectively pessimism versus optimism, original sin versus perfectibility, the rule of force against the law of love, the Lord God Jehovah against Jesus Christ. Stanley's view was: 'I always feel that the fever is not far off, but if it were not for that, I think his influence and example and sweet patience and grand hope that everything will come out all right at last would have an effect on me.'[49]

They sailed past Bangwe Island to Kigoma. The forested scenery was so spectacular that even the cynical Stanley was forced into exclamations of wonder; the natural beauty surpassed anything he had seen all the way from Bagamoyo to Ujiji. Livingstone was as enthusiastic as his young companion; six years' exposure to Africa had not jaded his appetite for the wonders of nature. Stanley continued enraptured: 'The lake was quite calm; its blue waters of a dark-green color, reflected the serene blue sky above. The hippopotami came up to breathe in alarmingly close proximity to our canoe, and then plunged their heads again, as if they were playing hide-and-seek with us.'[50]

At Niasanga, their first stopping-place, Stanley shot a dog-faced monkey, 4 feet 9 inches from nose to tail and weighing 100 pounds. Livingstone was out of action with diarrhoea, from which he was a chronic sufferer, so Stanley passed the time admiring the abundance of bird life: wagtails, crows, turtle-doves, fish-hawks, kingfishers, whydah birds, the *ibis nigra* and *ibis religiosa*, geese, paddy birds, kites and eagles.[51]

A four-hour pull on the oars brought them next to the River Zassi, where the mountains rose sheer from the lake to a height of over 2,000 feet. Stanley found Zassi the most beautiful spot yet; surrounded by a group of conical hills, it surpassed even his hitherto favourite, Lake George on the River Hudson. On the fourth day out they came to Nyabigma, a sandy island in Urundi which offered a 20-mile prospect between the two capes of Kazinga and Kasofu. On the mainland he could descry an alluvial plain into which five large rivers fed; all the rivers were hedged by a thick growth of *matete* or elephant grass which formed an impenetrable jungle.[52]

At Nyabigwa they prepared for a possible battle with the Warundi ahead and distributed ten rounds of ammunition to each man. Stanley shot another monkey and noted the same pipe-smoking phenomenon among the locals that he had observed at Zassi.[53] At Mukungu, on the fifth day out, they received the expected demand for *hongo*. Stanley was fascinated to see how an old campaigner like Livingstone dealt with tribute. Sure enough, he proved an experienced negotiator and insisted on a sheep being brought to them before he paid the *doti* of two and a half cloths. Unfortunately his circumspection was not matched by his followers. The *mateko* or sub-chief brought a 3-gallon pot of sweet liquor for the two headmen, Susi and Bombay. The two men were soon gloriously drunk, and in the morning found that the Warundi had stolen all Livingstone's sugar, a bag of flour, 500 rounds of cartridges, ninety musket bullets and the expedition's sounding-line.[54] Stanley was furious with Bombay: 'It was only the natural cowardice of ignorant thieves that prevented the savages from taking the boat and its entire contents together with Bombay and Susu as slaves.'[55]

On the sixth day they coasted close to the low headlands formed by the rivers feeding into the alluvial plain. The streams that ran down the sheer mountain side to the lake formed a dangerous surf, capable of capsizing the boat and pitching them all into the crocodile-infested waters. Stanley was amazed at the fearless insouciance of his oarsmen, but their aplomb turned to over-confidence when they assumed that the next village after the headland of Kisunwe was one of the few hospitable spots along the lake shore. When the expedition tried to land it was greeted with threats, then with showers of stones.[56]

At this point there arose the first clear difference in method between Livingstone and Stanley. Livingstone always believed in pacific settlement of disputes; Stanley's reflex action was to use force. Stanley begged the doctor to let him loose off a couple of shots at the stone-throwers. Livingstone's reply was stoical: 'What is the use? Let them be. We are safe. Let us bless God for that.' He placed his hand gently on Stanley's to calm him. Stanley acquiesced: 'I laid down the gun thinking what a pity it was that I should not send them home to meditate, and learn that some people had their wits about as well as they.'[57]

Faced with this hostility, the expedition camped briefly at Murembwe point, which was protected on the landward side by thick jungle. Ferrajji brewed up Mocha coffee while Livingstone explained the unwonted belligerency as due to Arab raids. Then they pressed on towards Cape Sentaheyi, but darkness came on so that they were compelled to put in to another sandy strand. The fires they lit attracted interlopers, and when four more scouting parties came up to reconnoitre, Livingstone agreed with Stanley that this boded no good. After supper they pushed off again, just in time, as a sizeable war party was gathering. They rounded Cape Sentaheyi and after six hours' pulling at the oars put in to the fishing village of Mugeyo where they were allowed to sleep unmolested. At dawn they continued and reached the village of the friendly Warundi of Magala, having rowed 40 miles in eighteen hours.[58]

Though well-disposed the Warundi of Magala reminded Stanley of the Wagogo in that they were 'profound starers'. In the afternoon the *mutare* came and for two *doti* provided a very good food supply. He warned them, however, that if they proceeded they would become snarled up in one of Mukamba's wars, so that unless they intended to join one side or the other they should go back. But the lure of the Rusizi River, the hoped-for effluent that would lead them on to Lake Albert and the Nile, was too strong. They decided to persevere.[59.]

On the eighth day of the joint expedition, a violent storm overtook them while they were half-way between Urundi and Usige. Their canoe yawed fearfully in the wave trough. In terror they put about and made for the village of Kisuka, where they heard further rumours of local wars, of raids and counter-raids. Even more depressingly, their local informants were adamant that the Rusizi flowed *into* Lake Tanganyika. To fill the cup to overflowing, Stanley went down with a fever that made him a mere passenger for three days. The canoe continued passed the broad delta of Mugere to Mukamba's village, where Livingstone put Stanley in a hut and nursed him back to health with 'tender and fatherly kindness'.[60]

Mukamba's people had never seen a white man before, but their chief was friendliness itself. The morning after their arrival, he appeared with presents of a sheep, a goat and an ox in return for nugatory *hongo*. He informed them that the Rusizi delta was just two days' journey away. On the second evening at Mukamba's, Livingstone's headman Susi again showed his liking for alcohol by getting hopelessly drunk and climbing into bed beside Livingstone. Thinking he was Stanley, Livingstone said nothing until the inebriate Susi pulled the blankets over himself, leaving Livingstone cold and uncovered. At this point the doctor discovered the identity of the culprit. In the ensuing hullabaloo Stanley was woken up. Left to himself, he would have set about Susi with a rod, but Livingstone simply gave him a perfunctory slap to wake him then rebuked him sternly: 'Get up Susi, will you? You are in my bed. How dare you, sir, get drunk in the way, after I have told you so often not to?'[61] The crestfallen Susi slunk off, leaving Stanley to marvel at the doctor's Christian forbearance.

Next day Mukamba came to say goodbye. He loaned them a second canoe to get to his brother Ruhinga's country. It was unfortunate that shortly after Stanley and Livingstone's visit Mukamba died, so that the white man was then perceived as 'bad medicine'.[62] Nine hours' rowing brought them to the head of the lake at Mugihema, the territory of Ruhinga. Cutting diagonally across the lake, the expedition gazed on the rich, flat country at the Rusizi delta, teeming with the finest herds Stanley had yet seen in Africa: goats, sheep and cattle in their thousands. The headwaters of the lake around the delta unfortunately abounded in less desirable creatures: crocodiles.[63] To their great disappointment they discovered that the Rusizi incontestably flowed *into* the lakes, so that there was no question of an effluent that would take them on to Lake Albert and the Nile.[64] Nevertheless, they contended themselves with the thought

160

that they were actually exploring a river that had eluded Burton and Speke.[65]

On the second morning at Ruhinga's Stanley took ten strong paddlers and set off for another look at the Rusizi delta, almost as if he hoped that a second reconnaissance would after all reveal it as an effluent river. But it was even more abundantly clear on this outing that the Rusizi flowed *into* not out of Lake Tanganyika. Stanley found that it was nothing like so large as the Malagarazi; it surpassed it only in its infestation with crocodiles. Stanley then proceeded to a bay in the west, to which the mountains descended sheer, before returning to Livingstone at Mugihema.[66]

Ruhinga, the chief, was not so dignified as his brother Mukamba but even more amiable and with a much better knowledge of the country. He provided the explorers with much valuable information about the country at the northern end of the lake; Stanley was able to determine from his intelligence that Lake Albert was nowhere nearby, so that Sir Samuel Baker's calculations must have been awry by some two degrees of latitude.[67] Ruhinga also regarded the coming of the two white men as a good omen. He had been languishing from sickness and recovered at about the time of their arrival. Sumptuous festivities heralded his recovery. The women celebrated the event by smearing their heads and faces with flour; Stanley shot a brace of geese, a duck, a crane and an *ibis religiosa* to provide delicacies for Ruhinga's table.[68] Ruhinga graciously reciprocated the gesture by sending the white men an ox, three sheep and some milk, from which Stanley's men churned butter – always a great treat in Stanley's eyes. Ruhinga further showed his appreciation by sending the explorers a keg of his home brew and they responded by inviting him to take Mocha coffee. The first rain since Stanley's arrival at Ujiji also fell while they were at Mugihema. Their prolonged, enjoyable stay was topped off when Mukamba came on a visit to his brother and there was a further feast.[69]

The only thing that marred their stay at Ruhinga's was illness. First Livingstone was laid up with bilious fever. No sooner was he recovered than Stanley went down with a severe attack; he remained at half-strength for five days and was unable to make a formal goodbye to Mukamba when he left on 5 December.[70] But Stanley always remembered the nights at Mugihema as the time when he and Livingstone became really close. Livingstone was a fountain of anecdotes. He spoke at length about the famous Burton and Speke feud, of the 1864 Bath confrontation and of Speke's death (which the doctor was certain was accidental, not suicide).[71] He told a hilarious story of how the freemasons had offered to make him a member in Glasgow on the grounds that membership would do him a lot of good in Africa! He spoke of how irritated he was by people who thought his refusal to lecture at a moment's notice derived from a desire for an enormous fee.[72] One night after Livingstone had been out taking longitudinal observations, he and Stanley fell into a lively argument over the respective merits of Disraeli and Gladstone, Livingstone supporting Disraeli and Stanley Gladstone. Despite the warmth of the dispute, when an attack of Stanley's fever brought the discussion to an abrupt end, Livingstone at once reverted to paternal solicitude.[73]

Stanley was so impressed by Livingstone and his instinctive rapport with and sympathy for Africans that he even felt ashamed of himself, and looked about for ways of proving that his own harsh methods were warranted. One night he found what he was looking for. Peeping through a crack in his hut, he saw Selim on his knees, with his head well back and his mouth under a dripping honey bag. The spectacle seemed an object lesson in mindless hedonism. Stanley was unable to resist the temptation to call Livingstone to witness the scene; the doctor turned away with a disgusted expression on his face.[74]

On 7 December they quit Mugihema and pushed on to the boundary of Uvira. Ruhinga had told them that Usige was a district of Urundi and that all local chiefs were vassals of King Mwezi Kissabo the Fourth.[75] But quasi-feudal bonds masked all kinds of differential local reactions. When camped within sight of the village of King Mruta, both Livingstone and Stanley agreed that they did not like the look of things. They decided not to stay in Kavima, but headed south in the teeth of a gale. They hid in a little quiet cove hidden by reeds, disembarked and built a thorn fence as protection during the night. At dawn after breakfasting on coffee, cheese and *dourra* cakes, they steered south from Kukumba point, intending to coast along the western coast of the lake for a while before crossing to Ujiji.[76]

They found the western shores of the lake steeper and loftier than the wooded heights of Urundi or Ujiji. The *mvule* tree was much in evidence. They made about two-thirds of the distance to Cape Kabogi before camping for the night at a group of islets, one of which Stanley named New York Herald Island.[77] On 9 December they came to the territory of the Wasansi at Cape Kabogi, on the coast of Uvira. They put in to nearby Cape Wasansi in the teeth of another gale and spent the night, unaware that the Wasansi took them for Arabs and hence as enemies.[78]

In the morning, while his men prepared breakfast, Stanley was drifting back into a half-sleep when he was aroused from his doze by the words:

'Master, master, get up quick! Here is a fight going to begin!' He stumbled to his feet to see seven or eight of his people crouched behind the canoe with their guns primed, surrounded by a yelling mob. There was no sign of Livingstone; Bombay informed him that the doctor had gone off on an early morning reconnaissance with Susi and Chumah. Stanley quickly sent off two men to find him, but they had not been gone more than a few minutes when Livingstone himself arrived on the scene, to find Stanley sighting down his Winchester. Calmly Livingstone approached the mob ringleader and asked what the matter was. The man replied that the Arabs were traditional enemies of the Wasansi ever since an Arab grandee at Ujiji had beaten up one of their chiefs for straying too near the Arab's harem. Livingstone nodded, rolled up his sleeve, pointed to the colour of his skin and asked the Wasansi to take notice that he was a white man, not an Arab. This produced a great effect and the two ringleaders were beginning to subside when a drunken headman lurched into the arena, cut himself with his own spear and then claimed the 'Arabs' had wounded him. Again Livingstone's powers of conciliation were called on, and again he managed to persuade the Wasansi to disperse peacefully.[79]

But Stanley had had enough. He ordered the tents struck, the canoes launched and the baggage stowed and implored Livingstone to come away. Livingstone acquiesced in this usurpation of his authority. They struck across the lake from Cape Lumumba and, after an eighteen-hour voyage over two days via Zassi and Niasanga, they arrived back at Ujiji on 13 December after a twenty-eight-day, 300-mile round trip. The return home could have been achieved faster, but Stanley was again taken with fever and Livingstone, out of compassion, obligingly headed the canoe for the nearest landfall on the evening of the 12th.[80] The journey had been abortive in the sense that it was now clear there was no connection between Lakes Tanganyika and Albert but Livingstone still continued to cleave to the hope that Lake Tanganyika might yet link in some other way with the Nile, possibly via the Lualaba.[81]

Back in Ujiji, which this time they entered quietly, without any firing of guns, but to the plaudits of the Arabs, Stanley marshalled his thoughts and impressions of Livingstone.[82] He began the process of 'appropriating' Livingstone, presenting him as a man mistaken by the world, slandered as splenetic, misanthropic, demented, unscientific, uncommunicative, cur-mudgeonly, hypocritical, but uniquely understood and appreciated by Stanley.[83] 'God forgive them for such thoughts. In this prosaic age I have not heard of or seen a man more worthy of honor from his white brothers and I am certain I will die in that opinion.'[84] On the contrary, argued Stanley, Livingstone possessed a unique charm, capable of affecting both African tribesmen and the hard-bitten Arabs of Ujiji, as well as all open-minded white men.[85] Moreover, so far from being a po-faced dour son of the manse, Livingstone had a wonderful sense of humour and enjoyed a good laugh. He had the rare knack, too, of finding joy in another's good fortune, as when Stanley found telegrams from Paris and a letter from consul Webb awaiting him in Ujiji, to which Livingstone's response was, 'And I have none. What a pleasant thing it is to have a real and good friend!'[68] Significantly, too, Stanley, who had attributed Shaw's downfall to his avidity for sexual intercourse with black women, praised Livingstone for not having taken an African 'wife', as the scandal-mongers alleged. Stanley laid this particular rumour at two doors: that of the 'sex-obsessed' Burton and that of Kirk, a notorious retailer of gossip and tall tales.[87]

Meanwhile Livingstone himself had to decide what his next step should be. There seemed to be a number of choices. He could try to link up with Samuel Baker in Equatoria by travelling via the Rusizi and Urindi to the Victoria Nyanza, thence through Unyoro and King Mutesa's country. He could return with Stanley to the coast, then home. Or he could set his sights on Manyema and the Lualaba, in which case the supplies Stanley had already given him were inadequate and he would need to come back with Stanley as far as Unyanyembe to pick up the next consignment of his trade goods and hire fresh porters. After a good deal of reflection, he decided to return to Unyanyembe and wait there until Stanley sent up fifty hand-picked *pagazis* from Zanzibar.[88]

Next Stanley and Livingstone turned to the immediate question of the route back to Unyanyembe. They sketched out a route that would take them away from the war zone and out of the orbit of rapacious tribes like the Ha. First they would go south for seven days on the lake as far as Urimba; then they would cut across the uninhabited forests of Kawendi. Twenty days of marching should take them to Unkonongo, then they would head north for twelve days through Unkonongo and allow a further five days for the final stretch to Unyanyembe.[89]

The rest of December was spent getting the expedition in shape. The first thing was to secure enough canoes for the week southward on Lake Tanganyika; then they needed an adequate supply of saddles and a flock of milch goats to provide milk as they went, on the assumption that each goat would provide a pint of milk. To show his 'filial' deference, Stanley personally worked on a saddle for Livingstone's donkey so that the doctor could ride all the way to Tabora.[90] Unfortunately, the 'trials' on the finished saddle were not propitious: Livingstone's donkey was evil-tempered and threw its rider several times, so that Livingstone was sceptical of his ability to ride the beast even with Stanley's saddle.[91]

While he worked with Selim on the saddle, Stanley proposed that Livingstone write a series of letters to the *New York Herald* (at a rate of £20 per 3,200 words) exposing the evils of the slave trade. Livingstone seemed doubtful whether enough *Herald* readers would be interested; Stanley, however, pointed out that such material would undoubtedly be syndicated, so that the doctor's pleas would reach a mass audience in a nation of nearly twenty-five million people.[92]

On 18 December Stanley again went down with fever and remained more or less convalescent until Christmas, listening to the thunder and heavy rain lashing down on the lake. When Livingstone had finished his long prayer meetings, habitually ending with the reading of a chapter from the Bible, which he then translated into Swahili and expounded for his men, he would come and chat to Stanley about a variety of subjects: the detested missionaries on his Zambezi expedition, his campaigns against the slave trade, his early life in Scotland. He told Stanley that Lord Palmerston had once asked him what honour he would most like, to which Livingstone replied that he wanted nothing for himself but for Africa would like a treaty with the Portuguese outlawing the slave trade. Palmerston abruptly changed the subject.[93] Sometimes Stanley would be half-asleep when Livingstone came into his room, whereat Livingstone would begin to talk to himself as though to an audience. The first time this happened, Stanley asked with a start to whom Livingstone was talking: the doctor laughingly told him to take no notice, it was a habit picked up in solitude.[94]

Ever afterwards Stanley treasured the golden memories of those magical evenings in Ujiji with Livingstone:

I never fancied myself more like a newspaperman than I did when at Ujiji with such an attentive listener as Livingstone. Then we sat until late in the evening long after the sun had set, long after the noise of ramblers and loungers of Broadway had ceased and long after the stars had appeared in the milky heavens above. I had something to say the whole time, something new to relate which drew from my listener sympathetic exclamations. I never thought I had such a good memory. A hundred events that I had already consigned to oblivion as things of no concern were recalled and dressed up as my fluency allowed.[95]

The most sustained conversation Stanley held with Livingstone at Ujiji in December was on the 21st when Stanley had recovered well enough to be out of bed. An accomplished amateur drawer, he began to sketch Livingstone as he wrote up his journals. The initially desultory conversation developed in some surprising ways. As he sketched, Stanley noticed that the doctor had a curious habit of catching his journal whenever he changed the position of his legs, indicating some form of paralysis in his left arm. Livingstone explained that the injury dated from his celebrated mauling by a lion in Mabotsa in 1843.[96] He asked Stanley to feel his arm. Stanley did as requested and perceived that the left arm was broken half-way between the elbow and the shoulder but joined in such a way that it felt as though the inner rim of the lower piece had been attached to the outer rim of the upper, resulting in an overlap of the lower half of the upper arm with the upper half of the lower arm. When the doctor stretched out his arms, Stanley could see that the left arm was considerably shorter than the right.[97]

The gruesome story of Livingstone and the lion led the two men by association of ideas to talk of other encounters with animals dangerous to man. Stanley told the tale of Simba's being taken by crocodiles in the Malagarazi; Livingstone, too, had a fund of horror stories involving crocodiles. Stanley blurted out his feelings of extreme hatred towards the reptiles: 'Ever since [the Malagarazi] at every opportunity I have lost no chance to pour lead into them. I do not think I hate anything as I do a crocodile.' Even the normally gentle Livingstone was disposed to agree: 'Yes, they are very cruel creatures and numbers of times they have caused me great grief.' They both agreed that there were some manifestations of the dark side of nature that it was difficult to adjust to.[98]

Eventually Livingstone insisted on getting on with his work without interruption. As Stanley continued with his sketching, he noticed that, by contrast with himself who was thirty but looked forty, Livingstone was sixty but looked forty-five. He had cut off his beard when Stanley arrived and now shaved every day.[99] His hair was still basically brown, though flecked with grey. His skin was much smoother and less wrinkled than when Stanley first met him six weeks before. He had discarded the scarlet jacket of coarse red flannelling that he wore at the famous meeting, and now wore a suit of dark Norfolk grey tweed that Stanley had bought in Bombay, but which had needed alteration as Livingstone was much bigger in the chest than Stanley.

By this time Stanley's feelings for Livingstone were clearly those of a son for an adoring father. Yet it was typical of his fragile core identity that

Stanley had to justify the very obvious ways in which he was a **different** personality from his admired mentor. Livingstone's superior memory bothered Stanley, so he attributed it to the fact that Livingstone did not smoke 'so that his brain is never befogged even temporarily by the fumes of the insidious weed'.[100] Naturally, Stanley could not bring himself to admit that Livingstone might actually have had a better natural memory or that he lived in his own inner world more harmoniously so could retain more. Still less could he have conceded that his own powers of retention were impaired by the need to remember all the lies he had told and make them coherent!

It emerged later that Stanley dreaded that if Livingstone had really got to know him, warts and all, he would have despised him, that he would have realised Stanley was fundamentally unlovable and unworthy of the doctor's esteem.[101] Stanley therefore insinuated to his readers that Livingstone allowed his beloved Africans to take advantage of his kindly nature. This was Stanley's way of coming to terms with the undoubted efficacy of Livingstone's pacific approach to Africa, which Stanley envied but could not imitate. He summed up the differences between himself and Livingstone as follows:

I am more than ever convinced that the people at Zanzibar who pretended to know Livingstone and told me such extraordinary things about him must have been dreaming. He no more resembles their Livingstone than I do. My impression is that he would rather be killed himself than be compelled to kill another, even if he is a black man. At the same time on three or four occasions I think he has allowed himself to tell me incidents wherein he showed himself capable of a flaming anger. 'I came near shooting him' is an expression I have observed to escape him and the provocation was doubtless strong, but he has never done so, and if it came to the pinch my belief is he would resign himself to other alternatives rather than to it. I admire this as I say but I am afraid that I could not yield my life to every Tom, Dick and Harry who chose to demand it. The waste of good material for bad would strike me as wrong . . . I wish to harm no one quite as little as the Doctor. The wish to do them some good is just as spontaneous in me as it is in him, but where we differ is, that whereas every instinct is prompt in me to resent evil or a deadly menace – he seems indifferent almost to carelessness. Perhaps the thirty years difference in age has something to do with it.[102]

The relationship with Livingstone was the most significant of Stanley's life. He was arguably the only person Stanley ever respected, and certainly the only one to whom he was genuinely prepared to defer. Yet Stanley drew the line at accepting the doctrines and way of life of even such an impressive father-figure. The trauma of St Asaph's was too deeply etched. There is both sadness and defiance in Stanley's conclusion that Livingstone's modes could never be his: 'My methods, however, will not be Livingstone's. Each man has his own way. His, I think, had its defects, though the old man, personally, has been almost Christ-like for goodness, patience and self-sacrifice. The woodenheaded world requires mastering as well as loving charity.'[103] 'Mastering the woodenheaded world' provides as concise a summary as any of Stanley's life project.

9

As the rainy season began and Stanley slowly recovered from his fever, he realised with a tinge of regret that the halcyon interval at Ujiji was at an end. The long trek to Tabora could no longer be delayed. They waited just long enough to celebrate Christmas, but their best-laid plans were ruined when the cook Ferrajji over-roasted the meat and burnt the custard.[1]

On 27 December they left Ujiji in two detachments: Stanley and Livingstone went south by canoe while a shore party followed by land. Altogether forty-eight souls accompanied the two white men westward, including women and children. There were three canoes in the lake party. On his boat Stanley ran the Stars and Stripes up on the end of a punt-pole; Livingstone good-humouredly pretended to be jealous of the flag's eminence and managed to pin a Union Jack on a length of palm.[2] The oarsmen were in great heart at the thought of returning to Unyanyembe and sang rousing songs while they pulled at the blades. Such was their gusto that the shore party driving the goats, sheep and donkeys, had a hard job to keep up with them.

The first stop was Ukaranga at the mouth of the River Luiche, which was flooded with the rains. They transferred the donkeys and goats to the canoes to get them to the other side. Next day, still striking south through hippo-infested waters, they paused briefly to take a cup of coffee and some sweetened vermicelli at the camp of one of Livingstone's favourite Arabs (Mohammed bin Garib); after eighteen hours' rowing they reached the mouth of the Malagarazi (2 p.m., 29 December), then waited three hours for the shore party to catch up with them.[3]

The next day was spent transporting the whole caravan over the Malagarazi. On 30 December they carried out the same manoeuvre to pass the River Rugufu. Since this river teemed with crocodiles, Stanley assuaged his wrath towards the saurians by shooting one. They were now making for Urimba, a six-day trip by water with no prospect of food *en route*. Stanley therefore took the precaution of purchasing four days' rations for four *doti*. He and Livingstone were particularly solicitous about the shore party, which contained the women and children; this detachment had set out from Ujiji with eight days' provisions and now received another four days' rations. In addition, for this stage of the journey, they transferred the children and the weakest goats to the canoes and gave the luggage to the shore party. The precaution was necessary, for they were now striking into unknown territory, where no Arab or East Coaster had ever penetrated.[4]

The days that followed were nervous ones. The canoes reached Urimba on 3 January, after wasting much ammunition on the way by blazing away at hippos and crocodiles, not only to keep them away from their frail craft, but to alert the shore party as to their whereabouts. But at Urimba not only was no food available – the locals were themselves in a state of semi-starvation – but no one had heard anything of the land detachment. Stanley took Kalulu and his double-barrelled Reilly rifle out on a hunting expedition to get meat. He espied a huge herd of zebra and began to stalk them, but his stalk turned into fiasco as he found himself tangled up in a morass of low prickly shrubs. Then, when he tried to sight down his rifle, a swarm of tsetse flies alighted on the barrel and bit him on the nose. He managed to get off a lucky shot that downed a zebra, then capped his feat by bringing down a goose on the wing. Exhausted by his efforts, he lapsed into a semi-feverish state for a couple of days.[5]

To show the land party the way, Stanley and Livingstone had run up an immense flag on a 20-foot long bamboo pole that was wedged on the very top of the tallest tree. On the third day at Urimba the exhausted land party came in. Livingstone waited until Stanley had recovered from his fever before ordering them on (on 7 January 1872). Then the united caravan struck east inland, through the Loajeri valley, still seriously short of food. Their luck held. That very afternoon Livingstone pointed to the other side of a deep crevasse. An immense cow buffalo was grazing there. Three well-targeted shots from Stanley despatched the animal; the expedition now had a meat supply. While Stanley and Livingstone dined that night on the tongue and other choice pieces, they tormented each other with talk of food: mince pies, buckwheat cakes, East River oysters.[6]

It soon became evident that the expedition guide did not know the country he claimed to know, so Stanley put himself at the head of the caravan and steered it by compass. He led it across the swollen River Loajeri, through a gap in an arc of hills that teemed with game, especially zebra and buffalo, and on through alternating tall grass and beautiful parkland. Trekking through the tall grass was particularly exhausting for Livingstone, as it showered rain on the travellers at every step.[7]

In the evenings they comforted themselves with wide-ranging conversation. Livingstone spoke with sadness of the death of his wife and his son Robert and with real passion when he touched on his two favourite topics: the abortive Zambezi missions and the Portuguese and Arab slave trades. He spoke of his many friends: James Young, a fellow medical student at Glasgow, Cotton Oswell, Murray, Frank Vardon. He declared his conviction that Gordon Cumming the lion hunter had built up the 'king of beasts' absurdly; Livingstone, who was in a position to know, felt that the lion's reputation far outstripped his reality.[8] Stanley continued to marvel at his phenomenal memory and ability to quote from the poets, even though the only volumes he had ever seen on his shelves were the Bible, prayer books and religious concordances. Stanley noticed too that when it came to Africa Livingstone was more interested in ethnology than topographical geography. He was amused that Livingstone had little interest in the arts: 'Livingstone tells me that he has only been twice at a theatre in his life and would not give a sixpence to see the best play ever acted.'[9] But he was delighted when the doctor, reminiscing about his early life as a missionary, suddenly took a sideswipe at his *bête noire*, Tozer: 'these weak, dandling creatures who call themselves missionaries ... Tozer, bishop of Central Africa as he is called, has not yet ventured upon his diocese. Central Africa indeed!'[10]

But these pleasant camp-fire chats were interludes only in the grim struggle for survival in the wilderness. On 12 January, after crossing several ranges, the weary expedition confronted a raging torrent. To lift the men's spirits before battling with the flood, Stanley set out in the afternoon to hunt. But instead of small game, he ran smack into a herd of elephants. Stanley judged it wiser to retire than try conclusions with these forest monarchs, 'especially with a pea-shooter loaded with treacherous sawdust cartridges in my hand'.[11] The day turned into a series of misfortunes. First he was stung by a wasp, then arrived back in camp to find that the men had eaten up all their reserve rations of dried meat. Three foodless days now yawned in front of them. As a finishing touch, at dusk that evening while Stanley and Livingstone were taking tea outside their tent, a herd of elephants rumbled by in the middle distance. Too exhausted for another joust with them, Stanley sent out his two *wangwana* hunters, who later returned, unsuccessful. Livingstone tried to comfort Stanley for his fruitless day in the bush by telling him tales of the great elephant hunters, underlining how difficult it was for anyone but an expert to down the great beasts.[12]

On they went, up and down ridges, through torrents, in forests never before seen by white men. Despite the pleas of his *pagazis*, Stanley insisted on steering by compass and chart across the long series of longitudinal ridges that paralleled Lake Tanganyika. Livingstone had full confidence in his young companion. Stanley found time to comment on the extreme beauty of this country to the east of the Malagarazi and to marvel at the colonies of an unknown species of reddish monkey they encountered, but after six days of existing on mushrooms and forest fruit, his followers were exhausted.[13] The very fact that the need for meat was so pressing seemed to affect Stanley's marksmanship adversely. On 15 January he had a good chance to make a killing among herds of hartebeeste and zebra, but overanxiety led him to shoot wide. Even such shooting chances came rarely because of the incessant rain and poor visibility: 'A thick haze covered the forests; rain often pelted on us; the firmament was an unfathomable depth of grey vapor.'[14] Moreover, the presence of numerous lions, whose roaring plagued them day and night, disconcerted his Zanzibari hunters, who were apathetic even in face of a reward of five *doti* offered for each animal slain.

By 17 January they were all at the end of their tether. As always with Stanley, a mixture of anxiety and guilt brought out his worst side. It was his custom to walk in the relative cool of the morning, then ride his donkey in the humid heat of the afternoon. But because Livingstone could not ride his donkey he trudged all day long. Stanley's response to the situation was typical of him: 'To see the old man tramping it on foot like a hero makes me a little ashamed – and sometimes an unsavoury thought comes into my head that he does it to vex me. He must be a rider – having been in Africa – but it is an odd taste to prefer walking to riding. However, if he won't, he won't and there's an end on't.'[15]

Yet relief was at hand. On 17 January they ascended a ridge in the beautiful rainswept parkland and were able to make out their old camp in the Mrera valley. Soon they were recognised and showered with congratulations on their safe return from Ujiji. The people brought food for the famished travellers: maize, sweet potatoes, beans. Livingstone was in poor physical condition: 'The doctor's feet were very sore and bleeding from the weary march. His shoes were in a very worn-out state, and he had so cut and slashed them with a knife to ease his feet that any man of our force would have refused them as a gift.'[16]

Next day they pressed on, in better spirits after some solid food. Even though they were now in known territory, the guide managed to lose his way again, so Stanley reverted to leadership of the caravan. By now his shoes were as bad as Livingstone's. Yet he was cheered by the fecund change that had come over the land since his journey to Ujiji: 'the wild grapes now hung in clusters along the road; the corn ears were advanced enough to pluck and roast for food; the various plants had their flowers; and the deep woods and grasses of the country were greener than ever.'[17] Livingstone was delighted with the profusion of plant life around them and insisted on stopping a few moments on the road to show Stanley the gum copal tree, the chilli and the sarsparilla plant.[18] The lifting spirits of the party seemed vindicated by two events on the 19th: first they reached Mpokwa's deserted village and slept in the huts, two of which seemed to have been expressly prepared for their use; then Stanley succeeded in shooting two zebras, which provided over 700 pounds of meat or about 16 pounds per person.[19] Stanley was especially delighted with his feat as he had dropped both beasts with his wrongly sighted O'Reilly rifle. The lean days seemed behind them.

Yet the zigzag nature of their fortunes was underlined next day when Stanley took aim at two separate herds of giraffe and succeeded only in wounding a female, which got away. Livingstone was at his most paternal over this incident and blamed it on Stanley's defective bullets. 'It was not the first time that I had cause to think the doctor an admirable travelling companion; none knew so well how to console one for bad luck – none knew so well how to elevate one in his own mind . . . he was a most considerate companion, and, knowing him to be literally truthful, I was proud of his praise when successful, and when I failed I was easily consoled.'[20]

The pendulum swung back next day when Stanley succeeded in stalking and killing a giraffe, fully 16 feet 9 inches tall, and weighing nearly 1,000 pounds. Stanley jokingly remarked to Livingstone that he wished the giraffe and zebra could be domesticated for, mounted on a zebra, a man could ride from Bagamoyo to Ujiji in a month.[21] But again Stanley's see-saw fortunes were in evidence, for he went down with fever and was ill for three days. Livingstone nursed him and treated him with the 'Livingstone pills' – his own antimalarial concoction of quinine, rhubarb, three grains of resin of julep and two grains of calomel.[22]

The two factors of enforced rest, galling for a hard-driving achiever like Stanley, and the necessity to feel gratitude to a benefactor, clearly triggered the dark impulses within, for 27 January, the first day back on his feet, saw the only serious, albeit momentary, rift between himself and

Livingstone. To make up for lost time Stanley cracked on the pace of his column towards Nisonghi. On the way they were attacked by a swarm of wild bees, who bit and stung unmercifully, turning the marching column into a wildly careering, panic-stricken mob. Stanley took two nasty bites on the nose and one on the finger during a pursuit of half a mile.[23] Livingstone fared even worse. Ironically, because of his poor health and aching feet, he had finally been persuaded to ride the donkey. When the bees attacked, instead of bolting, the donkey rolled over and over on its side, exposing Livingstone to the full fury of the insects. For all his years in Africa, being so badly stung was a novel experience for the doctor: 'I never saw men attacked before: the donkey was completely knocked up by the stings on the head, face and lips and died in two days in consequence.'[24]

On arrival in camp, Stanley sent some men back down the trail to assist Livingstone. They found him resting under a tree and offered to carry him the rest of the way. Livingstone reacted angrily: 'Get away with you – do you think I am a woman?' When this was reported to Stanley, he feared that Livingstone would be in a foul temper from the fall and the stings and would blame Stanley for having pressed on so fast. He ordered Ferrajji to prepare the best supper he could concoct and ordered Susi and Chumah to be at the ready, to pull off his boots and generally soothe him. While Ferrajji got to work on a meal of meatballs, custard and tea, Stanley asked his scouts to report to him the minute they saw the doctor approach.

Once they reported, Stanley hid behind a tree to observe. Livingstone limped slowly into camp and went to his tent, where Susi and Chumah washed his feet, then led him to the table where the aromas of Ferrajji's cooking were wafting around. Livingstone sat down and began to eat. Leaving ten minutes for the food to take its effect, Stanley sauntered over and said, 'Good evening' as though nothing had happened that day. Livingstone looked very grim at first but as he ate he began to relax, then allowed himself a diplomatic reprimand. 'Well, I thought you were going on to Unyanyembe without stopping. It is rather a long march is it not?' Stanley apologised and Livingstone allowed himself to be won round. 'Before long the doctor was in his usual sweet temper and we laughed over our misadventures. But a good hot meal is a great restorer of the spirits!'[25]

They pressed on, across three streams to Mrera. The terrible rain that had dogged them all the way from Urimba continued. At Mrera they met an Arab caravan and learned the first full news of Shaw's death, which Stanley attributed to drunkenness and debauchery.[26] Both Stanley and Livingstone were now beginning to suffer from food fantasies. They were no longer actually short of food, but they were starting to tire of the monotonous diet of salted giraffe meat, pickled zebra tongues, sweet potatoes, tea and coffee. Stanley was relieved to find that among Livingstone's human weaknesses was a concern for his stomach. Despite aching feet, fog, dew, rain and drizzle, Livingstone continued to gorge himself like a trooper. 'Among the blessings of this life I count meat, bread, good fresh butter,' Stanley noted in his diary.[27]

Yet Livingstone was in good spirits on this latter part of the journey to Unyanyembe. He fascinated Stanley with his profound knowledge of Africana: trees, fruit, woodcraft, anthropology. He still took with him everywhere five exotic parrots he had acquired in Manyema. He confided in Stanley his excessive dislike of the Portuguese, and they found a common interest in etymology. Stanley retained particularly fond memories of the doctor's good humour during a five-hour march through a forest that seemed alive with elephant herds.[28] There was just one macabre moment when, on passing a bleached skull in the depth of the forest, Livingstone expressed a desire to be buried in the stillness of such a forest. On an impulse, Stanley reverted to his Persepolis behaviour and carved his and the doctor's initials on a tree.[29]

On 3 February Stanley succumbed to yet another attack of fever, accompanied by severe pains in the back and loins. Livingstone dosed him with an emetic and gave orders that he be carried in a cot. In his lucid moments Stanley wondered whether it was his fate to follow Shaw to a Central African grave. Livingstone reassured him that this attack was merely due to the recent exposure to wet and damp; if he was going to die of fever, he would have passed away in Ujiji.[30]

By the time Stanley recovered, they were once again at the rich game country of Gombe (7 February), and by the creek, still swarming with hippos and crocodiles. Seeing that they were now within a week of journey's end, Stanley sent Bombay, Ferrajji and Chowpereh on ahead to Unyanyembe to bring back medicines and letters. Since he knew Gombe to be a hunter's paradise from his visit on the outward journey, Stanley set off to add something to the cooking-pot. He saw a lion lurking in the long grass and tried to stalk it, but the big cat made off apace.[31] Lions on land and crocodiles in the water were the bane of Gombe. Next day Stanley succeeding in shooting both an eland and hartebeeste but a pride of lions made off with the kill before he could retrieve it.[32]

At Manyara they were very hospitably received and given a present of sweet potatoes by the chief. Stanley started to appreciate the force of Livingstone's arguments in favour of Africans: 'Here was an instance of that disposition to sincere friendship with meritorious strangers which I ascribe to the chiefs in general in Central Africa where they have not been spoiled by the Arabs.'[33]

By 11 February they were at the palisaded village of Kwikuru, now well into the original theatre of the war between the Arabs and Mirambo. During Stanley's absence the tide had turned in favour of the Arabs (but it was to turn again in Mirambo's favour in June).[34] In particular, the Tabora sheikhs had taken heart from Stanley's exploit in opening the road to Ujiji and had resumed their caravans there. While Stanley and Livingstone halted a day to obtain provisions for the last lap of their journey to Unyanyembe, they discussed the doctor's future plans, once he had obtained his stores. Livingstone said he intended to strike south of Lake Tanganyika to the Lualaba and solve once and for all the question of the ultimate source of the Nile; he estimated that the journey would take him eighteen months, but to Stanley it seemed like a task that would occupy at least two years.[35]

They fell to talking about the reception of Livingstone's work in England. Stanley said that he had seen many favourable reviews of Livingstone's book about the Zambezi; Livingstone replied that most he had seen were unfavourable. Stanley pointed out that Livingstone's reputation was unimpeachable and that if he had ever received bad reviews, this would have been because of the 'new journalism's' desire for 'good copy'. Livingstone's response reveals shrewdness: 'You are very kind, I am sure, but I am thinking that you have also a pretty way of saying pleasant things to one who is low spirited. I return you the compliment you paid me the other day.'[36]

They marched on from Kwikuru on the 13th. Stanley was again very ill and had to be carried, as he was unable to ride his donkey. He was in a sorry state at the end of the day's trek: 'I am in such a state tonight that I can neither lie down or sit quietly in one position long. Livingstone is calmly asleep. I am nervous and my head is very strange. I have the most fearful dreams every night – and I am afraid to shut my eyes, lest I shall see the horrid things that haunt me. I will go walk-walk-walk in the forest to get rid of them.'[37]

Part of the feeling oppressing Stanley was a presentiment of evil. This seemed amply borne out when he arrived at Ugunda next day and met Ferrajji and Chowpereh, who had brought back a sheaf of letters from Tabora. The first one Stanley opened was bad enough. It contained all the recent news, including a graphic account of the bloody horrors of the Paris Commune, which drew from Stanley the comment: 'Oh France! Oh

Frenchmen! Such things are unknown even in the heart of Central Africa.'[38]

But the second letter he opened was even more of a bone-chiller. It was an irate communication from consul Webb to say that the cheque Stanley had left with him had been bounced by the *Herald*'s New York bankers and that Bennett had disclaimed all responsibility for the expedition's expenses. After reminding Stanley of all he had done for him, Webb pointed out that he would be ruined if the debt was not repaid: 'I am distressed not only in my private capacity as a gentleman and businessman but also as a consular official.' Other letters confirmed the story of the bounced cheque. Stanley noted in his diary in great distress: 'There was not a doubt of it! Bennett was about to treat me as I had heard he had treated others of his unfortunate correspondents.'[39]

Stanley's first instinct was to share his sorrows with Livingstone, but when he saw the look of quiet pleasure on the doctor's face as he read the long-delayed letters from his children, he did not have the heart to intrude his own problems. Crushed by the thought that he would have to pay off the entire debt out of his own savings, Stanley had no stomach for the other letters in the bundle. After about an hour he drearily opened the third letter from the *Herald*. It was from Zanzibar, dated 23 December 1871, and contained a missive from London, date 25 September 1871, informing Webb that since Levien had now been replaced at the *Herald*'s London office by Hosmer, the bureau was prepared to cash all drafts from Stanley.[40]

Mightily relieved, Stanley chatted to Livingstone about the Franco-Prussian war and the Commune without revealing the emotional turmoil he had just lived through. Livingstone was in great form after the letters from his family. He commiserated with Stanley about his insomnia and confided that the long years in Africa meant that he could no longer sleep comfortably in a four-poster bed but tossed and threshed in it like a buffalo.[41]

There were no further incidents on the march to Unyanyembe. They entered Tabora on 18 February in triumph, flags flying and guns firing, on the fifty-fourth day after leaving Ujiji.[42] They went immediately to the *tembe* at Kwihara, where, it transpired, they had arrived in the nick of time. The headman Asmani sent by Kirk had been pilfering the stores and was discharged. Even greater depredations had been carried out by Said bin Salim, who blamed the obvious inventory shrinkage on 'white ants', but, as Stanley sardonically observed: 'the brandy bottles most singular to relate had also fallen a prey to the voracious and irresistible destroyers –

the white ants – and by some unaccountable means they had imbibed the potent Hennessy.'[43]

Stanley immediately got out his trade goods and made over to Livingstone the surplus not required on the journey to the coast: this included twelve bales of calico, fifteen bags of beads, thirty-eight coils of brass wire, a boat, bath, cooking pots, twelve copper sheets, trousers and jackets and, most importantly, a tent – for on the return from Manyema Livingstone had been without one.[44] All in all, Livingstone now possessed four years' supplies; his only shortage lay in manpower.

They settled into a comfortable routine in the *tembe* which, compared with the hut at Ujiji, seemed like a palace. The *tembe* at Kwihara was already well on the way to acquiring legendary status as a 'hotel' for European travellers.[45] The sensation that Unyanyembe, with its plentiful stores, was a demi-paradise after their recent sufferings seemed to draw substance also from the elements, for the teeming rain that had accompanied them all the way from Ujiji suddenly ceased and glorious weather supervened. Livingstone gave thanks after the first morning coffee by holding an impromptu religious service, attended by a surprising number of the men.[46]

The last four weeks with Livingstone at Kwihara saw Stanley's relationship with his surrogate father at its deepest. Two days after arriving they decided to celebrate with a late Christmas dinner to make up for the one Ferrajji had spoiled at Ujiji. The after-dinner conversation showed the two men at their warmest and frankest yet. Livingstone gently chided Stanley for his excessive speed of marching, pointing out that he himself liked to do no more than 5 miles a day, so that he could make a thorough exploration of any aspect of the flora and fauna on the route that took his fancy. But to show that he harboured no grudge, he made Stanley his 'honorary son' by putting him in charge of his dead son Robert's affairs. He wrote to his daughter Agnes that all Robert's effects should be sent to Stanley in London, as the 'American' would be trying to find a secure resting place for her brother's bones at Gettysburg.[47]

Stanley for his part recorded his pleasure that the doctor seemed to look much younger now than on their first meeting in Ujiji. This was mainly a matter of diet: Livingstone in normal circumstances had a voracious appetite, and Stanley estimated his weight at Unyanyembe to be around 180 pounds, though he could never persuade his mentor to weigh himself.[48] He was a very close observer of the doctor. He noticed that whenever he was about to begin a story he always held up a crooked forefinger. There is a novelist's perception in his description of Livingstone in full flight. 'The loose front teeth which play while he talks add to the appearance of age a great deal. He uses humorous Scotticisms frequently . . . he is full of sly jokes. When he begins one of his funny stories, I see how it is going to end by the gleam in his dark hazel eyes, the pucker gathering about his eyes – the uplifted forefinger.'[49]

Every evening after dinner in the *tembe* Livingstone would discourse on some new topic that revealed further aspects of his personality. He complained bitterly about the Royal Geographical Society and its stinginess. They had not treated him well in any aspect of his life and work: they wanted basically to reap the benefits from his labours without making any financial outlay to support it. They would plagiarise his maps and doctor the letters he sent home so that they fitted in with the RGS view.[50] The one good thing about the Society, for Livingstone, was its dinners; among the items in the 'gorgeous entertainments' the RGS laid on for its explorers were 'juicy marrow bones' and Devonshire cream. 'You will think of me when you taste those marrow bones at the Geographical and the Devonshire cream in London,' said Livingstone with a wistful smile.[51]

But Livingstone's conversation was not all complaint and food fantasy. He embarrassed Stanley by placing Christianity firmly at the forefront of the daily agenda in Unyanyembe, plying the younger man with questions as to the suitability of the African for receiving the Gospel. Stanley prevaricated: spreading the Word would take a long time with 'such a stupid and wicked people'. Livingstone ignored the slur on his beloved Africans and asked how Stanley would go about the task of proselytising. It was perhaps typical of Stanley's habitual large-scale response to Africa that he suggested sending a thousand missionaries, all to be concentrated in the powerful hegemonic tribes. Inevitably, such religious conversations brought Livingstone back to one of his pet obsessions – the abortive Zambezi missions. Those years had thrown a chink of light on the Dark Continent, but the ineptitude of his comrades had allowed the darkness to descend again. Livingstone ended his long peroration on his incompetent toilers in the vineyard by quoting Burns:

See, yonder, poor o'erlaboured wight,
So abject, mean, and vile!
Who begs a brother of the earth
To give him leave to toil![52]

Livingstone's monomania about his 'betrayal' by his co-workers on the Zambezi expedition eventually led Stanley to reassess his mentor.

Whereas at the outset he had been bowled over by the fact that Livingstone was a truly Christian man and not a misanthrope, after four months in his company Stanley started to think that he was perhaps incapable of true Christian forgiveness and not quite so perfect as he initially thought him. 'I have had some intrusive suspicious thoughts that he was not of such angelic temper as I believed him to be during my first month with him – but for the last month I have been driving them steadily from my mind.'[53] However, he conceded that on the march back from Ujiji he had formed a balanced view and seen Livingstone whole, neither as misanthrope nor as subject for hagiography.

The slightly jaundiced tone with which Stanley recorded his impressions of his mentor in early March is explicable in terms of his own shame, for Livingstone had recently graphically demonstrated the supremacy of his own method of treating Africans over Stanley's. At Kwikuru, while Stanley was recovering from a bout of fever, he remonstrated with the cook for not cleaning the coffee pot properly. The cook, Ulimengo by name, retorted scornfully that he was used to working for Livingstone, and what was good enough for the 'big master' ought to be good enough for the 'little master'. Enraged by this 'impertinent' reply, Stanley seized a club, fully intending, at his own admission, to brain Ulimengo. While his Zanzibari followers were restraining him, Livingstone walked into the scene of bedlam. 'Gently, there! What is the matter, Mr Stanley!' he said kindly. Breathlessly Stanley blurted out his explanation. Livingstone lifted his hand, curled his forefinger and said, 'I will settle this.'[54]

Livingstone then called Ulimengo before him and rebuked him publicly. Did he not realise that all the food and stores they had came from the 'little master' and they were all his *mbengis* (guests)? He went on to explain that Stanley was the real leader of the expedition: 'I am only the big master because I am older.' Ulimengo was so chastened by this that after apologising to Stanley he asked to be allowed to kiss his feet. Livingstone, doubtless not feeling that Stanley had acted entirely correctly, would not permit this. Having dismissed Ulimengo, he took Stanley aside and calmly got him to see the error of his ways. 'Come now, you must not mind him. He is only a half-savage and does not know any better. He is probably a Banyan slave. Why should you care what he says? They are all alike, unfeeling and hard.' The upshot was that that evening Stanley shook hands with Ulimengo and absorbed a signal demonstration that civil reprimand was preferable to the club or the whip.[55] Unfortunately this was not a lesson that Stanley retained very long.

Any signs of less than saintly demeanour that Livingstone was display-ing at Unyanyembe can in any case largely be attributed to Stanley himself, for it was in the *tembe* at Kwihara that he whipped up the doctor's anger against Kirk to curdling point. But it is important to be clear that Livingstone already had a jaundiced view of Kirk before Stanley came on to the scene. The fact that Stanley had an independent grudge against him simply allowed two separate streams of resentment to flow into one. Livingstone's bitterness towards Kirk had many causes. He blamed him for inertia and failing to exert himself sufficiently to make sure supplies and letters got through to Ujiji quickly. He censured him for using unreliable slave labour to escort his effects to Unyanyembe and for using incompetent or dishonest agents. And he suspected Kirk of trying to force him to return home before his work in Africa was done.[56]

Within a week of meeting Stanley at Ujiji, Livingstone was bombarding his contacts in England with complaints about Kirk. As yet he did not make an official complaint, but in a letter to his daughter Agnes on 18 November he wrote the following: 'He has got by my influence to the top of his ambition – an acting consul and a political agent – husband of a wife and two children – and I may go to my grave before he will stir hand and foot for me.'[57] Livingstone further objected to Kirk's reported remarks to Stanley that Livingstone's task was 'to clear up Lake Tanganyika from the must left on it by Burton'. Who did Kirk think he was? His attitude evinced all too clearly the unmistakable signs of the professional bureau-crat in thrall to the Foreign Office mentality – that same Foreign Office whose underling had so insulted Livingstone in London by his 'instruc-tions': 'this was so insultingly nauseous from a mere jack in office that I never could quote it.'[58]

But at Unyanyembe in February and March Livingstone publicly pointed the finger at Kirk. He was particularly infuriated by Foreign Secretary Lord Granville's remarks in the House of Lords: that all Livingstone's wants had been supplied. So far were they from having been supplied that it was only Stanley's advent that had saved him from starvation at Ujiji.[59] Moreover, it was simply the chance observation of Livingstone's effects in Tabora that had led Stanley to lock them in the storeroom in the *tembe*. In addition, the entire Sherif episode was Kirk's fault. As far as Livingstone could make out, it was Kirk's intention to compel him (Livingstone) to give up and return to England, possibly with a view to getting hold of the precious research notes and publishing them himself. How else explain the incident at Ujiji when Kirk's hirelings had refused to hand over the Enfield rifles sent from Zanzibar for

Livingstone's use and Stanley had had to send an armed party to recover them?[60] 'Dr Kirk's eagerness to appropriate the infamy of having told slaves to force me back is incomprehensible.'[61]

Far the worst of Kirk's faults, in Livingstone's eyes, was having hired 'slaves' instead of free men: 'By some strange hallucination our friend Kirk placed some £500 of goods in the hands of slaves with a drunken half-caste tailor as leader . . . it is simply infamous to employ slaves when any number of freemen may be hired!' 'Tell Kirk not to believe every Banyan's tale. It makes him a jape and not a disciple of David Livingstone.'[62]

By the time Stanley was ready to leave for the coast, Livingstone had decided on two methods of humiliating his 'treacherous' former aide Kirk. In the first place, he wrote to the Foreign Office with an official complaint about the way his affairs had been handled from Zanzibar, which Kirk had no choice but to send on.[63] Secondly, he ordered Kirk to hand over to Stanley the £500 sent out from London to fund his work and to assist Stanley in finding fifty new porters and supplies.[64] This was an open snub, for it in effect announced to the world that Livingstone had no confidence in Kirk and had found someone else to supplant him.

But Stanley was also responsible for some more elevated correspondence from Livingstone, more in keeping with the popular image of Livingstone as saintly bearer of light in the Dark Continent. His pleas that Livingstone should write an open letter to the *New York Herald* in denunciation of the slave trade finally bore fruit. The right angle, Stanley hinted, was Livingstone's oft-expressed admiration for Abraham Lincoln. Interestingly, the letter Livingstone wrote, shortly after Stanley's departure, was a *mélange* of Stanley and Livingstone. It contained all Livingstone's passion about the evils of slavery and worked in his contempt for the present crop of missionaries in general and Tozer in particular. It then dilated on the affront to civilisation offered by the slave trade in an era of technological change, instancing all the examples Stanley had rehearsed to him (the Suez Canal, Pacific railways, railways in western Asia and India, the proposed Panama Canal, telegraph, steamships etc.). It finally exhorted all Americans to honour the memory of the 'good and great President Lincoln' by opposing the African slave trade as vigorously as they opposed slavery in Brazil.[65]

The last weeks together in Kwihara were painful for both men, conscious of the imminence of separation. With no rain to hinder them, Stanley's men made rapid progress in the preparations for the trek to the coast. Stanley's packing was impeded by just one incident when a black fly crawled under his pyjamas and bit him. The bite became a boil which awoke him from a delightful dream and was so painful that he consulted Livingstone about it. Livinstone conjectured that the fly must have secreted an egg. He squeezed the boil, an egg sac popped out, and the pain ceased almost at once.[66]

Stanley continued to press Livingstone to come home with him to restore his health, but Livingstone insisted that his work was not yet finished and if he had to die soon, he would prefer it to be in Africa.[67] Stanley found something Arab-like in the way Livingstone seemed to subscribe to *kismet* or *baraka*: 'Livingstone takes life in the same cool and assured manner [as the Arabs] as if it had been whispered into his ears – the assurance of enjoying a few more decades. Strange people here. I wish I could have the same comfortable feeling about longevity, but my shrunken muscles and whimpering stomach urge me to leave the black man's land before another bout of fever lays me low under the sable soil of this malicious clime.'[68]

For his part, as the time for parting drew near, Livingstone again proposed that Stanley accompany him to the Lualaba. Once more Stanley protested that it was impossible. Livingstone then pleaded with him at least to stay until after the next rainy season. But Stanley was now impatient to be gone: 'I have done my duty strictly by him and now another duty seizes upon me to sever us.'[69]

Their intimacy deepened. Stanley, with his mania for neatness, was particularly impressed with the doctor's scrupulous care with his materials: 'his boxes appear like new, his compasses and instruments are in first rate order. His journals are clean and orderly kept – blotless – as if a copyist had been lately transcribing them.'[70] More and more Livingstone confided in him, about his admiration for Lincoln (after whom he had named an African lake), about the chronic diarrhoea he suffered from (and which had nearly carried him off in 1854 on the way to St Paul de Loanda), about his grief for Manimokaya, his faithful servant and path-finder to Manyema (who died in early March).[71] Livingstone encouraged Stanley's project to write a book about the 'finding' at Ujiji and offered to help him find a publisher; he wrote a letter to the house of John Murray on his behalf. He sympathised with Stanley in his problems with the 'incorrigible Bombay' and quoted his favourite Scotticism: 'a stout heart to a stae brae'.[72] Only one false note was struck during the month at Unyanyembe. Seeing him in one of his reveries, with brows puckered and right forefinger bent, Stanley ventured: 'A penny for your thoughts,

Doctor.' Livingstone was momentarily disconcerted and irritated: 'They are not worth it, my young friend, and let me suggest that, if I had any, possibly, I should wish to keep them!'[73]

At last their final Sunday together came round. Stanley finished packing the gifts for the Webbs of Newstead and the doctor's children, then attended the service, slightly longer than usual, where the congregation prayed for Stanley's safe arrival at the coast. Livingstone led the prayers then read the 35th Psalm and preached on it, referring to Stanley as his 'friend and brother'. Later, after breakfast, Livingstone outlined his proposed route to the Lualaba, and Stanley reiterated that the round trip would occupy at least two years.[74]

Monday 12 March saw a farewell dance for the men. Livingstone sat up late finishing his letters, while Stanley went over to Tabora to fetch the Arab correspondence he had promised to take to Zanzibar. Then came the last day. The minutes flew by and Stanley felt sorely tempted to delay his departure. His time with Livingstone had been simply too happy and 'the farewell, I fear, may be forever.' Livingstone came to him and thanked him fulsomely for all he had done and for saving his life in Ujiji. Such an expression of gratitude from a man he so admired was too much for Stanley. He burst into tears and sobbed 'as one only can in uncommon grief . . . his sudden outburst of gratitude, with that kind of praise that steals into one and touches the softer parts of the ever-veiled nature, – all had their influence; and, for a time, I was as a sensitive child of eight or so, and yielded to such bursts of tears that only such a scene as this could have forced.'[75]

As they folded up Livingstone's journal in several wrappings of cloth, Stanley broke the sad, embarrassed silence. 'Tomorrow night at this time you will be quite alone, Doctor.'

'Yes,' said Livingstone, 'this house will look as though a death had taken place. Had you not better stop until after the rains which are now nearly over?' Stanley shook his head. He had set himself a target of forty days in which to reach the coast and nothing, not even his love for Livingstone, would stop him.[76]

On 14 March they were both up at dawn and ate a sad breakfast together. Then Livingstone accompanied Stanley a couple of miles to the slope of a ridge. As they walked together, he repeated his determination not to return home until he had found the true sources of the Nile. Stanley made a final entreaty to the doctor to come home. Livingstone declined. Then they looked back from the hill at the *tembe* where they had spent so many happy days together.

'My dear Doctor, you must go no further. You have come far enough. See, our house is a good distance now, and the sun is very hot. Let me beg of you to turn back.'

'Well,' he replied. 'I will say this to you: you have done what few men could do. And for what you have done for me I am most grateful. God guide you safe home and bless you my friend! And may God bring you safe back to us all, my dear friend! Farewell!'[77]

They shook hands. Stanley saw a look of suppressed emotion in Livingstone's eyes and he came close to breakdown himself. 'March!' he ordered sternly to his men. The only way he could keep a dry eye was by putting space between him and Livingstone as quickly as possible. Finally he allowed himself a last look at his mentor. 'We came to a ridge and I looked back and watched his grey figure fading dimmer in the distance for a presentiment or suggestion stole into my mind that I was looking for the last time at him. I gulped down my great grief, and turned away to follow the receding caravan.'[78]

For both men, it was the end of their most (one is tempted to say 'only') successful human relationship. Livingstone immediately went back and sent a postscript after Stanley to tell him, should he meet any more of Kirk's 'slaves' on the road, to send them back to Zanzibar. Livingstone had just one more year of life remaining but for the rest of it he continued to extol both Stanley's bravery and his filial qualities.[79] 'Like a son' is the almost Homeric epithet Livingstone used thereafter whenever referring to Stanley.[80] His opinion of Americans was miraculously transformed too (he still imagined that Stanley was an American). He habitually contrasted Kirk's 'lazy indifference' with Stanley's energy and courage, and encouraged his daughter Agnes to assist him in the writing of his book: 'it will in his hands do us no harm for the Americans are good and generous friends.'[81] When Horace Waller counterattacked on Kirk's behalf and tried to drive a wedge between Livingstone and Stanley by asserting that the latter used the famous explorer to produce a best-seller, Livingstone simply bounced the criticism back: 'I am told by Kirk that Stanley would make his fortune out of me, if so he is heartily welcome, for it is a great deal more than I could make out of myself.'[82]

Stanley was even more affected. 'In all fiction I know no moral hero greater than David Livingstone' was one of his milder later assessments. On the road back to Bagamoyo he reflected that if Samuel Baker deserved a baronetcy for naming Unyoro or Lake Albert, what did Livingstone deserve for discovering half a continent?[83] 'Supposing that all west of the Hudson and Albany was all a blank unknown to us – crowd that with immense lakes and noble rivers etc. – and you will have some idea of what Livingstone has now done for African geography.'

But the pang of the first afternoon apart from Livingstone was the worst wrench Stanley had experienced since his sudden disappearance into the maw of St Asaph's at the age of six. The father-son motif appears in the diary entry written that evening: 'I felt very lonely all afternoon – as if I had but just parted with my own family. Pity that partings should be necessary . . . I never thought while being a victim to its fever that I should leave Central Africa with a pang but it was so, and only because of a white man . . . I cried at parting with the good doctor . . . and I had to turn away rather suddenly.'[84]

When he camped next day, Stanley felt so despondent that he wrote an agonised letter of longing for the lost 'father', so revealing of emotional hunger that Stanley, on reflection, did not send it. But it may stand as a fitting epitaph to the strength of what was on paper the unlikeliest of close relationships:

My dear Doctor,
    I have parted from you too soon. I feel it too deeply. I am entirely conscious of it from being so depressed . . . In writing to you, I am not writing to an idea now, but to an embodiment of warm good fellowship, of everything that is noble and right, of sound common-sense, of everything practical and rightminded. I have talked with you; your presence is almost palpable, though you are absent . . . It seems as if I had left a community of friends and relations. The utter loneliness of myself, the void that has been created, the pang at parting, the bleak aspect of the future, is the same as I have felt before when parting from dear friends. My dear doctor, had I not turned away from you quickly at taking our farewell I would have appeared weak and were not the Arabs present? Could they have understood my feelings? I doubt if you can understand them thoroughly but there I do you a wrong, and you will please forgive me.
    Why should people be subjected to these partings, with the several sorrows and pangs that surely follow them? It is a consolation, however, after tearing myself away, that I am about to do you a service, for then I have not quite parted from you, you and I are not quite separate. Though I am not present to you bodily, you must think of me daily, until your caravan arrives. Though you are not before me visibly, I shall think

of you constantly, until your least wish has been attended to. In this way the chain of remembrance will not be severed.

'Not yet,' I say to myself, 'are we apart' and this to me, dear Doctor, is consoling, believe me. Had I a series of services to perform for you, why then, we should never have to part. Do not fear then, I beg to ask, nay to command, whatever lies in my power. And do not, I beg of you, attribute these professions to interested motives, but accept them, or believe them in the spirit in which they are made, in that true David Livingstone spirit I have happily become acquainted with.[85]

· 10 ·

LIKE his short-legged prototype Odysseus, Stanley was aware that potentially the greatest danger to any enterprise occurs just near the end, when the safe anchorage is all but established. He therefore took the utmost pains to ensure that his journey back to the coast would be as risk-free as he could contrive it. While he had learned from Livingstone the advantages of being conciliatory and courteous to the tribes, he still believed in the big stick as much as the soft voice. Every night he loaded all his guns and placed a brace of pistols under his pillow. The boxes containing the cartridges were unscrewed and prepared for immediate action. In his mind he sketched out a variety of plans to meet all possible contingencies: night attacks, assaults by day, mutinies, desertions, epidemics.

Stanley was in a great hurry to get to the coast. He knew the rainy season was coming, he wanted to obtain the fifty porters for Livingstone, and he himself wanted to make an end of the expedition. There seemed a good chance that his estimate of a forty-day march might not be absurdly optimistic. They were marching back over terrain they had already traversed, Stanley was by now an old Africa hand and no longer the tiro he had been on the outward journey; most of all his men had their faces towards home and were motivated in a way inconceivable on the way to Ujiji.

Nevertheless, the blistering early pace of the march, through rat-infested Rubuga and Tura, past forests of baobab, had the *wangwana* straggling and complaining.[1] By 20 March, in western Tura, with both rain and fever commencing, his men were begging to be allowed a halt. But Stanley would allow no let-up in his pace. Through the formidable river of Kivala they waded, on through the lotus blossoms of Ziwari and into the dense woods of the Wakumba people. The Wakumba were no military threat and habitually preferred to allow safe passage to caravans that carried firearms. And still the heavy rains beat down.[2]

As they crossed the border between Ukumbu and Ugogo, Stanley was again subjected to the peculiar staring curiosity of the Wagogo when seeing a white man that had so irritated him on the outward trip.[3] The other clear sign of Gogo territory was the gum-tree, which now joined the familiar thorn, tamarisk and mimosa. Ugogo in the rainy season was preferable to the scorched plain of June; now grapes hung thickly in clusters along their path.

At Kiwyeh they heard the booming and bellowing of war horns and braced themselves for an attack. But the din turned out to be the Wagogo sallying forth to do battle with Hehe raiders. The expedition watched rapt as the Gogo tribesmen gathered in the panoply of war: head-dresses of ostrich or eagle feathers, knee-straps and anklet bells, assegais, knob-kerries and shields. Then column after column swung off into the forest, more than 1,000 warriors in all. This was a sobering spectacle: Stanley realised how very little chance even the strongest caravan stood against a sustained assault by such numbers; typically it fuelled in him fantasies of bestriding Africa with 500 European riflemen.[4]

Next day the fantasy of violence came close to reality. At Khonze, remarkable for the mighty globes of foliage which the giant sycamores and baobabs put forth above the plain', some renegade Wanyamwezi who had intermarried with the Wagogo attempted to extort cloth from them by a show of force. Stanley ordered his men to load their guns, then advanced on the leader of the hostiles, seized him by the throat and threatened to blow his head off if he spoke again. He then compelled acceptance of a very light *hongo*.[5]

Light tribute was the surprising outcome of their progress through the much-dreaded Ugogo. At Kamenyi this was due to the fact that the chief had known Burton and Speke but at Mapanga, on 2 April, they had to live through some nail-biting moments. As they traipsed through the forest, they were suddenly accosted by forty yelling spearsmen. Stanley pondered the inevitable losses in a fight between his forty guns and the opposing spears. He decided to negotiate. The leader of the spearsmen asked what they meant by bypassing their village without paying *hongo*. In his best learned-from-Livingstone manner Stanley answered calmly that his caravan was in a great hurry to reach the coast; they did not stop for the simple reason that they were living on the breadline themselves and had nothing to offer.[6] To his great relief, the leader of the spearsmen started to laugh; why, he said, we are in no better position than you, for we were cutting wood when the call to arms came and we are in no mood to fight. To laughter all round a nugatory tribute was agreed. The spearsmen accompanied them part of the way along the trail, while the leader explained that the Wagogo were reasonable people: they did not try to extort blackmail from those who had nothing.[7]

Next the expedition passed Kulabi, penetrated a thorny jungle, then traversed a naked, red-loamy plain. Quenching their thirst on brackish water, they pressed on in the teeth of a storm and came to the territory of Mvumi, last of the Gogo chiefs. On 5 April they plunged into the wilderness and marched nine hours, past herds of rhino, quagga and antelope. With loud hurrahs they said goodbye to Ugogo and pressed on through the rain, which at least gave them plentiful supplies of fresh water.[8]

On the 7th they entered Mpapwa in pelting rain, having come 338 miles in twenty-four days. They looked for the remains of Farquahar, hoping to bury his bones, but could find no trace of them.[9] Next day Stanley noted the spot where his dog Omar had died. He was delighted with the progress they were making, largely attributed to the much lighter loads they, as a homeward-bound caravan, were carrying.

But the real force of the *masika* hit them once they entered the Mukondokwa valley. The rivers were now mighty brown floods, the banks brim-full, the nullahs full of water, the fields inundated. The rain cascaded down, causing a dramatic change in vegetation; this time the trails were covered with tall grass, higher than a man's head, intertwined in tangled heaps and swathes. On 11 April they spent five and a half hours crossing flooded fords before camping on a hill opposite Mount Kibwe at Kadetamare. The local chief was fond of strangers and to show his partiality sent them a 5-gallon jar of the local brew; in return Stanley gave him a generous *doti*.[10]

On 12 April they got to the mouth of the Mukondokwa pass – the gateway to the tableland of the interior – 'after six hours of the weariest march I had ever undergone . . . close to the edge of the foaming angry flood lay our route, dipping down frequently into deep ditches, wherein we found ourselves sometimes up to the waist in water, and sometimes up to the throat. Urgent necessity impelled us onward, lest we might have to camp at one of those villages until the end of the monsoon rains; so we kept on, over marshy bottoms, up to the knees in mire, under jungly tunnels dripping with wet, then into sloughs arm-pit deep. Every channel seemed filled to overflowing, yet down the rain poured, beating the surface of the river into yellowish foam, pelting us until we were almost breathless.'[11]

Stanley noted in passing that Usagara would be the perfect base for a major missionary effort, since it unlocked Central Africa. But most of his time was spent in a literally breathless fight to survive against the fury of wind and rain and the jeopardy of engorged, overflowing rivers. 'This and the following day will long be remembered in the memories of the several members of the expedition for the fatigues and hardships incurred on those marches.'[12] At night they battled with swarms of black, voracious mosquitoes while the rain pelted down unceasingly. By day they were starting to find the rivers unfordable because of the deluge.

A perilous river crossing by a tree bridge on the 13th saw all of Stanley's ruthlessness on display. One of his bearers, Rojab by name, was crossing with the box containing Livingstone's journals and letters when he lost his footing and fell into a hole in mid-river. Miraculously Rojab managed to retain his footing but the risk to the precious box drew from Stanley an angry roar: 'Look out! Drop that box, and I'll shoot you.' It was of a **piece** with the 'little master's' methods that Rojab received no plaudits **for** saving the box; for his fumble he was cautioned never to carry valuable effects again.[13]

To their chagrin this perilous crossing proved to be but a feeder to the main river, which boiled and seethed with wild, white churning waters. They constructed a raft from four trees, but it was immediately swept away in the roaring torrent and vanished into the whirling currents. Greater ingenuity was called for. They tied together a rope 180 feet long, then secured it around Chowpereh's body. Though swept downstream, he managed to reach the other side and lashed the rope to a tree. Then the expedition's members were hoist across the raging river in turn. But it was still too dangerous to risk the precious letter-box. Temporarily baffled, Stanley pitched two camps, one on either side of the river.[14]

In the morning the river was still rising. Stanley cut two slender poles, then tied sticks across them to make a kind of primitive handbarrow on which a box could rest when lashed to it. He figured that two men swimming and holding a rope, with the ends of the poles on their shoulders, should be able to ferry across a 70-pound box. He then chose twelve of the strongest swimmers, fortified them with brandy and divided them into six teams, who relayed the box across the river with ease.[15]

Seven hours' splashing through marshes and bogs brought them to Rehenneko. Stanley then ordered a four-day rest before they pressed on to struggle with the Rudewa and Itronga Rivers. A seven-hour forced march through slush, mud and mire, plagued all the way by gadflies, brought them to the edge of the dreaded Makata swamp. The only factor in their favour now was that the rain had stopped.[16]

The crossing of the Makata was as much a nightmare as Stanley had feared. They began the crossing already exhausted, since clouds of mosquitoes had prevented any sleep before midnight; thereafter they were bitten and plagued so grievously that 'when the horn sounded there was not one dissentient among them'.[17]

Into the Makata they plunged. They were up to their armpits, then up to their knees, then up to their armpits again, wading on tiptoe, supporting the children above the water. Beyond the swamp proper stretched a lake where four overflowing rivers converged. After sloshing through this for 6 miles, they came to the little Makata River, very deep at the centre and rising, with a current running at 10 knots. There was not a spit of dry land anywhere in the middle to rest a single bale of cloth. The tallest men waded into the 50-foot wide stream, half swimming, half treading water, probing and testing to find the shallow spots. Eventually they found a crossable route and waded back into the centre up to their necks to help the shorter and less able across. The crossing took two hours. They had entered the Makata swamp at 5 a.m. and it took them until 3 p.m. to get clear of it.[18]

On 25 April they were outside Simbawenni. The swollen river had rushed on the city with *tsunami*-like ferocity a few days before and swept away the entire front wall of the proud stone city, causing the destruction of fifty houses and great loss of life. Once again Stanley had arrived at the right time, as he acknowledged: 'I consider our delay at Rehenneko to have saved us from much peril if not death. Everything so far associated with this expedition has turned out for the best.'[19]

At Mussoudi too they found that the flooded rivers had acted like a tidal wave and swept away scores of villages with heavy loss of life. All that was left was debris and detritus piled high where there had once been houses. On they pressed through Kisemo and into a jungle, teeming with bird life and also with boa constrictors, some of them between 12 and 15 feet long.[20] The plague of boas continued in the next jungle, beyond Msuwa, full of impenetrable thorn bushes and spear-headed cactus: 'could a bottle full of concentrated miasma be used, what deadly and unknown poison – undiscoverable – would it make. I think it would act quicker than chloroform and more fatal than prussic acid.'[21]

In this dreadful jungle beyond Msuwa all of Tanzania's 114 varieties of snake seemed to have gathered in reptilian convention. There were boas in the trees above their heads and night-adders and cobras on the ground below. Stanley considered that this infernal forest topped the seven plagues of Egypt since, in addition to malaria, suffocation, miasma, stench, thorns under foot, spear cactus catching in clothes and bundles, and knee-deep mud, there were boas, poisonous snakes, scorpions and red ants to contend with.[22]

On 2 May they were at Rosako. Here at last they were within the Zanzibar ambit and Stanley was able to read back copies of the *New York Herald* from which he got his first glimmerings of the hostility his expedition had already engendered. He learned too that the exceptionally rainy season they had trudged through was but an echo of disastrous conditions off the coast, and that the mountains west of Simbawenni had actually protected them from the worst fury of the elements. A great hurricane had all but overwhelmed Zanzibar, destroying virtually every ship in the harbour.[23]

Two days later they crossed the Kingani, which now resembled a sea, in canoes, and on 6 May reached Bagamoyo at sunset. They had covered 525 miles in fifty-two days. It was an outstanding achievement, overshadowed by Stanley's more famous journeys, but in technical rate-per-day terms arguably his most successful ever. If fear of the water often denotes fear of one's own passive tendencies, it is clear enough that this was one psychological disability that Stanley, with his compulsion for continual action, did not suffer from.

While Stanley trudged down a palm-fringed street of mud houses, a red-headed young man in topee and flannels hailed him from one of the better-quality white houses. 'Won't you walk in?' he said. 'What will you have to drink – beer, stout, brandy. By George, I congratulate you on your splendid success!' The young man turned out to be Lieutenant Henn, who had just arrived as part of an expedition (sponsored by the RGS) to relieve Livingstone.[24]

It was the Mirambo war which jolted the RGS out of its previous complacency about Livingstone. It was clear that the road from Ujiji to the coast was blocked and there was a strong possibility that Livingstone's supplies had been destroyed; it was also obvious (or so it seemed) that there was no chance that Stanley, known to be in Unyanyembe, could reach the doctor.[25] In one of its fits of periodic compassionate concern, the British public responded to an appeal for funds with £4,000. The RGS set up an expedition and appointed to its command naval Lieutenant L. S. Dawson, who had recently surveyed the Yangtse and the River Plate.[26] Henn, Stanley's Bagamoyo host, had been named as his second-in-command. The third white member was Oswell Livingstone, aged twenty, the doctor's youngest son. In Zanzibar they also persuaded the Methodist missionary, the Revd Charles New, who had some experience of African exploration (he had recently climbed to the snow-line on Mount Kilimanjaro), to join the expedition. It was a pure fluke that New was in Zanzibar at all, for he had boarded the *Abydos* in Mombasa under the impression it was to sail straight to England.[27] But no sooner had the expedition members crossed to Bagamoyo, on 27 April, than news came in that Stanley had 'found' Livingstone. Dawson at once took the view that there was no longer any point in his project, threw up the command and returned to Zanzibar. Over drinks in Bagamoyo Stanley further persuaded Henn that Livingstone needed no relief expedition, but only the fifty porters he was pledged to obtain for him.[28]

Next day Stanley met Oswell Livingstone and put the same points to him. The young Livingstone dithered, then solved his vacillation by returning to Zanzibar to consult with Kirk. He finally decided to go home when a dispute between Henn and New as to who should now have the command (the older man with experience of Africa or the young naval officer officially designated as second-in-command) led both of them in turn to resign.[29] Stanley felt that young Oswell was wrong. It was right that the now pointless expedition should be wound up, but that was no reason why Oswell should not accompany the porters back to Unyanyembe. Oswell later justified himself by saying that in his delicate state of health (he had a bladder complaint as well as attacks of malaria and dysentery) he could not face the swollen, waterlogged country between the sea and Ugogo. Kirk concurred in this wholeheartedly, but in going home Oswell was giving significant hostages to fortune, as well as valuable ammunition to Stanley in his later propaganda battle with Kirk.[30]

While the fiasco of this RGS expedition was being played out, Stanley crossed to Zanzibar (7 May). He was greeted cordially by consul Webb and congratulated by Tozer and Kirk, as yet not suspecting the storm that was to burst on him. Stanley was startled, on looking into a mirror, to find that his hair was growing grey. He was almost unrecognisable, so much so that when he ran into his old friend Captain H. C. Fraser and greeted him, Fraser replied, 'You have the advantage of me, sir.'[31]

Stanley at once discharged his men and rehired twenty of them for Livingstone's expedition. He parted on bad terms with Bombay: 'Stupid Bombay, though he had more than once expressed his scorn of dirty money was glad to take a present of $50 besides his pay.'[32] Then he assembled fifty-seven men, all of whom were paid $20 in advance, and engaged a young Arab to head the caravan. Oswell Livingstone handed over clothing, provisions, money and fifty carbines from the stocks of the original RGS expedition. Stanley devoted extraordinary care to the choice of the fifty-seven, as on their performance his reputation with Livingstone would ride. He rejected Oswell Livingstone's Mombasa men and all obvious slackers and bounty jumpers; by the time he dispatched his party of sixty-four to Bagamoyo on 27 May he was well satisfied that Livingstone would have no cause for complaint.[33]

By now Kirk had learned of Livingstone's displeasure with him and suspected Stanley of having put the doctor up to it. He had no choice but to forward Livingstone's letters impugning him to London, and (humiliatingly) to hand over the £500 to Stanley, but he swore that he would never do anything for Livingstone again except on a direct order from the Foreign Office. In private Kirk described Livingstone as a 'damned old scoundrel';[34] when told he planned to visit America after finishing his African work, he remarked caustically: 'I am now glad to think it is not likely to be for three years.' When Stanley suggested that Kirk might like to take charge of despatching the caravan for Livingstone, Kirk declined curtly as 'I am not going to expose myself to needless insult again.'[35] Stanley had now laid firm foundations for one of the many bitter enmities of his life. Kirk immediately went over on to the counterattack. If there had been any problem in the arrival of Livingstone's supplies, this was mainly because Stanley's secretiveness about his true aims worked against the doctor's true interests; he also intimated that it was Stanley and Stanley alone who was responsible for the breakup of the Henn/Dawson expedition.[36]

Nor did Stanley make any friends among the other Englishmen in Zanzibar. When he lectured Dawson on duty, Dawson stormed angrily out of the room. Oswell Livingstone was abashed by the lectures he received on filial responsibility. New, too, was irritated by Stanley's treatment of him. While admiring his energy and courage, he soon spotted that he was no angel and found his duplicity particularly trying: Stanley 'blames me for not doing that which he avers it was unnecessary for anyone to do and which he justifies everyone concerned in it for abandoning.'[37]

Having completed the task he had promised to perform, Stanley wrote his last letter to Livingstone from Africa. 'Permit me to wish you joy of your plum pudding. And now, my dear and good friend, I have done to the utmost of my ability what I have promised . . . All I can now, is to wish you the blessing of God, and the beneficent Providence who has watched over you so long.'[38] The fifty-seven men arrived safely at Unyanyembe, and Livingstone later testified that all but one had given the most sterling service.

Stanley now had to reach the telegraph at Suez to learn what Bennett required of him next. He began negotiating with the owner of the steamship *Africa* to take him to the Seychelles to catch the Mauritius mail. The discussions were difficult, for the owner wanted $900 for the charter. Stanley intended to take New, Henn and Oswell Livingstone with him; he had offered Dawson passage, but Dawson was so angry with Stanley that he left on the *Mary Away* for the Cape of Good Hope expressly so as not to have to travel with him.[39] But at last they fixed a price and the four men embarked (29 May).

The *Africa* rolled, pitched and lumbered along at a top speed of 7 knots in a most wearisome way 'but it is better than staying forever at Zanzibar'.[40] They arrived at Port Victoria, Mahe Island in the Seychelles on 7 June, only to find that the French mail had left just twelve hours before. They rented a pleasant villa nicknamed 'Livingstone Lodge' at £30 a month, and there Stanley, New, Oswell Livingstone and a Mr Morgan lived, with Kalulu and Selim as servants, for a month while they waited for a ship (Henn stayed in a hotel).[41]

The month in the Seychelles was an oasis of quiet and reflection for Stanley. He climbed the highest hill behind Port Victoria with Oswell Livingstone and returned exhausted, full of praise for the young man's pluck but puzzled by his excessive taciturnity: 'I cannot make young Livingstone out at all.' In the end Stanley concluded that Livingstone's excessive reserve derived from a deeply rooted suspicion and prejudice inculcated in him by Kirk for Stanley and all his works. Scornfully Stanley recorded how many young men seemed bowled over by Kirk, purely through their immaturity and inexperience. For Stanley, Kirk was a prima donna and a congenital liar and it was at his baneful door that the débâcle of the abortive RGS expedition should be laid.[42]

On 2 July, Stanley, young Livingstone and the others were the guests of the British resident Hales Franklyn. Henn came from his hotel to join them and upstaged the other guests by playing the piano, singing Irish songs and making such a great hit with the ladies that Stanley was jealous: 'He is a star of the first magnitude, and I am naught, for I cannot converse with the fair sex, nor sing a song, nor play on the piano.'[43]

On 4 July a ship came at last. They embarked on the *Danube*, of the Messangeries Maritimes line, bound for Aden. One of their fellow passengers was Bishop Ryan of Mauritius and his curate, who also found young Livingstone silent as a sphinx 'as though he was offended at everybody'.[44] On 10 July they reached Aden, where they were due to transfer to the French mail steamer from China, the *Meikong*. Stanley cabled for confirmation that he was to return to Europe and not go on to China. His cable crossed with one from Hosmer in London that in effect carried its own answer and set the seal on his achievement:

Mr Bennett sends following. You are now famous as Livingstone having discovered the discoverer. Accept my thanks, and whole world. Recruit your health at Aden or elsewhere. Forward by special messenger Livingstone's letters and anything further you may have. Accept in addition assurance fellow correspondent that more splendid achievement, energetic devotion and generous gallantry not in history human endeavour. Hosmer.[45]

Stanley now had the world-wide fame he hungered for, and would shortly have money too from his book on the Livingstone expedition. But what of his status as African explorer? What general judgement can we form on the basis of his first eighteen months as an adventurer and discoverer in Central Africa?

Stanley mastered the intricacies of African travel, the nuances of *hongo*, *doti* and porterage, with remarkable speed. He claimed to have learned all there was to know during the three months' march to Unyanyembe, after which it was simply a question of honing and refining his craft.[46] Part of the judgement may be allowed to stand. Stanley had an extraordinary gift for knowing just how far he could push his *pagazis* and how much he could ask them to carry, before their discontent would boil over into outright mutiny.[47] He also learned that the usefulness of donkeys in Africa was limited, as their loads would catch in the brambles, branches and thorn bushes along the caravan trails.[48]

But Stanley as an explorer can be faulted in two areas: one venial, the other more serious. The trivial fault was a tendency towards hyperbole and journalistic 'expedient exaggeration': for instance, later travellers demonstrated that many of the accounts given in *How I Found Livingstone* were embellishments, since Stanley – located where he said he was – could not have seen the geographical features he purported to be describing as an eyewitness.[49] Along with this went a certain sloppiness: describing a swamp as a 'pond', and so on.[50] Part of this derived from his instincts as a journalist; he realised that too many scholarly qualifications and caveats would bore his readers. But another part came from his own temperament: Stanley was always too impatient, too concerned with achieving the grand effects, to be meticulous over small details.

Yet the inaccuracies in Stanley's travel accounts – and it must be stressed that there are few – had a deeper aetiology: his pathological desire not to share the glory with others, and to mock and disparage the discoveries and achievements of other travellers. Part of the difficulty of the outward journey to Unyanyembe was caused by Stanley's determination not to follow Speke's route but to blaze a trail of his own. Additionally, he was adamant that this achievement should be incontestably his own. So, although Farquahar was a trained navigator, Stanley deliberately did not use his skills. All Stanley did was use a watch and pocket compass to record the direction and duration of the daily march. There was no accurate astronomical plotting; in addition, Stanley's method of 'dead reckoning' was thrown out because he began his march during the rainy season, in a part of Africa where magnetic variation is notoriously high.

At every possible occasion Stanley tried to score off previous explorers, especially Burton and Speke. Some of his shots were wild, as when he claimed that the 'Kazeh' of Burton and Speke's narratives was unknown to the locals, only to be corrected by Verney Cameron who pointed out that Kazeh and Tabora were one and the same.[51] Stanley's animadversions tempted his rivals to go over on to the attack. Stanley made lavish claims for the mineral wealth of Africa: 'underneath the surface but a few feet is one mass of iron ore, extending across three degrees of longitude and nearly four of latitude.'[52] Joseph Thomson, the Scottish explorer and a geologist himself, called this statement 'the unrestrained exercise of fancy'.[53] But sometimes the counterattack went too far. When Stanley said that Lake Ugombo was 3 miles long and 2½ miles wide, Cameron commented that Stanley must have been dreaming.[54] But the truth was that the two men had seen the same thing at different times of the year; seasonal fluctuations transformed the lake almost out of recognition.[55]

Sometimes Stanley's geographical assessments were incorrect simply because at this stage of his African career his knowledge of Swahili was deficient. He simply noted down the phonetic equivalent of what he had heard, so that 'Nsisi' became 'Imbiki' and 'Ngererengeri' became 'Lungerengeri'. Two other associated problems were that many places were named after their current chief or after familiar objects. Stanley says he stopped at 'Mrefu' which means 'tall' or 'long', at 'Mtoni' which means 'river bed' and at 'Misonghi', which means a large, round hut.[56] Another problem about Swahili was secondary meanings. His porters used the word 'Mkali' (hot) to describe the terrain between Ugogo and Tabora, when on his own admission it was not hot on the plateau. The probable explanation is that the *wangwana* were using the word in its secondary meaning of 'unpleasant' or 'difficult' as an anticipatory description of the rigours to come.[57] Again, Stanley thought the local people had simply covered Farquahar's body with leaves, which was why he went to look for the corpse to bury it. But since the Swahili use the same word for 'grass' and 'leaves', what the people of Mpapwa meant was that they had grassed his body over, i.e. buried it.[58] Similarly, Stanley was adamant that 'Unyamwezi' meant 'The Land of the Moon' whereas later scholars favoured 'The Land of the West'.[59] On the other hand, Stanley is not as poor on proper names as some of his more astringent critics make out, and any deficiency in Swahili was something he certainly made up in later years.[60]

By and large, though naturally subject to later corrections, Stanley's geographical observations were surprisingly accurate.[61] When it comes to the peoples Stanley encountered, his anthropological flair is idiosyncratic. Stanley is good on the people who pose, or might pose, a personal threat to him and his expedition, and often made careful notes on the tribes who were friendly to him. But in peoples who posed no military threat, were distant from his line of march, or were known to him only by reputation, Stanley showed little interest.[62] He was impatient with the complexities of tribal politics and, while he appreciated the significance of the Hehe, the Gogo and the Ha, he dismissed the crucial Kimbu peoples in one brief sentence.[63] Nor was he much interested in the complexities of kinship, chieftainship or stratification in African societies.[64] The fact that he was no precisian also helps to explain why Stanley never realised, either on this expedition or any of his subsequent ones, the precarious knife-edge on which most African economies subsisted. Also, the reputation of African warriors tended to be made by their contact with European explorers. Stanley encountered Mirambo in dramatic circumstances, so the fame of Mirambo was placed before a wider audience. The Nyamwezi chief Nyungu, arguably as important as Mirambo, never had the same reputation because he never swam into the ken of the great explorers. In October 1871 Stanley narrowly missed meeting him on the borders of Mangala's Kimbu chiefdom (Iswangala Kamanga).[65]

Yet if he showed no real interest in tribal organisation and politics, Stanley did manifest a genuine feeling for the black man, possibly because chieftains and porters were no threat to his personal prestige. He did not have to put them in their place as possible rivals to his authority or as claimants to new discoveries. Stanley always claimed that his experiences in the *ante-bellum* South were crucial in this regard.[66] He despised the 'Yankee' notion of effortless white superiority over the black race. When consul Webb asked him in Zanzibar if he thought negro teeth had nerves, Stanley was not amused: 'As even then I had extracted about one hundred negro teeth to relieve my poor men from their tortures, my stare at Captain Webb was sufficiently expressive.'[67]

Under Livingstone's influence, too, he began to take a more positive view of Africa and to see it as a potential cornucopia, a further refuge for the 'huddled masses' of the world and a living refutation of Malthusianism. Here we may discern the experience of the West and the frontier as being decisive, rather than the South.[68] The obvious obstacle in the way here was tropical disease: after all, Stanley himself had suffered twenty-three separate attacks on his first journey.[69] No one knew better than Stanley himself the problem of the tsetse fly, even though the connection between insects and fever had not yet been made.[70] It was Dr Donald Ross of the Indian Medical Service who finally showed that the deadly African fever was a virulent form of malaria transmitted, not by climate or 'miasmata', but by the anopheles mosquito. At the same time, Dr Walter Reed proved that yellow fever, another medical scourge, was also mosquito-borne.

Amazingly, even after all Stanley had written, majority opinion, including that of the explorer Thomson, continued to hold that the tsetse fly was unknown between Zanzibar and Ujiji. This conjured visions of the end of *pagazis* and porterage charges and a future of African travel based solely on ox-trekking.[71] This consoling myth was finally exploded in 1878 when Edward Hore forwarded a specimen to Zanzibar and Kirk unhesitatingly identified it as the tsetse fly: 'it is established beyond all doubt that the line of road . . . is swarming with the fly.'[72] Stanley's response might well have been 'I told you so': he was in a good position to know what he was talking about for, aside from his personal experiences, Livingstone and Frank Vardon had encountered the tsetse in 1846–7 along the Limpopo; Vardon had actually brought the first specimen back to England.[73] Later travellers in Tanzania recorded their incredulity that Stanley's assertions on the prevalence of the tsetse could have been doubted; exactly ninety years later a pair of adventurers following in his footsteps encountered a cloud of the insects almost exactly where Stanley had, at Maledita.[74]

Yet it was not just in the general accuracy of his observations that Stanley showed himself to be an ideal African explorer. He was more capable than most men of reclusive self-denying existence. His sole 'vice' was chain-smoking; the familiar picture of Stanley is of a man puffing pensively on cigar or cheroot.[75] He neither drank nor was sexually active. Nor did he sublimate his instincts in big-game hunting – an activity he despised.[76] One of the items in Stanley's repertoire of abuse of Kirk was the consul's taste for hunting: 'When I started from the coast I remember how ardently I pursued the game; how I dived into the tall, well grass, how I lost myself in jungles; how I trudged over the open plains in search of meat and venison. And what did it all amount to? Killing a few inoffensive animals the meat of which was not worth the trouble. And shall I waste my strength and energies in chasing game? No, and the man who would do so at such a crisis as the present is a –'[77]

The hardest part of exploration for some men (and this applies particularly to polar exploration) is the degree of instinctual renunciation it involves. In this respect Stanley's sexual personality was ideal. The alternation of redemption through the suffering of swamp, starvation and disease with the derivation of pleasure from the infliction of cruelty tends to make Stanley's journeys almost a classic story of externalisation. His own deep unconscious guilt meant that he himself could never be to blame for any mistake. He rewarded good work with grudging praise and bad work with the most stinging reproaches. No one reading his treatment of Shaw and Farquahar can doubt the sadistic impulse; the savage beatings administered to Selim and Bombay even while in the throes of sickness warrant the description 'lustful pleasure'.[78] His habit – which was to recur in later expeditions – of leaving behind wounded or sick companions without taking proper thought for their safety goes beyond conventional ruthlessness. It must not be forgotten that all five white men who accompanied Stanley on his first two expeditions perished in the depths of Africa.

It has been speculated that Stanley obliterated all mention of his own sexuality in his published accounts of his travels as this would draw attention to the sadistic impulses of which he was himself dimly aware.[79] But there is no mention of sex even in his private diaries, except routine denunciations of men like Shaw who, in Stanley's view, sacrificed their own well-being to the cravings of the flesh.[80] Coupled with the cruel treatment of his companions and servants, the apparent absence of sexuality is itself circumstantial evidence for the fundamental personal ambiguity (at the sexual level, sado-masochistic) that we have postulated.

Other pointers are provided by Stanley himself. The fear of real human intimacy, as opposed to an idealised fantasy version, is everywhere apparent in his life and writings. On his expeditions Stanley habitually dined alone and slept alone in his tent. He had no sense of humour about himself and was hypersensitive to criticism. He expected people to dislike him and felt that every man's hand was turned against him: 'I make enemies every day of my life,' he observed.[81] He was obsessed with the notion that his mediocre contemporaries sensed his greatness and conspired against him to topple him, out of the hatred felt by the nonentity for the man of genius. Exploration, notionally a means to an end, became an end in itself. 'I have had no friend on any expedition, no one who could possibly be my companion, on an equal footing, except while with Livingstone . . . though altogether solitary, I was never less conscious of solitude . . . my only comfort was my work. To it I ever turned as a friend. It occupied my days and I dwelt fondly on it at night.'[82] Such was the man who directed his steps towards Europe in July 1872.

11

ON 11 July the steamer *Meikong* arrived from China and Stanley and party embarked. At Suez he received orders to send on Livingstone's two letters for the *Herald*, ahead of his other despatches, so that Bennett could make the greatest possible éclat. The plan was for the letters to be copied in London, then posted to New York. Stanley was to come on slowly, so as to arrive in London fifteen days after receipt of the Livingstone letters. The timing was contrived so that Stanley would arrive in London just when the *Herald*'s news burst on the world.[1]

This placed Stanley in a dilemma, between his moral master and his material one. He could not disobey Bennett, yet he had given his word to Livingstone that no more than forty-eight hours would elapse between publication of the doctor's 'open letters' and the despatch of private correspondence to his family. To this end he had already booked passage to Marseilles.

At Port Said Stanley dismissed Selim with £33 severance pay after two and a half years' service, plus £2 passage money for the journey from Port Said to Jerusalem.[2] Then he continued with Kalulu to Marseilles. The *Meikong* passed Stanley's old stamping grounds in Crete, then threaded its way up the Mediterranean past Messina, Rhegium, Sardinia and Corsica.[3] They docked at midnight on the 23rd, and Stanley at once went in search of the London bureau chief George Hosmer, who had travelled to the south of France to meet him. At 2 a.m. he found him at his hotel, already asleep. Bleary-eyed, Hosmer staggered from his bed and roused the correspondent of the *Daily Telegraph* who was sharing a room with him. They obtained the best wine available at such an hour and sat up till morning toasting Stanley's success.[4] Hosmer informed him that, owing to the special nature of his commitment to Livingstone, Bennett had decided to honour it, even though the cost of sending the despatches to New York by cable would be £2,000. This meant there was no longer any special reason for delay, since the *Herald* would now release its scoop in London on the same day as the reports appeared in the newspaper in New York.[5]

Stanley spent the 25th and 26th buying appropriate clothes for his appearance in Paris, as he was still dressed in his rather shoddy Zanzibar outfit. Then on the 27th he and Kalulu took the train to Paris. When the express sped into a tunnel, Kalulu immediately crawled under a seat in terror, thinking that in the white man's country darkness fell instantaneously. When the train emerged into the daylight, Stanley persuaded the boy to come out, and Kalulu was just starting to regain his composure when the locomotive again roared into a tunnel. Kalulu gradually got used to this and lost his fear, but he remained disconcerted by the cacophonous whistling of passing trains and the 'flying countryside'. But by Lyons he was reasonably adjusted, and when they descended from the train to dine, Kalulu acquitted himself well with a knife and fork, his only mistake being to take an overdose of mustard so that his eyes watered. Stanley tried to remedy this with ice-cream, but Kalulu found this too cold and wanted to spit it out. Out of deference to the 'little master' he swallowed it. A warmhearted French matron sitting opposite described the boy as a '*pauvre ange*'.[6]

Paris, reached on the 28th, was a whirl of congratulatory luncheons and dinners. The day before, the first of Livingstone's letters to Bennett had been printed in the London *Times* and the *Telegraph*, and the scale of Stanley's achievement was starting to dawn on the popular imagination. The Americans in Paris particularly lionised Stanley and he was taken under the wing of US Minister Washburne, who invited him to breakfast with General Sherman. Sherman magnanimously rated Stanley's journey above his own march to the sea. Stanley repaid the compliment by asking Sherman if he had ever met him before. Sherman shook his head. Stanley then rattled off large chunks of the speech Sherman had delivered to the Sioux at the North Platte Conference in 1867, to Sherman's considerable astonishment.[7]

On 29 July Stanley was at a banquet with eighty luminaries of Paris society. On the 30th he handed over Livingstone's Foreign Office despatches to the British Embassy; the somewhat frosty reception alerted him to a general British resentment that an 'American' had tracked Livingstone down. Perhaps in response to this, Stanley rather let his mouth run away with him, for he received a curt two-word message from Bennett: 'Stop Talking' – for Bennett, Stanley was in danger of playing his best cards too soon.[8] It was hard for Stanley to remain silent, for his suite at the Hotel du Helder was thronged with callers. This was not to his taste. As he recalled wearily on the 29th: 'Already I have heard enough to make me wish that Bennett had not chosen me to seek Livingstone. I get no pleasure at all in these crowds of curious callers or in their grossly worded congratulations. I have a presentiment also that with this sudden fame that has come to me, the annoyances will be quite as great as any pleasure and profit that may be derived from it.'[9]

His conviction that he was destined to make enemies every day of his life was borne out by a trivial incident at the hotel. Stanley was entertaining two guests when a card was sent in from the Reuters man, Edward Viruard, who had saved his life in 1868 when swimming in Egypt. Stanley sent word for Viruard to wait five minutes, but Viruard chose to take this as an insult and stormed off: 'He is too full of himself now to think of early friends.'[10] The bitterness over this 'rebuff' was eventually to lead to Viruard to attempt blackmail on the man he had rescued.

But Stanley was often his own worst enemy. This was underlined on 31 July when Washburne and the American colony gave a farewell banquet for him at the Hotel Chatham. Nearly a hundred guests were present in the new dining-room of the hotel which had been specially refurbished for the occasion. It was a hot night, the hotel windows were thrown open, and a throng of onlookers in the courtyard beyond gazed in at the proceedings. Overcome by the occasion, Stanley allowed himself to launch into a violent attack on Kirk.[11] It was particularly unwise to use an American venue for such a verbal mauling, for Kirk's powerful friends in London could now sally forth to his defence under the banner of patriotism and anti-Americanism, and there is no doubt that Stanley's performance that night further hardened opinion in England against him.

Stanley crossed over to England on the first day of August in sombre mood. The only thing that cheered him about Paris was Kalulu's sensational social success, particularly among Parisian women. A contemporary described the success as follows: 'Kalulu never allows his admiration to overstep his patriotism. His native Chambezi is ever to him the finest of rivers, and his description of its beauties and amenities represent it to be vastly more civilised than the most advanced districts of England. Since his introduction to French society his mental powers have been rather taxed but so far he has proved equal to the occasion. His first taste of wine, combined with the excitement of travelling by express, made him a decidedly hilarious companion.'[12]

After the disastrous and embarrassing meeting at Dover with his uncle Moses Parry and his step-brother Robert, Stanley travelled up to London and ensconced himself in the Langham Hotel. To his mortification he found himself in a hornets' nest of controversy. Many London newspapers doubted his claim to have found Livingstone. Others queried or belittled the achievement. Stanley found himself the focus of a three-headed beast of resentment. There was jealousy that an American newspaper correspondent had upstaged and humiliated the RGS Livingstone Relief Expedition. There was disbelief in his story because it emanated from 'that detestable newspaper'. There was animus from the English establishment because of his attacks on Kirk in Paris.

When it was first known that there was a possibility that Stanley might meet Livingstone in Central Africa, the attitude of the Royal Geographical Society was positive.[13] The explorer James Grant, who had known Stanley in Abyssinia, had great faith in his ability to succeed.[14] But the RGS line changed when its own expedition floundered into fiasco and especially when Dawson made his official report to the Society: 'Though I do not begrudge Mr Stanley his well-earned success, it would be distasteful to me, if not to both of us, to travel in company . . . I cannot but feel pain that he [Livingstone] should have adopted the course of forwarding his documents and correspondence through an American agent, and jealously avoided making known what his recent discoveries may have been to his former friend and fellow-traveller Dr Kirk.'[15]

The response of the RGS was twofold. While Grant continued to foster the idea that Stanley had not in fact met Livingstone at all, Sir Henry Rawlinson systematically attempted to belittle the achievement. Grant's line was that the abandonment of the RGS expedition by Dawson and Oswell Livingstone was a bad mistake, since there was no proof that Stanley had found Livingstone.[16] Rawlinson went much further. He coupled sarcasm at the *Herald*'s expense ('our transatlantic cousins, among whom the science of advertising has reached a far higher stage of development than in this benighted country') with a clear attempt to demean Stanley: 'There is one point on which a little *éclaircissement* is desirable, because a belief seems to prevail that Mr Stanley has discovered and relieved Dr Livingstone; whereas, without any disparagement to Mr Stanley's energy, activity, and loyalty, if there has been any discovery and relief it is Dr Livingstone who had discovered and relieved Mr Stanley. Dr Livingstone, indeed, is in clover while Mr Stanley is nearly destitute . . . It is only proper that the relative position of the parties should be correctly stated.'[17]

Such leads from Sir Henry Rawlinson and other RGS luminaries encouraged the worst excesses of the English press. When Stanley arrived at the Langham Hotel at the beginning of August, he found himself the butt of a sustained attack in the *Standard*, the gist of which was that he was a forger and a charlatan. After condescendingly declaring that Stanley's claims would have to be sifted by 'experts in African discovery' (to which Stanley in his diary rightly appended 'sic'), the *Standard* proceeded to cast doubt on the American's account of his adventure on a number of grounds. Why did Livingstone not return with Stanley? Why did the doctor not communicate with anyone other than the *New York Herald*? Why had Livingstone not been relieved for four years and what had Kirk been doing all this time? Why had the RGS expedition turned back? Surely it was obvious that the letters purporting to be from Livingstone had been written by Stanley himself. They were not written in the true Livingstone style. How could Livingstone have such an extensive knowledge of American literature? And would he really have dilated on the feminine charms of the Manyema women? No, for any thinking man, Stanley's imposture was palpable.[18]

These kinds of taunts were widespread in the London press. The *Echo* suggested ironically that perhaps Livingstone's letters to the *Herald* had been written by mediumistic means. Stanley dealt with the insinuations decisively. He appealed both to the Livingstone family and to Lord Granville, the recipient of some of Livingstone's most important private letters.[19] Granville consulted with Lord Lyons, the British ambassador in Paris to whom Stanley had delivered Livingstone's Foreign Office despatches, and with his other officials, then wrote an authoritative letter to say that no serious doubt could be entertained as to the authenticity of the letters. On 2 August Stanley met Tom Livingstone and handed over the doctor's private journals. Tom, who was much more like his father than Oswell, quickly perused the diaries then wrote a letter stating that the journals were 'his father's and no other's'.[20] Corroboration from these two sources dealt the *coup de grâce* to the theory of Stanley as charlatan/forger.

But by now the third wave in the Stanley controversy was washing in to England, as Livingstone's letters revealed the depth of his bitterness towards Kirk and Kirk in turn mounted a counterattack. Livingstone's letter to Sir Roderick Murchison (the president of the RGS who died in 1871) was particularly incisive. He contrasted the 'lazy' Kirk with Stanley 'the good Samaritan' and the altruism of the American with Kirk's desire for salary and status as consul – particularly reprehensible since Livingstone had 'made' Kirk. Kirk had pleaded that the Mirambo war prevented supplies from getting through to Ujiji; how then had Stanley managed it? Moreover, while Stanley exhilarated the doctor by promising to obtain fifty fresh porters at Zanzibar, all Kirk could suggest was that Livingstone should go home, as he was a tired old man, and let someone else finish his work.[21]

In reply Kirk wrote to Lord Granville to point out that he had no such sum as the £500 Stanley pestered him for in Livingstone's name, that Stanley had wrecked the RGS expedition by insisting that Livingstone would receive relief only from Stanley himself, that he deeply resented Livingstone's 'grossly unjust and ungrateful' behaviour: 'I shall here add, as otherwise my conduct may be misrepresented, that Mr Stanley, in order to evade blame, if his men did not reach Unyanyembe in time, applied to me to see them started off after his departure from Zanzibar: this was positively and at once declined, and I informed him that I could not, after what Dr Livingstone had done and said, act in any but an official capacity.'[22]

The dispute rumbled on and has never been wholly satisfactorily resolved to this day. Livingstone made partial amends to Kirk by telling Lord Granville that he regretted that Kirk should have taken the attack on Sherif as an attack on himself; he explained both to Granville and to Kirk that the nub of his complaint against Kirk was that he had allowed himself to be bamboozled into sending out slaves instead of free men.[23] Kirk was later exonerated in an official enquiry by Sir Bartle Frere which, however, strikes one as distinctly unsolomonic in its judgement. After conceding that Livingstone's complaints were justified, and allowing that Stanley's efforts had alone saved him from destitution, Bartle Frere concluded that Kirk was not to blame for the failure of Livingstone's supplies to arrive.[24] This most unsyllogistic conclusion was not helped by the admission that 'Mr Stanley's own convoy would have failed to reach Ujiji but for his presence with it' for it was precisely the contrast between Stanley's energy and Kirk's fecklessness that Livingstone had been labouring. Nevertheless, many later historians have been content to accept Bartle Frere as the last word on this affair, even though there are many issues in the anti-Kirk indictment it fails to answer or even to address.[25] The fact that Stanley's methods were brutal, that he was an habitual liar, that he undoubtedly influenced Livingstone against Kirk, should not seduce us into the unwarranted conclusion that Kirk was beyond reproach.

The Kirk affair was also the proximate cause of Stanley's meeting with Livingstone's old associate Horace Waller. All Livingstone's letters to Waller were full of extravagant praise of Stanley; more worryingly for Waller, they contained many acerbic asides on Kirk, whom Waller worshipped as a 'man of Africa' second only to Livingstone himself.[26] Waller was determined not to like Stanley, and on his visit to him at the Langham Hotel he found ample ammunition for his dislike. Waller was

Henry M. Stanley aged twenty

Stanley relaxing on the downs above Brighton, August 1872, just before
doing battle at the British Association meeting

Stanley in 1874, at the time of the 'romance' with Alice Pike

Stanley with his gun-bearer and servant Kalulu

Stanley's party on the lower Congo, 1877

The earliest known photograph of Mutesa, kabaka of Buganda

Stanley entering Bagamoyo, May 1872, with Selim and Kalulu

'Image-making'. A formal pose with Kalulu, London, 1872

James Gordon Bennett, proprietor of the *New York Herald*

Livingstone in 1864, on his last visit home

'Dr Livingstone, I presume'

Livingstone and Stanley going from Ujiji to Rusizi River. From a sketch by Stanley

Stanley's 1874 expedition. 'The travelling procession interrupted'

Stanley and his men at Zanzibar after tracing the course of the Congo, 1877

Through the Makata swamp

Mount Kiboué and the Mkondokwa Valley

Hauling canoes up Inkisi Falls. From a sketch by Stanley

The village of Manyema. From a sketch by Stanley

Stanley with admirers in Paris, January 1878

one of those Englishmen who had an exaggerated respect for the small change of social etiquette. When Stanley wrote to him from Paris to introduce himself, he protested that if he could have foreseen the enmity he would incur for going to find Livingstone, he would have thought twice about the assignment. Waller conveyed his reactions to Livingstone: 'Well, this was pretty strong from a man I had never written to, spoken to, and knew as little of as I did of Adam.'[27]

Stanley for his part had good reason for coolness to Waller. Waller it was who had boasted that Stanley would fail in his quest for Livingstone since 'only the steel head of an Englishman could penetrate Africa'.[28] Since reports of Stanley's denunciation of Kirk at the Paris banquet were now appearing in the English press, the omens for a successful encounter at the Langham Hotel were not propitious.

The meeting took place on Saturday 3 August. Stanley began by trying to wrongfoot Waller. He said it was a pity that Waller had not made an appointment. Waller replied that he had announced his intention to call on him in a letter he had sent to the Hotel du Helder in Paris. Stanley retorted that he had received no such letter. But a little later Stanley quoted a phrase from one of Waller's recent letters to *The Times*. This was a bad slip: Waller had written no letters to *The Times* and the phrase in question came from the letter to Stanley that he claimed he had not received. Waller moved in for the verbal kill. He pointed out that the quotation Stanley had used could only have come from Waller's letter to him. Instead of being taken aback at such exposure, Stanley simply shifted his cigar to the other side of his mouth and changed the subject abruptly.[29]

Waller came away from the meeting shaken. Stanley had brushed aside his convoluted explanation about how he came to use the 'steel head' expression. When Waller taxed him with having called Kirk a traitor, Stanley simply denied that he had used that word. Waller sat down to try to discredit Stanley with Livingstone. He referred to his 'pretty strong' reputation in Abyssinia, narrated the 'barefaced lie' in which he had caught Stanley out and added: 'I confess, doctor, I did feel very sorry for you and very sorry for Kirk.' But he rather spoiled his defence of Kirk by suggesting that a Livingstone/Kirk imbroglio was an affront to Christianity and that the rift between them could have been compassed only by the powers of darkness. It was unlikely that Livingstone would ever see the man who had saved his life in that light. Waller compounded his tactlessness by hinting that the balance of Livingstone's mind might have been disturbed when he made his accusations against Kirk.[30] But he did at least have the grace, in advance of Lord Granville and Tom

Livingstone's pronouncements, to scout as absurd any suggestion that Stanley had forged the letters from Livingstone.[31]

The destruction of the absurd canard that Stanley was a charlatan led many doors to open. The most significant was an invitation to read a paper at the Brighton meeting of the British Association on 17 August. There were also letters of congratulation from Agnes Livingstone and invitations to stay in aristocratic houses.[32] Stanley's immediate problem was to find a publisher for his projected book on Livingstone. The doctor had given him the name of the prestigious house of John Murray, but Murray's irritated Stanley by not giving him an immediate reply. Harper's of New York made an early offer of 10 per cent on retail prices, but Stanley decided to accept the bid from Sampson and Low that guaranteed him 50 per cent of the profits with a £1,000 advance payment. The New York firm of Scribner and Low offered a further £1,000 for American rights, on condition that they shared illustration costs with Low's.[33]

But as Stanley sat down to work on the book, he was disconcerted to find the rhythm of work vitiated by two things. One was the receipt of a letter from John Camden Hotten, recently a plagiariser of Mark Twain, which informed him that he would be working on a rival book on the 'finding of Livingstone' which he promised would not cover the same ground. Stanley was coldly angry: 'This man's consummate impudence is too astounding. Out of jail I did not suppose such men could exist.'[34] The other, even more unsettling, barrier to uninterrupted writing was a spate of anonymous and begging letters and requests from his family for financial hand-outs.

A diary entry for 6 August illustrates the problem. 'My stepfather has now called on me at the Langham Hotel. I discover a disposition among the members of my father's family to indicate to me very plainly that having acquired this wearying newspaper fame, I must pay in cash handsomely to all and every member.'[35] Again on 12 August: 'I have not only numerous public enemies but many venomous private enemies – whose bitter hate is excited because I will not satisfy their greed for gold. I lent £100 to mother and £15 to sister Emma and £10 to a cousin – but I seem to have a host of half brothers, cousins in Wales and Liverpool, uncles and aunts and a stepfather who have itching palms. There also seems to be an universal demand from Wales that I should discover myself freely to all the world – probably that Welshmen may share in the newspaper glory that surrounds me . . . I really do not know to what length my greedy stepfather will drive his wife. I offered to settle on her £50 as long as she lived, but she laughed at it and asked for double, which would mean a capital of £3,300 or thereabouts in the three per cent – which I have not got and which will take me perhaps a couple of years more to scrape together – and there are constant demands of me besides.'[36]

But it was not just his family that tried to apply the bite. The anonymous letters were wounding but could be ignored – 'You detestable Welsh Yankee – what right had you to put your finger in our English pie.'[37] The begging letters were more troublesome for, if ignored, they tended to graduate to blackmailing screeds: 'Ten guineas this day or look out for tomorrow's papers!' All kinds of people claimed kinship and hence financial assistance. The more subtle tried to elicit compassion. The most ingenious claimed a direct blood link. Nine separate women claimed to have been separated from their sons at an early age and were sure that Stanley was the lost child. Some of these women dogged his steps for years. On one occasion he had to call the police and on another the hotel staff had to eject a number of simultaneous competitors 'so fierce were they for my embraces'.[38]

Apart from the Livingstone book and the plague of letter writers, Stanley had to prepare himself for the Brighton meeting. He suspected that the RGS was trying to discredit him with the press while being polite to his face, and that the public squabble between the Society secretary Clements Markham and the members of the failed Livingstone relief expedition (Dawson, Henn, Oswell Livingstone) was a Trojan horse to disguise the RGS's insidious campaign against their real target.[39] Rawlinson's excuse for why no one from the Society had met him when he arrived in London was lameness itself: 'I regret that you should have arrived in London at a time when all who would have been most desirous to welcome you had already left town or were on the point of doing so.'[40] More suggestive, and more sinister, were the reports appearing in the newspapers that the RGS intended to 'pulverise' Stanley when he spoke at Brighton.

Stanley travelled down to the coast on 14 August as the special guest of Dr Burrowes, Mayor of Brighton. It was on Friday 16 August at 11 a.m. that he made his appearance before the Geographical Section of the British Association. Nearly 3,000 people packed into the concert room in Middle Street to hear his address. The 200-foot long hall, and the gallery that ran round its sides, were thronged with people. A row of VIP chairs at the front facing the stage (on which was hung a map of Africa) was festooned with scarlet cushions. Among the celebrities present was the exiled Emperor Louis Napoleon, the Empress Eugénie and the Prince Imperial, Stanley's patron Baroness Burdett-Coutts, the Bishop of Chichester and several Members of Parliament.[41]

The official title of Stanley's address was 'Discoveries at the North End of Lake Tanganyika' but Stanley was encouraged to give a general account of his travels to find Livingstone. The idea was that this part of the meeting would be followed by questions, there would then be readings from Livingstone's letters and a geographical critique from Colonel Grant. The start of Stanley's speech was unpromising. Stage fright led him to make three false starts, and when he finally got into gear, the tone was not quite what the august gathering of scientists and geographers had expected. 'I consider myself in the light of a troubadour, to relate to you the tale of an old man who is tramping onward to discover the source of the Nile.'[42]

Stanley then continued in the journalistic vein he was to make so familiar with the later publication of *How I Found Livingstone*. After a concise survey of his African journey and meeting with Livingstone he referred to the criticism that had been made of him in the press, by jealous foreigners and even by the RGS itself, and declared himself open for questions. Stung by the criticisms of the RGS, the president of the Geographical Section, Francis Galton, then arose to remind the audience rather tartly that they were gathered to assess new geographical discoveries in a spirit of dispassionate scientific enquiry and not to listen to sensational stories.[43] This, naturally, angered Stanley and he decided to return contempt for contempt. When Galton, in a spirit of 'scientific enquiry', asked whether the waters of Lake Tanganyika were sweet or brackish, Stanley burlesqued the childish (and hence, by implication, insulting) question by replying that he could not hope to find nicer or sweeter water in the world with which to make a cup of tea.[44]

This drew ripples of laughter from the audience. Much encouraged, Stanley set about his other critics. The Germans were simply jealous: 'I never yet heard of an Englishman who had discovered anything, but a Herr of some sort came forward and said that he had been there before.'[45] This worked on the strong element of anti-German prejudice in the audience (especially with Napoleon III present) and provoked loud guffaws. William Cotton Oswell, the big-game hunter and Livingstone's first collaborator, got to his feet to say that whereas Livingstone was the true old African lion, the gentleman on the platform was the real true young African lion.[46]

Stanley sat down, well satisfied. Then the RGS launched its counter-attack. Grant and Dr Beke criticised Livingstone strongly for identifying the Lualaba as a feeder for the Nile. Rawlinson pretended that there had never been any Society jealousy of Stanley. Worst of all, Galton asked Stanley if he would be willing to clear up the many speculations in the press about his nationality and origins. Incensed as much by the humbug of the RGS as by the attacks on his mentor and burning with indignation that his humble origins might soon be on display for the world to see, Stanley sprang to his feet and hit back angrily. He accused Rawlinson of drawing maps of Africa to suit his own prejudices then rounded on the 'experts'.

> Colonel Grant says that Dr Livingstone has made a mistake about the river Lualaba, but I want to know how a geographer resident in England can say there is no such river when Dr Livingstone has seen it? Dr Beke, living in London, and never having been within two thousand miles of the spot, declares positively that Livingstone has not discovered the source of the Nile, whereas Livingstone who has devoted thirty-five years to Africa only says he *thinks* he has discovered it. I think if a man goes there and says 'I have seen the source of the river', the man sitting in his easy chair or lying in bed cannot dispute this fact on any grounds of theory.[47]

Galton sensed that the meeting was getting out of hand and that a major scandal might be brewing. In some haste he closed the meeting but not before allowing himself the last word in his concluding remarks when he said with some asperity that a man in London might well have access to more information from books and maps than an explorer on the spot. Somewhat perfunctorily he proposed a formal resolution of thanks which was carried to loud cheers.[48]

Stanley was assured on all sides that he had scored a triumph but he was nettled by the snide insinuations of the RGS, angry that they had doubted the word of his mentor Livingstone and, most of all, he smarted under the humiliation of Galton's queries about his origins. He was in raw and vulnerable mood the following evening at a banquet held in his honour at the Royal Pavilion by the Sussex Medical Society.[49] When called upon to reply to the toast, he began to speak of his admiration for Dr Livingstone. After so many years away from polite society, and used to haranguing recalcitrant tribesmen in a histrionic style with much arm-waving and body language, Stanley forgot the necessity to underplay to an upper-class English audience. In addition his physical appearance was unprepossessing and he seemed ill at ease in evening dress. The combination made Stanley appear a somewhat ridiculous figure to the assembled surgeons. As he rehearsed a dramatic confrontation with the Ha, one of the doctors burst out laughing. Stanley immediately unstoppered the magma of his wrath. The violence of his pent-up rage was breathtaking. Bitterly he lashed his audience. He was sick and tired of all the sneers and insults, the canards and innuendoes. If the English excuse was that they were not used to American ways, this was a singularly inappropriate argument for professional men to use. Did they ask a man's origins before they operated on him? Come to that, had Livingstone asked his nationality before welcoming him? No, enough was enough. To general astonishment, Stanley made a stiff bow and walked out of the room.[50]

It was only with great difficulty that the Mayor of Brighton persuaded Stanley to stay on to the end of the scheduled week of activities so that he could attend the formal civic reception.[51] The RGS tried to play down the consequences of their own boorishness. Grant wrote on 21 August: 'What sensations they have had at Brighton in the Geographical Section! and to wind up with Mr Stanley showing that he has a very thin skin. I am very sorry for the occurrence, though it is very laughable for, after his daring achievement, he need have feared no silly laugh from an ignorant listener. It is to be hoped that the newspaper report is exaggerated.'[52]

The bruising experience at Brighton caused Stanley much private anguish, but publicly he retaliated by raising the temperature in his propaganda battle with the RGS. An obvious pretext was the new expedition being formed to succour Livingstone and the inevitable reflections this prompted on the failure of the earlier one. Stanley's technique was to insinuate that the RGS had chosen the previous expedition's personnel with insufficient care and that the expedition itself had ultimately been scuttled by Kirk.[53] But his sniping backfired when he used the injudicious word 'daunted' to describe Henn's reaction to the area between Bagamoyo and the River Kingani. To avoid a libel action, on the ground that he had accused Henn of cowardice, Stanley was forced to backtrack hastily and publicly.[54]

But he exercised no such restraint in going for the throats of the RGS grandees. In a letter to the *Daily Telegraph* he took on all his tormentors at once.

Let it be understood that I resent all manner of impertinence, brutal horse-laughs at the mention of Livingstone's name, or of his sufferings ... all statements that I am not what I claim to be – an American; all gratuitous remarks such as 'sensationalism', as directed at me by that suave gentleman Mr Francis Galton ... [Grant] chose to deliver himself of his unwise theories respecting Livingstone's discoveries ... though Sir Henry Rawlinson is great in cuneiform inscriptions and Assyrian history, his ideas respecting Central African rivers and watersheds are wild, absurd and childish, to use the mildest terms.[55]

Stanley's worst fear was that his origins and parentage would be exposed. When he went out to Africa he thought that Livingstone would be the only source of interest to the public but now he found to his horror that he was an equal source of interest to the public – which interest, however, he refused to indulge 'for I am sure that it was not to discover myself that Mr Gordon Bennett commissioned me to go to Africa, but to find Livingstone.'[56]

Stanley was particularly enraged at the determined efforts of the Welsh to claim him as one of their own. 'Wherever I go, I find one or two more Welshmen who are determined to let the public know that I am a compatriot. Some of them claim the privilege of old friends, force an entrance into the anterooms of the lecture halls, and bawl out in long-forgotten Welsh a strange greeting. Then, perceiving me to be rather surprised at their barbarism, they slink away angered, protesting against what they call my pride.'

Stanley found that Welshmen could not forgive him for not proclaiming his origins from the rooftops, even though there was an unbridgeable chasm between him and all things to do with Wales, and not just in the mundane consideration that ninety per cent of the people he met abroad were superior in most things to the Welsh. They were also more congenial, 'were it only for the reason that they assisted me to banish from my mind the unpleasant recollections of boyhood – that sordid life that appears to me like a nightmare ... there is no danger that I shall ever forget my parentless and abject condition in Wales, but I do not see the use of permitting myself to be branded with the hideous stigma.' He and the Welsh were poles apart: 'They cannot understand why I should not be proud of the little parish world of North Wales, and I cannot understand what they see to admire in it.'[57]

To throw his pursuers off the scent, Stanley deliberately obfuscated his origins. He would mix a little truth with a lot of falsehood, or a lot of truth with a little falsehood, depending on his audience. One constant in his stories was that he was a native Missourian.[58] Thereafter he varied the ingredients. The usual story was that he had been born in 1843 and had run away from Missouri to his early seafaring life.[59] However, sometimes he claimed that the year of his birth was 1844 and that he had enlisted in the Civil War in 1862 at the age of eighteen.[60] With amazing lack of concern for coherence he would at other times claim that he was eighteen in 1857 and had fought in the Indian Mutiny![61] But it has to be remembered that Stanley's main aim was to mystify and confuse, not to present a coherent story. He was fortunate, for in this period only relatively minor newspapers printed accounts of his origins that came close to the truth.[62]

That his childhood and early life were Stanley's Achilles heel was quickly recognised by his bitterest enemies in the RGS. Sir Henry Rawlinson and, to a lesser extent, Grant were coming to feel that the continued wrangling with Stanley was serving merely to lower the Society in public esteem, but the hardliners, Clements Markham, Galton and W. Carpenter, were bent on a conspiracy to reveal the truth about Stanley's shame and illegitimacy to the world.[63] Angered by the *Daily Telegraph* letter impugning the RGS, Markham took up the gauntlet on the Society's behalf and tried to put the upstart in his place. Some of the anger and dislike is evident in a letter Markham wrote to Stanley on 4 September, rejecting his claim to be a suitable recipient of the RGS gold medal on the ground that his geographical observations were not scientifically arrived at.[64]

The way this correspondence developed is highly revealing of the public and private face of both men. Stanley retorted to Markham's patronising epistle by reiterating that he should have the medal, since Livingstone had promised him that such would be his reward; furthermore, he on his side would withdraw his uncomplimentary remarks about the RGS only when Galton apologised for 'sensational' and for doubting his nationality. He then proceeded with a spirited defence on his observations.[65] Markham replied emolliently if patronisingly: 'I am very glad you have done such good work by dead reckoning (as we call it at sea) ... next to actual observation dead reckoning is most valuable. I will also give you full credit respecting the map. I really mentioned that you were not a fractional observer with a view to explaining the reason, if the medal was not awarded to you and with no ill-natured intention whatever.'[66]

But in private Markham fumed that Stanley was a blackguard, attempting to browbeat and blackmail the Society by using the magic aura of Livingstone's name. Stanley on his side was so angry with the initial supercilious letter that he leaked it to the *Daily News*, together with a running commentary mocking Markham's remarks. Then, in a wonderfully insolent touch, Stanley wrote to Markham denying that he was the source of the leak and urging him not to publish their correspondence. Markham bridled and ended a curt reply testily: 'I must remind you that when you write to honourable men and mark your letter private, it is quite unnecessary to urge them not to publish it as retaliation.'[67]

Since Galton refused to apologise, Stanley renewed his attacks on him.[68] But already the tide in the battle between Stanley and the RGS was turning in the former's favour. There were two main factors in this: the press backed the 'intrepid explorer' against the stuffy establishment; and Stanley received the irresistible accolade of Queen Victoria.

The volte-face in the press was largely the result of a brilliant campaign conducted by Bennett and the *Herald*. Gambling that Stanley would ultimately be successful in his quest for Livingstone, Gordon Bennett lashed the *Herald* into its worst frenzies of anti-British sentiment. First, it disingenuously claimed to know nothing of the Stanley expedition, and quoted Kirk's reports from Zanzibar as if they were red-hot news.[69] When finally flushed into the open, the *Herald* claimed that its objective in sending Stanley was not a scoop but the promotion of civilisation, science and humanity and the enhancement of the prestige of the 'fourth estate'.[70] It subtly advanced the notion – which was swallowed whole by Living-stone himself – that in sending Stanley to Central Africa it had more interest in the doctor's welfare than the British government itself.[71] Further to obfuscate his cunning purposes, Bennett sent out another 'special', Alvan S. Southworth, to 'find' Samuel Baker in the Sudan. Southworth's jingoistic Yankee sentiments were almost the mirror image of Waller's 'steel head of an Englishman' comments.[72] It has to be conceded, too, that this kind of twisting of the lion's tail played a part in the RGS's anti-Americanism in August 1872.

The initial scepticism in England about whether Stanley had actually met Livingstone in Africa further played into Bennett's hands, in an era when Fenianism and the Alabama dispute meant that anti-British senti-ment was already running high in the USA and especially in New York. Bennett stoked up the fires. He encouraged his rivals in their scepticism.[73] In New York the *Sun*, animated by an ancient grudge between its proprietor Charles A. Dana and Bennett, duly obliged it. It was the *Sun* that published all Noe's revelations, but it went on to make the unwarranted inference that so many of Stanley's enemies made: that because he was a proven liar, *nothing* he said was true.[74]

But the *Sun*'s cynicism was a bagatelle alongside the propaganda advantage given Bennett by the attitude of the British press. He waited until the largest conceivable number had denounced Stanley as impostor, fraud, charlatan and forger before releasing Livingstone's confidential letter to him which contained such powerful circumstantial evidence of authenticity that all doubters were at once silenced.[75] The *Herald* then counterattacked the RGS, stressing its ingratitude, its blinkered xenophobia, its myopic defence of Kirk, and its curmudgeonly refusal to give Stanley his due.[76] This gave the British press pause. They had been badly wrong about Stanley when they accused him of fraud. Perhaps their earlier unequivocal support for the RGS was equally misguided. Perhaps the real problem was that men like Sir Henry Rawlinson had feet of clay and were simply not big enough to admit it.

A further fillip to the pro-Stanley campaign was provided at the end of August when the journalist Winwood Reade wrote a withering critique in the *Pall Mall Gazette* of the mindless way British opinion had received the first two Livingstone letters.[77] He pointed out that the canard that Stanley himself wrote the letters was untenable even on internal evidence. The objection had been that Livingstone wrote with an eye to human interest stories rather than as a dour missionary. But, said Reade, that was precisely the point. Everyone agreed that Stanley was not stupid, yet only a very stupid forger would make an error like that. An ingenious charlatan would try to get inside the notional Livingstone, and saturate his pronouncements with reverential allusions and references to the workings of providence. Only someone who had actually met Livingstone would know the truth which was, as Stanley pointed out, that the 'rollicking' quality of the letters was pure Livingstone since 'for genial, kindly humour, for keen sense of the ludicrous he might be editor of Punch'.[78]

For all these reasons the RGS was already in full retreat in the battle for public opinion even before Windsor Castle took a hand. On 27 August, while Stanley was in the thick of newspaper stories about his nationality, he received sensational news. First there came a gift of a gold snuff box from Queen Victoria in token of her admiration. The box was inlaid with blue enamel and bore the legend 'VR' in diamonds, emeralds and rubies. Then there followed an invitation to attend on her Majesty at Dunrobin Castle on 8–9 September.[79]

Immediately Stanley sensed a changing atmosphere. On 4 September Sir Henry Rawlinson, who was to present him to the Queen, wrote a very conciliatory letter extending the hand of friendship: 'There may be very naturally a feeling of disappointment at your "having taken the wind out of our sails" and perhaps in some cases there may be individual jealousy, but as far as I can judge the Geographers as a body . . . rejoice in the honours you are receiving.'[80] Behind the scenes even greater activity took place. Lord Granville sent a confidential message to Markham and his fellow conspirators that they should on no account take any action that might redound to the detriment of the monarch, now that the gracious sovereign had seen fit to wrap Stanley in her mantle; any unwelcome publicity about the explorer would be received at Windsor with the greatest disfavour.[81]

The prospect of an interview with the Queen saw Stanley through the nasty patch when Noe's revelations were being widely bruited and was instrumental in persuading him not to sue the *Sun* for libel. As yet, though, he was not disposed to accept Rawlinson's olive branch, since the president had not publicly recanted on 'sensationalism'.[82]

On 9 September Stanley arrived at Dunrobin Castle, ancestral seat of the Duke of Sutherland, and dined that evening with Lady Churchill, while the Duke, Lord Granville and Sir Henry Rawlinson dined with the Queen. Once the sovereign had retired, the two parties met in the smoking room and began to discuss Gladstone and Disraeli. Stanley was appalled at some of the indiscretions committed by Granville, but was delighted to find that he had been assigned a better bedroom than Rawlinson.[83]

The morning of the 10th was spent in receiving instructions from Rawlinson on how to behave at the coming reception. About noon Queen Victoria and Princess Beatrice entered. They all bowed, and Rawlinson introduced Stanley. Stanley was enraptured with 'this lady to whom in my heart of hearts next to God I worshipped'. To him she conveyed a definite charismatic aura; though aware of her own inaccessibility she was serenely proud rather than forbiddingly haughty. A ten-minute conversation on Africa ensued. Stanley was relieved to find the Queen even shorter of stature than he was himself, though with similarly unforgettable eyes which revealed 'a quiet but unmistakable kindly condescension and an inimitable calmness of self-possession.' The smallness of the sovereign recalled his aunt but 'what a difference between the subdued imperious-ness and regal consciousness of one, and the sociable housewifeliness of the other'.[84] The Queen asked why Livingstone would not come home and how long it would take him to finish his work. Stanley explained the situation. A second interview with the monarch took place, then on the third morning Sutherland whisked Stanley away on his private railway to Inverness, whence he caught the London express.[85]

After the audience the Duke of Sutherland asked how Stanley had liked her. 'Splendid,' he replied. Sutherland then muttered something about the Queen being a good little woman who had a bee in her bonnet. Stanley's sentiments of rapt admiration were not however reciprocated by the sovereign and her entourage. Colonel Ponsonby found him 'rough looking' but very agreeable and an accomplished conversationalist with an unbounded admiration for Livingstone.[86] The Queen herself was more critical and referred to the interview twice, in a letter to the Princess Royal and in her own journals. The letter contained the following: 'I have this evening seen Mr Stanley who discovered Livingstone, a determined ugly little man – with a strong American twang.'[87] Even more interesting, as denoting the background research done by her intelligence departments on Stanley, is the journal entry: 'The Duke presented Mr Stanley, the discoverer of Dr Livingstone, who calls himself an American but is by birth a Welshman. He was, however, brought up in America and looks and speaks like an American. He has a very determined expression and is not particularly prepossessing.'[88]

This seal of royal approbation largely silenced the critics. On his return to London, Stanley found a letter from Bennett, granting him the requested six months' leave of absence on full pay (£400 p.a.) on condition that Stanley crossed to the USA once he had finished his book, in order to milk the Livingstone story further.[89] Stanley continued to scribble away furiously, ably guided by his editor Edward Marston. To economise on precious time he adopted a policy of sending Kalulu out to act as his proxy in response to social invitations. After one such tea, with Lady Franklin, Kalulu returned beaming at the way he had been petted and spoiled.[90] Yet finding uninterrupted leisure for writing was still difficult. Fame exacted a heavy price at all levels, as when Stanley had to sit all afternoon for a partner from Madame Tussauds who came to make sketches for their planned wax model of him.[91]

Stanley's enemies in the RGS had been thwarted in their more sinister designs by the bestowal of royal favour, but they still had many anti-Stanley options left to exercise. The principal one was the denial of the Society's gold medal, which public opinion now increasingly demanded for Stanley's achievements. Rawlinson was disposed to make the best of a sorry affair, but Galton, Markham and Grant remained intransigent. Markham's attitude is best conveyed in his unpublished history of the RGS:

> I met Charlie Forbes, a great friend, who pointed down with his stick and said 'the Society is going down, down, down in public estimation.' I replied, 'Damn public opinion. The fellow has done no geography.' But Sir Henry Rawlinson was weak and got alarmed. When he consulted me about the medal, I said 'to give the fellow a jolly good dinner for finding Livingstone would be proper but it would be a desecration to give him a Royal award.' Nevertheless, the Council was specially summoned and Stanley was voted a Gold Medal several months before the time laid down by our rules.[92]

Markham's opinion was shared by many RGS diehards. Dr Beke stated: 'As regards Mr Stanley, I think he is being *overrated*, just as he was *underrated* at first.'[93] Grant's objections were especially vociferous. He reminded Rawlinson of the personal attacks Stanley had made on him and others (especially in the 27 August *Daily Telegraph*) and went on: 'If such a fellow is worthy of the honours of the Geographical Society, it must clearly follow that the safest way to Geographical honours is to insult the President and Council of the Society.' He suggested that if Stanley was to receive an award it should be one hundred guineas prize money and honorary life membership of the Society instead of a gold medal, 'for if you examine the list of gold medallists, Mr Stanley has not done enough to be ranked with any of them . . . if Stanley has done any real geography, by all means let him be rewarded, but at this distance I cannot see what title he has to the distinction of our Society's medal.'[94]

But Rawlinson had keener political antennae than the hardliners. He had access to the establishment, and he knew from his talks with Sutherland, Granville and others that the élite was concerned at the damage to Britain's reputation being caused by the RGS's apparently dog-in-the-manger recalcitrance. He ordered Markham to swallow his objections and make peace between Stanley and the Society. Markham therefore invited Stanley to dine with him at home, when Burton and Verney Cameron would also be guests. On arrival, Stanley was disconcerted to find that Markham used a system of signs to discriminate between his guests and indicate his differential preferences for them. Thus Stanley received one finger of the right hand to shake, Cameron, a naval officer, got two, while Burton was given an entire hand.[95]

This was a dangerous game to play with the prickly paranoid Stanley. Although Stanley enjoyed the evening and got on well with Burton – 'Markham makes a kindly host in his own house – though outside he is somewhat uppish in manner' – Stanley did not forget the slight and dealt with it in two ways. First, to show the Society that it could expect no compromise from him in return for any honour awarded, he returned to his public indictment of Kirk.[96] Secondly, he inveighed against Markham for allegedly supporting an anti-Livingstone clique and promoting a chimerical notion of ascending the Congo from its mouth to relieve Livingstone that way. Rather than wasting time on schemes that were impracticable, and would be undesirable to Livingstone even if they did work, it behoved the 2,500 RGS members to contribute £10 each to a special fund. With £25,000 at his disposal, a professional explorer could uncover all of Africa's remaining secrets.[97]

It was now clear to Rawlinson and the Society that they had to accept Stanley on his own terms or not at all. Stanley's indomitable will finally won the war of attrition. On 21 October, at a dinner given by the Council of the RGS, Stanley was formally made a gold medallist.[98] Sir Henry Rawlinson made a conciliatory speech, defending the Society against the charge of having been cold and vindictive towards Stanley. He pointed out that the RGS had at no time aligned itself with those who claimed that Stanley had not found Livingstone.[99] Mark Twain, who was present, was deeply impressed: 'Rawlinson stood up and made the most manly and magnificent apology to Stanley for himself and for the Society that ever I listened to; I thought the man rose to the very pinnacle of human nobility.'[100] But Stanley, brooding and vengeful, did not see it that way. With the perseverance of monomania, he continued to harp away on the theme that Galton had never apologised for 'sensational'; accordingly, far from acknowledging Rawlinson's gesture, Stanley omitted all mention of it in his diary.[101]

Royal audiences and disputes with the RGS apart, September and most of October were spent hard at work on the Livingstone book. Stanley used the public appearances to promote interest in Africa, as when he received the freedom of the London Turners' Company at the Guildhall and urged British expansion into the 'Dark Continent'.[102] But before he left for the USA at Bennett's bidding, it was necessary for him to visit the land of Livingstone's birth. The tour of Scotland was a fairly complete triumph. There was little of the cavilling and sniping that had attended him in England. The Scots took him to their bosom as the rescuer of one of their greatest sons. Everywhere there were cheering crowds at railway stations, at every civic lunch there were ovations; the fact that he had twisted the tail of the *English* lion certainly did not dispose the Scots against him.[103]

Stanley's first stop was Glasgow, where he noticed for the first time how typically Scottish Livingstone's physiognomy was.[104] Next day he lectured in Hamilton and received the freedom of the city there. Here he met the extended Livingstone family, first the doctor's two sisters, who impressed him by the forcefulness of their personality (especially the elder one).[105] In the evening he went driving with Livingstone's daughter Agnes, who had from the earliest days expressed her belief in him and who exclaimed after reading the letters from her father: 'Oh that man Stanley, if I had a crown of gold and gems I would put it on his head.'[106] They struck up an immediate rapport, but Stanley's disdain for the 'common clay' was reinforced when their horses bolted after a political demonstration in the city centre and their carriage came near to overturning.

The lecture tour continued: Inverness, Aberdeen, Greenock, Paisley, Ayr, Helensburgh, Edinburgh. At Wemyss Bay he was the guest of the

Scottish MP Grieve. Honours, freedoms, acclamations rained down on him. His lecturing technique was to tell the same basic story about his finding of Livingstone, then add different anecdotes on each separate platform: for example, at Glasgow he gave vent to his hatred for crocodiles, at Hamilton he concentrated on his previous American experience; in other towns it would be the Ha, or Mirambo that elicited the telling story.[107] Whatever his experience at Brighton (and later in the USA), in Scotland at least there was no criticism of the style, content or delivery of his lectures.

After adding three further lectures (in Dunfermline, Liverpool and Manchester) to an already crowded schedule, Stanley returned to London to put the finishing touches to his book. But he could never steer clear of controversy for long. On 4 November he attended a great anti-slavery meeting at the Mansion House, at which the other speakers were Bishop Wilberforce and Sir Bartle Frere. It did not take Stanley long to upset his audience. He pointed out that the much-vaunted campaign against the Zanzibar slavers by the Royal Navy was less impressive when viewed at first hand, since the main result of releasing slaves from Arab dhows was that they were then indentured in the Seychelles, in effect exchanging one form of slavery for another. 'That is not true!' thundered the Lord Mayor. Stanley gave him one of his basilisk looks, repeated the charge, and said that Sir Bartle Frere, outward bound to Zanzibar on an anti-slavery mission, would shortly see the truth of it for himself.[108]

By now word of Stanley's Scottish success had followed him south of the border and he was in demand as a speaker both in England and for later engagements in the USA.[109] One public lecture in Maidstone afforded him particular enjoyment because of an incident on the train journey there. Stanley had hoped to have the compartment to himself but a typical English gentleman got in and struck up a conversation, not knowing whom he was addressing. The subject of Stanley came up. The gentleman described him as a Yankee rogue, 'the biggest impostor of the age'. Stanley let the man jabber away and soon discovered his prejudice to be the result of rabid anti-Americanism. As it happened, the man got out at the stop before Maidstone. Stanley kept him talking at the carriage window until the train began to pull away from the station, then handed him his card. In the light from the gaslamp Stanley was able to see the stupefied, incredulous reaction, which he found just compensation for the insult.[110]

Both Bennett's urgings and the amounts of money being offered for his American lectures led Stanley to wind up his affairs in London as fast as possible. After a round trip London–Liverpool–Manchester–London between 6 and 9 November, Stanley booked passage for New York on the Cunard steamer *Cuba* and departed on the 9th. Within days of his departure *How I Found Livingstone* was published, more than 700 pages long, with six maps and fifty-three illustrations by himself. It sold by tens of thousands and was into its third edition by Christmas. Florence Nightingale famously called it 'the very worst book on the very best subject I ever saw in my life', and there is some truth in the charge.[111] It is a volume marred by egocentricity. Stanley sustained his vendetta with Kirk in the book, and the long passages of self-justification were tiresome, but at its best, in its descriptions of the Mirambo war, the ordeal with the Ha, the crossing of the Malagarazi and the meeting with Livingstone, it deserved its phenomenal success.[112]

The three and a half months Stanley spent in Britain in the late summer and autumn of 1872 have often been identified as *the* crossroads in Stanley's life, his period of simultaneous triumph and disaster. How accurate is this assessment? Is it true that in these months the potentially positive aspects of Stanley's personality were killed off for good, and if so, why?

There is some evidence that even at the physical level Stanley in 1871–2 crossed an invisible watershed. From a young man, he became a prematurely middle-aged one. There was still the same indomitable set of features: thick-set, well-knit, barrel-chested, deeply tanned with large, dark, intelligent eyes, a general self-assertive, aggressive, bulldog demeanour, the same evidence of decisiveness and determination.[113] But his hair was rapidly turning grey. An early attempt to dye it turned into disaster when Stanley used a dye with an emerald hue and his hair turned green. He had to keep himself in hiding in his rooms at Duchess Street (to which he moved from the Langham Hotel at the end of August) to reverse the effects of the pigmentation, since an explorer with green hair would have excited universal derision.[114] But the grizzled hair was only part of the ageing process. Whereas the younger Stanley was prepared, and almost too prepared, to take risks, the middle-aged Stanley began to approach African exploration with circumspection. He invented a special form of headgear – the 'Stanley cap' – out of some tent cloth or twill, lined with native grass and set off with the leather peak of an old cap. He had discovered that the 'regulation' pith-helmet was inconvenient, since when he threw his head back the helmet tipped over his eyes.[115]

Yet if Stanley was ageing prematurely, his mental processes at this time were even more significant. A general feeling of disenchantment led him to violently anti-English feelings and a reassessment of his time in Africa. The disenchantment with the English particularly centred on their lack of fairness – exactly the quality they prided themselves on. Typical to Stanley's mind was the fabricated 'Stanley' dispatch that appeared in the *Spectator* in August. According to this fictitious 'report', Stanley was said to have told Livingstone that Horace Greeley would be Democratic candidate for the presidency in 1872. This was supposed to have drawn from Livingstone the following outburst: 'Hold on! You have related to me many stupendous things and with a confiding simplicity – I can peacefully swallow them down, but there is a limit to all things. I am a simple guileless Christian man and unacquainted with intemperate language, but when you tell me that Horace Greeley is to become a Democratic candidate I cast the traditions of my education to the winds and say, I'll be damned to all eternity if I believe it. My trunk is packed to go home but I shall remain in Africa, for these things may be true after all; if they are, I desire to stay here and unlearn my civilisation.'[116]

Having printed this nonsense, the *Spectator* then had the effrontery to 'refute' it as bogus, on the grounds that Livingstone would not have used profane language. But as Stanley pointed out, the 'story' was spurious on internal evidence; neither Livingstone nor Stanley could have known anything about Horace Greeley, since he did not announce his candidature until 1872. The true moral of the story, for Stanley, was that the English were cowards. Instead of the manly American tradition of settling disputes with pistols, the English resorted to calumny and slander. On his way through London to Abyssinia in January 1867 he bought an English newspaper and thought it more respectable than the hideous rags in the USA.[117] But now he was undeceived. American editors might be bullies but 'his English contemporary is in my mind more like an old shrew with his venom-laden pen and his effeminate malice . . . their propensity to nagging at a man marks the unmanliness to which their excess of laws have [*sic*] reduced them.'[118]

The result of the sustained vilification Stanley endured in the English press in August 1872 left him permanently scarred: 'I am slowly discovering that this life with all its gay colour and glare only consists of an unusual amount of envy with the slightest tincture of real esteem . . . I can count my friends on my fingers but my enemies are a host and command the entire press. Every mail also brings numerous proofs of English hate.'[119] This prompted two reflections: one that fame was an illusion; two, that the life of an African explorer, with all its hardships, was actually preferable to life in English society. On the first point, he noted: 'I have smacked my lips over the flavour of fame – but the substance is useless to me – as it may be taken away at any time. What a pity I did not go on to China without telegraphing Mr Bennett.'[120] Again, contrasting the anguish of his life in England with the toil of life in Africa, he remarked: 'One brings me an inordinate amount of secret pain, the other sapped my physical strength but left my mind expanded and was purifying.'[121]

Two things in particular seemed to strike deep wounds at the core of his identity during this period in England. One was the paradox that to taste fame as an international celebrity, he had to risk contumely arising from his 'base' origins.[122] The worst ordeal of his months of fame was when someone at a banquet called for information on his early life. The other cross he had to bear was the sniping at Livingstone, his true 'father'. As well as being traduced as hard, morose, impossible and a hypocrite, Livingstone was frequently portrayed as 'something like an adulterer', a man who had married an African princess or retired into an Arab harem.[123] Frank Harris, who had observed a white girl living in an African tribe, later asked Stanley if perhaps he had found Livingstone by tracking 'parti-coloured offspring' across Africa. Harris, who really did have the sex-obsession Stanley attributed to Richard Burton, was disconcerted when Stanely reacted angrily to the suggestion and dismissed the explorer as merely humourless.[124] There was more to it than that. One of the reasons why Stanley regarded Livingstone as a true mentor and father was that he seemed in his daily life as chaste as Stanley himself. Stanley could therefore sustain himself with the thought that he was as 'normal' as Livingstone. Any suggestion that Livingstone might be a normal heterosexual male (and thus clearly *unlike* Stanley) caused him excessive anxiety.

Profound considerations merged with trivial ones. Part of the legacy of Stanley's deprived childhood was that he always fretted over the expenditure of money. Because his photograph was everywhere and he could not walk anywhere in London without being pestered, he was forced to travel by cab: 'Cab fares were a heavy tax though they cost less than running the gauntlet between the crossing sweepers, the sly kindred and lost Americans (all after money).[125] When all these anxieties combined with the jealousy of other journalists and the resentment of the RGS, Stanley often found himself wishing that Bennett had chosen someone else to find Livingstone. The thought particularly impressed him the day he saw his name on a *New York Sun* banner headline. After ULYSSES S. GRANT, DRUNKARD came HENRY M. STANLEY, VILLAIN, FORGER AND PIRATE. At this point Stanley confided to his diary in despair: 'I would willingly give them all [the newspaper cuttings] for a day of that boyhood when I was blissfully obscure. I once thought that a press notice of me was "Immortality", but alas, I have found that that kind of "Immortality" means only abject slavery.'[126]

Some English observers agreed that Stanley had had a raw deal. As Stanley sailed away to New York, *The Times* recorded this verdict: 'We cannot think without shame and indignation of the conduct of the Royal Geographical Society in this matter.'[127] But more usual was the response that Stanley's view of the RGS was typical Yankee chip-on-the-shoulder, like Nathaniel Hawthorne's complaint about Lord Lansdowne. If the RGS did not at first believe the story about the finding of Livingstone, why then, whose fault was this? What was the credibility of a known anti-British rag, the leading exponent of 'yellow journalism' supposed to be, after all?[128] As for the Kirk controversy, Stanley had ultimately done himself more harm than good by plugging away at this theme, and in any case it had produced the 'spin-off' of the Bartle Frere mission to Zanzibar, for which the *Herald* was now shamelessly and mendaciously taking credit.[129]

It would be a mistake to spirit away all the real anti-Stanley and anti-American feeling into the ether of Stanley paranoia. Much of it was real enough, but it should be viewed in the sort of perspective Stanley always refused to entertain. The first point was that there was nothing particularly personal in the bad treatment Stanley received. All explorers who came before English audiences could expect a bruising time. When the French explorer and discoverer of the gorilla, Paul du Chaillu, came to London in 1861 to address the Ethnological Society, a member of the audience queried his veracity as if he were a criminal on trial. The quick-tempered du Chaillu suggested that in his country such matters were settled by a duel. After a few more unsatisfactory exchanges, du Chaillu jumped over the benches to where his tormentor (one T. A. Malone) stood and spat in his face. When Malone appealed to the chairman, Chaillu yelled 'Coward' at him.[130] Alongside this exhibition, the action and reaction at Stanley's lecture in Brighton was mild indeed.

Even more telling was the amount of support Stanley was able to enlist right from his earliest days in England. If we accepted Stanley's own account, we would have to conclude that he was indeed, in his own description, 'a perfect Ishmaelite, with his hand against every man, and feeling every man's hand was raised against him.'[131] But in fact very many notable English men and women rallied to his standard: Edwin Arnold, editor of the *Daily Telegraph*, William Cotton Oswell, John Murray the publisher, Lord Kinnaird, Sir Thomas Buxton, Lady Russell, Lady Jane Russell, Baroness Burdett-Coutts, and J.B. Braithwaite the leading English Quaker. America was represented by Mark Twain, then visiting in Britain. Perhaps the most significant of all these friends were the Webbs of Newstead Abbey.

The Webbs were close friends of Livingstone, ever since Old Etonian William Webb met Livingstone on a hunting expedition in Africa. But the driving force in the family was Emilia, a woman in her late thirties with six children. Without having met Stanley she had an intuitive sense from the newspaper reports of the Brighton meeting of the kind of wounded, vulnerable being Stanley really was. She extended an invitation to him to stay at their splendid country seat of Newstead Abbey, 11 miles from Nottingham, Stanley accepted and was housed in the wing occupied by Livingstone himself on his last visit to Newstead in 1864.[132]

Emilia Webb was one of the few women Stanley trusted. She had the rare gift of making acquaintances want to unburden their souls to her. Within a very few days at Newstead Stanley told her the 'shameful' secrets of his infancy. He behaved to her six children as a favourite uncle and romped with them in the woods in a most un-Stanley-like way. Stanley worshipped Emilia just this side of idolatry and was prepared to defer to her opinion in a way that would have been unthinkable with other women.

The underlying psychology of the relationship again reveals Stanley caught in the either/or posture towards women: either unattainable idol or carnal whore. The reasons for this deep-seated attitude derived ultimately from his promiscuous mother but had been reinforced by the culture Stanley grew up in, especially that of the American South where white women were idealised as 'ladies' while black women were regarded as carnal and seducible. Emilia Webb was the 'lost mother' as Livingstone had been the 'lost father'. That Stanley regarded her in a maternal light is clear from the childish petulance and jealousy he exhibited whenever she invited other guests to Newstead. Emilia intuited something of this for she remarked that a good woman would be the making of Stanley, 'only she would have to care for him *enough*' (in other words act like a mother).[133] She herself was secure in Stanley's esteem, for as a married woman she was 'safe' – Stanley would never have to put his real feelings for her to the test by forcing them through the prism of carnality and thus compelling an integrated response (neither madonna nor whore) towards her. So it was that the few days spent at Newstead in 1872 were as much an oasis in Stanley's troubled life as his months in Ujiji with Livingstone had been. Ahead of him stretched more arid emotional deserts than he could imagine.

12

DESPITE the victory over the RGS, the completion of his book and the new-found friendship with the Webbs, the Stanley who boarded the *Cuba* for New York on 9 November 1872 was not a happy man. He confessed that the three months in England had been a turning point: 'All the actions of my life, and I may say all my thoughts, since 1872, have been strongly coloured by the storm of abuse and the wholly unjustifiable reports circulated about me then.'[1] Stanley was in general the sort of person who ignores a hundred plaudits to worry away at a single insult, who dismisses the dozens of favourable developments to brood over the handful of unfavourable ones, who, child-like, remembers the wicked witch even when the fairy story has come through to a happy conclusion. But as a special source of anguish he had the myriad lampoons spawned by 'I Presume' to deal with. The (in retrospect) singularly infelicitous four words with which he had greeted Livingstone at Ujiji had entered the language and legend of England and coursed through the bloodstream of popular culture. 'Dr Livingstone, I presume?' became the last refuge of the scoundrel keeping failure at bay in the music halls. The October issue of *Tailor and Cutter* showed one dummy addressing the words to another.[2] Stanley came to dread the time he would be introduced to new contacts: he could almost predict the 'Mr Stanley, I presume' that would be the inevitable response.

The exploit that had brought him fame and fortune and ushered him into the presence of the greatest man of his lifetime was to end, it seemed, because of a single error of verbal judgement, in everlasting mockery. Stanley's response was to harden himself and to stifle the few softening human impulses that remained. If Emilia Webb had made him look at a caring maternal woman in a new light, there was a much greater countervailing force at hand to fuel his misogynism. For among the audience at his last lecture in the Manchester Free Trade Hall was Katie Bradshaw, née Gough-Roberts, now heavily pregnant with her second child by her architect husband. When Stanley departed after the lecture to the house of the president of the Manchester Chamber of Commerce, Katie took a cab there and sent in her card, asking for an interview. Stanley, angry not just at her 'treachery' but at the report that she had shown the 'unspeak-able' John Camden Hotten the biographical letter he had written her early in 1869, refused brusquely and demanded the return of his personal letters. Bridling in turn, Katie told Stanley's valet that if he wanted them he would have to come in person to ask for them.[3]

The memory of Katie's 'insolence' was obviously still smarting as Stanley crossed the Atlantic. He was in a violent temper, not just because of the slowness of the ship, but because its best quarters had been reserved for 'the ladies'. Not content with that, these pampered women then objected when he smoked in the public lounges and insisted he go on deck to indulge his vice. Stanley was livid: it was typical of the scheming ingratitude of women to allow the male sex to pay for their idleness in the most salubrious sections of the liner while humiliating them by insisting that they smoke under a canvas awning in a hatchway.[4]

Stanley soon had a more concrete focus for his misogynism. As the most celebrated passenger on the *Cuba* he was seated at the captain's table, where he had a pretty young woman as a dining companion. At first all went well. The girl seemed captivated by Stanley's tales of Africa. Then, to Stanley's intense chagrin, one of their fellow diners, a young empty-headed aristocratic *flâneur* who spent his time smoking cigarettes and yawning with 'boredom', cut in. One day at dinner he mentioned that he knew how to make an exceptionally good salad and gave the recipe. The young woman at once transferred her attentions to him.[5] Stanley simply could not understand how a stupid youth, with no conversation and not a single idea in his head, whose sole accomplishments seemed to be knowing how to make a salad and smoking cigarettes, could be preferred to the most famous man of the year. Insult was added to injury by the fact that the young fop wore a monocle; Stanley always had a violent prejudice against men with eyeglasses.

Stanley concluded both that women were impossible and that he could never be a lady's man. But the truth was that the young woman in question almost certainly picked up the essential oddity of his sexual persona; it was not so much that he did not know how to treat women, as that he frightened them by the impossibly high level of his expectations. Stanley's gaucherie with the female sex was usually attributed to his long absences in Africa, removed from polite society. But this was to make the symptom the cause. As a fellow journalist Thomas Stevens shrewdly observed: 'He would have been too scared to have seriously sought her hand, simply because she was young and beautiful. Mr Stanley thinks a lovely young woman a sort of wingless angel and a superior being who was made for rough man to admire at a respectful distance, but not to be approached too closely without sacrilege.'[6] With Stanley, the madonna/whore syndrome was part of a more general personality disorder, in which he simultaneously yearned for affection while taking steps to ensure that any real possibility for a close affectionate relationship was destroyed.

There was a curious sequel to this failed relationship. At a banquet in New York on his first night Stanley suddenly learned that his erstwhile protégée had fallen overboard when the ship was docking at the wharf and almost drowned. It was an uncomfortable reminder of the demise of his grandfather. Then the young Rowlands had wished that he might escape the promised beating, and, *mirabile dictu*, Moses Parry had dropped dead in the fields. Now, the vehemently hostile feelings he harboured towards the female sex had, almost, or so it seemed, brought about a young woman's death. Stanley at once rushed to her bedside where he was relieved to find her much recovered. But so great was his guilt that his reaction when she shortly afterwards married the monocled fop was mild.[7]

On 20 November the *Cuba* arrived in New York. In the Hudson River was a *Herald* steamer bearing a 'Welcome Stanley' banner, which promptly took the hero on board and whisked him away; customs formalities were waived. His first stop on land was the *Herald* office, where he was irrationally miffed to find the reporters carrying revolvers.[8] Stanley always liked the thought, when in polite society, that he was really a warrior who had the ultimate drop on the supercilious 'gentleman' who patronised him, by virtue of his superiority as a shootist. Armed reporters and sub-editors seemed to call this assumption into doubt; it was therefore necessary for him to browbeat the *Herald* staff with his superior knowledge of rifles to establish that he was really the 'top gun'.

But in worrying about his fellow hacks, Stanley failed to see where the real threat to him lay. By this time Gordon Bennett had begun to worry that he might have conjured up a sorcerer's apprentice. He was jealous of Stanley's fame, and resentful that it was Stanley, not the *Herald* and still less Bennett himself, who had got the credit for relieving Livingstone. His reporter's reception by Queen Victoria at Dunrobin Castle particularly annoyed Bennett. He himself despised the British and their monarchy, but he knew that the monarchy both enjoyed huge prestige in Europe and sold papers in America. Bennett brooded on the monster he had created. When he sent Stanley to find Livingstone, Stanley was a nobody. Now he was a celebrity, and all on Bennett's back. Bennett had conceived the expedition, financed it (albeit grudgingly), picked up all the associated expenses (such as the cabling of Livingstone's letters), and for what? He had not received so much as a syllable of thanks from the British while Stanley was lording it in London as if it were his own personal fortune that had made the discovery of Livingstone possible.[9]

When he heard of the sums Stanley stood to earn from the exploit, Bennett was even more angry. Apart from the advance on royalties of $10,000 paid for *How I Found Livingstone*, Stanley was to receive a guaranteed minimum of £10,000 for his American lecture tour, plus all expenses. It was a reasonable inference that Stanley might hope to net $50,000 in all, after all costs had been defrayed.[10] For once Bennett agreed with English critics of Stanley. The discoverer of Livingstone would henceforth enjoy an income of at least £500 a year for the rest of his life, while the doctor himself, after more than thirty years in Africa, still had no salary from the British government, nor so much as a penny in guaranteed pension. This was a literally preposterous situation. But while Stanley was being lionised as the great American hero, it would be impolitic for Bennett to strike back at him. His chance for revenge, he decided, would come later.

Stanley's triumphant landing at the Battery was the signal for junketings on a scale far eclipsing those in Britain. A long caravan of carriages accompanied him in procession up Fifth Avenue to his hotel. His suite was inundated with reporters (the familiar chant 'Mr Stanley, I presume' predictably went up), and there were so many flowers in the rooms that at first he fancied himself back in tropical Africa. That evening he attended a banquet then went on to see a Broadway farce, *King Carrot*, which burlesqued the stuffed shirts of the RGS.[11]

The days that followed were a period of unqualified success. He was the toast of the town: reception followed reception, banquet followed feast.[12] Kalulu, dressed in page's outfit, was almost as much a sensation as his master; by now he had overcome his earlier aversion to European clothes.[13] But the rich fare triggered a minor attack of African malarial fever, so that Stanley after a week decided to spend more time at home in his suite in the Fifth Avenue Hotel and to take greater care with his diet.[14]

At the beginning of December he commenced the much-trumpeted series of American lectures. On the evening of 3 December he appeared at Steinway Hall to deliver the first of them. All tickets for the four-lecture series had been sold and there was brisk business on the black market. Great things were expected, but they did not materialise. Stanley had made a number of bad judgements that worked against his success even before he opened his mouth. In the first place, on the advice of his agent, he had divided his speech into four parts, each part of the 'serial' to be given on successive nights. But, much more seriously, remembering how controversial his 'popular' Brighton speech had been, he decided both to discipline himself and make his material more 'scholarly' and to refrain from extempore speaking, as it was then that he seemed always to be carried away into indiscretion.

Also working away against ultimate success was the fact that in the first flush of the heady days in New York Stanley had already exposed his best cards. He had already delivered the thundering denunciation against the evils of drink in Africa that he had first unburdened himself of in England in August.[15] And on 25 November at a dinner given by the *Herald* club he had repeated the flourish that had first brought the house down in Scotland. His trick was to start by saying, 'I may be called a forger . . .' then pause while he drew from his pocket the dark blue consular cap with the gold braid around it that Livingstone had given him as a keepsake at Ujiji before continuing, 'but I would like to know if I could forge Livingstone's cap.'[16]

The Steinway Hall lecture began to a capacity crowd. Behind Stanley was a large map of Africa, the Stars and Stripes, and dozens of bouquets. To one side of the stage was a table laden with African weapons and artefacts. On the other side sat two guests of honour: Kalulu and Livingstone's brother John who had come down from Canada for the occasion.[17] The audience buzzed with expectancy, awaiting a roistering evening, and perhaps more of the famous Stanley indiscretions and personal attacks. What they heard was an unpleasant surprise. Determined not to endure another Brighton, Stanley emulated the dry Teutonic academician at his worst. There was not a single anecdote, no levity, no jokes, simply a plethora of unpronounceable names that seemed to go on much longer than the actual one and a half hours.[18] In so far as the lecture was controversial, it was merely because the content was un-acceptably eccentric. A thumbnail sketch of African exploration from the days of Bartolomeu Diaz was followed by a 'proof' that Darwin was insane and that Christianity was bound to succeed in the Dark Continent. Stanley's delivery was poor: he could not be heard beyond the first ten rows and when after an unconscionable interval he glanced up from his prepared script it was to find that all but these ten rows had decamped.

The remainder, too polite to depart, remained remarkably quiet and no sound of approval was heard to emanate from them.[19]

This was disaster of the first magnitude. No more signal miscalculation could be imagined. As one student of Stanley has commented: 'It was as though he had indeed been touched with a curse which made him do everything backwards. The detailed scientific discourse which he gave at Steinway Hall ought to have been given at Brighton, and the light-hearted narrative offered to the Emperor ought to have been given in New York.'[20] Yet this was just the sort of opening the brooding Bennett had been waiting for. He gave the nod to his reporter George Seilhamer to prick the Stanley bubble. If he could kill off the lecture series, Bennett would have evened scores with his 'uppity' employee.

The review in the *Herald* next morning was devastating. Stanley was 'intolerably dull . . . his elocution is bad . . . his manner of treating his subject was not such as to ensure a forgetfulness of his faults of oratory . . . he talked commonplaces . . . his anecdotes were spoiled in the telling . . . his voice was pitched in a sing-song and doleful monotone . . . Mr Stanley has utterly mistaken the necessities of the platform . . . it would be cruel to him not to say so . . . Mr Stanley still betrays some of the vices which are the necessary blunders of the tyro. He speaks too fast in his eagerness not to bore his hearers, the consequence is that they sometimes fail to understand the force of what he has said . . . the subject matter was a trifle abstruse for his audience.'[21]

Stanley tried to pull his chestnuts out of the fire. He had a brochure printed containing the following: 'Born New York City, 1843, ran away to sea, joined the Union Army, then became a war correspondent.' It was typical of this broadsheet's commitment to accuracy (for, apart from the war correspondent bit, every statement in it was false) that it also quoted Stanley's greeting to Livingstone as 'Dr Livingstone, I *believe*.'[22] But Bennett had done his work too well. When even the *Herald* admitted that its own man was a flop, there could be little incentive for the crowds to turn out. Although Stanley's second lecture was better delivered and stuck to the finding of Livingstone, the word had got about and the hall was only one-third full.[23] The series petered out in fiasco. On the night of the third lecture, the dedicated handful of would-be listeners was turned away at the hall by a janitor who told them that the talks were cancelled as the box-office receipts were no longer even covering expenses.[24]

This was disaster on a scale not experienced even in hostile Britain. The plain fact was that the organisers had badly miscalculated; what was wrong was not the lectures or their delivery but the fact that at bottom the

American people, unlike the British, had no real interest in Africa.[25] But Stanley, typically, saw the whole thing as a conspiracy, especially when he learned that Bennett, whom he suspected of having set him up, had suddenly quit New York in his yacht for Paris, significantly leering at Seilhamer as he walked up the gang-plank. But if Stanley saw his experience in New York as tragedy, New Yorkers saw it as farce. A ludicrous show at the Theatre Comique on Broadway called *Africa* presented African explorers much as Groucho Marx portrayed them sixty years later in *Animal Crackers*. Following the usual 'cast of thousands' portraying Mirambo, slaves, cannibals, concubines and other fictitious 'characters' the curtain rose for the last act, wherein Stanley met Livingstone at Ujiji. When the words 'Dr Livingstone, I presume' were pronounced the audience would collapse nightly into hopeless, hysterical laughter.[26] By mid-December the Stanley saga was as much a joke as air-raid wardens in World War Two. The *reductio ad absurdum* was reached when a false Stanley appeared in Pittsburgh and was treated royally for two days as the guest of the city.[27]

Severely wounded in his pride and self-esteem, Stanley left the Fifth Avenue Hotel and took rooms on East 20th Street. He now waited for the storm of ridicule to blow itself out. The New Year saw diary entries of the utmost banality: '1 January 1873. Called on Misses Battersby, 122 Madison Avenue. Called on J. G. Holland, the novelist and poet. Edward King of the *Boston Journal* left yesterday for Philadelphia.'[28] Stanley kept his head down while the new star of the lecture circuit, Professor John Tyndall, received the accolades from the *Herald* that Stanley might have had but for Bennett's spite.[29]

It was the middle of January before Stanley felt it was safe enough to venture into public again. The occasion was the Correspondents' Club in Washington. Since this was a tribute by fellow journalists he thought himself secure from the kind of public lampooning he had sustained in New York the month before. But he had misjudged the mood. There was still life in 'I presume', as Stanley learned to his very great cost. William Copeland of the New York *Journal of Commerce* composed a spoof epic poem called 'Stanlio Africanus' in which he worked in references to his friend L. A. Gobright of the Associated Press. After the banquet, toasts and speeches were over, Copeland was 'persuaded' to declaim his ode. It was fairly obvious imitation Longfellow but at the twelfth stanza the smoothness of the trochaic dimeters, in the style of 'Hiawatha', was suddenly broken with the surprise staccato line 'Mr Gobright, I presume.' Like all catch-phrases, 'I presume' had already acquired humorous connotations out of all proportion to its intrinsic mirthful worth. To Stanley's stupefaction, the banqueting room rocked with laughter. He slunk away to his hotel room, having endured the ultimate humiliation.[30]

For three months Stanley, the stricken African lion, licked his wounds. In some ways the period January–March was the lowest point of his adult life. From being world-famous as the discoverer of Livingstone, he had now reached the pass where he dared not stir out into the public gaze, lest he endure another 'I presume' débâcle. He worked on a fictional book, based on Kalulu, in which he transmogrified his servant into a young African prince.[31] Stanley was now almost completely in the world of fantasy. Bennett had had his revenge, more completely than he could ever have hoped or expected.

It is possible that Bennett deliberately left Stanley in limbo in the USA, hoping that further rebuffs and humiliations would be visited on the man who had stolen his thunder. If so, he was disappointed. After the bruising Washington experience, Stanley lay low on full salary and awaited the word from Paris. At last, at the beginning of April 1873, it came: Stanley was ordered to report to Bennett in Paris. 'I presume he thinks it is about time I proceeded to work again,' he noted. 'I think so too and infinitely prefer it.'[32]

On 8 April Stanley began his eastward transatlantic crossing. As always, he chafed at the slowness of the Cunard vessels.[33] In England he allowed himself a few days' leave with the Webbs at Newstead; Kalulu disappointed Stanley by failing to win a running race against Emilia's daughters.[34] Once in London he left Kalulu in the hands of the Rev. J. Conder who ran a school in Wandsworth. Kalulu was quite an intelligent boy and within a month was making his first faltering steps at reading English; he could also write his own name.[35]

On 2 May, ironically the day after Livingstone died on the borders of Katanga, Stanley reported to Gordon Bennett at the Hotel des Deux Mondes in Paris. Bennett was in a vile temper, seemingly unassuaged by his reporter's humiliation in America. He made no mention of increasing Stanley's salary, even though, at £400 p.a., it stood at exactly the same level as in 1869 when he was a nobody. Stanley was forced to press the issue, to get an increase to £1,000 a year, but his bitterness towards Bennett for making no spontaneous offer was palpable.[36] He was not to know that Bennett thought that, with his royalties and lecture fees, he had already been paid way above the market rate for the Livingstone exploit.

Though not mentioning money, Bennett quickly came to the point of the interview. Spain was again ablaze but this time the main threat to the government came from the Right rather than the Left. There had been many changes since Stanley was there in 1869. Prim had been assassinated in 1870, then on 16 November of that year Amadeus of Savoy had been elected king. His abdication in February 1873 signalled the collapse of the experiment with constitutional monarchy and opened the floodgates to power-seekers from Right and Left.

For four months Stanley divided his time in Spain between the Carlist uprising of Navarre and the radical challenge in the South. Then Bennett, realising that the Spanish agony was going to be more protracted than he had expected, recalled Stanley to Paris and gave him a fresh assignment: to cover the Ashanti war in West Africa. The Ashanti campaign was in many ways an epigone to the 1868 Abyssinian affair, with Sir Garnet Wolseley and his Highlanders playing the role of Napier and the Irish troops before Magdala. In technical military terms the campaign was another success, but after defeating the Ashantis and burning their capital Kumasi, Wolseley hurriedly retreated, leaving the political context much as he had found it.

Stanley had arrived at the Gold Coast at the end of October 1873. The war was over by early February and Stanley left the 'white man's grave' with few regrets. When his ship put into Sao Vicente Island in the Cape Verde group on 25 February 1874, he learned of the death of Livingstone at Ilala near Lake Bangweolo the previous May. He became seized with the idea that it was his mission to continue Livingstone's work: 'Dear Livingstone! Another sacrifice to Africa! . . . May I be selected to succeed him in opening up Africa to the shining light of Christianity! . . . May Livingstone's God be with me, as He was with Livingstone in all his loneliness. May God direct me as He wills. I can only vow to be obedient, and not to slacken.'[37]

Livingstone's death had been reported in Europe at the very moment Wolseley's expedition was getting to grips with the Ashanti.[38] But still to come was the news of the astonishing nine-month journey Livingstone's servants Susi and Chuma had made across Africa, from Katanga to Bagamoyo. After finding their master dead at his bedside in a kneeling position, they had at once determined to take his body back to Zanzibar. First they cut out his heart and entrails and buried them in a tin box, so that the core of Livingstone would always remain in Africa. Then they dried the body in the sun for a fortnight, wrapped it in calico and fitted it into a cylindrical bark sarcophagus. The package was then sewn into a sailcloth and lashed to a pole that two men could carry. Under Susi and Chuma's directions, the whole Livingstone expedition then spent from

May 1873 to February 1874 threading their perilous course back to Bagamoyo. The Foreign Office thereupon issued precise instructions. After a medical examination to establish that the body was indeed Livingstone's, the coffin was put on board the next mailboat for England, accompanied by another of Livingstone's 'faithfuls' Jacob Wainwright.[39]

Stanley arrived in Lisbon on 9 March, and transferred from the *Dromedary* to the *Garonne* for the final leg of his homeward journey, to Liverpool. The mouth of the Tagus brought to mind the early Portuguese explorers of Africa, about whom he had lectured so disastrously in New York, especially Vasco da Gama.[40] From Liverpool he proceeded to London and arranged to meet up with the Webbs of Newstead, who had Livingstone's last letter in their possession. Almost his first act on arriving at his favoured Langham Hotel was to write a long letter to Agnes Livingstone, setting down his impressions of her famous father.

> I was stricken dumb and I cannot give you a description of the misery I feel. How I envy such a father! The richest inheritance a father can give his children is an honoured name. What man ever left a nobler name than Livingstone? Written words, my dear Miss Agnes, however eloquent, would fail to express the sympathy I feel for you, and I feel too abashed by the subject to attempt it. The very name of Livingstone has a charm in it for me. I loved him as a son, and would have done for him anything worthy of the most filial. The image of him will never be obliterated from my memory. It is so green with me when I think of the parting with him, that I almost fancy sometimes that it is palpable, and while I think of him I shall think of his children, more especially of his favourite daughter, and of the deep love he bore for her.[41]

Stanley's secret resolution to complete the work of exploration started by Livingstone was further inspired by two things: on 6 April the Webbs arrived in London and handed over the doctor's last letter; and on the same day came reports that the latest attempt to chart the River Congo had failed.[42] The question still remained unsolved: was the Lualaba the feeder for the Nile, as Livingstone thought, or did it flow into the Congo?

On 15 April the ship bringing Livingstone's body docked at Southampton. Four days earlier Stanley had travelled down with the Webbs to be on the dockside as a reception committee.[43] The coffin came ashore to a twenty-one gun salute, was whisked away to London by special train, then lay in state for two days at the Royal Geographical Society. Tearful crowds filed past to pay tribute to Britain's greatest Victorian hero.[44]

Then on 18 April came the state funeral in Westminster Abbey. A long train of carriages, including one sent by the Queen, filled Broad Sanctuary. Inside the Abbey was the greatest crowd seen since Prince Albert's funeral, with more than 900 reserved seats. The coffin was borne slowly down the nave. The congregation sang the 90th Psalm to Purcell's music. In front of the coffin walked Livingstone's two sons and his father-in-law Robert Moffat.[45] There were eight pall-bearers. Stanley was in the front row with Jacob Wainwright. Then came Waller, Kirk (on leave in England at the time), Webb, Oswell, Steele and Young. Behind the coffin walked the missionary Roger Price and Kalulu, dressed in a grey suit. In the congregation, seated next to the Prime Minister, were the two Livingstone sisters Stanley had met in October 1872, both of them on their first trip south of the border. The Dean (also named Stanley, as it happened) read the burial service. A wreath from Queen Victoria was placed on the coffin. The congregation sang Doddridge's 'O God of Bethel by whose Hand' to the tune by Thomas Tallis. Canon Conway preached the sermon. Then Livingstone's body was interred in the nave close to that of Marshal Wade.[46]

Stanley returned to the Langham Hotel to ponder his next step. Whatever the sadness it occasioned, Livingstone's death at least opened up the possibility that Stanley's career might be rescued from the doldrums in which it had lain since 1872. Stanley was determined to be the man who carried on Livingstone's work in Africa, but the problem was how to bring this about. If he approached Bennett directly for the funds for a fresh expedition, the jealous Bennett would certainly turn him down. The trick was to force Bennett's hand.

Fortunately, one of Stanley's powerful friends had already come to the conclusion that Livingstone's work had to be finished and that only Stanley was capable of the task.[47] Edwin Arnold (later Sir Edwin), editor of the *Daily Telegraph*, poet, orientalist and fellow of the RGS, was one of the few Englishmen to have been completely won over to Stanley in 1872.[48] Arnold persuaded the *Telegraph* proprietor Edward Levy-Lawson to put up £6,000 for an African expedition to be led by Stanley, on the understanding that Bennett and the *New York Herald* would match the figure pound for pound. Naturally, when Arnold mentioned the proposition, Stanley jumped at it.[49] Now it was just a question of waiting for Bennett's answer to the cable inviting him to participate. Bennett was in a quandary. To agree would be to advance Stanley's career. Yet to refuse ran the risk that the *Telegraph* would find another co-sponsor; Stanley would simply resign from the *Herald* to head the expedition and both

239

reporter and African scoops would be lost forever. Bennett felt that he had no choice. A terse and charmless 'Yes' was cabled across the Atlantic.[50]

Five months' preparations now ensued for the expedition that was confidently billed by both the sponsoring newspapers as the greatest ever to be sent to Africa and the one with potentially the most sensational consequences; where nations sent armies, this project, backed by the despised 'Fourth Estate', would bring 'peace and light'.[51] Offers of help from wealthy individuals and organisations flooded in. There was Angela Burdett-Coutts, one of the wealthiest women of the age and an admirer of Stanley since 1872.[52] There was William Mackinnon, like Stanley a Celt and self-made man from humble origins, who had made a fortune from Indian commerce and founded in 1863 the British Indian Steam Navigation Company.[53] His interest was particular, since in 1872 Mackinnon's company opened the first regular steamship service between Aden and Zanzibar. Then there was the Peninsular and Oriental Shipping Line, which made available various free facilities.[54] The White Star Line gave Stanley free passage to and from America in return for the publicity. All in all, 'invitations to dinner and to parties and to spend a month or so in the country were so numerous that if I could have availed myself of them in succession years must elapse before any hotel need charge a penny to my account.'[55]

Once news of the expedition was made public, Stanley was inundated with volunteers. He received more than 1,200 applications, 700 from Great Britain, 300 from the USA and about a hundred each from France and Germany, including three generals and five colonels. All the military volunteers had impeccable credentials but it was otherwise with the would-be civilian intake, which was distinguished by its extreme eccentricity. Many of them alienated Stanley at once by boasting of their 'street wisdom' and how they were 'up to every dodge', of how they had seen, done and knew everything. One madman proposed that he and Stanley should journey alone and unarmed through Africa, disguised as black men. Another suggested taking a tramway and a locomotive, of which he would be the driver. Yet another, a pre-echo of Kipling, suggested that he and Stanley set themselves up as kings in Africa. The most *outré* suggestion came from a man who claimed to be an expert in poisons and suggested that, instead of taking guns and ammunition or paying tribute to the 'nigger' chiefs, they would be able to poison them all as they went. Stanley reserved an especial contempt for the French and German applicants, many of whom offered as valuable attributes the ability to cook *biftek* or, even more idiotically, offered to interpret at the various 'hotels' at which the expedition would be staying during the crossing of Africa![56]

All of this evoked scorn and derision in Stanley. He inveighed at the mob of imbeciles who would 'take me up in balloons or by flying carriages, make us all invisible by their magic arts, or by the "science of magnetism" would cause all savages to fall asleep while we might pass anywhere without trouble. Indeed I feel sure that, had enough money been at my disposal at that time I might have led 5,000 Englishmen, 2,000 Frenchmen, 2,000 Germans, 500 Italians, 250 Swiss, 200 Belgians, 50 Spaniards, 5 Greeks, or 15,005 Europeans to Africa.'[57]

However, Stanley did feel the need to take a handful of European companions with him. Typically, he decided they should all be from a lower social class, so that there could never be any question of a challenge to his authority. Three men only survived his severe winnowing process. One was Frederick Barker, a clerk at the Langham Hotel, who pestered and wheedled him until Stanley gave in. The other two were the Pocock brothers, two Medway sailors and fishermen recommended to him by Arnold; Edward Pocock, their father, skippered the Arnold yacht at lower Upnor on the Medway.[58] They would be particularly useful to him, Stanley decided, because of their knowledge of boats. Among other innovations on this expedition he intended to take a specially designed boat, constructed by James Messenger of Middlesex. 40 feet long, with a 6-foot beam and 30 inches deep, of ⅜-inch thick Spanish cedar, the boat was in five detachable sections, each of 8 feet, on paper ideally suited for Africa's rivers. Stanley nicknamed this craft the *Lady Alice*, for reasons which he never publicly divulged.

The reason was particularly intriguing, for by the time the African expedition was announced, Stanley had embroiled himself with the third of his unattainable dream women. It was of the essence of Stanley's relationships with women that he had to light on someone who would reject him. This was because at the unconscious level he wanted to be rejected. At the conscious level this meant becoming entangled with women who were quite obviously unsuitable, in terms of class, culture or age. On 13 May at the Langham Hotel, he made the acquaintance of the Pike family. This was after the Livingstone funeral but a month before the announcement of the African expedition. At the time Stanley was in a fallow period, working night and day on the book that would become *Coomassie and Magdala*. But, perhaps significantly, Stanley had just been visited by one of the voices from his past. Virginia Ambella renewed contact, this time from an address in Athens, to indicate that she was still available as a wife. Stanley brushed the suggestion aside curtly: 'It is hopeless to expect that I can love again where that love was rejected in such an abrupt manner.'[59]

The Langham Hotel was the most modern and spacious in London and as such a great favourite with visiting Americans. One of Stanley's fellow guests was a Mr Aronson from New York (whom Stanley did not like). On 13 May Aronson invited him to join his guests at dinner and Stanley, out of boredom, accepted. Two of the Pike girls were to be there, Nettie and Alice, daughters of Samuel N. Pike, a German-Jewish immigrant to the USA who had made a fortune out of distilling whisky in Cincinnati and built the Grand Opera House there.[60] Nettie came to the table first. Stanley found her good-looking but rather 'fast': 'her hair was done up in what I believe are called frizzles, which is a lot of untidy hair hanging over the forehead. She had an enormous chignon, talked disgustingly loud.' Nettie got into a close conversation with Aronson, so that when Alice came and sat down, Stanley had her to himself for a long period. She was only seventeen but when he spoke to her, she turned her face around in a self-contained way that contrasted strikingly and favourably with the more volatile Nettie. Stanley observed her closely and his later jottings are revealing on what he considered desirable in a woman:

> While her manner was constrained even to being frigid, the style of her hair and dress, diamonds and such, indicated 'fast' or inordinate vanity with over-much wealth to gratify it or absolve her from following what may be called good taste. Her eyes were of a bluish grey, were very large and seemed capable of expansion. Her mouth was large but well-formed, her nose had a certain Jewish fullness at the point with the slightest possible rise half way down. Her face was pallid, forehead was broad, temples prominent, her 'frizzles' however hung as thickly over the forehead that they marred what would otherwise have been a very attractive face . . . when she rose from the table I noticed her figure was very elegant. The carriage of her head indicated that she was cool and self-possessed and that if she does not know much of society she had a lower opinion of society than she had of herself.[61]

Soon they were joined by Mrs Pike, a recent widow of about forty, stout and good-tempered. After dinner Stanley accompanied the Pike ladies to their suite of rooms at the Langham. During dinner the three women had declared great interest in his forthcoming African journey, but further questioning had revealed a woeful ignorance of African geography and, added Stanley waspishly, 'I fear of everything else.'

During the next few days Stanley's interest in Alice Pike was further enhanced by a series of meetings and drives in Hyde Park. He was attracted physically, while repelled morally. Alice, it was plain, was a coquette and a *capriciosa*. She had a number of suitors, among them an elderly judge called Mumford in St Louis. Another was a French nobleman, whose private letters she read out for the general amusement. Nettie, too, while admitting that she cared nothing for Aronson, encouraged him in his slavish admiration. Stanley's ambivalent reaction to this pair of flirts is well conveyed in one of his diary entries. 'I fear if Miss Alice gives me as much encouragement as she [Nettie] has been giving him [Aronson] lately, I shall fall in love with her, which may not perhaps be very conducive to my happiness, for she is the very opposite of my ideal wife.'[62]

A few days later this impression was reinforced. One morning he called to see the Pike girls at their suite, and Nettie was called downstairs to deal with another of her conquests. Stanley was left alone with Alice. Alice produced another letter from the French Count Portales, read out a section which was overly euphuistic and collapsed with laughter as she read it. Stanley was most disconcerted. 'It impressed on me the necessity of being very circumspect and I mentally vowed that she would never receive a declaration from me . . . I have discovered that however pretty, elegant, etc she may be, she is heartless and a confirmed flirt.'[63] The fear of being laughed at behind his back was in Stanley's case almost pathological; given that this was Alice's way, no worse choice of wife could be imagined.

Yet by mid-June, just when the African expedition was being confirmed, he entered the following in his diary. 'This day I saw my fiancée Alice, for so I must call her, depart from Liverpool by the *Russia* with her family for New York. She has sworn undying fidelity to me and our parting was very tender.'[64] Clearly the physical impact of Alice had for the moment swept aside his reservations. As soon as he had tied up the London end of the expedition with Levy-Lawson and the *Daily Telegraph* people, Stanley found the excuse to follow Alice across the Atlantic in the alleged need to consult with Bennett in New York. With free passage given him by the White Star line, there was no financial impediment to the chase. On 24 June he left Liverpool on the *Britannic* and arrived in New York on 4 July.[65]

There was a strong contrast between the public and private parts of

Stanley's American mission. Bennett went out of his way to snub the man who, he felt, had manoeuvred him into another African venture that would redound purely to Stanley's fame. After keeping him dangling for several days around the *Herald* offices with the usual lame excuses about being 'in a meeting', Bennett finally consented to see him at 10.30 a.m. on the morning of 8 July. When Stanley stepped into Bennett's office to speak, 'Jamie' cut him off brusquely, saying he was too busy to talk now – it would have to wait until Friday. As Stanley remarked, for once with understatement: 'This is rather an unkind way to receive one whom he is about to send to explore Africa.'[66] When he did eventually manage to see Bennett, the proprietor simply handed him on to the editor Conway, who gave him his instructions verbally and conveyed the deep unhappiness of all at the *Herald* headquarters about the 'enforced' collaboration with the *Daily Telegraph*.[67]

The quest for Alice fared better, or so it seemed. On Sunday 12 July Stanley signed a marriage pact with her at her home at 613 Fifth Avenue, the millionaire quarter of Manhattan, made fashionable by the Astors and Vanderbilts. 'We solemnly pledge ourselves to be faithful to each other and to be married to one another on the return of Henry Morton Stanley from Africa. We call God to witness this our pledge in writing.' The pledge was reinforced after a dinner on 17 July. They returned to the Pike house on Fifth Avenue and during an intimate talk in the parlour, Alice told him: 'You must hurry and do your work in Africa, and when the two years are gone, if you come to claim me, I will marry you, so help me God.'[68] Alice explained that it was in deference to her mother's wishes that she had decided to postpone the marriage for two years, but that at the end of that time she would marry him with or without her mother's consent. After saying this, she raised her lips 'in tempting proximity' to his. He kissed her on the lips, eyes, cheek and neck and she kissed him in return.[69]

Next day Stanley left New York for Liverpool on the *Celtic*. Alice repeated her vows and promised to write to him often. She and Nettie went down to the pier to see him off. 'I clasped her hands to bid her goodbye. She gave me such a look – a long, earnest, wide-eyed look, during which I thought that she was striving to pierce the dark, gloomy picture, but I turned away and the spell broke.' Once on deck he waved dismissively to tell them not to wait around. At the second wave, they moved off. 'Alice kissed her hand to me, and resolutely turned away, a seeming self-possessed maiden but hiding, I know, some pang at parting.'[70]

· 13 ·

Back in London Stanley put the finishing touches to the expedition. Despite his experiences with domestic animals on the Livingstone expedition, he decided to take a quartet of dogs with him: a mastiff, Castor, a retriever, Nero, a bulldog, Bull, and a bull-terrier, Jack.[1] These he sent ahead with the Pococks and Barker to wait for him at Aden. After signing formal contracts with Stanley on 4 and 5 August, his three white companions shipped out from Southampton on the *Mongolia*, bound for Aden via Malta, Alexandria and the Suez Canal.[2] Stanley remained at the Langham to tie up loose ends, such as whether the British India Company could take the *Lady Alice* on from Aden to Zanzibar. Then in mid-August he left for Zanzibar on the BISN steamer *Euphrates* for Zanzibar.[3]

The Pococks arrived in Aden on 2 September and Stanley a week later, with the *Lady Alice.* Uniting the two parties, they sailed on to Zanzibar, reached on 22 September. It was fortunate for Stanley that there was a skilled carpenter on board the *Euphrates*, for he found that the boat sections, instead of weighing a maximum of 120 pounds each (and as such suitable for being carried by two men) weighed anywhere between 280 and 310 pounds. It took the carpenter two weeks to remodel the sections.[4]

At Zanzibar Stanley found many changes. Since he had been there last, in 1872, the Bartle Frere mission to the Sultan had succeeded in abolishing slavery on the island.[5] Tozer had gone, replaced by Dr Edward Steere, a man universally liked and praised even by Stanley.[6] Even better, Kirk was in England on leave and as Acting Consul and Political Resident there was Captain Pridaux, one of the Magdala captives.[7] Stanley and his party stayed at the house of Augustus Sparhawk (now working for the Bertram Agency) in Shangani. Stanley was by now convinced he had made a wise choice with the Pococks, whom he found not just sober, civilised and industrious but very good singers and musicians.[8]

He set about recruiting porters from among his beloved *wangwana*.[9] Chowpereh agreed to join provided Stanley vaccinated his son against smallpox. Others of his veterans who were prepared to sign were Ulimengo, Rojab, Manwa Sera and Mabruki. The troublesome Bombay was not in any case available this time, since he had already accompanied Verney Cameron into the interior.[10] But Stanley was able to recruit forty-seven of the men he had sent to accompany Livingstone on his last expedition. Additionally, he engaged a further 200, largely on the personal recommendations of his veterans.

Stanley spent a tedious first week in Zanzibar organising this greatest ever foray into the heart of the Dark Continent. He discovered that whereas barter goods had gone down in price in Zanzibar since 1872 because of uncertainties about the trade of the interior, the cost of porters had doubled. Stanley lost no opportunity in shifting the blame for this to his rival, attributing it to the 'somewhat inordinate liberality of the Cameron expedition'.[11] He tried out his inflatable pontoon, designed by J. C. Cording of London to help in fording flooded African rivers, and made of thick india-rubber cloth. The only relaxation was horseback riding in the interior of the island every evening after dinner, or sightseeing. Yet, apart from the Mnazi Moya (One Coconut Tree) at Shangani Point, there was little enough to see – just a harbour filled with every conceivable kind of ship, from British warships to Arab small craft, sometimes as many as 150 at anchor together.[12]

By the end of September Stanley had had enough. Leaving the final administrative details to Sparhawk, he took his companions over to the mainland to explore the Rufiji River.[13] After several weeks' exploration, they returned to Bagamoyo and thence across the channel to Zanzibar. A further month on the island was necessary before the vast expedition was finally ready to depart. Stanley paid out £1,300 in advances to his *wangwana*; the formal contract of service, dated 15 November 1874, specified that the men of Zanzibar were to remain with Stanley 'for two years or until such time as he may require them or until such time as he no longer needs their services.'[14] Stanley took with him into Africa 18,000 pounds of trade goods, arms and *matériel* – 8 tons divided into loads of 60 pounds each for his 300 porters. His three white companions toiled away at the boats to make them manoeuvrable and weatherly on the treacherous African waterways. Barker and the Pococks timidly asked (and received) permission for a Union Jack to be flown, since this was an Anglo-American expedition.[15] The simplicity of Stanley's two young fishermen is best illustrated by a visit to Zanzibar of HMS *Thetis* during which the crew put on a performance of *The Merchant of Venice*. It is quite clear from Pocock's diary entry that he had never before heard of the play.[16]

At last all was ready. On 12 November 1874 six Arab vessels conveyed the expedition across the straits to Bagamoyo. But before the march could get under way there were problems. Stanley's men proved unruly and undisciplined. After one affray Stanley placed a dozen men under arrest. When his drunken followers continued to run amok, he called in the aid of the governor of Bagamoyo. But when his severity in turn threatened to make a bad situation worse, Stanley was reduced to asking the governor for lenient treatment for his followers. It became clear that the problems would be resolved only when Bagamoyo was left far in the rear. Stanley tried to encourage his men by pointing out that the 60-pound loads would reduce to 30 pounds within the year.[17]

The only point of interest for Stanley in Bagamoyo was to see the vastly increased rate of missionary activity there. But Stanley, never a friend to missionaries, criticised them for trying to take the African straight from barbarism to Christianity, without satisfying the intermediate stage of material want.[18] For once, Stanley the hard driver was criticising people for trying to go too fast. The missionaries, in turn, remembering how Stanley had pilloried them in *How I Found Livingstone*, were wary. When Stanley returned to dine at the Holy Ghost Mission, the fathers made sure that this time there was no champagne, that the explorer was served only simple fare.[19]

Finally, on 17 November, having secured six riding asses for the expedition, one each for the Europeans and two in reserve for the sick, Stanley was able to give the order to march into the interior.[20] Many thought he was going to a certain death, but Stanley was unworried by this. As he wrote to J. R. Robinson of the *Daily News*: 'Now that I am face to face with inhospitable Africa there is something, it seems to me, which grinds out all hope of return. At the same time I cannot say that I feel any melancholy at the hopeless prospect, but rather a careless indifference as to what Fate may have in store for me. I say truly that I don't care whether I return or not. I have disciplined myself to look at my long journey in this light. If I return, it is well, if not, then it is well again, for I shall cease from being troubled or annoyed.'[21] He ended by pointing out that Livingstone had preferred to die in Africa rather than endure the sustained hostility of people in England, and he himself felt the same way.

What light does this curious avowal of the death instinct throw on the relationship with Alice Pike? There are good grounds for thinking that both partners to the New York marriage 'contract' were acting in bad faith, Alice fundamentally unserious and caught up in the sentimentality of the moment, Stanley unconsciously willing his own ultimate rejection. There is something decidedly curious about a man who professes love for a woman, then disappears into the heart of Africa for three years. Equally, it is hard to take seriously the coquettish outpourings of a rather empty-headed seventeen-year-old for a dour thirty-four-year-old explorer. That the Stanley-Alice Pike romance was foredoomed becomes very clear when we examine the correspondence between them. Stanley's 'love letters' were better suited for the columns of the RGS *Journal*. Alice's letters are a farrago of social gossip and girlish chatter about dances, clothes, weddings and music lessons. She manages at once to convey the impression of being offhand about his deeper feelings and serious in her calculation that she will have a pretext for not writing to him once he heads into the Dark Continent. The restless tone of the letters makes it seem always unlikely that she would keep to the terms of the engagement.

On 13 October Alice writes:

My dear Morton,
    I have not had a line from you in perfect ages, so wasn't I delighted on my return from a harp lesson to find, as I supposed a letter awaiting me . . . Although you have been kind in getting me so many pretty things you have been real mean about writing. You never write to me any more and I just want to know why??? I am real angry with Central Africa.[22]

Two weeks later she complains that she has not heard from him even though she writes every week. The level of communication is well conveyed by the following: 'I do love opera but I can hardly ever go, for Ma will not let me go out with gentlemen except one or two I have known for ages, or in a party.'[23]

But most revealing of all is her reply to Stanley's farewell letter from Zanzibar.

Why did you not tell me you would be gone for more than two years? I did not expect you to be back on the very day or month, but I was hardly prepared for a whole year over the time. And suppose you are not home, then where will you be? Dead or still seeking the Nile? What a change these years will make in me! I will have seen something of the world by then, will I be changed for the better or not. I may be affected and proud and you will not like me at all. Then my past habits might change perhaps, I may be dead long before the three years have passed. We cannot tell. I might become very poor and have to support myself. I can do nothing but sing. I would have to go on the stage. I would be compelled to for there is nothing else I can do well. Of course you would be too proud to marry me, an Opera singer. If I should lose my money I would marry any *rich* man who would have me, to save myself from the stage . . . Don't for Mercy's sake, get jealous of Hall, he is the best friend I have, he is only twenty-one, I have known him ever so long. By this time you must know you will have no further fear from others. That is wrong what you said about they wouldn't like me unless I gave them some encouragement, it is natural they should like me. I give them no more encouragement than talking to them, singing and dancing, and it is really no fault of mine if they are conceited enough to think I will accept them, if they only ask me. I have the most horrid sore finger all blistered from playing the harp. I am getting along quite well with it, only I never practice.[24]

The absurdity of such a letter, addressed to a man about to brave the dangers of unknown Central Africa, is evident. The fantasies of poverty seem particularly odious from the daughter of a millionaire. But instead of lamenting Stanley's inability to discriminate between immature women and those of greater emotional solidity, we should ask whether there was not method in Stanley's madness, whether he had not deliberately (albeit unconsciously) chosen an impossible object for his affections. We have established that Stanley in his oscillations between opposite polarities – sadism/masochism, homosexual/heterosexual – clearly manifested a schizoid personality disorder. The schizoid personality typically combines a desperate need for love with an equally desperate fear of intimacy. Stanley dared not make close contact with a woman for fear that any love given him would be withdrawn. Humiliated, unloved, despised, feeling himself the unworthy recipient of any apparent affection, Stanley constantly turned to African exploration as a means of re-establishing his identity. There is a motif of redemption by suffering both in the choice of Alice and in the penetration of Africa.[25] The implausibility of an enduring relationship with Alice Pike, then, derives from something deeper than Alice's essential flightiness and frivolity.

Stanley's unconscious wish to be rejected was soon granted. On 11 January 1876 Alice married Albert Clifford Barney of Dayton, Ohio, himself the heir to a huge railway fortune. Nine months later she gave birth to a daughter. In later life she became a playwright and patroness of

249

the arts.[26] She and Stanley never met again. When she wrote to congratulate him on his emergence from Africa in 1877 she excused herself thus: 'You must know, by this time, I have done what millions of women have done before, not been true to my promise ... No doubt before long you will think it a gain, for Stanley can easily find a wife all his heart could desire to grace his high position and deservedly great name.' But she began the letter with words that, in the light of Stanley's psychic turmoil, have an extra dimension of irony: 'Poor Stanley! How much you have lost, but your gain has been great indeed.'[27] She could not have understood that the gain and the loss for Stanley were one and the same.

What were Stanley's intentions when he set out from Bagamoyo in mid-November 1874 on what would prove to be his greatest African expedition? In following the established caravan route at first he was partly trying to build up his men's confidence and partly trying to avoid the territory of the Masai, for whom he had an exaggerated respect.[28] Once beyond the orbit of the Masai, he intended to strike north-westward to Lake Victoria to establish who was right about this great stretch of waterway. Speke thought Lake Victoria was just one vast lake, Burton thought it was a cluster of several smaller lakes, while Samuel Baker thought that Lakes Albert and Tanganyika were one and the same.[29] The way to solve all this was to circumnavigate Lake Victoria and Lake Albert, visiting the great King Mutesa on the way, and possibly to end with a visit to Gordon in Equatoria – Gordon who had no interest in exploration as such.[30] Finally – 'beyond this point the whole appears to me so vague and vast that it is impossible to state at this period what I shall try to do next.'[31]

The first part of the march to Lake Victoria was something of a rerun of 1871. But this time it was the *masika*, and as they slogged through the familiar Usagara and Ugogo country, they had to endure deluges of rain. Christmas Day 1874 saw the four white men huddling in their tents in wet clothes and blankets while flash floods outside produced a torrent that could convert a plain into a swamp in fifteen minutes.[32] They slurped and squelched through Ugogo, following a more northerly itinerary than in 1871, then crossed into Ukimbu, where no white man had ever been seen before.

Then they began to head north towards Lake Victoria. But at the village of Vinyata they became embroiled in sustained warfare with the hostile Waturu people. For a time it was touch and go whether the explorers would survive. In order to take the war to the enemy, Stanley divided his seventy effectives into four 'moving squares'. Unfortunately, the leader of one of these squares disobeyed orders; he and twenty men were lured out of range of their comrades and slaughtered to a man. Only quick thinking by Stanley prevented a second square from being overwhelmed. Learning from his mistakes, Stanley formed all his men into one bristling formation, resembling the Roman 'turtle'. His concentrated firepower then carried all before it. In a series of running fights the Waturu were completely defeated; the expedition could proceed in safety.[33]

But victory had been won at a price. At the end of January 1875 Stanley held a muster and found that half those who had started from Bagamoyo were dead. Apart from battle casualties, large numbers had perished from the aggravated effects of disease. Edward Pocock, who had caught fever on his first day on the African mainland and never recovered, died on 17 January. Among the *wangwana* there was a huge death-toll, from a plethora of illnesses: dysentery, bronchitis, pneumonia, ophthalmia, rheumatism, sciatica, asthma, dropsy, emphysema, erysipelas, elephantiasis.[34]

Further gruelling marches had to be endured before they came in sight of Lake Victoria on 26 February 1875. Frank Pocock was the first to espy the distant glistening waters, thus becoming the fourth white man to see Victoria Nyanza, after Speke, Grant and Chaillé-Long.[35] The porters burst into songs of joy at sight of the lake; universal joy was constrained only by the knowledge that Barker was now very ill with fever. A day later brought them to the small conical huts of the village of Kaduma on the lakeside, where they hired quarters. Euphoria was general at the thought of a long-earned rest. In 103 days they had come 720 miles from Bagamoyo – an average of 7 miles a day.[36]

It had been a great feat of marching, but the human cost was extraordinarily high. Out of 347 persons with whom he had started, Stanley had lost 181 through battle, famine, illness and desertion. One white man was dead and another seemed likely to die. Against this was the rapport that Stanley had established with Frank Pocock, and Pocock with the Zanzibaris. Pocock had no feeling of racial superiority about him. He was full of praise for Manwa Sera: 'Such a nice man . . . like a father. When we were in a desert he went twelve miles among wild beasts for water for the white men, a turn I shall never forget.'[37]

Frank Pocock wrote to his parents of his homesickness: 'I dreamed last night that I was at home eating fine things, but I awoke and found myself in Central Africa.' As they relaxed on the lake shore, Stanley too waxed nostalgic. He wrote to Alice Pike to tell her with pride that the *Lady Alice* had been carried 720 miles across Africa and spoke of his future plans. 'You asked me if we could not get married at once on my return, to which I answer that it shall be as you desire. The very hour I landed in England, I should like to marry you, but such a long time must elapse before I can see you that even to see your dear face again appears to me as a most improbable thing.'[38] Unknown to him, Stanley's fantasy romance had become a true fantasy, as much a dream as Pocock's reverie of the Medway.

14

S TANLEY allowed his men just one day of total relaxation. On the night of 28 February he gave a banquet and allowed extra 'pocket money' to Pocock and Barker in the form of beads and cloth with which to buy extra food.[1] Next day he announced his plans for an immediate circumnavigation of Lake Victoria. To begin with he would take a small party north to locate the capital of Mutesa, King of Uganda. The rest of the *wangwana* were to be divided into eight squads of twenty men each, with an experienced NCO to guide each squad. All would be armed either with Sniders or percussion-lock muskets; the NCOs additionally would be armed with revolvers. Stanley gave specific instructions that in any armed clash with enemy forces during his absence, his men should open fire at a distance greater than 40 yards; the men of Ituru had shown what would happen if an enemy closed the range below this distance, when spears became as deadly as bullets. The dreadful casualties in the battle at Vinyata still preyed on Stanley's mind; he had come to realise that there were African warriors 'rivalling the Apache in ferocity and determination'.[2]

It took Stanley just seven days to have the *Lady Alice* ready for its first real trial by water. He took with him ten men and large stocks of food (600 pounds of flour and 200 pounds of dried fish) to barter with the tribes.[3] The local chief Kaduma was an alcoholic, so Stanley decided he would be useless as a guide on the trip north. But the tall tales his people recounted of the horrors to be encountered on Lake Victoria further demoralised the *wangwana*, who had already protested to Stanley that they were not sailors and knew nothing of boats. Stanley had to use a mixture of cajolery and browbeating to get the men he had picked into the boat.[4] Even as they rowed away from camp on 8 March, the men looked back fearfully, sighed dolefully and hoped all the time for the signal to return.

Morale sank even lower as *Lady Alice* picked its way past Nathari Island at the mouth of the Shimeeyu River in the teeth of a ferocious gale. Next day the waters were as placid as a pond, but again nature intervened against them in the shape of a trio of hippos who rushed at them open-mouthed on the shores of Manassa and drove them off.[5] The hippopotami of Lake Victoria were very aggressive and often chased the boat; on one occasion they bumpèd over the spine of a hippo, who bade fair to shake the craft to pieces. Being spilled into these waters was mortally perilous, since the lake was infested with crocodiles, which, to Stanley's interest, lived here in a state of peaceful symbiosis with colonies of monitor lizards.[6]

They rowed east along the southerly shore of Speke Gulf, confirming that explorer's observations on Ukerewe, before turning north along the coast of Uriruri. They passed Ukara Island, later an especial haven for explorers of East Africa.[7] So far they had met only Sukuma peoples, but as they paddled farther northward Stanley noticed a different dialect creeping in: the population was mixed, part Sukuma, part Shasti.[8] They were finding it extremely difficult either to confirm or deny the Speke thesis that Lake Victoria was a single large waterway. For example, Stanley set down the Majita peninsula as two islands, did not spot that Baringo was a separate lake, and missed the Kavirondo Gulf altogether, as it is shielded from Lake Victoria by an island.[9] However, there could be no mistaking the fact that the people of Kavirondo were utterly different in language and culture from the Sukuma.[10]

But along the northern coast of Lake Victoria they ran into their first group of hostile tribesmen. At Ngevi Island, the locals brandished spears at them but bolted in terror when Stanley fired warning shots in the air with his revolver. Next day they returned, to insist that the strangers visit their king. Stanley pretended to agree to this, then hoisted sail and swept past them. But a ferocious gale that night forced them to make landfall in the country of the Waruma. Something about their demeanour made Stanley suspicious and he ordered his men to stand ready.[11]

Another gale, complete with hailstones, supervened the following night. Then, next morning, the Waruma attacked. Beaten off by a fusillade from the Sniders, they next launched a fleet of thirteen war canoes just as the *Lady Alice* was getting under way. To avoid conflict, Stanley allowed them to approach, but was forced to fire over their heads when they tried to seize the oars. Sheering off for a moment, the war canoes again came in close and the warriors taunted Stanley by pointing out the beads they had stolen during the land attack. Infuriated by this, Stanley opened up with his elephant gun, which at once smashed three canoes and killed four men. After he had holed the others below the waterline, the *Lady Alice* put about while their tormentors slowly sank in the water.[12]

Making good speed, they entered Napoleon Channel (later Napoleon Gulf) and soon passed a great river flowing away northwards (afterwards identified as the Victoria Nile at Ripon Falls). They explored the Buvuma Islands at the entrance to the gulf.[13] After failing to find Speke's Luajerri River, they sailed west along the northern shore of the lake, past Ikira, Kriva and Ukafu, and entered the territories of King Mutesa.[14] They passed the word to the warriors who accosted them that they were bound for the court on an embassy. On 3 April the Kabaka's ambassador arrived in a flotilla of large canoes to accompany them on the last stretch. He wore a bead-embossed head-dress above above which waved a long plume of white cocks' feathers. About his person was a long crimson robe and a snowy-white long-haired goatskin.[15]

On 3 April they completed the last stretch of the journey together, 'the king's canoes making a fine appearance'. On 4 April they arrived at Mutesa's hunting camp at Usavara, where they were welcomed by the Katekiro, the Kabaka's prime minister; after being greeted by a volley of musketry, the strangers were feasted on chickens, eggs, bananas and sweet potatoes by 2,000 of the king's excited followers. Ten oxen and sixteen sheep and goats were slaughtered in their honour. Stanley himself was lodged in a special house.[16] Stanley passed the Katekiro's interrogation with flying colours and both sides fell to mutual admiration. Mutesa's people seemed as different from the other denizens of Lake Victoria as Kansas whites from the Choctaws.

5 April 1875, the date of Stanley's meeting with Mutesa, was one of the decisive dates in the confrontation of European explorer with African indigenous power. It bore comparison with Moffat's meeting with Msilikazi in Matabeleland or Livingstone's with Sekeletu, the Makololo chief. A less happy precedent that might have been in Stanley's mind was the disastrous *rencontre* between Kabba Rega and Samuel Baker in Unyoro three years earlier. The actual meeting was certainly dramatic. Walking from his quarters, Stanley soon found himself in a broad street, 80 feet wide and half a mile long, lined with Mutesa's personal guards and servants. At the extreme end of the street sat the Kabaka in his house of audience. To the firing of guns, waving of flags and beating of drums, Stanley advanced slowly up the avenue. Mutesa arose, a tall, slender figure in Arab costume. He approached a few paces, held out his hand mutely, and the two men stood gazing at each other while the drums

continued their deafening tattoo. Then silence fell. Mutesa sat down and invited his guest to follow suit.[17]

Seeing before him a 'most intelligent, humane and distinguished prince', Stanley was unable to recognise the Kabaka in Speke's unflattering portrait. Around thirty-four years of age (the same as Stanley), Mutesa deeply impressed him by his quiet dignity and his vast superiority in intelligence to the Sultan of Zanzibar. 'His face is very agreeable and pleasant, and indicates intelligence and mildness. His eyes are large, his nose and mouth are a great improvement upon those of the common type of negro . . . his teeth are splendid and gleaming white.'[18] A heathen in Speke and Grant's day, Mutesa now professed Islam. All his officers wore Arab dress and affected Arab ways. Taken by surprise at the level of civilisation at the court, Stanley rounded on Speke in his writings and accused him of luring him almost to his death by his inaccuracies; believing in Speke's portrait, he had come close to insulting Mutesa by offering him the sort of childish trinkets appropriate to the savage tribes of the *hongo* system.[19]

Rapport between the two men was immediate. Next day Mutesa held a naval review to show off his power. Then he asked Stanley to demonstrate the force of his weaponry to the women of his harem. Getting off a lucky shot from a moving canoe, Stanley killed a crocodile stone dead from a range of 100 yards. Deeply impressed with this marksmanship, which he considered probably run of the mill with white men, Mutesa tried one of the rifles himself, but it fractured in his hands, and some very quick technical explanations were called for from Stanley to avert the suggestion that this was a bad omen.[20] Once restored to full favour, Stanley penned this portrait of the king.

In person Mutesa is tall, probably 6' 1" and slender. He has very intelligent and agreeable features, reminding me of some of the faces of the great stone images at Thebes and of the statues in the museum at Cairo. He has the same fullness of lips, but their grossness is relieved by the general expression of amiability blended with dignity that pervades his face, and the large lustrous lambent eyes that lend it a strange beauty, and are typical of the race from which I believe him to have sprung. His colour is of a dark red brown, of a wonderfully smooth surface. When not engaged in council, he throws off unreservedly the bearing that characterises him when on the throne and gives vein to his humour, indulging in hearty peals of laughter. He seems to be interested in the discussion of the manners and customs of European courts, and to be enamoured of hearing the wonders of civilisation. He is ambitious to imitate as much as lies in his power the ways of the white men. When any piece of information is given him, he takes upon himself the task of translating it to his wives and chiefs, though many of the latter understand the Swahili language as well as he does himself.[21]

On 8 April the Kabaka's court moved from the hunting village to Mutesa's capital at Ugalla, a three-hour march away over rude roads. The highway improved dramatically just before the capital.

As we approached the capital, the highway from Usavara increased in width from twenty feet to 150 feet. When he arrived at this magnificent breadth we viewed the capital crossing an eminence commanding a most extensive view of a picturesque and rich country teeming with gardens and plantains, and beautiful pasture land . . . the vast collection of huts crossing the eminence were the Royal Quarters, around which ran several palisades and circular courts, between which and the city was a circular road, ranging from one hundred to two hundred feet in width, from which radiated six or seven magnificent avenues, lined with gardens and huts.[22]

Stanley was given a 'garden villa' of a marquee shape to live in. He was invited to the palace that very afternoon for the first of a week-long series of chats, during which the intimacy and mutual regard of both men deepened.[23] Stanley had already seen that he could score a great publicity coup if he could declare to the world that the kingdom of Uganda was open for missionary work. He therefore continually urged on Mutesa the advantages of converting to Christianity. The Kabaka had no intention of apostasy from Islam, but he realised the advantages that could accrue to him, not least in the technology of war, from closer contact with Europeans. Accordingly, he pretended a deep interest in the Christian faith and expressed a wish to be converted. Stanley triumphantly made him a present of a Bible. Mutesa artfully questioned him on what was so good about the Gospel. Mention of the brotherhood of man, the equality of women and the absence of slavery produced a glazed look in the king. Then Stanley produced his trump. He claimed that there were eleven commandments; the eleventh, inverted by Stanley himself, ran thus: 'Honour and respect kings, for they are the envoys of God.' This was closer to the language Mutesa understood, and his features lit into a smile. He said that in that case he would certainly embrace Christianity.[24]

Stanley was completely taken in and announced to the world that Uganda was a rich vineyard for England's missionary toilers.[25] In London the call created a sensation, and eager acolytes flocked to the missionary standard, but Mutesa's later behaviour made it crystal clear that he had made the credulous Stanley his dupe.[26] Here was a signal instance of one of the weaknesses in Stanley's personality. He was always prone to overrate his own persuasiveness and to imagine that he possessed the ability to win people round to his point of view. It did not occur to him, *as long as they appeared deferential*, that they might be gulling him.[27]

There was a specific reason why Mutesa contemplated calling in the power of Europe to redress the balance in Africa. He was aware of growing pressure on his kingdom from the Egyptians in the north, especially since Colonel (later General) Gordon had become governor of Equatoria province. That pressure seemed to take a concrete form a few days after Stanley's advent when, coincidentally, an envoy from Gordon, Colonel Ernest Linant de Bellefonds, arrived in Ugalla.[28] His coming illustrates the extreme complexity of Central African power politics in the 1870s.

In 1869 Khedive Ismail (whom Stanley had met that year at the opening of the Suez Canal) appointed Samuel Baker as governor of Equatoria – the area of the Upper Nile between Fashoda and Lake Victoria. His brief was to extirpate the slave trade and bring the headwaters of the Nile under Egyptian control. In 1870 Baker left Khartoum for Gondokoro, 'capital' of the province of Equatoria. Baker had been chosen as governor because of his earlier (1863) exploration of Lake Albert and the kingdom of Bunyoro, then ruled over by Kamrasi. Bunyoro was one of two powerful Bantu kingdoms in the lake regions, the other being Buganda. Buganda, on the north-west side of the lake, was the dominant power in the area during this period.[29] When the Europeans first encountered the kingdoms, Buganda played the Inca to their *conquistadores*, with the rival state of Bunyoro as the Aztecs. In other words, the power of Buganda was on the ascendant while that of Bunyoro was declining.[30]

In 1872 Baker, after a year of ineffectual blood-letting in a war against the slavers at Gondoroko, headed south with an army of about a thousand well-armed Sudanese and Egyptians, bent on the annexation of Bunyoro. Kamrasi's successor, Kabba Rega, had no intention of submitting to Egyptian rule. He forced Baker to make a humiliating retreat out of his kingdom, after coming within an ace of annihilating his invading army. In 1873 Baker resigned and was replaced as governor of Equatoria by

'Chinese' Gordon. I April 1874 Gordon arrived in Gondokoro, determined on southward expansion. His ambitious plans included exploring
the Nile between Lakes Albert and Victoria with a view to steamer
communication; occupation of the plateau between the two lakes; abandoning the Nile as a principal artery of communication between Cairo and
Equatoria and its replacement with an overland route to the East African
coast.[31]

Clearly these plans posed a threat to both Buganda and Bunyoro.
Militarily it might have seemed that Gordon lacked the capability to
implement such grandiose plans, but the Khedive's attack on and occupation of the Sultan of Zanzibar's garrison forts north of Mombasa in
1875 showed that Egyptian will at least was not lacking.[32] The Khedive
was clearly a hothead. When he first heard of Stanley's expedition, he told
Chaillé-Long that the desire to complete Livingstone's work was merely
the ostensible object of the Anglo-American expedition. Its real objective
was to plant the British flag in Uganda. Accordingly the Khedive was keen
that Gordon, Chaillé-Long and his other lieutenants should beat Stanley
to the punch.[33] This was the genesis of the Linant de Bellefonds mission
to Mutesa. Gordon was playing for time, hoping forlornly to get the
Kabaka and Kabba Rega to negotiate away their territorial rights while he
and the Khedive considered whether they really did have the resources for
military conquest in Central Africa.

This explains both the much greater coolness with which Mutesa
received Bellefonds, as compared with Stanley, and the sustained interest
that Gordon and all his lieutenants showed in Stanley's movements in
1875-6.[34] From Gordon's point of view, not only might Stanley's
'meddling' wreck his own designs against Mutesa, but Stanley, with his
retinue of *wangwana*, had to be considered as in some sense the Sultan of
Zanzibar's man and hence the enemy. Stanley's notion of meeting up with
Gordon for joint action against the slavers was egregiously naïve. Gordon
made it clear that he would allow no Zanzibari soldiers on the soil of
Equatoria. If Stanley made his way into the province, he, Gordon would
send him politely on his way to Khartoum.[35]

This complex background to the Bellefonds mission at Mutesa's court
in no way diminished the pleasure that Stanley took in the Frenchman's
company, largely because he was unaware of its wider implications.
Bellefonds arrived in the Ugandan capital on 11 April and at first mistook
Stanley for Verney Cameron.[36] That mistake corrected, the two men
spent three stimulating days in each other's company. Bellefonds, at his
initial interview with Mutesa, found himself having to confirm the truth of

the Stanley verson of Christianity. But afterwards: 'On leaving the king I went to breakfast with Mr Stanley, and we chatted together a long time, stretched out on our straw, smoking and taking our tea. These were for us happy moments – like a splendid meteor, the duration of which was like that of a shooting star. Each one of us found in the other a brother and opened his heart to him. Stanley told me about the fatigues and difficulties of his journeys, the hostility he had encountered among certain peoples whom he had been forced to fight – he gave me geographical information of the greatest interest.'[37]

Stanley for his part was even more glowing: 'The meeting, though not so exciting as my former meeting with the venerable David Livingstone, at Ujiji in November 1871, still may be said to be singular and fortunate for all concerned. In Colonel Bellefonds I met a gentleman extremely well informed, energetic and a great traveller.'[38] Their conversations ranged far and wide, over Mutesa, religion, the geographical details of Uganda and the Sudan, the future of Africa. They even swapped items of cuisine. Their opinions differed only on how to treat the Africans. Bellefonds was stiff and reserved with the Ganda people, while Stanley encouraged them to swarm all over his courtyard. It was good luck for Stanley that Bellefonds was a Protestant, against the run of probability for his country-men, since he was able to tell Mutesa the same story about Christianity. The Kabaka was amazed that two men who had never met before could independently give accounts that squared with one another. It was a genuine loss to Stanley when he heard later that Bellefonds had been killed fighting the Bari on his way back to Gordon's headquarters.[39] On his side the Frenchman paid full tribute to Stanley's already remarkable achievements since leaving Zanzibar five months earlier; if he were an Arab he would still be floundering through Ugogo.[40]

On 14 April Stanley informed Mutesa that he had to return to see how his expedition was faring at Kaduma's. The Kabaka was sorry to see him go; his encounter with his fourth white man had left him both stimulated and content.[41] With Bellefonds he returned to Usavara (Murchison Bay). There he said goodbye to the Frenchman and set off along the western shore of the lake, aiming to return to Kagehyi, where his men were camped, after a complete circumnavigation of the lake. Mutesa had assigned Stanley thirty canoes under the command of his admiral Magassa, but Magassa, a notorious prima donna, was not ready to sail on the 17th.[42] He suggested that Stanley would do better to go on without him, while he assembled the promised canoes from the Sesse people.[43] Taking some of the Ganda with him as an escort, Stanley set out to explore the 'Alexandra Nile' and the Ripon Falls on the north-west coast before sailing due south.

Once out of Mutesa's domains, Stanley began to encounter sharp signs of hostility. At Makongo on the coast of Urongora he was menaced by a war party. In face of such a welcome he withdrew to Musira Island 3 miles away. There he threw off the troubling company of his indisciplined Ganda escort by allowing himself the luxury of a quiet stroll in the woods. Next day Magassa's standard was sighted fluttering in the breeze; he appeared to have assembled the canoes promised by Mutesa. Stanley signalled to him to follow and cast off. Magassa acknowledged the signal and promptly ignored it. Alone again, Stanley put into Alice Island, where his men at once despoiled the local fishermen of their catch. To avoid bloodshed Stanley had to restore the stolen goods and compensate the fishermen. Camped in the shadow of a 50-foot basalt cliff, Stanley worked hard to establish good relations with the people of Alice Islands. The islanders were friendly enough but their prices were exorbitant. Stanley decided there were better pickings to be had elsewhere. After vainly waiting for Magassa until noon on 28 April, he set course for Bumbire Island.[44]

They reached the island after sunset in another tropical downpour. They anchored under the lee of the island in the darkness and huddled there wretchedly all night, cold, hungry and miserable. Bumbire was a large island, 11 miles long by 2 miles wide, hilly, clothed in short grass and with a large population of some 4,000. As *Lady Alice* drew into the shore next morning, they were assailed with war cries. Stanley's inclination was to shove off again, but his men were hungry and he yielded to their blandishments.[45]

No sooner had the keel of the boat grounded than the Bumbire people rushed it and dragged it high and dry on to the shore. Literally scores of tribesmen were needed to do this, as combined boat, crew and baggage weighed more than 4,000 pounds. Stanley's natural instinct was to shoot it out then and there. He raised his revolver to fire but Safeni, wisest and most diplomatic of his Zanzibari bodyguards, counselled him not to. Unconvinced, Stanley sat down in the stern sheets and awaited the crisis he was sure would break, for all around him the locals were yelling and screaming with demented fury.[46]

Negotiations for *hongo* commenced amid this angry tumult. For three hours Safeni bargained with Shekka, the Bumbire chief. After viewing the cloths and beads on offer, Shekka retired to consider. He returned with a promise of food in return for large *doti* but immediately showed his treachery by ordering his warriors to seize the boat's oars. He then began again to talk emolliently, but Stanley guessed that it was only a matter of time before the Bumbire repeated the performance, this time with the guns. He continued to negotiate through Safeni, master of tongues and dialects. First he promised twenty cloths for the return of the oars, then offered to make blood-brotherhood with Shekka. Both offers were refused.[47]

At 3 p.m. Stanley's worst fears were realised when Shekka and 300 warriors appeared in warpaint at the brow of a hill no more than 300 yards from the *Lady Alice*. Presently drums were heard beating the call to arms. More tribesmen appeared daubed in paint. Shekka sat on the ground and began to exhort his people. When he had finished, fifty of the boldest rushed down to the water's edge to admonish Stanley to prepare his guns, as Shekka was coming to cut his throat. They bore off the Zanzibari drum as a trophy. While they were occupied in showing this triumphantly to Shekka, Stanley shouted to his men to push the boat into the water. With a desperate heaving effort, the eleven-strong crew lifted it off the ground and shot it into the water. The impetus of the craft into the lake bore them all quickly into deep water.[48]

The Bumbire people, meanwhile, uttering a furious howl of disappointment and baffled rage, came running like dervishes towards their canoes at the lakeside. Stanley discharged his elephant gun, loaded with two large conical balls, into their midst. He then pulled one of the crew out of the water and told him to help his floundering comrades aboard while he kept the enemy at bay. He next fired his double-barrelled shot-gun, loaded with buckshot. The roaring explosion from this did terrible damage. The tribesmen fell back up the slope of the hill. It was now time to get *Lady Alice* out of the cove before the warriors manned their canoes and sealed off the exit.[49]

Stanley ordered his men to tear up the seats and floorboards and use them as oars. They began to paddle away while Stanley picked off the most prominent of his pursuers with the deadly elephant gun. Among the first to fall victim was Shekka's war chief. On clearing the cove they were intercepted by two more canoes full of warriors, shooting out of another inlet. Stanley let them approach to within 100 yards before unleashing a killing fusillade from the elephant gun, now loaded with explosive balls. Four volleys were enough to kill five men and sink both canoes. The enemy sheered off, having taken casualties later discovered to be fourteen dead and wounded.[50]

Yet even as they seemed to be reaching safety, Stanley's men came under attack from a wholly unexpected source. Two large hippos dashed on them open-mouthed. Stanley dispatched one at 10 yards' range and wounded the other. From the shore the watching tribesmen hooted with derision and frustration. 'Go and die in the Nyanza!' They salved their wounded pride by firing a few arrows at the vanishing *Lady Alice*; these dropped harmlessly into the water.[51]

But the danger was not yet over. It was 5 p.m., they had four bananas between twelve men and had no idea where to go. All night, all next day and the following night they paddled, out of sight of land, battered by gales and surrounded by crocodiles ready to devour them if the storms capsized the boat. Even if they were wrecked on an uninhabited island, they would surely die of slow starvation. Stanley always regarded the day after the first Bumbire encounter as the most desperate of his life.[52]

By the morning of 30 April the dozen-strong party had had just a third of a banana and a cup of coffee each since 10 a.m. on the 27th and had rowed sixty-eight hours in the meantime. Exhausted and in desperation they made landfall at 2 p.m. on an island christened Refuge Island by Stanley. The *wangwana* made a fire while Stanley and Safeni scoured the island for food. Stanley managed to shoot a brace of ducks; his men meanwhile had uncovered bananas and berries. That evening they feasted on duck, banana, berries and coffee: 'The tobacco gourd and pipe closed one of the most delicious evenings I ever remember to have passed.'[53]

Next morning Stanley found himself feverish, the result of rain, famine and exposure. He rested a day on Refuge Island before the expedition paddled on through calamitous waters and freak waves in Speke Gulf to haven at Kagehyi.[54] They reached home base after a fifty-seven-day absence to hear bad news on a number of fronts. Frederick Barker had died twelve days earlier, foaming at the mouth and breathing painfully at the end. Frank Pocock, who conducted the burial service, felt very lonely as the only white man in charge of 153 *wangwana*. He himself had been very ill with fever, which he tackled by lying on hot stones and drinking brandy.[55] In addition, there had been a serious threat to the expedition from two different directions. First there was a conspiracy to attack the camp and pillage the stores, led by Kaduma's brother Kipingiri and Kurrereh, chief of Kyenzi. They tried to inveigle Manwa Sera into the plot, but he divulged it to Pocock, and the whole scheme aborted when Kaduma, for all his inebriation, decided to remain loyal to Stanley.[56] Then fears arose among the men that Stanley would not return. The Zanzibari Msenna had declared that he would lead sixty members of the expedition back to Unyanyembe on 6 May; Stanley's timely advent nipped this scheme in the bud.[57]

All in all, though, Stanley had grounds for his hearty congratulation of Frank Pocock on the way he had handled things in his absence, especially the way he had got on to such good terms with Kaduma.[58] The *wangwana* were well fed and the differential dietary experiences of Pocock and Stanley revealed themselves in weights of 162 pounds and 115 pounds respectively; Pocock's complexion was the colour of milk while Stanley's resembled that of a Red Indian.[59] Not surprisingly after his privations, Stanley went down with fever and was laid up for five days.[60]

When he had recovered, Stanley learned with petulant impatience that Magassa still had not arrived with the thirty canoes promised by Mutesa. Having cleared up most of the problems relating to Lake Victoria, Stanley was eager to press on to Ujiji and Manyema, but the route westward was said to be impassable because of the continuing Mirambo wars. King Rwoma, lord of the Zinza state of Bukara from 1864 to 1895 (when he was killed fighting the Germans), an ally of Mirambo, was said to regard white men as 'bad medicine' on the basis of some tall stories retailed to him. A tentative overture was met with the response that Rwoma would fight him if he came that way.[61]

Accordingly Stanley tried to obtain canoes locally for the passage to Uganda and thence westward. His first act was to send Pocock to treat with Lukongeh, ruler of Ukerewe, for the purchase of such canoes. Lukongeh was an amiable though wily ruler who managed to live at peace with the whites for years before the Germans defeated and deposed him in 1895.[62] But Pocock was the first white man Lukongeh had ever seen. After promising him canoes, he kept him hanging around his kraal for days of infuriating delay. The mission finally aborted when Lukongeh made an offer of canoes with crews; Stanley had ruled this offer out in advance in his instructions to Pocock, for fear of outbreaks of fighting between the Ukerewe men and the Zanzibaris.[63]

Stanley, who had been racked with fever during Pocock's absence – but had still managed to shoot an 11-foot long boa constrictor that slithered into camp – saw there was nothing for it but visiting Lukongeh himself.[64] He crossed the Speke Gulf to the Ukerewe capital of Msossi and on 31 May came face to face with Lukongeh. The king received him on a knoll on a plain, seated on a throne, surrounded by hundreds of spearsmen and archers. Light-coloured and affable, aged about twenty-eight, Lukongeh recalled Mutesa in his conspicuous robes of red and yellow silk and damask cloth. He proved as interested in matters European as the Kabaka (and professed the same 'expedient' interest in Christianity), even though he later admitted that Stanley lost caste when he told him that the USA had no king or queen.[65]

Stanley came straight to the point. He wanted the canoes without strings, not subject to the whims of Ukerewe oarsmen.[66] If that was impossible, he wanted a cast-iron commitment from the king that his men would take the Anglo-American expedition to Uganda along the Uzinza coast. At first Lukongeh alleged that all his canoes were rotten and he did not want the responsibility for white men drowning on Lake Victoria. But when he came to Stanley's tent surreptitiously and saw the trade goods spread out on the floor, he became keen to trade and promised that he would have his canoes. He asked his guest for the magical powers of the Europeans; when Stanley refused, the king merely interpreted this as 'playing hard to get'.[67]

On 6 June the king again visited Stanley secretly at night with his chief counsellor. He proposed that thirty canoes, with two oarsmen each, should accompany him back to Kagehyi on the pretext of accompanying the whole expedition back to Ukerewe. Once there, Stanley should seize the canoes and the paddles. This was the only way the king could accommodate Stanley's wishes, for if he ordered his men to Uganda, they would not even go as far as Kagehyi. But as an earnest of his good faith Lukongeh offered his nephew as a guide over the perilous waterway to Uganda. So it was that next day Stanley returned to his base with twenty-seven canoes.[68]

Once at Kagehyi, he ordered the *wangwana* to seize the canoes and oars. Then he issued an ultimatum: either the rowers could accompany them to Uganda or they could return home in relays; he would allow them just four canoes for the homeward passage. At this, and misunderstanding the presence of Lukongeh's nephew in the white man's party, the Ukerewe men sprang to arms. Finding themselves staring down the barrels of massed Sniders, they quickly desisted. None of the forty-five men volunteered for the onward journey to Uganda but accepted the four canoes for home relay.[69]

Stanley now prepared to take two-thirds of the expedition across the lake to Uganda. He provisioned for a long voyage at a grain auction and recaulked and replanked Lukongeh's rotten canoes; the king, it seemed, had not been exaggerating when he said that his canoes might take the white man to the bottom of the lake. Yet on 20 June the expedition was ready to sail: 150 men, women and children were embarked, together with 100 loads of cloth, beads and wire, eighty-eight sacks of grain and thirty cases of ammunition.[70]

The first day on the lake brought them close to utter catastrophe. Stanley was at first delighted with the way his men had picked up the art of paddling. But as they tried to 'island hop' among the Miandereh group, the waves began to make up and they found themselves rowing against an increasingly heavy swell as a light gale began to blow. Intense darkness overtook them; they paddled on in the inky blackness by the light of wax tapers. It was impossible for one boat to see another but they kept in touch with shouts and the measured, rhythmic plash and beat of oar and paddle. Now and then Stanley waved a flambeau through the dark wastes as a beacon. After three hours of this tentative progress, the first cries of alarm went up. 'The boat, the boat!' came the shout, as if from drowning men. Locating the sinking canoe, they could discern the heads of several men swimming away from the rotting wreck. Stanley ordered the men taken aboard the *Lady Alice*. A box of ammunition and 400 pounds of grain had gone to the bottom with Lukongeh's putrid canoe.[71]

Half an hour later another canoe went down. This time five guns and four sacks of flour were lost. When the survivors were redistributed in the remaining boats, they brought the teetering craft to the very edge of capsize. If the winds increased in velocity all would be lost, for the *Lady Alice* was already up to its gunwales, with a complement of twenty-two men and thirty loads. Stanley altered course for the nearest of the islands. Across the Stygian gloom he bawled his latest orders. If any more canoes sank, the men were to jettison the cargo (but not the guns) and cling to the wreckage until he could devise means of rescuing them. If anyone lost his gun, he would be left to drown.[72]

Almost on cue, two more canoes at once began to sink. After reiterating his orders, Stanley commanded his oarsmen on the *Lady Alice* to haul for the shore. An hour's heroic, superhuman pulling at the oars brought them to landfall on one of the Miandereh isles. Quickly disembarking men and goods, the *Lady Alice* set off into the lake to pick up survivors. Two of the most weatherly canoes accompanied her. By this time there had been a veritable epidemic of sinkings. But the recovery rate of *Lady Alice* was superlative. All men, women and children in the water were brought to safety, and some of the rotten canoes were even refloated and taken in tow. All told on that dreadful night the expedition lost five canoes, five guns, a case of ammunition and 1,200 pounds of grain – a truly devastating setback palliated only by the absence of all human loss. Stanley conceded that his action in leaving men in the water for two hours, at the mercy of any cruising crocodiles, might have appeared inhumane, but he faced the possibility that the entire party could be lost in mid-lake if the *Lady Alice* had become overloaded and foundered.[73]

After a halt next day to recaulk and patch up the canoes, they made their way gingerly to Refuge Island – a slow, careful seven-hour paddle. Stanley left behind the third of the party that could not be accommodated on the canoes with instructions to negotiate peace with the people of Ito and Komeh Islands, who had been hostile during his circumnavigation. These negotiations were successful and within days the whole party was reunited on Refuge Island, where Stanley was pleased to see his people going over every inch of their canoes in minute examination.[74]

Leaving Pocock and Manwa Sera with forty-four men to construct a defensive stockade on Refuge Island, Stanley set out for Kagehyi to bring back the remainder of the expedition. He took the *Lady Alice*, seventeen canoes and 106 men. Pocock spent the time until his leader's return hunting and shooting crocodiles, for which species he had picked up Stanley's aversion. His men even managed to find a nest of fifty-two crocodile eggs on which they feasted – Pocock found them very indigestible, with the size and texture of a goose's egg.[75]

Stanley's party meanwhile was caught in yet another storm, in which three canoes and thirteen men became separated. Two of them made landfall in Lukongeh's country, whence he returned them to Kagehyi; the other canoe and crew, after getting to land, deserted across country to Unyanyembe. On arrival at Kagehyi on 1 July, Stanley made a fortunate purchase of a thirty-seater canoe he dubbed 'the hippopotamus'.[76] But then he had to confront two ticklish situations in quick succession. First, a fight arose among the *wangwana* which left two men dead from stabbing. Kaduma and the Zanzibari NCOs decreed the death sentence for the two culprits, but Stanley intervened and commuted this to 200 lashes apiece followed by six months in chains.[77] Next he was alerted that Kaduma had been listening to his brother Kipingiri and was disposed to acquiesce in a kidnapping of the white man. Stanley pre-empted this by not telling the chief when he was leaving, then shoving off before every last item had been loaded.[78]

The journey back to Refuge Island was uneventful. The entire expedition was reunited on 11 July, and Stanley found that Pocock had wrought wonders of diplomacy with the locals. Once he tasted his firepower and saw the strength of his fortifications, Kijaju, ruler of Kome Island off the Zinza coast, made friendly overtures and brought gifts.[79] The relief afforded by this good news allowed Stanley to relax; the pent-up stress burst out, prostrating him with a five-day bout of fever. But at least the seven days on Refuge Island put the expedition in good hearts. After exploring the island from top to bottom, his men had located copious supplies of fruit and wild dates. Stanley's real problem continued to be the canoes; after discarding the rotten ones he had only fifteen seaworthy craft left.[80]

On 18 July, following a feast in honour of Kijaju, with frenetic moonlight dancing a feature, Stanley took the king's guides with him over to the uninhabited island of Mahyiga, the most southerly of the Bumbire group. Then he ferried the expedition over to this foothold in relays while he pondered what to do about the menace of Bumbire, on the flank of his route to Uganda. As they entrenched their camp, they were reconnoitred by their old enemies from Bumbire. Stanley addressed them through Kijaju's guides. He demanded that Shekka return the stolen oars; the Bumbire scouts replied that Magassa now had them and had taken them back to Mutesa's court. The rumour was current that the white man had been slain and Magassa believed it.[81]

Attitudes hardened over the next few days while Manwa Sera gradually brought over every last man from Refuge Island. Another Bumbire canoe approached their redoubt on 23 July and its occupants showed their contempt in the well-understood African way by throwing up water in the air with their paddles. Stanley decided on a draconian response.

In the feudal hierarchy of Lake Victoria, Antari, king of the Ihangiro, held his lands from Mutesa, while Shekka of Bumbire in turn was Antari's vassal. Stanley decided to use this hierarchy ruthlessly. Antari had received orders to provision the Anglo-American expedition from Mutesa and had passed these on to the people of Iroba, neighbours of Bumbire. Stanley took thirty-five heavily armed men to Iroba, placed their chief and two elders under arrest and announced that they would be released when Shekka was given up. The ruthless scheme worked. On the evening of 27 July the Iroba brought in Shekka and his two sub-chiefs; Stanley had to interpose himself to prevent his men from murdering the hostages.[82]

Interrogation of Shekka revealed another twist in the skein. He told Stanley that Antari himself was preparing a large force to attack the expedition. Sure enough, next day a large force of Antari's men arrived to treat. Stanley allowed the armed envoys to land, under the watchful covering of Pocock and his riflemen. Antari's emissaries warned Stanley that in no circumstances would the king allow the expedition to proceed to Uganda. Stanley pointed out that he was the Kabaka's friend, reminded them of Antari's feudal obligations, and gave them until noon the next day to bring word of a safe-conduct, otherwise he would take Shekka and the others on to Mutesa to stand trial.[83]

It is important to be clear that at this stage in proceedings Stanley's later justification for the attack on Bumbire held good: viz. that he dared not attempt the perilous passage to Uganda in rotting canoes with such an enemy on his flank. He was still thinking of the dreadful experience the night the canoes sank on the lake and running it together with his earlier armed clash at Bumbire to produce a hypothetical picture of unparalleled catastrophe. But this excuse ceased to hold good once large numbers of Mutesa's Ganda appeared in their war canoes to assist him. The first of these allies was Sabadu, with six canoes, sent by the Kabaka to learn the truth of Stanley's alleged death on the lake.[84] Then there arrived eight more canoes under Mkwanda and two under Kytawa. Including his own force, his allies at Komeh and Ukerewe, plus the 250 Ganda arrivals, Stanley could now muster 470 fighting men, more than enough to overcome both Bumbire and Ihangiro. By the end of July his only worry was the food supply; he could no longer legitimately allege that he feared an enemy flank attack.[85]

Stanley's justification for his assault on Bumbire was therefore bogus. But the later criticisms of him for gratuitous aggression missed the dimension of face-saving involved in the complex manoeuvres during these days of late July and early August. Confident of his overwhelming military power, Stanley sent a message to Antari, offering to release Shekka and the other prisoners in return for a token payment of five bullocks and a number of spears and billhooks. This was letting the Ihangiro king off very lightly, but Antari ignored the offer. After waiting for three days without an answer, Stanley was infuriated to receive a defiant message that Antari would attack the expedition if the prisoners were not given up at once. In Stanley's mind that settled matters. Sabadu and Mkwanda were still dubious about the benefits of an attack, but then the Bumbire people played into Stanley's hands. A Ganda reconnaissance mission sent to the island was repulsed, with one dead and eight wounded. Sabadu and Mkwanda at once threw in their lot with Stanley and agreed on a punitive assault.[86]

4 August was the date set for the chastisement of Bumbire. At noon after a morning gale, a force of fifty riflemen and 230 spearsmen set out in six large canoes and the *Lady Alice*. Twenty rounds each had been distributed to the riflemen, all handpicked Zanzibari sharpshooters. Stanley had rehearsed his warriors thoroughly in the planned tactics. He intended to feign a landing at a point where the sun would be shining in

the enemy's face, then lure him on to killing ground under his guns. After two hours they pulled close to the 'hated isle'. The flotilla made as if to land, then rowed round the cove and, steering under the lee, entered a bay on the western side of the island. Through his field-glasses Stanley could see the heights of the hilly ridge crowded with his old foes. Panning along the shoreline, he also detected the main body of the Bumbire tribesmen in a plantain grove on top of the most southerly hill.[87]

Having now enraged the enemy by exposing his battle plan, Stanley ordered his men to paddle slowly for the opposite shore of the bay, where there were bare slopes with short green grass, as if intending to make landfall there. The stratagem worked perfectly. The Bumbire warriors raced them to the shore to contest the landing. All this took about half an hour. At the end of that time there were knots of tribesmen poised around every conceivable beachhead.[88]

Stanley came within 100 yards from the shore before forming battle line. He ran up both the Union Jack and the Stars and Stripes, then anchored the canoes together so that they faced broadside to the beach. He ordered a first volley fired at a group of about fifty warriors. Several at once fell dead and wounded. Seeing the danger of standing together, the tribesmen separated. Some advanced to the water's edge, slinging stones and shooting arrows; others retreated into the cane-grass, from which they discharged showers of arrows, all of which fell short. Stanley ordered the canoes to edge closer and delivered the next broadside from a range of 50 yards. A crashing, winnowing volley ripped the enemy ranks apart.[89]

The slaughter was terrific. Frank Pocock was one of those who mowed down the 'savages' just out of bowshot: 'They were very thick on the shore but in ten minutes they were thined [sic] from the fire of our rifles.'[90] After an hour of the most excruciating pounding, the warriors began to withdraw on to the slopes, out of range. As a *coup de grâce* Stanley again feigned a landing, then, as the Bumbire fighters raced back to close in combat, delivered a slaughterous volley that dropped them in their tracks.

Now the Ganda spearsmen screamed and pleaded to be allowed to land to finish off the enemy. With supreme discipline Stanley restrained them. Instead he had the interpreter announce to the stricken Bumbireans that it would be ever thus if they attempted again to insult white men and they could enjoy a repeat performance next day if they wished. There was cruelty in the taunt, but it was not just Stanley's blood that was up. Both the Ganda and the *wangwana* whooped and yelled with triumph. Just two of their number had sustained bruises from the rock-throwing. On the shore they counted at least forty-two enemy dead and over a hundred wounded. Maimed and lamed warriors could be seen limping off up the hillside.[91]

They returned to base that evening in a state of euphoria. Next day Stanley embarked 685 souls for the voyage to Uganda. At 9 a.m. they were again off Bumbire and a warning shot was fired to call the people to parley. The enemy, now well and truly cowed, signalled that they had no further hostile intentions. Stanley announced that he was taking Shekka on for trial before Mutesa. 'Old Shekka the king viewed his island as he passed it with sad, regretful eyes, and at the sight of it I felt more than half inclined to land him on the shore and then and there forgive him. Had he shed one tear I should have done so, or had he asked me, but the captive king, though sad-looking, was mute and tearless.'[92]

The news of the fearful chastisement of Bumbire travelled fast. For the next five days, as they plied along the coast to Dumo in Uganda, they were well received by excessively friendly chiefs.[93] Arriving off the mouth of the Alexandra Nile at Dumo, having lost five guns and a case of ammunition and one drowned man when a canoe capsized, Stanley learned that Mutesa was now waging war against his old enemies the Waruma. Frank Pocock, it seemed, was destined never to lay eyes on the Kabaka. Once again Stanley left him in charge of the camp while he himself went on ahead. But his long detailed list of instructions, even down to fire drills, shows the perennial Stanley dislike of delegating authority. There is something irritatingly patronising about his parting words: 'As you value our success, our common safety depends upon your sleepless vigilance and diligence in my absence. P.S. My last words are: Watch and sleep not over your duty and it will be for your benefit in the future.'[94] Pocock, as it turned out, found it extraordinarily difficult to maintain discipline during Stanley's absence. His bouts of fever made it impossible for him to obey his orders to the letter. Safeni's wife was egregiously insubordinate and insolent. There were daily squabbles over food. The *wangwana* tried to raid the arsenal for ammunition, against strict orders to the contrary.[95]

Hastening to the capital meanwhile, Stanley found that Mutesa had already gone on ahead to the seat of war. For the rest of August Stanley marked time. He confirmed that the Ripon Falls were the only northerly outlet from the lake, and had the sad experience of burying Jack the bull-terrier after it had been gored by a cow; only Bull the bulldog was left of the original canine quartet. After pondering his next step, he concluded that the obvious wisdom of holding aloof from Mutesa's wars was outweighed by the thought of the future assistance the Kabaka could give them. Accordingly he decided to catch up with Mutesa at the war theatre.[96]

There seemed even greater warmth in the Kabaka's greeting this time. Stanley was received in state by thousands of men standing in line. Mutesa made lavish promises of opening the area between Uganda and Lake Edward for his explorations. At the end of August Stanley watched as his protector reviewed his army, bound for the Waruma front. An estimated 150,000 warriors (Mutesa would never let Stanley inspect his muster-rolls) filed past the king, followed by some 100,000 women and camp-followers. 'Mutesa's face was covered with a whitish paste, his head was uncovered and he wore a blue check dress.'[97]

Stanley raised the issue of his captives. Sabadu confirmed his story of Bumbire in every detail. Mutesa was willing to order the immediate execution of Shekka and the others, but Stanley argued that the recalci-trant Antari should be given time to ransom them. This unwonted compassion from Stanley was not unconnected with the Bible lessons he read to the king. Mutesa evinced a taste for theology and was particularly enraptured by the notion of angels. A quotation from the Bible on this subject led to an immediate order from the king that the entire 'Good Book' be translated into Swahili.[98] Ecstatically announcing the ruler's sure and certain conversion, Stanley at once sent back to Pocock to have the copy of the Book of Common Prayer they had in camp sent on.[99]

But Mutesa's pragmatic reasons for 'conversion' soon became clear when he explained to Stanley that since the white man's technology was superior to that of the Arab, it followed that his 'magic book' must be superior to the Koran. This was a particularly urgent consideration to the king, since his war with the Waruma was not going well. Although Mutesa had overwhelming superiority on land, his enemy held the advantage on water and had just inflicted a humiliating defeat on the Buganda navy. 'Turn the other cheek' had not worked well; a peaceful embassy sent to the Waruma had been slaughtered to a man. It was in Stanley's interest in a double sense to assist the Kabaka in his war, both to restore Christian credibility and to enable himself to get away to Lake Tanganyika and the west.[100]

Stanley therefore advised Mutesa to build a causeway to link the headland of Nakaranga with Ingira Island. But this was constructed ineptly. A determined attack by the Ganda on Ingira Island was beaten off. There followed four fiercely contested battles on the lake, with great loss of life. Although the Ganda showed greater battle skills and coolness under fire, they were consistently overwhelmed by the greater courage of the Waruma. In desperation Mutesa asked Stanley for his guns and ammunition. The request was refused, on obvious prudential grounds: 'because I should be as one committing self-murder.'[101]

By the beginning of October the war had settled into a stalemate of attrition. Stanley made a final attempt to win the campaign for Mutesa by lashing together a number of canoes, building a platform over them and converting the whole into a sort of floating fortress. A bristling oblong stockade, 70 feet long by 27 feet wide, impervious to enemy spears, drifted towards the Waruma. After embarking 214 warriors inside the 'wooden horse' Mutesa presented the enemy with an ultimatum. The fortress was advanced to within 50 yards' range and the Waruma given the option of surrendering or being hacked to pieces. This did the trick. On 13 October the Waruma agreed to honourable peace terms.[102]

Stanley's stock with Mutesa was never higher. The Kabaka pledged an escort of 500 spearsmen for the expedition's journey to Lake Albert. Stanley, absurdly overrating the extent to which the Kabaka's writ would run in Unyoro, felt that he had already as good as achieved his objective: 'We shall travel as safe as though we were in bed at home.'[103] Mutesa he described as the most intelligent African he had ever known; his few faults were a susceptibility to flattery and (significantly in Stanley's book) 'he is too fond of women.'[104] But relations between Stanley and Mutesa plummeted after a dreadful incident on 15 October. A fire mysteriously began in the Kabaka's camp; Stanley and the able-bodied escaped up the mountain slopes but hundreds of women and children were trampled or left to die in the conflagration. Stanley suspected Mutesa of having deliberately started the fire, in frustrated rage that his 'cowardly' armies had not been able to annihilate the Waruma, and let his suspicions be known. Such was the regard Mutesa entertained for him that he actually gave categorical assurances that he had not compassed or contrived the fire.[105]

But Stanley was convinced that he had witnessed the dark side of his genial host, and determined to depart as soon as possible. On returning to Ugalla with Mutesa, he was delayed for a few days with another bout of fever. Then, after a formal leave-taking, he set out for Dumo, where he was reunited with Pocock after more than three months' absence.[106] The entire expedition was in good heart at the tidings that Mutesa's warriors would clear passage for them to Lake Albert. Stanley ought to have been warned of the limitations of Ganda power after their poor performance against the Waruma. But buoyed up by the Kabaka's assurances he allowed himself to distrust the evidence of his senses. He was soon to pay dearly for this lapse of judgement.

$$ \cdot \quad \underline{15} \quad \cdot $$

S TANLEY'S impact on Mutesa had been startling and his impressions of Buganda and its people very different from those of other early travellers.[1] It remained to be seen whether he could make the same headway with Kabba Rega and Bunyoro. Seven days after his return to Dumo, Stanley commenced the march towards the rendezvous point with his Ganda escort on the Katonga River. Striking inland from Lake Victoria, they travelled through beautiful valleys of palm trees and villages rich in bananas. Smooth rounded hills were separated by broad grassy vales, teeming with game. They had to wade through many streams and swamps up to their waists in water, ever on guard against the numerous leopards in which this region abounded.[2]

At Kikoma Stanley called a halt and waited for the man he had selected as guide to take the expedition on into Bunyoro. Mutesa had given him free choice, so Stanley had plumped for Sembuzi, one of the most intelligent Ganda chiefs, on whom the Kabaka ordained strict obedience to the white man.[3] Stanley spent the time at Kikoma amassing meat supplies. In a five-day period he shot fifty-seven hartebeeste, two zebra and a waterbuck. The region was fecund with game, being largely void of human habitation both because of the large numbers of lions and leopards who were a threat to human life and because this was a favourite location for raiders from Ankole.[4]

The one dark spot on Stanley's mental horizon was Frank Pocock's continuing propensity to fever. By now Stanley entertained a special regard for his one surviving white companion and he was beginning to regard him as a successful version of Lewis Noe or Edward King. Pocock's mixture of deference and efficiency suited the leader perfectly. 'Frank, you are the coolest man and the happiest I ever saw,' Stanley told him.[5] To the *Herald* he reported, rather patronisingly: 'He did not look very promising as a companion at first; I thought him rather slow. He has a host of virtues and not one vice, nor shadow of vice. He is a brave, honest, manly, patient young Englishman.'[6] Pocock for his part was gaining in confidence, fevers apart. He thought (with reason) that his disciplining of the men was more judicious than Stanley's and he was proud of the progress he had made in Swahili.[7]

On 12 December guides arrived from Sembuzi. They then essayed the crossing of the Katonga River; it took an entire day and four separate journeys to force the *Lady Alice* through the reeds. They finally met up with Sembuzi at Ruwewa but the Ganda chief, already late for the rendezvous, further irritated Stanley by insisting on another five-day halt before pressing on to the general rendezvous at Langurwe. Stanley rationalised his impatience by telling himself that at least Frank Pocock could get over his fever. He took his gun and went shooting. There was a skirmish with a hyena on the outskirts of the camp, then he downed an eagle with a nine-foot wingspan.[8]

Christmas 1875 was in many ways as depressing as the Yuletide the year before, but without the rain. At Langurwe, Stanley finally realised that he had been Sembuzi's dupe. Sembuzi had courted Stanley assiduously to get this position as the Kabaka's representative in the journey to Unyoro, but now, far from Mutesa's gaze, he acted more imperiously than the king himself. But Stanley was forced to grit his teeth and bear the impudence of this prima donna; the plain fact was that the Ganda outnumbered the men of Zanzibar twenty to one. The combined force numbered 2,270, with an effective fighting strength of 1,000, a hundred of whom had firearms.[9]

On 2 January 1876 this force finally crossed the frontier between friendly Buganda and potentially hostile Bunyoro. Stanley claimed to notice an immediate change in the terrain. North of the Katonga was rolling country crisscrossed by tributaries. But across the Bunyoro boundary, on the far side of the Nabwari River, this soft pastoral scenery gave way to rugged, mountainous country. Even the huts looked different, and while bananas were the staple in Buganda, here it was sweet potatoes.[10]

For ten days they trudged through grassland, on permanent alert in case the Bunyoro people attacked. Even simple grass-cutting tasks required an armed escort. The unremitting tension was trying on the nerves. The valour of Kabba Rega's warriors was exaggerated by rumour: they were said to be capable of lying in long grass with their spears and shields then springing up in ambush like tigers. Fleet-footed as deer, they had also trained savage mastiffs to fight for them.[11] Pocock later recalled:

'We travelled for several days, not seeing a single person. They had gone to earth for they are like rabbits, and they live chiefly underground. In time of war they put their cattle and women underground while the men fight. They have large dogs which they train to fight. They also dig elephant pits and holes to catch men. Several of our men were caught in them and went out of sight, but by screaming loud were heard and pulled out.'[12]

By 8 January they were on the east bank of the Mpanga River, at an altitude of 4,600 feet, the nights bitterly cold, with thick fog every morning. Ten hours' swift marching took them through an uninhabited strip of Ankole and back into Bunyoro in the district of Kitagwenda to the east of Lake George.[13] On the way they passed through Uzimba, where the country looked like Switzerland, but where the people scattered at their approach and tried to pick off stragglers from the column. They took a few prisoners and released them on condition they went back to the local chiefs and advised them of the expedition's peaceful intentions.[14]

On 11 January the expedition camped on a plateau 1,500 feet above Lake George, a small lake connected to Lake Edward by the Kazinga channel.[15] With difficulty Stanley persuaded Sembuzi to descend to the lake with the sections of the *Lady Alice* and launch the boat. Immediately large crowds of Bunyoro warriors barred the way. Sembuzi asked leave for the expedition to pass through Bunyoro peacefully. The request was peremptorily refused. The men of Bunyoro pointed out that Kabba Rega was already fighting with the white man (doubtless a reference to skirmishes with Gordon's forward positions in Equatoria); it followed that the newcomers must either retire or fight. Kabba Rega was in alliance with Mutambukwa, king of Ankole, so fighting could have only one result. As the Wanyoro contemptuously expressed it: 'It is true you have come, but tell us how you will get away from here? Can you fly in the air? If not, think of tomorrow and sleep on what we have told you.'[16]

To his anger and astonishment, Stanley realised that Mutesa's promises of safe conduct through Bunyoro and his 2,000 spearsmen availed him nothing. Furiously Stanley lashed out at Baker and Gordon for their meddling: 'Ever since Sir Samuel Baker and his Egyptian forces provoked the hostility of the successor to Kamrasi, Unyoro is a closed country to any man of a pale complexion, be he Arab, Turk or European. Besides, Gordon's officers in the north frequently engage the Wanyoro whenever they are met, and thus the hate which Kabba Rega bears to Europeans is not diminishing.'[17] Stanley was largely right. Kabba Rega objected to the presence of large numbers of Ganda from the rival Mutesa on his soil, wasting his substance, and he feared that Stanley's presence indicated a two-pronged attack from the white man, the whole engineered by Gordon, who was even then establishing military posts at Myuli and Masindi. But he did not want unnecessary bloodshed. He was prepared to let the expedition retire to the kingdom of Karagwe to the south.[18]

At this resolute performance from the warriors of Bunyoro, the Ganda began to panic. Sembuzi announced his intention to retreat. Angrily Stanley insisted on holding him to Mutesa's promise; if he would just get the Anglo-American down to the lake, the Ganda could depart, and good riddance. Sembuzi appeared to agree but then came back with word that lowering the *Lady Alice* to the lake was impossible: not only was there a sheer 50-foot precipice to the water but the enemy were massing in strength below.[19]

Stanley was still confident that if Sembuzi would just stay with him for two more days, they could launch *Lady Alice* and find enough canoes for the rest of his party. He sent the *wangwana* out to find canoes.[20] But at 5 p.m. on 12 January Sembuzi asked Stanley to attend a council of war. There, all the familiar arguments for retreat were rehearsed, and the decision to return to Buganda endorsed unanimously. Calmly Stanley tried to win the Ganda round. But he made no progress. Sembuzi reiterated that it would be difficult enough as it was to get back to Uganda in face of an enemy known to take no prisoners. To stay on even one day more was suicide.[21]

At that Stanley's patience snapped and he railed at the Ganda angrily. He taunted them with being cowards, knaves and traitors. Failing to make any impression on them, he returned to tell his men that there was nothing for it but retreat prior to trying another route. So much for Mutesa's assurance that Kabba Rega would not dare to oppose him if he entered Bunyoro under the Ganda banner. 'Honestly I do not suppose I have been guilty of such a harebrained scheme as this before. Looking calmly at it now, I regard it as a great folly.'[22]

Sullenly Stanley retreated, consoling himself with the new knowledge he had acquired about this utterly unknown region.[23] They marched in compact formation, 500 spearsmen in the front, 500 in the rear, with the others in a central cluster. Over the summit of Mount Uzimba they trekked and into the forest. They slept on the grass, hungry and tired, with fires burning all night to keep predators at bay. Sembuzi had to use the whip on his tired men to urge them forward. The Bunyoro tracked them at a safe distance, nudging and nagging the rear. Only once, on 15 January, was there a brief but furious attack on the rearguard, but this was beaten off without loss. At the Katonga Stanley and Pocock celebrated their

277

deliverance by slaughtering a bullock and roasting it – their first meat for fifteen days.[24]

Once across the border, at Kisweri, Stanley and Sembuzi parted company, on the worst of terms. Stanley sent a special courier to Mutesa, outlining the fiasco of the venture into Bunyoro and containing a detailed indictment of Sembuzi's conduct. He had added to his disloyalty in refusing to build a palisaded camp at Lake George by refusing to return three porters' loads of beads given him for carriage. Mutesa replied swiftly, since his prestige had taken a battering. He promised to provide 50,000 men to force passage through Bunyoro. He also informed Stanley that the recalcitrant Sembuzi had been placed in chains and all his property confiscated and ended with an assurance that he would do all he could to further the aims of the expedition.[25]

But Stanley had by now decided that Mutesa's assistance was more trouble than it was worth. Henceforth, he decided, he would rely on himself and himself alone. His next objective was the kingdom of Karagwe. He pressed on southwards to the River Kagera, taking potshots at hippo and other big game in the tedious evenings. On 19 February 1876 they crossed the half-mile wide River Kagera, adorned with speargrass, bullrush reeds and irascible hippopotami. On 25 February they were in Karagwe proper, at the Arab township of Kafurro, situated in a deep valley 1,200 feet below the tops of the surrounding mountains and at the source of streams flowing north and east to the Alexandra Nile.[26]

Kafurro's Arab magnates were Ahmed bin Ibrahim, Sayd bin Sayf and Sayd Muscati. They explained to him the politics of the kingdom. Far from being a vassal of Mutesa, as Stanley had imagined, the king of the Haya state of Karagwe commanded the resources of the third important African state in the Lake Victoria region. Mutesa and Rumanika were linked as sovereign rulers in mutual defence treaties.[27] Arab intelligence was first-rate. Ahmed bin Ibrahim had been in Karagwe twelve years and enjoyed excellent relations with both Rumanika, king of Karagwe, and Mutesa. Stanley asked about the prospects of penetrating westward from the state; Ahmed was dubious but offered to accompany Stanley to Rumanika's court to learn the king's disposition.[28]

On 28 February Ahmed and Sayd bin Sayf accompanied Stanley to Rumanika's capital, across a lake the explorer christened Lake Windermere. Rumanika Stanley found even more impressive than Mutesa. Where Mutesa had a volcanic temper, and was nervous and intense, the soft-voiced Rumanika was placid, mild-tempered and kind.[29] Dressed in a red robe, distinctive because of his Roman nose, Rumanika at 6 feet 6 inches towered over the diminutive white man. He was affability itself and gave Stanley leave to explore any part of his domains he wished. He provided him with guides and promised free subsistence.[30]

Elated, Stanley set out with Pocock to explore the region north to Mpororo and south to Ugufu. They launched the *Lady Alice* on Lake Ruanyara (the one Stanley had dubbed Lake Windermere).[31] After a boat race with Rumanika's men, they commenced the circumnavigation of the lake. Making their way through papyrus walls 9 feet wide, they spent the night among the reeds but were savagely attacked by a cloud of voracious mosquitoes.[32] Rumanika was as good as his word on the subsistence, for Stanley recorded laconically in his diary: 'Food was reluctantly supplied gratis by poor population.'[33]

After circling the lake, they entered the mouth of the Kagera, then descended the river, making careful observations all the way. They entered another lake, Ihema, on the Ruanda coast, outside Rumanika's orbit. Here, as the Arabs had foretold, they were greeted with hostile war cries. Stanley's contact with Ruanda-Urundi on 9–10 March was as fleeting as his twenty-four hours in Ankole two months before.[34]

Next Stanley told Pocock to take *Lady Alice* back to Kafurro while he visited the hot springs of Mtagata – a two-day march. The relaxed journey to this famous Central African spa enabled him to appreciate the wealth of Karagwe. He counted 900 head of cattle in a single herd. Even more impressive was the abundance of game. In particular the rhinoceros seemed to have a special stamping ground here. On the first day he saw three white rhino and four black. His guides urged him to shoot one but, short of ammunition and not certain of getting in a killing shot, he decided not to court the well-known risks from a wounded rhinoceros. However, next day his men complained of the shortage of meat, and Stanley felt his credibility was at stake. Just before dusk he managed to creep within 50 yards of a double-horned specimen and get a shot through the ear. The pachyderm keeled over dead in an instant.[35]

On 15 March he came at last to the fabled hot springs – a kind of Central African Lourdes: 'Male and female were seen lying pro-miscuously in the hot pools half asleep, while their itchy and ulcerous bodies were being half cooked.'[36] Such was the stability and peace of Rumanika's domain that Stanley was able to remain at leisure at the springs for three days, with as much unconcern as if he had been taking the waters at a European spa. Ever the Victorian amateur scientist, Stanley bottled some of the water and took it away for later analysis, just as he had done six years earlier in the Dead Sea.[37]

Arriving back at Kafurro on 19 March, Stanley spent a week in affable conversations with Rumanika before getting the king's consent to depart and a brace of guides for the journey to the south-west. Once again Stanley had mightily impressed an African potentate, so that traces of his visit lived on in local lore.[38] But the idyllic interlude with Rumanika had momentarily made him forget the harsh realities of normal African travel. It was something akin to culture shock to find the chiefs on the Karagwe borders as hungry for *hongo* as ever the Gogo and the Ha were. As usual, Stanley's response to a demand for excessive *doti* was to press on in forced marches, hoping to find more amenable hosts.[39] But famine in western Usui meant that four days' food ration now cost thirty-two *doti* of cloth. It was as well that he had acquired a new expertise as a rhino hunter and was able to kill three of the beasts for food.[40]

Stanley was now entering the region of his 1871 expedition to find Livingstone. This brought problems. He shrank from another encounter with his nemesis that year, the Ha, and was hemmed in on another side by the hostile country of Ruanda-Urundi. He decided to strike south to the Malagarazi, hoping that his luck would hold and that he would miss Mirambo, just as he had missed the *ruga-ruga* chief's great rival Nyungu both in 1871 and in January 1875.[41]

Now came famine and the rains. After being used to trading their cloths for goats, they found that not even millet was to be had for love or money. On emergency corn rations they struggled on, with morale lessening daily. As Pocock remarked: 'What is to be done except march to where we can get food, for the longer we stop here the worse it will be, although it is hard to march under a burning African sun for so many hours hungry, still it is better to go than to starve without a struggle.'[42] On 6 April even the burning sun disappeared. As they traipsed wearily up a hill, a dreadful thunderstorm descended on them. The resultant floods forced them to plough through mud and water up to their waists. A feverish Stanley fell from his donkey into a quagmire and had to be fished out.[43]

Still the hard-driving leader urged them on. He crossed the Nile/Congo watershed, the dividing line between the basins of Lakes Victoria and Tanganyika, on 10 April. Thenceforth their route lay away from the lacustrine territory of Lake Victoria, which had been their home since January 1876. They began to encounter increasing hostility. Chief Makorango sent an emissary to demand their presence. Stanley ignored this and got clear of the kingdom by two days of forced marches. This finally finished off Bull, last of the quartet of dogs. The hardships of these two days provoked another attempted mutiny, which he scotched by reducing the ringleader Msenna to the ranks.[44]

Beyond the famine-stricken Usambiro district Stanley headed for the territory of Urangwa. He felt himself beset on all sides by hostile tribes, all with a reputation for levying prohibitive *hongo*.

> Beyond the mouth of the Akanyaru I dared not go, as the natives of Kishakka on the left bank and Ugufu on the right bank are a great deal too wild. I find that the long-legged race inhabiting the countries west of Uganda, Karagwe and Ui have a deadly aversion to strangers. The sight even of a strange dog seems sufficient to send them into a mad rage and paroxysm of spear-shaking and bow-bending. They are all kin to the long-legged mortals of Bumbiri, who sounded the war-cry at the mere sight of our inoffensive exploring boat floating on the Victoria lake.[45]

After receiving a bullock from the chief of Urangwa in return for six *doti*, the expedition marched on to Serembo, only to hear the frightful news that Mirambo himself was approaching the town from the opposite direction. As he sat in a house once used by Speke, Stanley pondered the possible consequences of meeting the man he had fought against in 1871. A tumultuous welcome and the firing of 'Brown Besses' announced the coming of the black Napoleon. Learning that there was a white man in town, Mirambo asked for the symbolic token of the 'loan' of a gun and said he would not depart until he and the white stranger were friends. Stanley sent him a diplomatically worded reply, stressing that he was a man to be reckoned with.

> Tell Mirambo that I am eager to see him and would be glad to shake hands with so great a man, and as I have made strong friendship with Mtesa, Rumanika and all the kings along the road from Usoga to Unyamwezi, I shall be rejoiced to make strong friendship with Mirambo also.[46]

On 22 April the two men came face to face. Stanley found Mirambo deeply impressive and very different from his reputation. Expecting someone like Mutesa 'whose exterior would proclaim the man's life and rank', Stanley found Mirambo's meek demeanour disconcerting and at first suspected that he might be the victim of a practical joke. Aged about thirty-five, 5 feet 11 inches tall, carrying not a surplus ounce of flesh, handsome, soft-spoken and open-handed, Mirambo was quiet and un-assuming but amply conveyed the iron in his soul. Stanley liked to intimidate African chiefs by staring them out, but Mirambo met his gaze steadily – the first African who had passed that particular test.[47] This, then, was the 'Frederick the Great' of Africa who had paralysed the Arabs in five years of warfare and consequently tripled the price of ivory. Mirambo explained his fighting methods. He liked all his warriors to be very young and unmarried, so that they could travel fast and unencumbered with women. After a long talk in Stanley's hut, Stanley returned the visit at Mirambo's that evening. Mirambo wore an Arab coat, tarbush slippers and carried an Arab scimitar. They made blood-brotherhood, outdid each other in the generosity of the gifts they exchanged and parted on the very best of terms.[48]

Stanley later gave a fuller record of his impressions to Alice Pike:

> Throughout all my travels in Africa I have not yet met such dis-interested kindness as I have received from the great bandit Mirambo. He had 15,000 muskets with him, all handled by desperate fellows, but the minute their chief embraced me all the savages clapped their hands, and hailed me as a brother of their chief. Mirambo gave me oxen for beef and two milch cows with calves, and gave me five men to guide the expedition to safety through his country that no stray bandits might molest us. He is tall, large chested and a very fine specimen of a well-made man. Mild featured, nose regular, small mouth and has a splendid set of teeth. He is as quiet as a lamb in conversation, rather harmless looking than otherwise, but in war the skulls which line the road to his gates reveal too terribly the ardour which animates him.[49]

With Mirambo's 'safe conduct', Stanley pressed on with confidence to Lake Tanganyika, still through teeming rain. Able to browbeat the chiefs he met with the terror of Mirambo's name, he faced down the chief of Myonga who robbed Grant in 1861 and at Ubagwe upbraided the chief for his rapacity. Abashed by this eloquence from Mirambo's blood-brother, the chief became generous to the point of sycophancy.[50] But if they could get food, they could not control the rainy season. Again they found themselves wading through mud and water all day long; on the worst stretches, they were up to their necks in water for hours. The men went down with fever, among them Pocock. It was a measure of Stanley's regard for Frank that he consented to spend four whole days waiting in a village for him to recover.[51] The 1871 Stanley of Shaw and Farquahar would never have done so much.

At the beginning of May, learning of the ferocious reputation of the Watuta tribe, Stanley skirted their territory and marched south-south-west at great speed (a forced march of twenty miles) across an extreme strip of the territory. They came to the meeting place of the Gombe and Malagarazi Rivers, normally a plain, but a lake in the rainy season. Still bearing south-south-west they reached the stockaded village of Usagusi on 12 May, then linked up with an Arab caravan at Uvinza.

Uvinza, gateway to the crossing of the Malagarazi, was the scene of Stanley's 1871 confrontation with Nzogera and his son over *hongo* for the river passage. Rusunzu, the hawkish son of 1871, had now succeeded to his father's throne and proved as rapacious as ever. Having been paid one *hongo* for normal rights of passage through Uvinza, Rusunzu tried to mulct the expedition for an additional payment for the crossing of the swollen Malagarazi. Stanley pretended to open negotiations, meanwhile telling Pocock to assemble the sections of *Lady Alice*. Then, at the last moment, they launched the boat and got across without paying anything.[52]

The route to Ujiji now involved a detour if they were to avoid the territory of the dreaded Ha. Strangely enough, the Ha were quite ready to sell food to travellers beyond their border, so that the expedition was well victualled for the journey through the wilderness between Uvinza and Ujiji; what seemed to drive the Ha into extortionate frenzies was the thought of strangers on their sacred soil.[53]

On 26 May Pocock saw a mark cut in a tree by Verney Cameron's expedition. Next day at dawn they espied the waters of Lake Tanganyika from the top of a hill and at 3 p.m. in the afternoon they entered Ujiji, having travelled at twice the normal speed of Arab caravans since leaving Mirambo. Pocock estimated that they had now travelled 1,850 miles by land and 1,600 by water since leaving Bagamoyo.[54]

Ujiji inevitably conjured nostalgic memories of the famous meeting with Livingstone nearly five years before. 'From the fact that the imposing central figure of the human group drawn together to meet me in Ujiji is absent, Ujiji in spite of the beauty of its lake and the greenness of its patterns, seems strangely forlorn and uninteresting.'[55] The absence of Livingstone was not the only depressant. Ujiji was being so battered by the monsoon rains that its shoreline was 250 yards farther inland than in November 1871. Moreover, neither Stanley nor Pocock found a single line from home awaiting them. When a scouting party was sent east to Unyanyembe to see if there were any letters for them there, it promptly deserted.[56] By now, not having heard from her in eighteen months, Stanley must have realised that his romance with Alice Pike had foundered. Not yet admitting this, he addressed her a *cri de coeur*: 'Heavens and earth, what trick is this fortune has played me? What would you have done in a like case, oh my Alice? Tear your hair, clothes, and shriek distractedly, run about and curse the Fates? I did not do anything so undignified, but I soberly grieved and felt a little discouraged.'[57]

For a week Stanley was laid up with fever. Then, on 11 June, he commenced a circumnavigation of Lake Tanganyika in *Lady Alice*, leaving Pocock in charge at Ujiji. First he sailed south, along the coastline familiar to him from the first part of the journey to Tabora with Livingstone in January 1872. By 21 June he was near Karema in country pullulating with game: elephant, buffalo, waterbuck, eland, zebra. 'They graze boldly along the water edge and up to this day I have succeeded in bagging three zebra and an antelope.'[58] At Karema he added buffalo to the tally.

They came upon plenty of evidence of the recent presence of the dreaded Ndereh bandits: deserted villages, smoking and gutted settlements, mounds of human skulls. Soon they crossed Livingstone's route at Bisa on his last journey. Finding submerged islands and villages where the flood level of the lake had swept over them suggested to Stanley that, contrary to his hopes, there was no outflow from the lake – which later proved to be the case.[59]

On 7 July they passed the Rufuvu River in a violent gale and three days later ran into elemental violence of another kind: with the cessation of the rains in mid-June the elephant grass, high and thick as cane, had become parched and dry as tinder and now sparked into flame; a tremendous forest fire roared around them on the shore.

Finally on 15 July they camped at the mouth of the Lukuga River. This was one of Stanley's principal targets on the circumnavigation. Cameron had claimed that the Lukuga was an outlet for Lake Tanganyika, but had not sailed all round the lake to verify his hypothesis.[60] Content that he had asserted his supremacy as an explorer over Cameron, his rival as heir to the mantle of Livingstone, Stanley allowed himself to reveal an unwonted charming self: 'Let Cameron's friends, then, rest content, for in this letter I shall have to correct myself, Livingstone and Burton.'[61]

Stanley then proceeded to 'tidy up' Cameron's findings. He met chiefs who had known Cameron and Livingstone, reported on the great changes in physical appearance of the lake since his own visit in 1871, and sent back reams of data on the local geography, fauna and flora. He was particularly intrigued by reports that the Lukuga linked eventually with the Lualaba, for the Lualaba was the key river of the entire Anglo-American expedition, which would unlock the final secrets of the sources of the Nile and Congo.[62]

During the stay at the Lukuga they saw copious evidence of the slave trade against which Livingstone had preached so fervently. Slave caravans passed them, 1,200 strong; the mortality level among the slaves was astronomical and the survivors were weakened and emaciated. By introducing guns to the Wanyamwezi in exchange for slaves and ivory, the Arabs had in effect turned the whole Lake Tanganyika region into a kind of game reserve for slavers. The consequence was that all warlike tribes who resisted this slaving push were unwelcoming to strangers. On 27 July at the Nakasangara river, the Bembe people threw stones at them as a warning not to land. Farther up the western shore of the lake chief Kiunyu replied contemptuously to a request for grain: 'Are we slaves that we should grow grain for *your* use?'[63]

When Stanley tried to proceed farther north up the western shore of the lake, war canoes began to pursue the *Lady Alice*. Stanley decided on one of his exemplary 'lessons' with the Winchesters: 'Six shots and four deaths were sufficient to quiet the mocking.'[64] But the hostility of the people in this area made its impact. Reluctantly, he had to concede that his original ambitious project of striking out from Lake Tanganyika at Uzige to explore Lake Albert was impracticable. He heard rumours of Lake Kivu too, but all this territory to the west had to remain unvisited by Europeans for another twenty years.[65]

On 29 July Stanley arrived back at Ujiji after a fifty-one-day, 810-mile circumnavigation of the lake. He found that Pocock had been ill for much of his absence; for the rest of the time he had been depressed, sickened by the everyday cruelty and the casual attitude to human life in Ujiji. A typical incident was when a woman drawing water at the lakeside was taken by a crocodile; Pocock could find no other reaction than a resigned shrug of the shoulders.[66] But more serious from Stanley's point of view than Frank's state of mind was a smallpox epidemic that had broken out while he was away. The outbreak was now accounting for between forty and seventy-five deaths a day. Five of the *wangwana* had already succumbed and six more were seriously ill. But for the mass vaccination programme at Bagamoyo, the Anglo-American expedition would have been virtually wiped out; and it was the men who had evaded their shots then who were dying now.[67]

Stanley faced a dilemma. If he ordered his men out of Ujiji, he might cause even greater mortality. On the other hand, to stay was to risk decimation. The decision was made for the leader when he went down with fever. He convalesced by writing letters to close friends and to Alice Pike. A letter to Edward Marston, his editor on *How I Found Livingstone*, enabled him to broach the subject of Livingstone, whose absence continued to haunt Ujiji.

Think of the time when you first brought a splendid bit of pasteboard cover, rich in green and gold, whereon was stamped cunningly enough the pictures of two human actors in gold, saluting each other with doffed hats under the waving palms of Ujiji. Think of the reams of paper you have handled on which was written the word Ujiji. Can I think of Ujiji without thinking of Livingstone? Can I think of either without thinking of Marston?[68]

The letter to Alice Pike was one of Stanley's longest-ever 'love letters'. He began by relating some persiflage from Kalulu about her being 'Stanley's girl' and reminded her that by now Kalulu was almost unrecognisable physically.[69] He described the voyage of *Lady Alice* around Lake Tanganyika and said he thought of her on 4 July, wondering how differently that date would be celebrated in Philadelphia, especially in Centennial year. Then he came to the nub:

I have not received one encouraging word from you or any living friendly soul since I left Zanzibar twenty-one months ago. But I do not blame you, the letters were no doubt detained somewhere on the road. Then, my own darling, if by that name I may call you, let us hope cheerfully that a happy termination to this long period of trial of your constancy and my health and courage await us both, that the time may come when we can both laugh at these silent gloomy days to me, both be amused at our experiences, various and different as they are, and that our after lives will never be marred by such a long separation. If one knew that such a happy time would certainly arrive, one might be happy enough now, but we do not know it. The Omnipotent has wisely kept us ignorant, but instead of the wisdom and foresight, he has given us some hopeful hearts and sanguine minds which sustain us equally well and better serve us on such occasions as this.[70]

There are clear hints in this letter of the ambivalence characteristic of the schizoid personality: the hungry desire for intimacy coupled with the fear (or hope) that the writer will not be put to the proof.

At a muster held in Ujiji on 25 August Stanley found that of the 170 men still on his roll thirty-eight had deserted. Of the meagre force left he could trust only about thirty with guns. Morale was low at the prospect of an encounter with the Manyema cannibals. A quarter of the remaining *wangwana* had to be put under house arrest to prevent their deserting.[71]

The first task was to ferry the expedition from Ujiji to the western shore of the lake. Pocock and the advance party left on 30 August and established base camp at Mtowa on the far shore; Stanley and the rearguard joined them there on 4 September. But there were three more desertions – something that particularly angered Stanley, as he had just spent £350 on six bales of cloth which were distributed to his men as incentive payments. Stanley sent Pocock and Kacheche back to Ujiji to retrieve the runaways.[72]

Pocock's anger at the task assigned to him and his disgust with the routine brutality of Central Africa found expression in a confrontation with a slaver who owned the boat in which the white man crossed back to Ujiji. Finding himself packed like a sardine against the sweating bodies of hundreds of slaves, Pocock cleared adequate space for himself at gun-point, at the expense of forcing dozens of slaves off the boat and into the bush, whence they decamped into liberty. Once in Ujiji the determined and cross-grained Pocock secured the aid of the governor of Ujiji and was soon recrossing Lake Tanganyika with his prisoners in chains.[73]

Stanley was well pleased with Pocock's exertions, but his ego took another knock on 14 September when Kalulu himself deserted, only to be retaken next day. Stanley realised that it was the Arab settlements that provided the temptation to desert; before coming to Lake Tanganyika they had experienced almost no desertions. Accordingly between 16 September and 6 October he ate up the 200 miles to Manyema country, travelling at an average of nearly 10 miles a day. They passed the most astonishing variety of landscapes: conical hills, hot springs, wooded buffalo country (that afforded plentiful meat); then a long march from Kagongwe in Uvinza to Uhombo, remarkable for the fertility of its groves and its astounding physical beauty. 'It was the most delightful spot we had seen.'[74]

They crossed the watershed between Lake Tanganyika and the Lualaba and entered the region of Manyema on 5 October. Manyema had a dual significance. In the superstitious minds of the *wangwana* it was the abode of ferocious cannibals. But for Stanley it was the land whose glories Livingstone had sketched for him at Ujiji in 1871, a land, the doctor had said, containing Africa's most beautiful women. Once into the Lualaba hinterland, they encountered the most spectacular scenery yet: 'It is a most remarkable region – more remarkable than anything I have seen in Africa. Its woods, or forests, or jungles, or bush – I do not know by what particular term to designate the crowded, tall straight trees rising from an impenetrable undergrowth of bush, creepers, thorns, gums, palms, fronds of all forms, canes and grass – are sublime, even terrible.'[75]

In this land Stanley heard his first stories of the mysterious pygmy race who hunted elephants with poison darts, and sighted his first grey Manyema parrot with crimson tail. He found that Livingstone's reputation everywhere in the area was of the highest – a fact confirmed to him by the chief of the Luama tribe Mwana Ngoi, who had known Livingstone during his penetration of Manyema.[76] Contrary to Manyema's fearsome reputation, Stanley found the people of the area friendly, compassionate and humane.[77] They told him stories of gorillas, but from the coughs and growls Stanley heard at night he conjectured that the apes in question were actually chimpanzees.[78]

The aim of the expedition now was to follow the course of the Luama River, where Mwana Ngoi lived, down to its confluence with the mighty Lualaba and thence to the great trading town of Nyangwe. As they left the Manyema area they noticed that the friendliness of the native peoples they encountered rapidly vanished. Between Kabungu and Mtuyu the country was both populous and hostile. They had to proceed with caution, since an entire brigade could have been swallowed up in this country. The tribesmen on the banks of the Luama did not molest them, but followed out of curiosity, being particularly intrigued by their donkeys. They heard themselves being called by different names: sometimes *wasambe* – a word denoting those like the Arabs, who wore flowing costumes of cloth; sometimes *nivema* – whites.[79]

On 17 October, beyond Mpungu, they came to the confluence of the Luama with the Lualaba. The 400-yard wide Luama emptied into the pale grey expanse of the Lualaba, almost four times as broad, winding slowly from the south and meandering in a vaguely easterly direction. Before launching his boats on the mighty stream, Stanley decided to visit the Arab post at Kasongo on the Lualaba bank. The lord of Kasongo and the overlord of the entire area 350 miles from the western shore of Lake Tanganyika to Nyangwe was the famous Arab slaver Tippu Tip, whom Livingstone had met in 1867.[80]

Hamed bin Muhammed el Murjebi, known as Tippu Tip, born around 1840 to a family of prosperous Muscat Arab merchants, began his trading career at Unyanyembe under his father's aegis at the age of eighteen. The first Arab to penetrate the forest region west of Lake Tanganyika, by the early 1870s Tippu had a commercial and political empire based on slavery and the ivory trade. His political suzerainty over the 10,000 square miles of Manyema was based firmly on the firepower of his muskets, whose distinctive sound on firing was said to have provided him with his nickname.[81]

Though nominally subject to the Sultan of Zanzibar, all the Arab potentates of the interior (Unyanyembe, Ujiji, Manyema, Nyangwe) were in fact independent rulers. Far the most important was Tippu Tip. He possessed great political skills and was careful at this stage of his career not to embroil himself with his powerful neighbours, the Luba of Katanga.[82] His commercial acumen was legendary; it was said that through the ivory trade he could convert an initial capital of $3 into $1,000.[83] He had transformed the economy west of Lake Tanganyika from barter to currency; the standard unit of value and medium of exchange was the cowrie bead.[84]

But most impressive of all Tippu Tip's achievements was the way he had transformed Manyema into a slave state that resembled Zanzibar in the pre-Bartle Frere era. As in Zanzibar, there was a three-tiered social system based on slavers, middlemen and slaves.[85] The great slavers like Tippu inculcated aspects of the coastal culture, such as the use of Swahili as lingua franca, even though Arab culture and religion always ran skin-deep in Manyema. The key to the entire edifice of stratification was the *wangwana* or *petits Arabes* of the middle tier. Detribalised middlemen, recruited as adolescent males by the Arabs and ritually circumcised, the *wangwana* spoke a Swahili dialect called Kiungwana.[86] Existing in a twilight world between freedom and slavery, the *wangwana* were the NCOs of the Arab slavers and controlled the local Africans on their behalf. Their relationship with the Arab overlords was rather like that of the Sicilian *gabelotti* to the landowners, and they were later to become the cornerstone of Leopold's control of the Province Orientale of the Belgian Congo.[87]

Such was the power of the man Stanley met at Kasongo in October 1876. The anecdote Tippu Tip provides to illustrate their first meeting gives us clues to the character of both men. To overawe this formidable merchant of death Stanley boasted to Tippu that he had a gun that could fire fifteen rounds at once. When Tippu Tip asked for a demonstration, Stanley said it would cost $20–30, the cost of the ammunition. When the Arab gave an Islamically stoical shrug, Stanley relented and gave the desired demonstration of his firepower.[88]

But the most important consequence of the meeting at Kasongo was the information Tippu Tip provided about Cameron, Stanley's putative rival for the charting of the Lualaba River. After leaving England on the would-be definitive RGS expedition, Verney Lovett Cameron had made a leisurely progress through Arica. In August 1873 he had stayed at Unyanyembe in the *tembe* that Livingstone and Stanley had made famous.[89] It took him until December 1874 to reach Nyangwe, where he prepared for the descent of the Lualaba. But his men had refused to proceed any farther into the unknown Congo; they lacked sufficient canoes and were terrified of the ferocious reputation of the Upper Congo peoples. Tippu Tip himself had advised Cameron that the Congo was impassable; not even he, with his 'hordes', would dare to venture into those dark forests.[90] Faced with this advice, Cameron abandoned his pursuit of the Lualaba and cut across to the west coast of Africa by an easier route taking him through Portuguese territory. This meant that the great task of charting the Lualaba still remained for Stanley to perform.[91]

Since Tippu Tip had accompanied Cameron as far north as Nyangwe for an agreed sum, Stanley thought it might be possible to tempt him farther north as an escort in return for suitable largesse. But the Arab quickly turned his flank by showing Stanley his immense stocks of ivory, thereby demonstrating clearly that he did not need the money. Stanley tried a different tack and appealed to Tippu's prestige. Tippu replied that he would accompany him to Nyangwe as a favour, a gesture of friendship towards the white man. Even this decision caused ructions, as Tippu's lieutenants thought his magnanimity madness.[92]

Stanley then questioned him about the Lualaba and the chiefs who lay along its banks. Tippu's best intelligence was that the Lualaba flowed undeviatingly northward beyond the ken of trading man. What about Munza, the grand chief of the Mangbetu?[93] Why did Stanley want to know about him, Tippu asked. Stanley replied that he intended to travel north on the Lualaba to Monbuttu, then cut across west to the next watershed, be it the Nile or the Niger or the Congo.[94]

The next days were spent in protracted and arduous negotiations concerning the exact conditions under which Tippu and his men would accompany the Anglo-American expedition. After exhaustive consultations with his lieutenants, Tippu Tip agreed to escort the expedition for sixty days in return for full subsistence for 140 men and a fee of $5,000. There were many conditions attached to the deal. Each camp should be no more than four hours' march from the one before; there should be a day's rest for every two of marching; the money should be payable even if Stanley abandoned his march before the sixty days were up.[95]

While these tortuous negotiations were going on, Stanley discussed with Pocock their future strategy. There seemed no glory in simply following Cameron's southward route to the coast and besides, knowing Bennett, Stanley was sure the *Herald* would make difficulties over paying the *wangwanas'* passage back to Zanzibar from the west coast. Their best bet seemed to be to strike north, possibly returning to Zanzibar via Lake Victoria and Kagehyi. Even better might be the route via Munza's territory which would enable them to solve the Lualaba/Nile riddle and return via Gondokoro and Uganda, perhaps meeting Gordon on the way.[96] First, however, they ought to try for a clear resolution of the north/south question. They tossed a coin to decide the matter: 'heads' for the Lualaba and the north; 'tails' for Katanga and the south. The omens were not good. Six times the coin came down 'tails'. When they tried drawing straws, long for the north, and short for the south, the short straws were drawn every time.[97]

These academic lucubrations were interrupted by the news that Tippu Tip had agreed to the sixty-day march. A formal contract was signed, Tippu's men received an advance of cloth and their names were entered on the muster-roll of the expedition at the same rate as Stanley's men. Then for four days they marched through rolling, depopulated country full of ruined villages, sometimes through eight-foot high grass. To the east of them were the conical spurs of the Manyema hills; to the west was a rolling, marshy grassland extending to the Lualaba. The only incident *en route* was that Kalulu, newly restored to favour, was accidentally wounded by a loaded Snider.[98]

They reached Nyangwe late on 26 October 1876. The farthest outpost of the Zanzibar Arabs, it was perched on a high reddish bank some 40 feet above the Lualaba. Stanley found it riven by factionalism and rivalry between the various Arab slavers based in the town. There appeared to be three main coteries under the domain respectively of Myinyi Dugumbi, Mohammed bin Nassur of Kassessa and Muhammed bin Said of Mamba Mamba, a relative of Tippu Tip.[99] These three had carved up the local area and within a triangle hunted for blacks the way an English country gentleman would hunt for grouse, in a way that horrified Frank Pocock, already distraught at the experience of slavery in Ujiji.[100]

But Stanley found two other Arabs more interesting. One was Abed bin Salim, one of the founders of Nyangwe, who found the discipline of Stanley's *wangwana* impressive after a march of 338 miles from Lake

Tanganyika in forty-three days.[101] The other was Abed bin Juma, who seemed to confirm Livingstone's idea that the Lualaba flowed into the Nile.[102] Stanley also derived some bogus consolation from the peaceful demeanour of the Genia people on the left bank of the Lualaba. But it was a fallacious extrapolation as to what he would encounter later. The Genia were intrinsically pacific, and were also habitually left in peace by the Arabs, since their skill as boatmen made them useful.[103]

During the week spent in Nyangwe Stanley and Pocock virtually rebuilt *Lady Alice* for the coming voyage on the Lualaba while they continued to ponder their route. Despite Abed bin Juma, Stanley was virtually certain by now that the Lualaba must feed into the Congo, since it was too mighty a river at this southern latitude to be a tributary of the Nile. But he was still undecided whether to follow the Lualaba to the sea or simply follow it north until it swung west before aiming for Munza's with the aim of linking up the spheres of discovery of Livingstone and Schweinfurth. There was much agonising on the point between him and Pocock until 'one midnight we resolved together that it was our duty to try it'. Pocock again tossed a coin and this time the decision favoured following the Lualaba.[104]

But nobody could be *certain* where the Lualaba ended until its course had been traced. Stanley had earlier told Alice Pike that he would probably reach England in August–September 1877 if he emerged on the west coast, and some three months later if he came out at Zanzibar. Yet his letter to Edward King from Nyangwe revealed a fear that the Lualaba might, after all, be not the Nile but the Niger, in which case he would be lucky to emerge on the ocean before late 1879 or early 1880.[105]

At the final muster on 4 November Stanley counted 146 of his own men, armed with twenty-nine Sniders, two Winchesters, two double-barrelled shotguns and thirty-two percussion-lock muskets. Though only forty of these were reliable shots, Stanley took comfort from the force of more than 500 that Tippu Tip had assembled. Stanley, wrongly as it turned out, could not see how a party nearly 700 strong could be opposed.[106] They planned to travel in two detachments, a land party and a river squadron. The river section would have the advantage since, whereas a porter could carry 50–70 pounds for a maximum of 20 miles a day, a paddler in a trading canoe could transport 140–400 pounds a day twice that distance upstream and four times downstream.[107]

Stanley and Pocock were now (save for a few last-minute waverings) definitely committed to following the Lualaba to the end, lead where it might. Stanley summed up his feelings on the eve of launching into the unknown.

> Should my opinion be confirmed I should by following the Lualaba so far north, be taking the expedition beyond all power of aid or supplies from any quarter. Such a long distance beyond all calculation would waste every article we could possibly exchange for food. If the mere purpose of this expedition was to cross Africa, with the utmost confidence I declare to you that I could reach San Salvador in six months from Nyangwe; but I should then, like Cameron, have left the question of the Lualaba just where Livingstone left it, to be discussed upon the grounds of each man's opinions. If I merely struck direct west for San Salvador, how could I presume that the Lualaba is the Congo, or that it is not the Congo but the Nile or the Niger – whichever it may be? I should forfeit all right to be heard upon the subject or to be considered as one able to confirm any of the theories broached upon the subject. This would be lamentable . . . But, as neither conjectures, dreams, theories nor opinions will make one positive geographical fact, I propose to stick to the Lualaba, come fair or come foul, fortune or misfortune; and, that I may not be driven back by force, I have recruited the expedition to one hundred and forty rifles and muskets and seventy spears. The desertions and deaths from smallpox at Ujiji had thinned my companions to such a degree that we should have been only a sop for a ferocious tribe . . . it must be a very strong tribe indeed that can drive us back now. But what savages cannot do hunger may, if the Lualaba continues running so far north of the Equator. I have ample supplies for six months. Beyond that heaven knows what will become of us if we find ourselves at the confluence of these two rivers, the Lualaba and the unknown river, so far out of the way of supplies, with not a single bead or cowrie to buy food.[108]

Nothing more clearly demonstrates the uncertainty of success entertained even by the man of iron himself.[109]

· 16 ·

IN the 'global village' near the end of the twentieth century it takes an effort of imagination to appreciate that in late 1876 the African region north of Nyangwe was completely unexplored and unknown both to Arabs and white men. Stanley and Tippu Tip were now entering the true 'Dark Continent' – where none but local tribesmen had ever ventured before. The very audacity of his attempt intrigued his followers, who oscillated between terror of the unknown and pride in the courage of the 'little master'.[1] But Stanley himself displayed the insouciance that properly belonged to the unconscious rather than the rational calculation of odds: 'I believe I was made half indifferent to life by my position; otherwise I doubt if I should have deliberately rushed upon what I was led to believe – as my predecessors were – was almost certain death.'[2] So convinced, indeed, were the Arabs of Nyangwe that the white man was bent on a suicide mission that they refused to supply him with canoes.

The great trek into *terra incognita* began on 5 November. The expedition marched 10 miles over a rolling plain covered with grass. Ahead of them stretched a black wall of tropical forest curving away to the south-east. Even Stanley was rather daunted by the prospect as he stole a last look at green and inviting Nyangwe. Next day they said goodbye to the sunlight and plunged into the forest gloom. Here Stanley made his first mistake. He allowed Tippu Tip's warriors, brandishing flintlocks and bows and arrows, to enter the dark interior ahead of him. These came to an abrupt halt when they encountered the tangled undergrowth of the forest, and those coming behind cannoned into them, throwing the line of march into chaos.[3]

When order was restored, the expedition began to pick its way through 20-foot high undergrowth, fed by a feculent humus of fallen branches and rotten leaves. They marched in permanent twilight, soggy with dew under a fuliginous forest canopy, floundering through ditches formed by rivulets descending to the Kunda River. Their clothes were saturated with moisture. Stanley's white sun-helmet and puggaree felt as if they were weighted with lead. The atmosphere was stifling and sweat oozed from every pore. 'The path soon became a clayey paste, and at every step we splashed water over the legs of those in front, and on either side of us.'[4] Although the main expedition made camp at around 3 p.m. the boatmen did not get into bivouack until dusk, as the sections of *Lady Alice* had to be driven like blunted ploughs through the depths of the foliage.

8 November 1876 was a date recorded in sorrow by the two white explorers. 'Through dense forest, at intervals we saw an open space, then plunged in the same deep vales and high hills of forest and bush as before,' wrote Pocock.[5] Stanley's impressions were similar. The expedition crawled, tore and scrambled through the damp, dark jungle. The locals were surly and set spoked traps on which several of the men gashed their feet. Once on the crown of a hill they caught a distant glimpse of the Lualaba which seemed to the travellers like the promised land. Then back into the darkness they plunged, into a blackness so inky that Stanley could not see the words he scribbled in his notebook. They arrived in camp half-suffocated by the heavy fetid miasma of the forest. Stanley recorded the day's impressions.

Fearful time of it today in the woods – such crawling, scrambling, tearing through the damp cool jungles, with such height and depth of woods. Once we got a sidelong view from the limited growth of a hill over the wild woods around us which swept in irregular waves towards the Lualaba and of green grass plains on the other side of the Lualaba.[6]

The next day saw more of the same. They tried to cut their way through the tangle with axes and billhooks, so as to clear a way for the boat sections, but they could make it neither wide nor straight enough, as so many forest giants lay prostrate across their track.

Another difficult day's work in the forest and jungle. Our caravan is no longer the tight compact force which was my pride but utterly dis-organised; each one scrambling to the best of his ability through the woods . . . the path being over a clayey soil, is so slippery that every muscle is employed to assist our progress.[7]

By the 10th, in the country of the Regga, the expedition was exhausted, so Stanley ordered a three-day halt. Since Stanley had insisted on following a track through the territory of the warlike Regga, Tippu Tip raised his rate for the job from $5,000 to $7,000.[8] Such was the general despondency in the expedition that even the great Arab slaver's morale was low, and it seemed that money alone could palliate it. Certainly the folkways of the Regga were enough to demoralise the most sanguine traveller: so impregnable and secure were they in their forest fastnesses that many of them had never seen the Lualaba all their lives even though it was but 20 miles distant.[9]

When they resumed the march, the straggling problem of the boatmen and the complete absence of food forced Stanley to head for the Lualaba and cross to the western bank. It was taking the twenty-four men bearing the boat sections twelve hours to march 6 miles, so that at this rate every other day would have to be spent resting. The march to the Lualaba finished off Stanley's penultimate pair of shoes; Pocock was already on his last. As he drew the final pair from his stores, Stanley pondered the prospect of barefoot marching on the Congo. It was not inviting, for, as well as the wealth of small grey white-necked monkeys in the trees around them, they encountered other less welcome forest denizens: 10-foot pythons, gigantic puff-adders, and armies of deep-brown 'hot water' ants.[10]

At last, on 16 November, Tippu Tip's patience snapped. Not even the extra money could compensate for the daily agony. He complained of the length of the marches and pointed out that at their present rate of progress sixty camps could take a whole year to achieve. He therefore requested a dissolution of the original contract. Stanley doggedly held him to his word as an Arab gentleman. In that case, Tippu countered, after the sixty marches you must agree that I can take half the force back with me to Nyangwe. Angrily Stanley rejected this as nonsense. Not so, insisted Tippu: without this number of men I would be torn to pieces by the tribes on my way back. He put it forcefully to Stanley that if he did not agree to an amended contract, he and his men would return forthwith to Nyangwe. Angrily Stanley raged at him. Four hours' march a day would mean that the sixty marches would be equivalent to less than thirty normal days. Tippu Tip seemed to him 'bent on breaking the agreement or making money'. But Stanley's position was weak and he knew it. If the Arab turned back now, the entire Anglo-American expedition would disintegrate through desertion. With supreme difficulty the two men hammered out a compromise whereby Tippu Tip would escort Stanley as far as Kima-Kima on the Rumami River.[11]

On 17 November they left Uregga and entered the territory of Uvinza. On the river bank were the fishermen or Wagenya but ahead lay two warlike tribes, the Songola (Stanley's 'Wabwire') and the Kusu.[12] 'We crossed several lofty hill ridges, separated by appallingly gloomy ravines, through which several clear streams flowed westward, and after a march of eleven miles north-westerly through the dark dripping forests, arrived at Kampunzu.'[13] A 5-mile march through the forest west of Kampunzu brought them to a point at 3°35' south (41 miles north of Nyangwe) where the Lualaba proper ended and a new river began, which Stanley proposed to call the 'Livingstone'. Here the broad stream was 1,200 yards wide from bank to bank. They camped on the bank. The brown wave of the river flowed on, as gentle as a summer's dream, while Stanley contemplated the mysteries and dangers ahead.

That evening he harangued his men to the effect that destiny had led them to this confluence that they might follow the new river to the end. He asked for volunteers to follow the 'Livingstone' to its mouth. Only thirty-eight of the *wangwana* agreed to follow him; the other ninety-five sat tight-lipped. Tippu Tip and the other Arabs threw their weight into the balance, urging Stanley not to go on to certain suicide.[14]

It was not long before the local tribesmen visited them. Stanley started to bargain for canoes, without revealing that he already possessed the *Lady Alice*. His overtures were received contemptuously. The Lualaba people told him he would first need a heap of cowrie shells a cubit high. Appearing cowed, Stanley gave secret orders that *Lady Alice* be made ready. Suddenly he launched it on the river to general astonishment. His sharpshooters trained their Sniders on the shore while Stanley commanded the Wagenya of the islands to appear in camp that evening to make blood-brotherhood. The Wagenya agreed to become blood-brothers provided the ceremony was carried out on their island territory.[15]

Suspecting treachery, Stanley sent Kacheche and a company of men upstream, just four minutes away from the island, while Frank Pocock crossed over to make blood-brothers with the Wagenya. The precaution was justified: the relief force had to intervene quickly when the demeanour of the tribesmen towards Pocock turned nasty. Baulked of an obvious reconciliation with the recalcitrant Wagenya, Stanley decided to land his sharpshooters on the far bank so as to form a beachhead, pending the transfer of the entire expedition. He then floated down past the Wagenya village and called out to them that they were now between two fires, that resistance was useless. The Wagenya appeared to acquiesce in the *fait accompli*. The next step was to transfer the expedition to the far bank. On 20 November 458 souls with four donkeys and 150 loads of cloth and beads transferred to the right bank. Since the Wagenya still failed to co-operate, Stanley gave orders that all canoes were to be seized.[16]

Next day they discovered that the Wagenya were using Fabian tactics against them, leaving their villages deserted and melting into the forest rather than co-operate. They left behind a series of man-traps for the unwary. Stanley decided to divide his force for the passage downriver. He and thirty-six crack shots boarded the *Lady Alice* and the few canoes they had acquired, while Pocock, Tippu Tip and the rest of the expedition tracked them from the bank. They floated down the Lualaba to the confluence with the Ruiki. Whenever they approached a village, the inhabitants fled, crying out, 'Wasambye, Wasambye.'[17]

At 3 p.m. on 22 November they came to the black and sluggish Ruiki, 100 yards wide. Since the land party would be unable to cross, Stanley awaited them here. He built a strong camp and set sentries. The locals offered them food, but it was clear that this was with the intention solely of ridding themselves of their unwelcome visitors.

By the 24th, when there was still no word of the land party, Stanley began to regret that he had divided his force. He decided to take *Lady Alice* 10 miles up the Ruiki in hopes of finding Tippu Tip and the others encamped there. He left behind a small 'holding' force to guard the camp. By 2 p.m., after ascending the Ruiki for 10 miles, Stanley concluded he was wasting his time and commenced the return to camp. At 3.30 p.m. they heard the distant muttering of gunfire. Rowing at full speed they came to the Ruiki junction to find it blocked by Wagenya canoes, full of warriors in war panoply who were pressing the camp garrison hard. They had waited until word came in that the white man had departed before pressing their attack on the camp, but then, fortunately, had delayed too long before assaulting it. Stanley arrived in the nick of time to save his beleaguered rearguard.[18]

Finding the land party had now become an imperative. Stanley at once sent out Uledi the coxswain and five of the boatmen under cover of night to find Tippu Tip and Pocock. At 4 p.m. next day they returned with news that the main force had fallen foul of the even more formidable Kusu and had lost three men in arrow attacks. Four hours later Stanley was finally able to unite both sections of the hard-pressed and demoralised expedition. He then transported the entire party to the left bank of the Ruiki; an old man was shot by his bodyguard as he tried to repossess a canoe.[19]

On 26 November the united expedition proceeded downriver to Nakanpemba. This time the land and river parties kept in close touch, by visual contact whenever possible, otherwise by drum-taps. The Lualaba was about 1,700 yards wide on this stretch. At deserted Nakanpemba they found rows of human skulls in the streets. Again the locals melted away and had to be taken by force for questioning. The expedition now no longer thought of barter but took whatever it could lay its hands on. In one village they appropriated fifteen goats, though this did not go far among 458 mouths. The diet was supplemented by roasting ears of Indian corn and manioc. Fatigue and food shortages were already depleting numbers, especially among the land division. The attacks came not just from smallpox and dysentery but also from ulcerated feet caused by the entry of thorns and serrated stakes into the soles and shins of the marchers. Stanley was forced to improvise a floating hospital for the sick by lashing together six abandoned and unsound canoes.[20]

They glided below Nakanpemba at a rate of 1½ knots. Soon they heard the dull murmur of approaching rapids. Stanley ordered the land party to camp for the day while he edged cautiously along the left bank to explore. His reconnoitring took him perilously close to an ambush mounted by about fifty canoes in a hidden creek close to the Lukassa rapids. The enemy canoes were based on an island between the two arms of the falls. Stanley landed ten riflemen and in a brisk skirmish drove his opponents off the island: 'It was most undesirable to have an enemy lurking in the grass or the reeds below the rapids.'[21]

On returning to camp Stanley was alarmed to hear that Pocock had allowed four of his best men to shoot the rapids in one of the hospital canoes. They negotiated two of the falls but were predictably pitched into the water at the third. Though no lives were lost, three of the Sniders were borne away in the swirling waters. To add to this, the enemy canoes began to hover ominously close to the shipwrecked men until a rescue unit under Stanley and Uledi dispersed them. That evening Stanley upbraided Pocock angrily at the camp below the first rapids on the left bank 'with the noise of falling and rushing water all around us'. Yet his rebukes to Manwa Sera were even harsher, so acerbic in fact that the great Zanzibari captain stormed off to Tippu Tip's tent and vowed he would serve the 'little master' no longer.[22]

Again Tippu Tip and the Arabs besought Stanley to turn back. He promised a definite answer next day, but upstaged them by portaging the boat and canoes around the rapids and ascertaining that there were no more falls ahead. They continued to float down the Lualaba until 5 December, making 4 miles a day. The land party again lost contact, but this time Stanley was less fearful as it contained 350 men and 120 guns. Stanley and the river party meanwhile continued unavailingly to make overtures to passing canoes. The Lualaba at this point would suddenly narrow to 800 yards if a large island lay athwart it, only to broaden again to 1,700 yards. It was characterised by many sharp bends with frequent dangerous whirls and broad patches of foam on its face. At night they camped at the communal market-places on the bank which no chief could claim as his own – most of them wide grassy spaces under the shade of mighty trees. The river continued to run for most of its length in two broad streams, each about 1,000 yards wide, separated by large islands.[23]

On 5 December Stanley's progress was halted by rainstorms and food shortages. At Ikondu he faced the first of the many river battles he fought during his progress down the Lualaba-Congo. As he explored the right bank of the Lualaba, he was greeted with a shower of arrows from a crowd of warriors he estimated as about 500 strong. An answering volley from the Sniders killed three of them and wounded several. In the afternoon battle was rejoined. After much blowing of horns and conches eight war canoes approached *Lady Alice* and issued a formal challenge. Stanley issued forth to meet them, with twenty riflemen and his elephant gun. A crashing barrage from the booming elephant gun quickly sowed confusion among the warriors. They panicked and fled. A few minutes later their would-be confederates, another hundred tribesmen in seven canoes, approached Ikondu from the left bank but, seeing their comrades in full rout, sheered off at once.[24]

Victory on the water led to serendipity on land. Finding a large condemned canoe on the shore, Stanley gave his carpenters two days to patch it up and make it weatherly. Twelve men with axes working flat out produced in forty-eight hours a viable monster canoe. This was a valuable bargaining counter for Stanley in his wrangles with Tippu Tip. It proved that a flotilla of 'super-canoes' could be built, capable of floating the entire expedition downriver and thus undercutting Tippu's pleas for a return.[25] But if Stanley was now confident he could keep Tippu's party with him, he was shaken by the condition of the Arab's party when it came in on 8 December. Smallpox was making fearful inroads and would soon rage almost unchecked through the united party. In addition, the expedition was beset by dysentery, ulcers, itch, bronchitis, pneumonia, pleurisy, typhus, even cases of anal prolapse. Every day they tossed an average of three bodies into the river.[26]

Yet it was as well that the two vanguard sections of the expedition were united, for on 8 December at Unya-Nsinge, a large town 4 miles below the junction of the Lira and the Congo, they ran into their stiffest opposition yet. In the afternoon fourteen large canoes came upriver and challenged the strangers to fight. Stanley drew up his men on the bank. At 50 yards' range the warriors loosed their poisoned arrows. They then attempted to land to use their short stabbing spears. Stanley waited until the keels were scraping the shore before giving the order to open fire. His musketeers performed terrible execution. The stricken enemy retired to a range of 150 yards, from where they continued to yell defiantly. Stanley decided on a sortie. With a handpicked crew, including Tippu Tip, he made a sudden dash to midstream in a canoe, tempting the enemy into close range. Then, at a distance of 50 yards, Stanley's sharpshooters unleashed a devastating barrage. The enemy retreated in a chaos of floating hulks and upturned canoes. The expedition had not lost a single man.[27]

Stanley and Tippu dug in at Unya-Nsinge and waited for Pocock and the third detachment to come in overland. It was the 11th before this company came in, having been engaged in running fights on the way and, like Tippu's men, decimated by smallpox and disease. The smallpox was now at epidemic level. Three *wangwana* had succumbed on the march with Pocock and new eight more died, including the three favourite girls in Tippu Tip's harem. A further thirty were seriously ill on the hospital canoe.[28]

And still there was no respite from the hostile tribesmen. Tippu Tip spurned Stanley's offer of making the entire expedition riverborne and continued by land; Stanley took Pocock and Sheikh Abdullah (Tippu's second-in-command) on board *Lady Alice*. On 14 December at Mutako the river party ran into a well-planned ambush, beaten off at the cost of one arrow wound: 'The Mutako natives made a first-class plan of attack, two sides by water, one side by land, but it faded from their want of courage. One canoe sufficed to drive the water party, and two canoes the land party.'[29]

On the 18th they arrived at a market green between the island of Mpika and the left bank. Again the war-horns sounded for battle, but a fortuitous capture of the local headmen led to peace negotiations and the making of blood-brotherhood. But this peace proved a false dawn. They continued with confidence a further 10 miles by a channel between the river and a long high island, with banks 80 feet above the water. At the end of this 10-mile stretch the river widened to 2,000 yards. Just as they were about to debouch on to this open waterway, Stanley heard the familiar ping of arrows. One of the stewards on the hospital canoe fell transfixed. The whizz of arrows showered uncomfortably near Stanley's head.[30]

The expedition sheered off and landed at an untenanted market green.

Defences of brushwood fence were constructed. A shriek of agony rang out from one of the *wangwana* followed by the crackle of Sniders. There followed a cacophony of yells and war-horns, while arrows flew around the defenders from all sides. They just had time to complete the defences before Stanley's scouts returned with word that the enemy was approaching in strength.

A savage combat now broke out. The warriors flung themselves forward on to the killing ground in the 150 yards of clearing in front of the stockade. Plumes of smoke arose from the embrasures as the defenders poured a steady fire on their attackers. Uledi and Pocock were kept busy clubbing would-be deserters from the *wangwana* back into position. At dusk, having taken heavy casualties, the enemy retired but the night continued to be punctuated by the din of ivory horns and the whizz and ping of poisoned arrows. To sustain the sentries' vigilance, it became necessary for Pocock and Sheikh Abdullah to pour kettles of cold water over their heads. At 11 p.m. a surprise attack was beaten off, but throughout the night the depressing 'twit-twit' of falling missiles continued to aggravate them.[31]

In the morning they breakfasted cautiously. Then Stanley reconnoitred in the boat and discovered a large town just 500 yards away. This was Vinya-Njara, 125 miles north of Nyangwe. The depth of the hostility they had encountered now began to be explained, for Stanley's intelligence revealed that the Vinya-Njara people had called in the bellicose Kusu warriors to 'eat up' the interlopers.[32]

Stanley decided to occupy the southern village of the two that comprised the town, in order to provide rest and recuperation for the sick and a base camp for the daily-expected land party. Seventy-two men were now out of action with smallpox. Swiftly Stanley landed his forces and occupied the deserted southern village. He turned it into a defensive redoubt by constructing three stockades around the anthills that commanded the village, and felling trees to block the access trails. The Kusu responded by climbing tall trees and drawing a bead on anyone who showed himself in the broad streets. It became impossible for the expedition to bury its dead or attend to the delirious wounded.[33]

Stanley responded in kind to this fresh threat. He sent four sharp-shooters to climb the tall trees along the river bank and take out the enemy snipers. He himself pushed off from the shore in a canoe and by use of his field-glasses located the bowmen's main nests. A lucky shot managed to down one of the Kusu chiefs. Desultory firing continued all morning until noon when Stanley led a sortie that cleared the skirts of the southern village for the day. He then sent scouts to deploy in a crescent formation from beyond the ends of the village into the forest. Under this cover the rest of his men formed a line and began to cut down all the grass and weeds within 100 yards of the stockades. Next they constructed 15-foot high snipers' nests at each end of the village, so as to control all approaches.[34]

When the Kusu launched their belated counterattack on 20 December, the strength of the new defences shook them. They retired to plan an assault in maximum strength. At noon the attack came. 800 warriors in canoes flanked them from the river while the bulk of the Kusu forces charged in from the forest. The task of containing these hordes fell to the twenty sharpshooters in the nests. Stanley, Pocock, Abdullah and twenty others received the attack at the riverside. The *wangwana* behaved splendidly that day. After two years of gruelling discipline, Stanley could at last tell himself he possessed an élite fighting force.[35]

A desperate struggle now ensued. The outcome appeared uncertain and the war canoes were massing for a landing in strength when sudden whoopings and ululations from the Kusu announced to Stanley that his land party had finally arrived. The enemy was now outflanked and outgunned. In rage and frustration the oarsmen threw water towards them with upturned paddles in the now familiar gesture of contempt.[36]

The tide now turned in earnest. A large bribe of cloth secured the services of the forty original defenders for a daring commando operation to cut adrift the enemy canoes. Setting out at 10 p.m. on a rainy, gusty night, travelling with muffled oars, Stanley, Pocock and their élite squad achieved complete surprise and total success. Having cut adrift thirty-six canoes, they towed a further twenty-six back to camp. This was a crushing blow to the Kusu. When Stanley reconnoitred the enemy island base next morning in *Lady Alice*, he found they had fled. All that remained in the northern village now was a pitiful remnant who quickly made peace to avoid the occupation of their huts. Blood-brotherhood and the partial restitution of canoes secured a week-long peace, with no known enemy nearer to Vinya-Njara than 10 miles.[37]

But if Tippu Tip's coming at the eleventh hour secured a great military victory for Stanley, it also marked the end of his co-operation with the expedition. The final march to Vinya-Njara had convinced Tippu of the madness of the exploit he was engaged in. His men had lost their way several times on the jungle trails, they were short of food, they were daily shrinking in numbers through smallpox. On the afternoon of 22

December Tippu Tip informed Stanley that he intended to return to Nyangwe as soon as he had rested; this decision was non-negotiable.[38]

The news ran through the camp like electricity. The tired and dispirited *wangwana* saw in Tippu Tip's decision a unique opportunity to escape their bondage with Stanley. Bondage it truly was in their eyes, since their interpretation of their contracts was that they had agreed to serve for two years only, and they were already well into their third year. At the prospect of mass desertion on the eve of his final breakthrough, Stanley's spirits began to quail. He sat depressed in his tent for some hours. Finally, on the evening of 22 December he went to talk to Tippu Tip.

What happened next is disputed. According to Stanley he pointed out that Tippu Tip had not fulfilled the proper terms of their contract; however, he was willing to see him depart if the Arabs would help him force his *wangwana* into the boats. When Tippu demurred, Stanley threatened to denounce him before the Sultan in Zanzibar. Faced with this threat, Tippu simply passed the buck by threatening to shoot any of Stanley's Zanzibaris who tried to quit.[39] Tippu Tip's own version is different, more subtle and more convincing. He suggested that the best solution was for Stanley to enact a charade. Stanley should harangue the men, warn of the wrath of the Sultan if they backed out, and insinuate that the Sultan would recoup the expedition losses from the Arabs if it was forced to turn back. At this point Tippu Tip would make an apparently spontaneous entry on the scene and declare that he was not going to take financial loss because of the cowardice of the *wangwana*. He and his levies would then force Stanley's men into their canoes.[40]

However, some news of the intended comedy must have leaked out, for on 23 December the *wangwana* learned that Tippu Tip intended to shoot anyone from Stanley's party who tried to turn back to Nyangwe. A delegation came to see Tippu on the night of 23 December to point out that since their contracts had expired, they were perfectly entitled to return. Tippu repeated that he would not be ruined on their account and that he would shoot any unauthorised person who tried to return with him. The *wangwana* then lowered their sights and complained of Stanley's miserliness. To assuage this grievance, Tippu distributed nine bales of cloth which he then claimed back from Stanley as the price of success. He further promised that he would wait at Vinya-Njara a month to see if the expedition was turned back from the Congo.[41]

According to Tippu, Stanley was overjoyed and jubilant at the success of the Arab's stratagem, and it is true that in the privacy of his diary

Stanley later acknowledged his debt.[42] In Stanley's version he rewarded the Arab potentate with a draft for $2,600 and a promise of a personal gift of $1,000 when he got back to London.[43] In Tippu's version, the payment at Vinya-Njara was all in the form of promises, none of which were fulfilled. This left him with a legacy of bitterness against Stanley, who acquired the reputation in the Arab world as a master of double-cross and a man who did not pay his debts.[44] There was a further reason for the hostility towards Stanley later manifested by Tippu Tip. Tippu swore up and down that no man could travel down the Congo and emerge on the Atlantic coast; the feat was an impossibility. When Stanley achieved the impossible, Tippu Tip's own reputation as a man of peerless wisdom suffered. There was an issue of credibility in Tippu's later pique against Stanley, as well as justified resentment against a man who would not pay his debts.[45]

On Christmas Day 1876 Stanley announced to his captive *wangwana* that they would follow the river to the sea, wherever it led. He assigned his men to twenty-three canoes, each named after a Royal Navy East Africa cruiser. From now on the original Anglo-American expedition would proceed wholly by water, so that its speed would not be impaired by the need to wait for a land party to catch up. In the afternoon Stanley's men held an athletics competition against Tippu Tip's men. In one race Tippu Tip himself took on Frank Pocock over 300 yards and easily outstripped him. A dance by the men of Unyamwezi brought the festivities to a close. Next day Tippu Tip gave a farewell banquet of roast sheep to celebrate the departure of the 149 men, women and children who would go on with Stanley into the unknown.[46]

17

THE morning of 28 December 1876 dawned wet and misty. So thick was the river fog that departure was delayed until 9 a.m. Stanley's men then began pulling slowly over towards the left bank, a mile above Vinya-Njara. Stanley remembered the occasion as the saddest day he had spent in Africa.

> To the sound of the thrilling farewell song of the *Wanyamwezi* we took our seats, and formed a line in mid-river, my boat in front. The influence of the song, whose notes were borne in wild and weird tones across the river, proved too much for my people: they wept as though they were nearly heart-broken. 'Children of Zanzibar!' I shouted to them. 'Lift up your heads! Cry out, Bismillah! and dash your paddles into the water. Let the *Wanyamwezi* return to Nyangwe and tell the tale to your friends, what brave men those were who took the white man down the great river to the sea.[1]

Gradually the beautiful elegiac notes of the song being chanted by Tippu Tip's men grew fainter, then faded altogether. The expedition paddled on despondently, in silence. They passed fourteen densely populated villages without incident. But at the confluence of the Kasuku on 29 December the war drums sounded and flotillas of pirogues dashed out from either bank. Stanley veered towards the left bank and engaged the enemy in a parley, thus taking his fleet out of range of the spearsmen on the right. Then, at an appropriate point in the current, he allowed *Lady Alice* and the canoes to float under their own momentum. They were borne rapidly downstream past the gesticulating tribesmen on the left bank.[2]

Stanley was perplexed by the unremitting hostility of the tribes and disconcerted by the perpetual cries of '*Niama! Niama!*' ('Meat! Meat!'), an alarming sign of cannibalism.[3] At every curve and bend in the river the huge wooden drums sent ahead the message that strangers were coming, that fierce resistance should be mustered.[4] Even where tribes were not cannibals, they entertained the fear that the strangers must be slavers. Stanley had no time to stop to explain his mission. He was racing against time, for both food and ammunition were short and the expedition daily faced perils that thinned their numbers. A storm on 30 December sank two canoes; two men were drowned and four guns lost. That meant seven guns lost since leaving Nyangwe. Out of the 143 souls left (apart from two asses, two goats and a single sheep), 107 were enlisted men on wages but only forty-eight now possessed guns. Of these forty-eight only thirty-two were good fighting men, so that the effective fighting force (with Stanley and Pocock) was just thirty-four. By this time, setbacks and disasters failed to spark the men into thoughts of desertion. They embraced fatalism which Stanley found moronic: 'They are terribly dull people to lead across Africa. They smoke *banghy* [hashish] until they literally fall down half-smothered.'[5]

They continued past the confluence of the Urindi, hugging the right bank. At night they camped in dense low jungle, the haunt of elephant and hippo, where Stanley imagined their presence could not possibly be objected to. But he was wrong. Continual hostility forced them on, through rainstorms, past dark banks and low oozy mudflats and swamps, sometimes within an arm's length of elephant country – an impenetrable undergrowth of ferns, dates, palms, vines, capsicum, lianas, rattan leaves, camwood, bombax and teak. The forest hummed with the sounds of insects: ants, termites and mantises; Stanley allowed himself a jibe at armchair romantics who spoke of the 'silence of the forest'.

Armies of parrots screamed overhead as they flew across the river; aquatic birds whirred by us to less disturbed districts; legions of monkeys sported in the branchy depths; howling baboons alarmed the solitudes; crocodiles haunted the sandy points and islets; herds of hippopotami grunted thunderously at our approach; elephants bathed their sides by the margin of the river; there was unceasing vibration from millions of insects throughout the livelong day. The sky was an azure dome, out of which the sun shone large and warm; the river was calm, and broad, and brown.[6]

1876 closed with yet another threatened naval assault from two wings, out of which Stanley again talked his way through the interpreter Katembo. New Year's Day 1877 they began well with three hours' peaceful progress: 'The morning was beautiful, the sky blue and clear, the tall forest still and dark, the river flowed without a ripple, like a solid mass of polished silver.' They glided past several settlements and shouted peaceful slogans, but this tactic backfired when their pacific sentiments were interpreted as weakness. A net was thrown across the river to catch them, as if they were game. A cry went up: 'We shall eat *wajiwa* today!' The net infuriated Stanley. He hove to in *Lady Alice*, then allowed the war canoes to approach very close before opening up with his elephant gun. The enemy dispersed in terror at this awesome demonstration of firepower.[7]

When the river broadened out to 3,000 yards, with no islands and no settlements, hopes were momentarily raised that the expedition might win a respite. But soon more islands funnelled the river, and they became involved in a series of short, sharp fights. On 3 January they fought for three hours without pause, raking with bullets the combined forces of a powerful local confederation from both banks. During a lull in the fighting Stanley sent Katembo with shells as a peace offering for the chiefs, but they asked scornfully why they should settle for so little when they had the prospect of so much. Fighting was resumed. Stanley ordered his men to set up captured shields as bulwarks around the canoe; against their hide protection reed arrows tipped with poison clattered like hail. In reply Stanley ordered his men to load with brass slugs so as to overawe the opposition when they saw the fearful wounds such projectiles caused.[8]

Katembo tried again to negotiate a peace. This time he was more successful. Inter-tribal rivalries were breaking down the confederation of war, with the less bellicose elements now disposed to negotiate. Taking advantage of the split in the opposition, Stanley revictualled and got his men to weave ropes out of lianas and convolvuli ready for the rapids the locals told them were just ahead.

But the hardliners in the confederation – the tribe Stanley called the Mwana Ntaba – had not yet finished with him. On the afternoon of 4 January they launched a fresh attack, in huge 50-foot canoes of a crocodilian aspect. Stanley got his boats into a line, using the shields as bulwarks as before. Holding fire until the enemy was no more than 50 feet away, they then commenced a rapid, stuttering fire. They poured volley after volley into the painted warriors and ended the conflict by ramming an 80-foot canoe and pitching its occupants into the water.[9]

Shortly after the battle the expedition came to another confluence, with a river Stanley later named the Leopold. Here the 2,500-yard wide Congo turned sharply to the north-north-east. At once they heard the roaring of the cataracts the friendly Kankore people had warned them about. They were in fact at the first of the seven cataracts making up what later came to be known as the Stanley Falls. Stanley Falls extended for 56 miles. The first, second, third, fourth and fifth cataract came so close together that they were distinguished only by the number of distinct waterfalls. Though Stanley did not know it at the time, a 9-mile overland journey could take him safely past all first five cataracts. Then came 22 miles of navigable waterway before the fearsome sixth cataract – an absolute fall on the left side and a set of barely passable rapids on the right. 26 further miles of navigable river led to the seventh cataract, where the Congo divided into four channels.[10]

The first cataract at once posed unprecedented problems. At the Ukassa Falls in early December they had been able to float their canoes over the falls and pick them up on the other side of the portage. Here the waters were too turbulent. It would be necessary to drag the boats to below each fall. Yet even while Stanley pondered this problem, he was again assailed in the rear by the dauntless Mwana Ntaba. It was necessary to deal with them first. This time he improvised more skilfully. He landed a party under Manwa Sera, then turned his fleet broadside to the river. This meant that when the enemy came up to them, they would be caught between two fires. So it proved. A running fight from about 5.30 p.m. till dusk saw the warriors finally driven off. Landing by the lip of the falls, Stanley then had his men busy until 10 p.m. constructing a brushwood stockade.[11]

5 January 1877 was a grim date in the expedition's calendar. In order to get his canoes to the foot of the falls, Stanley had to send some of his men to cut a 20-foot wide road through the jungle. He used the older *wangwana* on this task, keeping back the younger ones to repel attacks from the determined Mwana Ntaba, who were now in league with the Baswa tribe from below the first cataract. Remaining on the defensive until 10 a.m., Stanley then sortied and in a five-hour combat succeeding in flushing the enemy out of the woods around the falls. They saw the enemy no more for two days, but the victory had been costly. The expedition had taken casualties of ten wounded and two killed. Of this duo Stanley wrote: 'To prevent them becoming food for the cannibals, we consigned them to the swift brown flood of the Livingstone.'[12]

Next the descent of the falls had to be compassed. Stanley ruled out the right-hand side of the cataract because of the enormous waves and decided to cut overland next to the left fork of the Congo. It took him no more than two hours to blaze a trail to the foot of the falls. Then he ordered his men to open up the trail to a width of 15 feet. Bringing the canoes as close to the lip of the falls as possible before landing them, he had them hauled overland along an expertly cut path through the tangle of rattan palms, vines, creepers and brushwood. The main obstacle was the rain and the fact that only half his force could be used; the other half remained above the falls on the look-out for the enemy.[13]

By the afternoon of the 8th they had passed the first cataract. The temptation now was to race downriver but almost at once they heard the minatory roar of another cataract. As they hugged the left bank, they heard again the drearily familiar sound of drums, conches and war-horns. Between Scylla and Charybdis, Stanley decided to deal with the Baswa first before tackling the second cataract. He landed on the Baswa stronghold of Cheandoah Island and put the enemy to flight, hauling in an immense quantity of bananas, chickens and eggs as well as thirty goats.[14]

From the cowed Baswa people they heard alarming rumours of a ferocious tribe of cannibals called the Bakumu, allegedly directly in their path on the left bank. Stanley's first inclination was to give them a wide berth but an inspection of the right-hand side of the Congo soon put paid to that idea:

> The whole face of the river was wild beyond description and the din of its furious waves stunning . . . we pushed a rotten and condemned canoe above the fall, watched it shoot down like an arrow and circle around that terrible whirring pool, and the next instant saw it drawn in by that dreadful suction, and presently ejected stern foremost thirty yards below.[15]

The only way to resolve the dilemma was to confront the Bakumu, defeat them, then drag the canoes overland through the dense forest overlooking the second cataract on the left bank. On 9 January they left Cheandoah Island and made for the left bank. As they neared a creek, they virtually collided with a Kumu party in full warpaint. After scattering them with a few volleys from the elephant gun, Stanley landed a party that flushed the remaining warriors out of two strongly defended villages and put them to flight.[16]

Next day they portaged the canoes down the second cataract in relays. The route around these falls was especially gruelling and seventy-eight hours were needed to complete the task. One sensational incident punctuated their labours. Zaidi, a veteran of the Livingstone expeditions, was flung into the water when his canoe was smashed. Just as he was about to be borne over the boiling lip of the main waterfall, the wrecked boat snagged on a pointed rock, about a foot above the surface. Zaidi was left clinging to the point of rock just yards away from where the waters boiled over into the whirlpools below. Various attempts to throw him a rope or to send a canoe attached to the shore by rattan creepers failed ignominiously. Then Stanley called for volunteers. After some hesitation Uledi, coxswain of the *Lady Alice*, was joined by Marzouk the boat-boy.[17]

Their comrades on the shore hauled on a length of cable while the two boatmen edged the canoe closer to Zaidi. They managed to secure a rope to Zaidi but then the cable snapped. The two men leaped for safety on to an outcrop of rock on the edge of the waterfall and pulled Zaidi to safety with them while the canoe was swept over the falls. Three men were now in a parlous position instead of the original one. 50 yards of boiling water and calamitous waves lay between them and their comrades. To the right of them was a fall 300 yards wide; below them was a mile of rapids and whirlpools. Dusk came on while rescue attempts were being made, so the effort was abandoned until morning.[18]

At dawn Stanley ordered strong rattans to be cut in the forest. Then they fashioned extra-strong cables which were anchored on the bank and thrown across the foaming flood to the outcrop. There the three men secured the line to the rock and prepared to swing themselves over the water, hand over hand. After many anxious moments, especially when Marzouk's strength seemed to be ebbing, all three men winched themselves manually back to the shore. It was a great triumph of the moral over the material and another successful test of Stanley's sterling leadership qualities.

Stanley's luck continued to hold. The Kumu left them alone while they continued to negotiate the third, fourth and fifth cataracts. One portage involved cutting a road 3 miles long, while being stung by red ants and gashed by spear grass, trying to conceal their endeavours from the enemy betimes. Stanley noted in his diary: 'The men's backs are covered with blisters, while my scalp smarts as if wounded with a fine steel comb.'[19]

No sooner were they clear of the fifth cataract, than they were attacked again, this time by the Asama people. Stanley counterattacked, dividing his force and landing on either side of the enemy. His tactical *élan* wrongfooted the Asama. While they pondered their next move, Katembo's eloquence persuaded them to make peace. Stanley cunningly sent back the prisoners he had taken, laden with peace-offerings of shells and beads. Convinced of the strangers' pacific intentions, the Asama people made blood-brotherhood and supplied them liberally with food.[20]

They resumed the voyage, still following the river north-north-east. On 19 January the expedition halted on the right bank on what was thought to be a market-place but within a minute a huge net had been thrown over them as if they were wild beasts. This kind of netting on the Congo always enraged Stanley. He ordered Manwa Sera to take thirty men and go upstream to set an ambush on the trail to the 'market-place'. Then he ordered the detachment he had kept with him to cut its way through the nets ahead of them. When the Wenya people saw this, they closed in for the attack, only to blunder into Manwa Sera's ambuscade. Stanley took two prisoners to guide him to the sixth cataract.[21]

The passage to the sixth cataract was predictably disputed, so that it was 23 January when they finally approached it, after running skirmishes with the locals. Their guides indicated a shallow channel 6 miles long that would take them through the sixth cataract. Despite the fact that this was, on paper, the most formidable obstacle in all the Stanley Falls, they got through without problems.

Later that day Stanley took observations and noted their crossing of the Equator. He decided to switch to the left bank. Suddenly his instruments indicated that the river was swinging decisively westwards. Here was the most powerful circumstantial pointer yet that the Lualaba really did become the Congo. But even while he congratulated himself, he heard the surge and thunder of the seventh cataract begin to sound in his ears.[22]

The roaring of boiling waters was soon counterpointed with another, even more familiar, sound: the sonorous booming of war drums. Stanley pulled into shore and drew up his men in a crescent-shaped formation. He planned to hold the Wenya at bay while Pocock began the portage of the boats around the seventh cataract. He constructed strong defensive redoubts at a point where a kind of dyke separated the right bank from an inhabited island. The strength of this position seemed to dismay the Wenya. They began to pull their people off the island.[23]

Stanley now had leisure to address himself to the seventh cataract. At this point the configuration of the Congo was thus. The river had narrowed from 2,000 to 1,300 yards; there was a 40-yard strip of water between the right bank and Wenya Island, then came 760 yards of Wenya Island followed by 500 yards of the main river. These 500 yards formed a spectacular waterfall, 10 feet deep, with 6-foot waves splashing up from it: 'Here was a stupendous river flung in full volume over a waterfall only five hundred yards across. The river at the last cataract of the Stanley Falls does not merely fall: it is precipitated downwards.'[24]

While constructing the overland road for the boats, his men were attacked front and rear by the Wenya and lost one killed by a knife. A gallant running action held off the Wenya until the canoes could be relaunched at the foot of the falls. Finally, by the morning of 28 January they were clear of the last of the Stanley Falls, after a twenty-two-day nightmare period since 6 January. Away from the deafening roar they sped. Still the river ran north by north-west, confirming that this was indeed the Congo. The 2,000-yard wide river forked into two equal branches past an island at the confluence of the Mburra River. Stanley chose the right branch but had to exchange volleys with the locals before the expedition could camp in peace at the south end of the island.[25]

On 29 January they floated on to a broad expanse of the Congo, now 2,500 yards wide, between high, steep, wooded banks. Here they were attacked by a new tribe (called by Stanley Yangambi) in full war paint, half daubed in white, the other half ochreous. After a running fight had failed to shake off their assailants, Stanley landed, constructed a *boma* and beat off a fresh wave of attacks on the shore. By now, after twenty-four fights, Stanley had perfected his defensive techniques. In each combat the women, children and other non-combatants would raise the sixty-four door-like shields in front of the forty-three riflemen, thus making them more effective than three times that number of undefended sharp-shooters. The steersmen, likewise protected, were able to manoeuvre in the current in the course of a running fight. Stanley's real worry was ammunition. If the expedition had to fight its way to the mouth of the Congo, it would surely run out long before then. They would then be easy prey for the first powerful war-party.[26]

The last two days of January seemed to confirm Stanley's worst fears. So far from lessening, the daily pressure seemed to be increasing. The strain on nerves of the constant drumming and conch-blowing could not be discounted. Stanley took to releasing his prisoners early to get some respite, as such release invariably brought a halt (albeit temporary) to the frenzied drumming.

Past the Ruiki River they floated, through perpendicular red cliffs 300 feet high, the enemy forever snapping at their heels. The banks were becoming lower. The picturesque cliffs, tall wooden ridges, and brown, red and grey bluffs seemed to have been dropped astern. At last they seemed to be emerging from the eternal forest as the river broadened to 3,000 yards, but all the *mangwana* were weary with the non-stop fighting. Even by clinging to the islands in the middle of such a broad river they were not safe. With cries of '*Niama! Niama*' daily arising around them, they seemed to have a straight choice: fight or be eaten. Stanley's preference was for the right bank, which was still more forested than the left. By now the left bank was out of sight if they hugged the right shore.[27]

But if Stanley thought he had worries enough, 1 February was to provide the crown of thorns. The day began promisingly. In brilliant sunshine they continued to cleave to the right bank of the Congo, which was steep, high and crowned with woods. They made good progress until about 2 p.m. when they came to the point where the mighty Aruwimi emptied into the Congo. At this confluence the most awesome display yet of military might barred the way. Fifty-four huge canoes lay ready in battle formation, in two 'horns', half converging on them from the Congo's right bank, half from the Aruwimi. In the first ten 'supercanoes' 500 warriors of the Soko stood ready to 'eat up' the Anglo-American expedition.[28]

Stanley at once perceived what a deadly threat this was. This flotilla far surpassed in size and numbers anything they had encountered hitherto. First he had to calm his men's nerves, badly shaken at sight of such a huge armada. Four of his canoe crews immediately became panic-stricken and tried to pull away downstream. Stanley cut off their getaway in *Lady Alice* and ordered them back into line. He passed the word that any canoe attempting to desert would be holed by the elephant gun. Then he formed a defensive formation in the narrows between the Aruwimi and an island, ranged around *Lady Alice*. Eleven double canoes were anchored 10 yards apart, with *Lady Alice* 50 yards in the van. Again the shields were raised to form a bulwark. Nervously the *wangwana* fighting men fingered their Sniders.[29]

Stanley ordered his men not to fire until the first spear was thrown. The fifty-four canoes began to swoop in on them, the two rows of paddlers upstanding, their bodies bending and swaying in unison as they chanted a blood-curdling chorus.

> Down the natives came, fast and furious, but in magnificent style . . . their canoes were enormous things, one especially, a monster, of eighty paddlers, forty on a side, with paddles eight feet long, spear-headed and really pointed with iron blades for close quarters, I presume. The top of each paddle shaft was adorned with an ivory ball. The chiefs pranced up and down a planking that ran from stern to stern. On a platform near the bow were choice fellows swaying their long spears at the ready. In the stern of this great war canoe stood eight steersmen, guiding her towards us . . . At a rough guess there must have been from 1,500 to 2,000 savages within these four canoes.[30]

The *wangwana* discipline held up superbly that afternoon. In full confidence of victory the Soko shot past them in the first monster and launched a fusillade of spears. There was a cacophony of deafening drums, braying horns and triumphant ululations as the spears sped through the air, to bounce off or impale harmlessly in the shield wall. Then came a devastating broadside in reply. At such a short range, the Sniders dealt out death for every bullet.[31] For about ten minutes a furious mêlée of close order combat ensued. Clouds of spears whistled and hissed around the defenders' heads but their rifles were already doing terrible damage. For a few minutes the outcome was uncertain; Stanley later confessed that the expedition was seconds away from being overwhelmed by sheer weight of numbers.[32] Then the Soko broke and fled, unable to take such dreadful punishment any longer. Stanley lifted the stone anchors and gave chase. He carried the fight on to the shore, raided the village of the now demoralised Soko, and turned repulse into rout. His triumphant soldiers staggered back into the boats laden with trophies: not just food in abundance, but 133 pieces of ivory plundered from the Soko's 'ivory temple' (value $18,000) which Stanley gave to his men as prize money.[33]

Following such a crushing victory, there was no further Soko resistance. After this, their twenty-eighth combat, the *wangwana* were all in. Moreover, Stanley was now seriously worried at the diminishing stocks of ammunition. He decided that thenceforth they must abandon the shore and glide down through the central islands. This seemed a feasible prospect, for the river after the Aruwimi junction was so broad that there were sometimes six distinct branches of the Congo, divided by islands.[34]

What was the reason for the unremitting hostility along the Lualaba and the Congo? To a large extent it was a function of the hoary old cliché: 'failure to communicate'. Stanley was travelling too fast to be able to stop and explain his mission to every tribe he came across, especially as this would remove the element of surprise if it came to fighting and thus use up even more of the perilously scarce ammunition. Stanley himself showed some appreciation of the position of his opponents in his despatches to the *Herald*:

The natives had never heard of white men; they had never seen strangers boldly penetrating their region, neither could they possibly understand what advantage white men or black men could gain by attempting to gain an acquaintance. It is the custom of no tribe to penetrate below or above the district of any other tribe. Trade has hitherto been conducted from hand to hand, tribe to tribe, country to country.[35]

315

Moreover, though the extent of cannibalism on the Congo in this era has been exaggerated, it did exist, and faced with the constant cries of '*Niama, Niama!*', it was probably more sensible for Stanley to shoot first and ask questions later.[36]

For their part, the Soko were alarmed by reports of a powerful tribe descending the Congo, led by a man with a face as pale as the moon. Nor was there any record in Soko tradition of a tribe on the move with so many canoes, except for war. For that reason they fought at the Aruwimi.[37] And if Stanley and the *wangwana* got the fright of their lives when they saw this formidable armada waiting for them at the Aruwimi junction, the culture shock for the Soko was even greater. The coming of men 'with sticks which sent forth thunder and lightning' was (not incorrectly in the light of future Congo history) interpreted by them as the advent of evil spirits and the harbinger of bad days to come.[38]

But the rationalisations possible later were no help to the beleaguered expedition in February 1877. For a time it seemed that many more battles would be their lot. Though the Congo was now between 5 and 8 miles wide and they were threading their way through a channel between a series of islands, they were not immune to hostile attacks. The Bemberri people refused to accept their peaceful overtures and replied with showers of stones and frenzied drum-beating. For all that, they did not attack but followed at a safe distance. For five days the drumming continued day and night, as the fugitives glided down narrow streams, between palmy and spicy islands, at risk from rocks, rapids, tribesmen and crocodiles. On the 7th the elements took a hand: heavy swells and howling winds buffeted the expedition, already weak from loss of food.[39] And still the drumming continued day and night, driving Stanley to the brink of endurance. Near to despair he recorded in his diary:

> Livingstone called floating down the Lualaba a foolhardy feat. So it is, and were I to do it again, I would not attempt it without two hundred guns. The natives, besides being savage, ferocious to an extreme degree, are powerful and have means by land and water to exercise to great lengths their ferocity. I pen these lines with a half feeling that they never will be read by another white person ... either bank is equally powerful, to go from one side to the other is like jumping from the frying pan into the fire. It may be said thus that we are now 'running the gauntlet'.[40]

Stanley's desire to conserve ammunition now led him to cut his rate of progress down the Congo in the interests of coaxing and conciliating the tribes to allow him food and free passage without a fight. An especially anxious day was spent on 8 February negotiating for food with chief Rubunga of the Poto.[41] The *wangwana* advised Stanley that Rubunga was stalling them, hiding away food supplies against the time of the fight. Stanley persisted in believing in the chief's good faith and was rewarded when Rubunga offered to make blood brothers and supply them with all the provisions they needed. The consequence was that for the first time in many weeks they could eat their fill – for food was cheap – rest free from anxiety, and get a good night's sleep.[42]

Rubunga also sent on envoys to introduce the expedition to Urangi, the next settlement along. When they moved out on 10 February, Stanley was in high hopes that word of his generosity at Rubunga's would precede him. And indeed at first the chief of Urangi received them hospitably. Then on 11 February the mood changed. Urangi decided to try conclusions with them. Again Stanley was obliged to form his canoes into a square and demonstrate the firepower of the Sniders on contumacious warriors. When the expedition raised anchor, Stanley was again pursued from island to island until, at the end of their territorial range, the Urangi marauders turned back. But shaking them off had been costly. Manwa Sera's party lost the eighth gun since Nyangwe. This made forty-eight guns missing since they had left Zanzibar.[43]

They continued gliding down through the Congo islands on narrow streams between palmy, spicy islands, full of cottonwoods, palms, guineas and tall cane. Unlike the Mississippi, the Congo appeared free of snags and sandbars. Gigantic trees on the bank were shrouded from full view by vines and creepers. Since the banks on this stretch of the river were only about 5–10 feet high, they were frequently flooded and mangrove swamps were the result. These swamps positively crawled with large crocodiles, and from the oozy miasmata issued forth armies of gadflies, mosquitoes and tsetses to plague the *wangwana*: 'The murmur of vast multitudes of these insects sounded during the night of our half-waked senses like the noise of advancing savages.'[44] On the increasing number of islands they encountered a wealth of wildlife: storks, cranes, geese, flamingos, ibises, egrets, kingfishers, snipe. Lemurs and monkeys teemed in the trees and hippos and monitor in the river. Big game was represented on the islands by elephants and herds of red buffalo.

Yet if ever Stanley was temped to daydream in the balmy, languorous humidity of the Congo, he was soon recalled to his present peril. On 13 February they rounded a bend suddenly to find themselves in the midst of a large cluster of villages. At once the war drums boomed and the horns sounded. To conserve ammunition, Stanley tried to float by without firing. The expedition was also dangerously light on weapons by this time, down to nineteen Sniders and twenty muskets (plus Stanley's personal arsenal). But the Marunja people sallied out in their canoes to meet them, and to his horror Stanley saw that they were armed with muskets. Fortunately their open-mouthed stupefaction at sight of Pocock and Stanley afforded a precious breathing space, so that firing did not commence until the expedition was almost clear of the village. In a 5-mile running fight the *wangwana* had much the better of the exchanges, but Rehani was shot dead.[45]

Even so, 13 February seemed in retrospect a bagatelle compared with what came next – what Stanley called 'the fight of fights'. On the 14th they arrived at the first village in the huge Bangala settlement that extended along the right bank. Stanley steered in between two islands, hoping to float by without being seen, but the sudden sharp taps of a kettledrum dashed his hopes. At once Stanley withdrew his flotilla from the shelter of the islands and commenced a dash downstream. Bangala canoes came rushing out from the shore towards them. An attempt at pacific overtures by the expedition was answered with lead. The Bangala were much more dangerous than the Soko at the Aruwimi junction, for they possessed Ashanti-style blunderbusses, loaded with jagged pieces of iron and copper ore. This time there was a real doubt about whether the bulwark of shields would be enough.[46]

This was the hardest-fought battle of them all. Sixty-three canoes assailed them at first and thereafter the Bangala fought in relays, with each successive village sending out its quota. The fight lasted from noon to just before sunset, during which time the expedition floated 10 miles down-river past the huge Bangala conglomeration of villages.[47] It was breech-loaders, double-barrelled elephant rifles and Sniders against Brown Besses loaded with slugs. Fresh supplies of ammunition had to be distributed to the *wangwana* riflemen. At first Stanley was fearful of the outcome. He counted 315 enemy muskets and knew that if the Bangala closed the range his tiny force would be outgunned.[48] Fortunately, the Bangala were so impressed by the long-range deadliness of the Sniders that they kept their distance; they had never seen weapons that could kill so efficiently. The walls of their huts were riddled with bullets and many goats and unwary spectators were killed or wounded.[49]

Around 2 p.m. Stanley began to fear the worst. There was no slackening in the enemy's impetus and the *wangwana* sharpshooters appeared off form that day. He himself for some reason seemed unable to hit any target.

Just as he was beginning to despair, there came a turn-round in fortunes. Suddenly every shot from the expedition seemed to find its billet. Stanley finally found the range and every round he fired in the last hour of the battle found its mark.[50] An uncertain combat suddenly turned into the equivalent of the turkey-shoots he had known from the deep South. The *wangwana* drew inspiration from his accurate volleys. An extraordinary display of gunnery from all members of the expedition finally dropped so many Bangala into the water that the pulse of their assault weakened and they at last began to disengage. Their mistake had been to fight outside a range of 100 yards. Had they dared to come closer in, their numbers would soon have told.[51]

The Bangala later explained their aggression by pointing out that they had never seen a white man before 1877, thought they must be envoys of the Ibanza or Great Spirit, but also considered them evil spirits because they were on the Congo. But the Belgian Coquilhat, who knew the Bangala well in the 1880s, thought their explanation should be taken with a pinch of salt, because of their known bellicosity.[52] The missionary Holman Bentley concurred, 'Anyone who knows the people can have but one opinion; being there, he [Stanley] had either to fight in self-defence, or walk quietly to their cooking pots, and submit to dissection and the processes of digestion.'[53]

The fight with the Bangala – 'the Ashantees of the Livingstone River' as Stanley termed them – was the most ferocious yet and boded ill for the remainder of the expedition, but though the thirty-first combat on the Lualaba/Congo it was destined to be the penultimate one.[54] Seeing that the right bank had brought them so many hostile contacts, Stanley switched to the Congo's southern shore. For the next three days they were unmolested and heard no drums. The problem now came from the elements, for strong winds blew upriver every day and cut down their rate of progress; even a 2-foot wave could be dangerous to a canoe. The dry season (there was no rain between 12 January and 5 March) produced many mirages: a small crocodile basking on the bank looked as big as a canoe. At night they were prey to clouds of mosquitoes: 'few slept and continually was heard the flip-flap of branches from the poor tormented soldiers'.[55]

On 19 February they reached the most enormous Congo tributary yet, greater even than the Aruwimi. Dubbing this the Ikelemba, Stanley found it to be 3,000 yards wide with a wine-dark colour that contrasted with the Congo's whitey-grey. Again short of food, Stanley made a supreme effort of conciliation with the Ruiki tribe and succeeded in revictualling the expedition.[56] They continued to tack between friendly and hostile tribes, crossing and recrossing from right to left banks. But already Stanley was growing confident that he could escape further battles, for the river was now so wide and divided into innumerable channels (some of these individual channels were 5,000 yards wide) that escape from attacks would always be possible. Whatever the depredations from mosquitoes, ants, gadflies and tsetses, they could at least enjoy reasonable security from human predators.[57]

They soon passed out of the territory of the Wangata or Bolumba peoples and entered the terrain of the Bolobo.[58] The river grew sea-like – they could no longer see its banks but only the islands. Sometimes the islands disappeared and they could gaze out over an uninterrupted width of between 4 and 6 miles. At last their usual contact with the riverine peoples was of a peaceful kind. They had more to fear from the river itself, as Stanley recorded: 'A hippopotamus attacked a canoe and snatched a paddle from a man's hand and almost upset the heaviest canoe we had. I believe he was so ferocious at sight of the donkeys, believing they were young of his tribe.'[59]

At the end of the month they reached the territory of the chief of Chumbiri. He was most friendly and made blood-brotherhood with Pocock. He warned them of a series of cataracts ahead, and offered guides to take them there, but wearied Stanley by continual changes of mind on the amount of *doti* he required: 'He is, though old and of a kindly aspect, a prodigious liar.'[60] Yet even the friendliest tribes practised routine cruelty. A man condemned for witchcraft was tossed into the river, gagged and bound hand and foot. The executioner taunted him: 'If you are a magician cause this river to dry up and save yourself.' The victim was swept downstream by the current. A huge crocodile tracked him for a while, then rushed on him and dragged him under.[61]

On 7 March after a long rest they resumed their voyage, but not before a 12-foot boa constrictor had crawled into the camp and caused a lot of commotion before being despatched.[62] They were now into the rainy season and were lashed by fearful gales. They camped in the forest but had another encounter with a snake when a young boy was attacked by a python. His shrieks brought help and the serpent made off, but half an hour later reappeared to attack a woman. This time the *wangwana* killed it; the python pegged out at 13 feet 6 inches long.[63]

These encounters with snakes were later read as bad omens by the Zanzibaris, for on 9 March the expedition was the victim of a surprise attack, 6 miles beyond the confluence of the Nkutu.[64] A grim hour-long fight ensued, in which fourteen of Stanley's men were wounded. But this, the thirty-second combat, proved to be the last. Its unexpected nature was later unravelled by the missionary Bentley. The Bolobo told him that since all the tribes of the Upper Congo had fought the white man, their own credibility required it. Otherwise the Congo legends and songs would record that while others faced the white man's bullets, the Bolobo hid in the grass like women: 'We should be ashamed to travel or to trade, so of course we went.'[65]

Having completed its great arc to the north, the Congo was now heading steadily south-west for the sea. The tea-coloured tributaries were changing the complexion of the river from whitey-grey to dark brown. The mainland was free from thick woods for the first time since Nyangwe. In their stead arose high, white cliffs with picturesque, precipitous shores. On the right bank were abundant herds of antelope and red buffalo, which Stanley dared not shoot for fear of arousing a general call to war. Then, on 12 March, the river broadened out into a kind of pool, surrounded by white cliffs like those at Dover. Stanley called the area Stanley Pool.[66]

The next few days were spent in negotiations and blood-brotherhood ceremonies while Stanley attempted to unravel the complex politics of this densely populated area. What he learned about the river ahead depressed him. It seemed that henceforth his battle would be with the river itself, not the tribes. So it proved. South of Stanley Pool was a stretch of cataracts that made Stanley Falls seem like child's play. Having survived thirty-two fights and a thousand other perils, the expedition came close to disaster on this impassable stretch of waterway.

The Livingstone became straitened by close-meeting up-rising banks of naked cliffs, or steep slopes of mountains fringed with tall woods, or piles above piles of naked craggy rock; and presently swept impetuously down in serpentine curves, heaving upward in long lines of brown billows, sometimes as though ruffled by a tempest, or else with a steep glassy fall, or else thundering down steep after steep, tossing its waters upwards in huge waves, with their crests dissolving in spray and mist; or at another bend boiling round isles of boulders, which disparted it into two branches with fearful whirlpools, with uprising whirling cauldrons; and as the magnificent river varied its wild aspect, so it raised its thunder, moan and plaint. At one time the rush sounded like the swash of sea waves against a ship's prow driven before a spanking breeze; at another time like a strong tide washing against the piers and buttresses of bridges, at another it overwhelmed the senses, and filled the deep gulf with the roar of its fury.[67]

They began the attempted descent of the falls on 15 March, lowering the canoes by hawsers through the boiling waters. The work was onerous. There was an ever-present danger of slipping on the wet rocks. Stanley himself tripped head-first into a 30-foot chasm and was lucky to escape with just a few rib bruises. The techniques tried successfully at Stanley Falls failed them here. Their best canoe 'London Town', 75 feet long by 3 feet wide was swept over the cataracts and lost. Even as they lamented this loss, two days later the canoe 'Crocodile' was swept over Rocky Island Falls. Six men were drowned, including Kalulu, who since Ujiji had been fully restored to Stanley's favour. For a fortnight Stanley scarcely penned more than a line in his diary, such was his depression.[68]

Still Stanley did not desist from the impossible task he had set himself. Even though he admitted that 'the most powerful ocean steamer going at full speed on this portion of the river would be as helpless as a cockle-boat,' he did not draw the obvious conclusion and abandon the attempt to follow the Congo by water. They were just 300 miles from the sea, and a 50-mile reconnaissance overland would have demonstrated conclusively that the Lower Congo cataracts were impassable. Yet he clung to his self-assigned task, with the result that in over four months they covered no more than 180 miles.

Was this fanaticism – the redoubling of effort when the rational goal is lost sight of? Was it a reluctance to abandon the Congo, in case some nitpicking RGS official later claimed he had not been all the way down by river? Was his judgement faltering after nearly three years of unremitting strain? Doubtless all of these factors played a part, but it is also possible to detect here an aspect of the masochistic redemption-through-suffering Stanley. When he was in this phase, the most likely sufferers were his white companions. Fortunately by this time he and Pocock had achieved an almost brotherly rapport that prevented Frank's being the victim of some sado-masochistic impulse. Pocock's patient stoicism, cheerfully submitting to Stanley's ever more desperate remedies, emerges clearly in his last diaries.[69]

The terrible battle with the cataracts continued throughout April. Hauling canoes round rocky points by cable worked as long as the ropes and hawsers did not snap, which they frequently did. There were many narrow escapes from drowning. By 21 April they had come just 34 miles since mid-March. The best-laid plans were devastated by the elements.

One canoe, being hauled by cable by no fewer than forty men, was yet torn from their grasp and sucked into a whirlpool. The problems of trying to control the boats with cables were intractable.

> Before us were long lines of brown white-topped breakers without any little indentation in the rocky shore to give us breath, so that the boat was urged along too rapidly and dragged the men behind too swiftly before they could secure their footing. Finally, to check the threatening hurried descent, the men were compelled to lie down on the rocks, but this was not enough. The boat dragged them over the boulders into the water.[70]

Stanley described another incident when he was struggling for his life in the raging waters: 'Waves whirled around like a spinning top, diving into threatening troughs and swirling pits, then jostled aside, uplifted by another wave and tossed upon the summit of another, while the shore was flying by us with amazing rapidity.'[71] And all this went on while the expedition was desperately hungry. Pigs and goats were plentiful but dear, costing three *doti* or a gun each. Economies were necessary, as they did not know how much longer they would have to remain on the river. The diet of yams, cassavas, groundnuts and bananas was far from balanced and contributed to the illnesses now becoming commonplace: ulcers, itch, dysentery.

Having come just 35 miles in thirty-seven days, Stanley tried a new tack and cut a portage through the mountains and then hauled the canoes over the hills to rejoin the river at Nsabi. There, having obtained permission from the local chief to cut down forest giants for timber, they built two new canoes: the 'Stanley' and the 'Livingstone'.[72] But before these could be launched, Stanley had to deal with a fresh crisis. He had already caught some of the most trustworthy *wangwana* out in petty pilfering from the expedition stores. But depredations from the local population were more serious, as they could precipitate another battle. He had long since warned his men that if caught stealing from the locals they would be surrendered to native law, which meant execution or eternal slavery.[73] Even so, now that Saburi and Rehani were taken prisoner by the locals, he spent a whole day and $150 of cloth to ransom them, while issuing a warning that the next men found guilty would not be so lucky.

Towards the end of May they launched the 'Livingstone' and 'Stanley', having waited until the rainy season was over. The tempests in early May had been frightful; the level of the river had risen noticeably. For all their exertions, they learned that there were still another five cataracts ahead of them. Frank Pocock was now seriously ill with ulcers. His feet were inflamed and oozing with sores after going barefoot for four months, during which time he worked from dawn to dusk.[74] His exertions in the past two months had been herculean, as his diary entries show.

16 March. Passed three rapids. Landed goods and let canoe down by ropes through roaring foam . . . Everyone very hungry.

28 March. Passed canoes down rapids and pulled them on shore.

29 March. Too dangerous to pass canoes in river, so had to pull them overland.

9 April. Halt to pass the canoes down. Got the largest canoe round the point with ropes.

12 April. Boat suddenly drops fifteen feet down a fall with Stanley in it. Had it been a canoe it would have been lost. The *Lady Alice* shot forward two miles in a few minutes. The escape was an act of providence.

30 April. This is the forty-seventh day of fighting with these rapids and likely to be fifteen or twenty days more.[75]

Lady Alice's coxswain Uledi was not available to Stanley when they set out again, being under close guard after pilfering. Later Stanley submitted him to his peers for punishment, but he was such a beloved figure that two of them offered to take his punishment. In a solomonic judgement Stanley freed Uledi, accepted the two others in lieu, then pardoned them. But while all this was going on, Pocock, unable any longer to walk, had taken over as *Lady Alice*'s steersman. His inexperience brought them close to disaster when he took the boat on to the worst part of the rapids and she was holed on the rocks.[76]

Making the usual one mile a day, the expedition reached Mowa. Here Stanley's habit of taking copious notes aroused the fears of the locals that this was 'bad medicine': it was an unheard-of practice, so must be a fetish or form of witchcraft. Stanley was requested to hand over his writings on pain of a declaration of war. Not wishing to sacrifice his precious notes, Stanley went into his tent and emerged with a pocket Chandos Shakespeare with a cover identical to his notebook, then publicly burned it to appease the Mowa people.[77]

During the stay at Mowa Stanley scouted ahead and saw that there were more fearsome rapids to come. An attempt to shoot the rapids at Zinga was abandoned, after Stanley came close to being sucked into the central whirlpool. He hurried on ahead to parley with the Zinga chief, leaving word with Pocock to follow him overland, for the rapids were too treacherous. Stanley was by this time genuinely solicitous of Frank's welfare, and worried about his virulent ulcers. The quiet reliable uncomplaining Pocock had completely won him over. Stanley was prepared to accept him as a friend, if not intellectual equal, and loved to spend the evening with him, smoking and talking. He could not have imagined that, having come so far with him, Pocock was about to depart this life.

Stanley was in a good mood on the afternoon of 3 June. His parley with the friendly Zinga chief had gone well. The expedition was already well within the orbit of European trade and the locals sold beeswax, indiarubber, palm oil and gum copal for beads; they did not fear the white man like the peoples of the Upper Congo. Well content with his negotiations, Stanley ascended an eyrie on the rocks and sighted his field-glasses upriver. He was alarmed to see an upturned canoe in the raging torrent of Masassa Falls, with three heads bobbing in the water.[78]

Then the news came in. Three men were drowned, and one of them was Frank Pocock. Whether because he could not bear walking on his ulcerated feet or because as a Medway fisherman and expert swimmer he genuinely scorned the perils of wild water, Pocock had insisted on shooting the falls in a canoe. When the *mangwana* remonstrated and repeated the orders of the 'little master', Pocock jeered at them for cowardice. To save face, ten of the Zanzibaris joined Pocock in the canoe. In less than three minutes it was swept over the falls.

> The canoe was in the middle of the great rolling billows with . . . flanks pitted with great whirlpools, into one of which the canoe was sucked bodily down to the bottom, and after a minute or so was shot up again with eight of the eleven that were in the canoe. Three out of the eleven were drowned and one of the three, to my surprise and my great grief was my faithful, honest, gentle Frank.[79]

Pocock's over-confidence in his abilities as a swimmer proved fatal. While surfacing Pocock struck his head on the bottom of the canoe and in his concussed state was drowned. His body was borne rapidly downstream, and eight days later a local fisherman found the bloated body of a white man – this was regarded as 'bad fetish'.[80]

Stanley was genuinely grief-stricken, as the immediacy of his diary entry makes clear.

Alas, my brave, honest, kindly-natured good Frank, thy many faithful services to me have only found thee a grave in the wild waters of the Congo. Thy many years of travel and toil borne so cheerfully have been but ill-rewarded. Thou noble son of Nature, would that I could have suffered instead of thee for I am weary, oh so weary of this constant tale of woes and death; and thy cheerful society, the influence of thy brave smile, the utterance of thy courageous heart I shall lack, and because I lack, I shall weep for my dear lost friend. 'And weep the more because I weep in vain.'[81]

Pocock's death brought Stanley close to nervous breakdown. The diary entries, full of illegible jottings, crossings-out and incoherent syntax, bespeak his deep distress. But he was jolted out of his depression by the catastrophic impact of Pocock's drowning on the *wangwana*. The stress of the *via dolorosa* over the rapids since Stanley Pool suddenly burst out. They mutinied openly, declaring that they would rather stay with the savages than follow a man whose payment was the wages of death.[82] The truth was that the men of Zanzibar might respect and fear Stanley but they had genuinely loved Pocock. 'Mabuiki' – their pet name for Frank – ate from the same pot as them, he shared the same hardships, his justice was the merciful New Testament kind rather than Stanley's wrathful Yahweh variety. For three days they mourned the loss of Mabuiki in a prolonged wake of lamentations and ululations. Eventually Stanley grew jealous and resentful. He upbraided the *wangwana*: 'Was he your father? No, I am your father; and would he have paid you your money in Zanzibar? No! I am the man you must rely on for your money, and now let us have no more crying like women.'[83]

Stanley's resentment that the Zanzibaris valued Pocock more highly than him accounts for the changed tone of his communications to Europe and America on Pocock's death, where he was anxious to escape any hint of culpability for the tragic accident.[84] After conceding: 'I feel his loss as keenly as though he were my brother,' Stanley told Pocock's father that his son's death arose from his contempt of water, for it was folly for a sick man with ulcerated feet to attempt to shoot Masassa Falls: 'The truth is that Frank died through his own rashness and his immense contempt for water.'[85]

There followed a long delay at Zinga while Stanley tried to pull his demoralised and rebellious expedition together. His men were surly and refused to work. There were significant desertions. Without Pocock the entire chain of command broke down. If Stanley had failed to realise how much he owed to his second-in-command, he paid for the error now. In mid-June, still at Zinga, his depression found expression in a significant diary entry:

> I have publicly expressed a desire to die by a quick sharp death, which I think just now would be a mercy compared to what I endure daily. I am vexed each day by thieves, liars and unconquerable laziness of the *wangwana*. I am surrounded by savages who from superstitious ideas may rise to fight at a moment's notice. Weeks are passing swiftly away and goods are diminishing until we have but little left, and at the rate we are going six weeks will suffice to bring us at death's door from starvation.[86]

The worst days at Zinga were 20–22 June. On the 20th thirty-one men under Safeni deserted without food, guns or ammunition, preferring to face the uncertain mercies of the tribes rather than continue with Stanley. Only great eloquence from Manwa Sera brought them back. Then on 23 June the rattan cables they were using to haul the 'Livingstone' canoe clear of the Masassa Falls snapped, pitching the boat and two of the best expedition craftsmen to their death.[87]

Finally, on 25 June, after an enforced halt of twenty-five days, they pressed on from Zinga with seven canoes and the boat. Zinga rapids was but the fifty-seventh in a series of seventy-four cataracts on the Lower Congo. The same agonising hauling and lowering around rocks and rapids continued until, by mid-July, the expedition was again in serious danger of famine and men were dying of dysentery. The *wangwana* responded by pilfering from the locals. This time Stanley's patience snapped. He refused to ransom a couple of the Zanzibar men caught red-handed by the Mata people. At this the other *wangwana* declared their intention of fighting to free their brothers. In that case, Stanley replied, he would press on downriver with all the loyal men and leave those who wanted to fight to stay and try conclusions with the locals. This was the last straw for Safeni, leader of the rebellious faction. By the end of July he was stark insane.[88]

Finally, by 30 July the column, still wrestling daily with the cataracts and now openly maddened by hunger, reached Isangila. This was clearly the 'Second Sangalla' charted by Tuckey, which meant it was established beyond all doubt that the Lualaba became the Congo. At last Stanley gave the order to leave the river and proceed overland to the sea. The *Lady Alice* was left to bleach above Isangila cataract. The expedition ascended to the tableland and began to march across country to Boma, just six days away. But their ordeal was not yet over. The trail was thickly strewn with splinters of suet-coloured quartz which increased the fatigue and pain of the famished marchers. They managed just 8 miles before collapsing in an uninhabited valley and drinking from rainpools. Stanley now began to fear that his men would expire from starvation on the very last lap. He asked the chief of Nsanda to send a courier to Boma with a distress call for food, addressed to the Europeans at the trading post there. Signing the letter 'Stanley', he produced an epigone to his 'Dr Livingstone, I presume' gaucherie by adding a PS: 'You may not know me by name: I therefore add, I am the person that discovered Livingstone in 1871 – H.M.S.'[89]

On 5 August 1877 Uledi and Kacheche departed with this message, guided by two of Nsanda's couriers. Stanley and the others trekked on wearily so as to be closer to the relief supplies. After narrowly avoiding an eleventh-hour battle over disputed *hongo* in southern Nsanda, they were overjoyed during the mid-morning march on 6 August to see in the distance Uledi and Kacheche returning with a caravan. They were saved. Eagerly they unpacked the goods and found all manner of luxury provisions: port, sherry, champagne, sardines, salmon, tea, jam, plum pudding. Enclosed was a letter from Messrs Da Motta Veiga and Harrison of the trading firm Hatton and Cookson, to whom Stanley dashed off an extravagant letter of thanks.[90]

They gorged themselves on the unparalleled richness of the diet, then marched on refreshed. Three days' trekking took them to Boma, an inland port sixty miles upstream from Banana on the Atlantic coast. They entered Boma on the 999th day after leaving Bagamoyo. Stanley had come through the Dark Continent. His 999-day epic was the greatest feat in the entire history of the exploration of Africa and one of the greatest achievements in *all* exploration. The workhouse boy from St. Asaph's now had a secure place in legend. As an explorer he had outstripped even Livingstone, his mentor. His was a name that would ever afterwards by mentioned with those of Cook and Columbus.

• CONCLUSION •

'THE human head once struck off does not regrow like the rose,' Richard Burton was warned as he set off for the forbidden city of Harar, whose ruler was reputed to behead all interlopers. 'Lord, let us kill this prodigy!' urged the officials and priests at the court of Mutesa when Speke arrived there in 1862, the first white man ever to reach Lake Victoria. Even the saintly David Livingstone, 'the father of the Africans' had to take up arms against hostile tribes on occasion. His fellow Scot Mungo Park was killed on the Niger while fighting off an assault with spears and arrows.

To run such risks argues for a kind of madness on the part of the nineteenth-century European explorers of Africa. In risk-taking ventures Stanley's samurai decision to launch onto the unknown Lualaba, in the teeth of Tippu Tip's predictions of fearsome opposition which were amply fulfilled, rates as at once the most foolhardy and courageous of them all. But Stanley had already demonstrated, on the Livingstone expedition, that he would stop at nothing to achieve his ends. This aspect of Stanley was truly Napoleonic. He lacked Livingstone's moral stature and Burton's immense erudition and anthropological curiosity. But as a pure technician in the art of African exploration he far outdid even the greatest of his rivals. The 1874–77 trans-Africa exploit was *the* outstanding feat in all European exploration of Africa.

Yet it was achieved at a great price, both in the lives of others and in psychic cost to Stanley himself. It was almost as though, having expended the last ounce of his willpower to come through to the Atlantic, he had also drained away the residue of humanity briefly instilled in him by the famous meeting with Livingstone. Ahead of Stanley in 1877 loomed a further twenty-seven years of life, but already his finest moments, both as African explorer and human being were behind him. 1877 marked the meridian point, when the influence of the saintly Livingstone started to fade and that of the evil genius King Leopold II began to appear. The Dark Continent left to Stanley to conquer now was one that could not be defeated as the Congo-Lualaba had been. For it was the dark interior of H. M. Stanley himself that stubbornly refused to yield up its secrets.

· NOTES ·

Guide to abbreviations used in notes

Add. MSS Additional Manuscripts, British Library
EHR *English Historical Review*
JAH *Journal of African History*
JRAI *Journal of the Royal Anthropological Institute*
MP Mackinnon Papers
NLS National Library of Scotland
PRGS *Proceedings of the Royal Geographical Society*
RA Royal Archives, Windsor Castle
RCS Royal Commonwealth Society
RGS Royal Geographical Society Archives
SFA Stanley Family Archives
SOAS School of Oriental and African Studies, University of London
TNR *Tanzania* (earlier *Tanganyika*) *Notes and Records*
UJ *Uganda Journal*
ZA Zanzibar Archives

Chapter one

1. Journal, 1 August 1872, SFA.
2. Journal, 18 August 1872, SFA.
3. See the perceptive comments in John L. Brom, *Sur les traces de Stanley* (Paris 1958), p. 289.
4. As Freud remarks: 'Unfortunately there is reason to distrust the autobiographical statements of neurotics. Experience shows that their memories introduce falsifications which are designed to interrupt disagreeable causal connections.' (James Strachey, ed., *Standard Edition of the Complete Psychological Works of Sigmund Freud*, 24 vols (1953–74), 21, p. 182.)
5. RGS, Stanley Collection, 16/4.

6. 'Stanley: a biographical notice', *Journal of the African Society* (1903–4), pp. 449–63.
7. Harry Johnston to Dorothy Stanley, 22 May 1904, SFA.
8. Lucy M. Jones and Ivor Wynne Jones, *H. M. Stanley and Wales* (St Asaph 1972), p. 13.
9. Ibid.
10. For James Vaughan Horne see Bob Owen, 'Stanley's Father, I Presume', *Hel Achau: Journal of the Clwyd Family History Society*, 15 (1985), pp. 23–7.
11. *Western Mail*, Cardiff, 22 May 1889. Stanley in the *Autobiography*, p. 39, cites a woman who claimed to have known Moses Parry to the effect that he had an eldest son called John. Stanley neither confirms nor denies this.
12. For Elizabeth Parry see Bill Wynne-Woodhouse, 'Elizabeth Parry of Denbigh, an extraordinary woman and H. M. Stanley, her son, an extraordinary man', in *Hel Achau: Journal of the Clwyd Family History Society*, 15 (1985), pp. 35–44.
13. These were named Elizabeth, Robert, Emma and James.
14. *Autobiography* (1909), p. 29.
15. Ibid., p. 7.
16. *The Times*, 31 December 1888.
17. *Autobiography*, p. 7.
18. Jones, *H. M. Stanley and Wales*, p. 7.
19. *Autobiography*, pp. 8–9.
20. In his unpublished draft notes for the *Autobiography* (in SFA) Stanley dealt at greater length with Sarah's fear of ghosts. Sarah was still alive in 1904, when she recalled that in 1872 Stanley gave her a bracelet he had acquired in Jerusalem (RGS 13/1).
21. *Autobiography*, p. 10.
22. Ibid., p. 12.
23. The date of his admission (Workhouse Admission and Discharge Book 1845–7, G.C. 6012 quoted in Jones, *H. M. Stanley and Wales*, p. 7.
24. Quoted ibid., p. 21.
25. Ian Anstruther, *I Presume: Stanley's Triumph and Disaster* (1956), pp. 10–11. For workhouse conditions in general at this time see the same author's *The Scandal of the Andover Workhouse*.
26. *Autobiography*, pp. 12–15.
27. *Western Mail*, Cardiff, 22 May 1889.
28. Ibid.
29. Jones, *H. M. Stanley and Wales*, p. 9.
30. Cadwalader Rowlands, *H. M. Stanley: The Story of his Life* (1872), p. 5.
31. Ibid.
32. The exact date is disputed. Jones, quoting Admission Book 1850–54, G.C./60/5, says 14 June 1851. Wynne-Woodhouse says 3 December 1850.
33. *Autobiography*, p. 29.

34. Ibid., pp. 13–15.
35. Journal, 10 July 1889, SFA.
36. Richard Hall, *Stanley: An Adventurer Explored* (1974), pp. 105–7.
37. *Autobiography*, p. 33.
38. See e.g. M. Luwel, *Stanley* (1959), p. 13; Byron Farwell, *The Man who Presumed* (1957), p. 5; Anstruther, *I Presume*, pp. 13–14; Frank Hird, *Stanley, the Authorised Life* (1935), pp. 19–20. So far as I am aware, the first biographer to draw attention to the general similarity of Stanley's picture of the workhouse and that of Dickens' *Oliver Twist* was Jakob Wassermann, *Bula Matari* (1932), p. 8. But not until the 1970s and the Joneses' *H. M. Stanley and Wales* were doubts expressed. The first categorical refusal to accept the story by a biographer occurs in Hall, *Stanley*, pp. 108–9.
39. *Western Mail*, Cardiff, 11 May 1889.
40. Wynne-Woodhouse, p. 41.
41. William Hoffmann, *With Stanley in Africa* (1938), p. 8.
42. For these fantasy episodes see *Autobiography*, pp. 35–40. Bill Wynne-Woodhouse is especially perceptive about all this: 'Stanley uses Moses and Moses's mother at Denbigh as characters in another fantasy about Mrs Roberts telling him of his family and parentage and prompting him to go to his putative grandfather John Rowlands where he was rebuffed.' (Wynne-Woodhouse, p. 41.)
43. *Autobiography*, p. 8.
44. For this point see Gerben Hellinga, *Henry Morton Stanley, Een Individual Psychologische Interpretatie* (1978), p. 40.
45. Birth register, St Asaph's registry, quoted in Jones, p. 13.
46. *Autobiography*, p. 45.
47. Cadwalader Rowlands, p. 51.
48. 'In time all friendship with any school fellow at Brynford was impossible. Most of the boys were uncongenial through their incurable loutishness. Few of them were clean or orderly, and their ideas of what was right differed from mine. They were vilely irreligious, and to my astonishment acted as though they believed manliness to consist of bare-faced profanity. Most of them snuffled abominably, while as to being tidy and neat, no savages could have shown greater indifference. It would be easier to transform apes into men than to make such natures gentle.' (*Autobiography*, p. 48.)
49. *Autobiography*, p. 48.
50. Cadwalader Rowlands, p. 53.
51. *Autobiography*, p. 53.
52. Ibid., pp. 53–4.
53. John Rowlands to Tom Morris, 2 June 1858, SFA. There are copies at RGS 1/1 and in the Wellcome Institute Archives (Ms. 169294).
54. Stanley's journal of his trip to France and Italy (20 March–5 May 1886) contains a first-page entry in Swahili about John Owen (SFA).

55. *Autobiography*, pp. 56–7.
56. It was typical of Stanley to give (in the *Autobiography*) an address (22 Roscommon Street) in a more 'upmarket' part of the city. See Hall, *Stanley*, p. 378.
57. *Autobiography*, pp. 58–9.
58. Ibid., p. 61.
59. In a curious way, being at large in Liverpool made Stanley feel free. See his 'autobiography' to Katie Gough-Roberts in 1869: 'At that time the boy could have cursed all nature, God and human kind, but he did not; he feared God and loved his kind and generous love, but hated his relations each and all of them. Through the streets of Liverpool Rowlands wandered wonderfully happy. Yes, actually happy. He was sixteen years [actually he was seventeen] but he was free; none could claim his allegiance, his love and respect, he was free.' (Jones, p. 21.)
60. *Autobiography*, p. 66.
61. This journal runs from 8 February 1861 to 15 August 1879 but contains two preliminary pages in Swahili covering events from his birth to July 1857 (SFA).
62. *Autobiography*, pp. 28–9.
63. After describing the fantasy embrace, Stanley says, 'The exhibition of fond love was not without its effect on me for I learned how a mother should behave to her boy.' (*Autobiography*, p. 38.)
64. Some contempt for women is evident in his early milieu. Stanley was told by his grandfather: 'Thou wilt be a man yet before thy mother, my man of men.' Again Stanley records: 'Though women might be taller, stronger and older than I, there lay a future before me that the most powerful women could never hope to win.' (*Autobiography*, p. 7.)
65. The classic statement of the Family Romance is in Freud (S.E. 14, pp. 236–41). Freud explains that the commonest cause of this syndrome is a desire to escape from the 'reality principle', when the adolescent sees its parents as they really are, warts and all, to the 'pleasure principle' of early childhood when the child perceives its parents as genuinely god-like and omnipotent. But this is only the most common species of the genus 'Family Romance'. For Stanley as a classic Family Romance candidate see P. Greenacre, 'The Family Romance of the Artist', *The Psychoanalytic Study of the Child*, 13 (1958), pp. 9–43. Cf. also Bernard C. Meyer, *Joseph Conrad: A Psychoanalytic Biography* (Princeton, 1967), p. 349. It is possible that the tale of Moses Parry's early opulence is itself an aspect of this fantasy (*Autobiography*, p. 39).
66. *Autobiography*, p. 26.
67. Ibid., pp. 11, 28.
68. Ibid., pp. 26, 36.
69. Ibid., p. 30.

70. This of course is the key element in the authoritarian personality as diagnosed by Alfred Adler, for whom the instinct to dominate, not Freudian libido, is the mainspring of human behaviour. A notable Adlerian interpretation of Stanley has been attempted by Gerben Hellinga in *Henry Morton Stanley: Een Individual Psychologische Interpretatie* (1978). Hellinga sees Stanley as 'a choleric with a personality disorder which Adler designates the Ruling Type'.

71. Cadwalader Rowlands, p. 52.

72. *Autobiography*, pp. xvi, 56.

73. For the neatness see *Autobiography*, p. 21.

74. Thomas George, *The Birth, Boyhood and Younger Days of Henry Stanley* (1895).

75. *The Times*, 24 December 1888.

76. *The Times*, 31 December 1888.

77. See e.g. A. G. Feather, *Stanley's Story* (1890, reprinted Chicago 1969); David Ker, 'Africa's Cortez', in J. Scott Keltie, ed., *The Story of Emin's Rescue as Told in Stanley's Letters* (Boston 1890), p. 17; Paul Reichard, *Stanley* (1897), pp. 3 *et seq.* E. Kerfyser, *Henry M. Stanley* (Brussels 1890), pp. 3–14, was the first account to make a definite link between St Asaph's and the man of the Emin Pasha Relief Expedition.

Chapter two

1. For the *Windermere* voyage see *Autobiography*, pp. 69–81.

2. Ibid., p. 78. Wassermann, *Bula Matari*, p. 16, says of this outburst: 'It is the attitude of a man of action who will be lost if he does not learn to mistrust.'

3. *Autobiography*, p. 81.

4. Ibid., p. 84.

5. Ibid., p. 86.

6. Ibid., pp. 87–9.

7. For the 'adoption' by Stanley senior see *Western Daily News*, Bristol, 22 January 1889. 'Morton' was adopted after he had tried and discarded 'Morelake' and 'Morley' (Wynne-Woodhouse, p. 40). This was not a sudden event but a gradual process. In 1869 Stanley signed his name on at least one occasion as Henry Morelake Stanley (see E. S. Balch, 'American Explorers in Africa', *Geographical Review* 5 (1918), pp. 274–81, at pp. 279, 281). In 1884 Harry Johnston dedicated *The River Congo* to Henry Moreland Stanley. When Livingstone met Stanley at Ujiji in 1871 he referred to him as Henry Moreland Stanley (Livingstone, *Last Journals*, 2 vols (1874), ii, p. 156).

8. *Autobiography*, p. 99.

9. Mary M. Shuey, 'Stanley in New Orleans', *South-West Review* 25 (1939–40), pp. 378–93.

10. Catherine M. Dillon, 'From Wharf Waif to Knighthood', *Roosevelt Review*, June 1944.
11. *Autobiography*, p. 101.
12. Stanley himself was aware of an eccentric component in his obsessive neatness for he says defensively, 'Envious or ill-natured people might have said it was fussy or officious.' (*Autobiography*, p. 102.)
13. *Autobiography*, pp. 106–11.
14. Ibid., p. 129.
15. Ibid., p. 137.
16. Mary M. Shuey, 'Young Stanley: Arkansas Episode', *South-West Review* 27 (1941–2), pp. 197–206.
17. *Autobiography*, pp. 111–13, 145, 161.
18. RGS 1/7.
19. Undated draft, miscellaneous papers, SFA.
20. The first biographer to spot the clues was Jakob Wassermann, *Bula Matari*, pp. 24–5.
21. *Autobiography*, p. 126.
22. Ibid., pp. 148–50.
23. Jones, *H. M. Stanley and Wales*, p. 22.
24. *Autobiography*, p. 156.
25. *How I Found Livingstone* (1872), p. 119.
26. For this see *Autobiography*, p. 21.
27. Ibid., pp. 152–3.
28. Mary M. Shuey, 'Young Stanley: Arkansas Episode'.
29. *Autobiography*, p. 167.
30. For his soldiering experiences in 1861 see ibid., pp. 167–85.
31. For Belmont see *Personal Memoirs of U. S. Grant*, 2 vols (New York 1885–6), i, pp. 271–81.
32. *Autobiography*, p. 184.
33. Ibid., p. 199.
34. Journal, 13 April 1862, SFA.
35. *Autobiography*, p. 206.
36. Ibid., p. 211.
37. Hellinga points out that there was a pathological element in the way the young Stanley was driven to become the leader in any social relationship of equals. He cites Adler's notion of the 'leader complex' (A. Adler, *Superiority and Social Interest*, 3rd edition, H. L. and R. R. Ansbacher, eds (New York 1973), p. 78) to explain Stanley's neurotic inclination in this regard.
38. Jones, *H. M. Stanley and Wales*, p. 22. The same story appears in *Saturday Review*, 5 July 1890.
39. *Autobiography*, p. 214.
40. 1862 Journal, SFA.
41. St Asaph Registry Office quoted in Jones, p. 17.

42. *The Times*, 31 December 1888.

43. Jones, p. 22.

44. Journal, November 1862, SFA; *Autobiography*, p. 219.

45. Hall, *Stanley*, p. 132, claims that this took place in Manchester. Other sources mention the Morrises in Liverpool as the donor. Since the phrase 'relations of his second father' comes from Stanley's 'confessions' to Katie Gough-Roberts (22 March 1869), to whom he had previously 'rubbished' the Morrises, it may well be that the Morrises *did* help him but that Stanley would not admit this to Katie.

46. Hall, *Stanley*, p. 133.

47. *The Graphic*, 17 October 1872; *Hamilton Advertiser*, 26 October 1872.

48. Thomas George, *Birth, Boyhood*, p. 103; cf. also Stanley, *Coomassie and Magdala* (1874), p. 375.

49. *Autobiography*, p. 220.

50. Hall, *Stanley*, p. 134.

51. *New York Sun*, 24 August 1872.

52. *Saturday Review*, 5 July 1890.

53. Wassermann, *Bula Matari*, p. 3.

54. To say nothing of the recently retired businessman whose forced retreat from the maelstrom often leads to mental breakdown (see ibid., p. 4).

55. Hall, p. 135, dismisses the idea of joining up to get 'copy' as a cub reporter and suggests that Stanley favoured 'the more genteel role of ship's clerk'.

56. Smith to Wellcome, 3 November 1907, RGS 14/2.

57. For Noe see Cadwalader Rowlands, pp. 157–74.

58. RGS 14/2.

59. As in Stanley's 'autobiography' to Katie Gough-Roberts (Jones, p. 22).

60. Smith to Wellcome, 27 October 1907, RGS 14/2.

61. For this battle see Stanley's autobiography to Katie Gough-Roberts (Jones, pp. 22–3).

62. Significantly, not even Lady Stanley (in the *Autobiography*, pp. 220–21) nor Hird (*H. M. Stanley: The Authorised Life* – a work of hagiography – pp. 43–4) quite dares to include this tall story. Stanley's impressions – both the events he actually observed and the products of his own imagination – are recorded in his journals under dates 20–25 December 1864 and 6–16 January 1865, SFA.

63. RGS 14/2.

64. *New York Sun*, 24 August 1872.

Chapter three

1. *New York Sun*, 16 August 1872.

2. Norman R. Bennett, *Stanley's Despatches to the New York Herald* (Boston 1970), p. 407.

3. Smith to Wellcome, 3 November 1907, RGS 14/2.
4. Journal, 14 April 1865, SFA.
5. Letters from Stanley to Noe's sister (19 April, 9 May 1865, SFA) definitely place him in New York until the latter date.
6. Richard Hall, 'Stanley in America', *Explorer's Journal* 54 (June 1976), pp. 78–83.
7. His remarks during the journey to find Livingstone are revealing: 'The fairest of Californian scenery cannot excel, though it may equal, such scenes as Ukawendi can boast of.' (*New York Herald*, 10 August 1871).
8. There are letters from Stanley from Black Hawk City dated 4 September, 19 October, 21 October 1865, 26 January 1866 (RGS 14/2).
9. RGS 1/3.
10. Ibid.
11. Hall, 'Stanley in America', loc. cit.
12. RGS 14/2.
13. To give just one initial example, Cook swallowed whole Stanley's story of having been a Civil War reporter for the *New York Herald* (Bennett, *Stanley's Despatches* pp. 430–31).
14. Bennett, p. 432.
15. RGS 1/3.
16. Ibid.
17. Journal, 27 May 1866, SFA.
18. Arrived St Louis 4 June. Left St Louis 9 June. Arrived New York 12 June (Journal, SFA).
19. Journal, 12 June.
20. *New York Sun*, 24 August 1872.
21. Bennett, p. 408.
22. Journal, 16 June, 11 July.
23. *Boston Evening Transcript*, 10 July 1866.
24. Bennett, p. 408.
25. RGS 1/3.
26. Journal, 28 August.
27. Journal, 3 September.
28. RGS 1/3.
29. Bennett, p. 409.
30. 'Adventures of an American Traveller in Turkey', (unpublished manuscript in SFA, hereinafter 'Adventures').
31. Ibid.
32. *New York Sun*, 24 August 1872.
33. Bennett, p. 410.
34. Ibid., pp. 410–11. The whipping incident is doubtless the reason why there is a page torn out of Stanley's journal between 8–18 September. Stanley later admitted he had beaten Noe, but said it was because of Noe's irresponsibility

in starting the bush fire. He claimed that he merely administered 'a few strokes of a switch'. (*New York Herald*, 26 September 1872.)

35. *New York Sun*, 29 August 1872.
36. Bennett, p. 411.
37. Ibid., p. 412.
38. Interestingly, we again see here the androgynous motif noted in the Williams boarding house in New Orleans.
39. 'Adventures', SFA.
40. Ibid.
41. Ibid.
42. Ibid.
43. Ibid.
44. Ibid.
45. Journal, 27 September.
46. Journal, 30 September.
47. Journal, 8 October.
48. Stanley's letter of 11 October 1866 printed in *New York Sun*, 30 August 1872.
49. Journal, 14, 16 October.
50. *New York Herald*, 7 September 1872.
51. Bennett, pp. 420–21.
52. *New York Sun*, 5 September 1872.
53. Journal, 25 October. Nevertheless, Stanley later forced Noe at gunpoint to sign a paper acknowledging that he had received one-third of the money (Bennett, p. 424).
54. Journal, 26 October.
55. The first newspaper account is in the *Levant Herald*, 17 October 1866. This was taken up by the *North Wales Chronicle*, 2 November, 22 December 1866. The international ramifications are described in the *New York Times*, 5 February 1867.
56. Journal, 7, 9 November.
57. Journal, 13 November.
58. Journal, 14, 15, 16, 19, 20, 21, 23 November.
59. Journal, 24, 26, 27 November.
60. RGS 14/2.
61. Noe to Dorothy Stanley, 8 October 1907, RGS 14/1.
62. Jones, *H. M. Stanley and Wales*, p. 18.
63. Cadwalader Rowlands, pp. 70–71.
64. RGS 16/4.
65. *Denbigh Free Press*, 24 May 1904.
66. *New York Sun*, 29 August 1872.
67. Cadwalader Rowlands, pp. 167, 172. Cf. also RGS 14/2. Stanley had already shown a disposition towards assassination. In Smyrna, although

virtually penniless, he originally hired a guide at $60 a month and expenses, but the man pulled out before the departure from Smyrna. When Noe asked at the time of hiring what Stanley would do when the man asked for his money, Stanley replied: 'I would tie him to a tree and blow his brains out, as I don't intend to have any man go back to Smyrna and let them know how we travel.' (Bennett, p. 409.)

68. Jones, p. 19.
69. Journal, 7, 8, 14 January 1867.
70. Not for nothing did we make the comparison with Senator McCarthy at p. 61!
71. Bennett, p. 443.
72. Cook to Stanley (n.d. but 1867), SFA.
73. See Morris's story in the *New York Herald*, 7 September 1872.
74. *New York Sun*, 26 September 1872.
75. Stanley to Gordon Bennett, 13 September 1872, in *New York Herald*, 26 September 1872; Dorothy Stanley to Wellcome, 1 December 1907, RGS 14/3.
76. *New York Sun*, 9 October 1872.
77. *New York Herald*, 29 August 1872.
78. *Chicago Times*, 31 August 1872.
79. Bennett, pp. 425–33.
80. For this point see Wassermann, p. 4.
81. François Bontinck, *L'Autobiographie de Hamed el-Murjebi Tippu Tip* (Brussels 1974), p. 178.
82. Rivals for what Hellinga, after Adler, calls Stanley's fictitious goals.
83. *Diary of A. J. Mounteney-Jephson*, ed. Dorothy Middleton (1969), p. 248.
84. *Autobiography*, p. 52.

Chapter four

1. Stanley's year on the plains in 1867 is covered in exhaustive detail in volume one of the two-volume autobiographical *My Early Travels in America and Asia* (1895).
2. *Autobiography*, p. 228.
3. There is some confusion about the exact date of Stanley's departure for Europe in December 1867 and even about which ship he sailed on. In the *Autobiography*, pp. 228–9, he claims he left in the steamer *Hecla* on 22 December 1867. In his journals (SFA) he says he departed New York on 17 December on the *Nebraska* and arrived in Liverpool on 29 December. The confusion is compounded for the different dates for departure from Liverpool to London and London to Paris given in the two different journals covering January 1868.

4. Journal, 20 January 1868.
5. See Part Two of Stanley's *Coomassie and Magdala* (1874).
6. Journal, 27, 28 June 1868.
7. *New York Herald*, 3 June 1868.
8. *New York Herald*, 23 December 1871.
9. Journal, 28 June, 17 July 1868.
10. Journal, 8 July.
11. Journal, 9 July.
12. *New York Herald*, 12 August 1868.
13. Stanley to Hekekyan Bey, 19, 24 June, Add. MSS. 37, 463 ff. 401–2.
14. Journal, 23 July.
15. For events in 1868 see Edouard Driault and Michel Lheritier, *Histoire Diplomatique de la Grèce de 1821 à nos jours* (Paris 1925), iii, pp. 239–88. A recent popular account is given in Douglas Dakin, *The Unification of Greece 1770–1923* (1972).
16. For *Herald* coverage, including Russian and American involvement with the Cretan rebels, see *New York Herald*, 11, 21, 30 March, 3, 20 April, 2, May, 20 June, 11 July 1868.
17. *New York Herald* 14 August 1868.
18. Journal, 11, 13, 15, 16, 17, 18 August 1868.
19. Journal, 19 August.
20. *Autobiography*, p. 231.
21. Ibid., p. 232.
22. Journal, 20 August.
23. *Autobiography*, p. 232.
24. Ibid., p. 233.
25. Ibid., p. 234.
26. Journal, 23 August.
27. Journal, 24 August.
28. Journal, 25 August.
29. Journal, 26–30 August.
30. Journal, 31 August.
31. Journal, 2 September.
32. *New York Herald*, 23 September 1868.
33. Journal, 4–8 September.
34. *Autobiography*, p. 234.
35. Ibid., p. 236.
36. Ibid.
37. Stanley to Hekekyan Bey, 14 September 1868, Add. MSS. 39, 463 f. 407.
38. *Autobiography*, p. 236.
39. Journal, 14–23 September.
40. Journal, 24–25 September.
41. Stanley to Hekekyan Bey, 26 September 1868, Add. MSS. 37, 463 f. 409.

42. *Autobiography*, p. 236.
43. RGS 16/23.
44. Ambella family to Stanley, 13 December 1868, SFA.
45. *Saturday Review*, 5 July 1890.
46. *New York Herald*, 8 November 1868.
47. Stanley's accounts diary, 1868. Even more surprisingly, Dorothy Stanley failed to spot the discrepancy between the dates given in the accounts and the *Herald* despatches and those in the journal, which she partially reproduced in the *Autobiography*. For one who was usually so eagle-eyed and so determined to suppress anything that did not redound to Stanley's glory, this is a classic case of Homer nodding!
48. *The Times*, 1 October 1868.
49. *The Times*, 13 October 1868.
50. From 21 September to 10 October there was a daily report on Spain in the *New York Herald*, culminating in a full-page spread on 11 October 1868.
51. Journal, 2, 3, 6 October 1868.
52. Journal, 8 October.
53. Journal, 10–11 October.
54. *New York Herald*, 22 October 1868.
55. *New York Herald*, 30 October 1868.
56. *New York Herald*, 31 October 1868.
57. *New York Herald*, 28 October 1868.
58. Journal, 13 October 1868.
59. For continuing 'saturation coverage' of Spain by the *Herald* after Stanley's departure see *New York Herald*, 2, 4, 5, 10, 12, 17, 19, 23 October 1868.
60. Journal, 14–15 October.
61. Journal, 16 October.
62. Journal, 17 October.
63. Stanley's servant in the 1880s, William Hoffmann, confirmed that this was a running sore with Stanley. From the moment of his expulsion in 1862, 'so Stanley used to tell me, he made up his mind that his natural feelings must be checked or at least hidden from the hurtful eyes of the world. He threw around his sensitive, affectionate nature a cloak of reserve through which only his closest and most intimate friends and companions could successfully penetrate.' (Hoffmann, *With Stanley in Africa* (1938), p. 12.)
64. RGS 16/4
65. Jones, *H. M. Stanley and Wales*, p. 11.
66. Cadwalader Rowlands, p. 73.
67. RGS 13/1. Catherine Maria Gough-Roberts, born 25 January 1849, was one of six children.
68. *Western Mail*, Cardiff, 11 May 1889.
69. Cadwalader Rowlands, p. 73.
70. Journal, 23, 24, 25, 26, 31 October, 6 November 1868.

71. Journal, 10 November.
72. John MacGregor, *The Rob Roy on the Jordan* (1869), p. 42.
73. Journal, 12 November.
74. MacGregor gave him a letter of introduction in case he ever did run into Livingstone. Livingstone knew the family and told Stanley that Rob Roy's family commanded the *Kent*, an East Indiaman (see *Journal*, 17 December 1871: 'I showed Rob Roy's introduction to the doctor today. He said he knew his mother and father as well – or his sister and father, I forget which.').
75. Journal, 21 November.
76. Journal, 23, 25 November.
77. Journal, 25 November.
78. *New York Sun*, 29 August 1872.
79. *New York Herald*, 9, 23 April 1868.
80. *New York Herald*, 2 July 1872.
81. For Stanley's reading see Miscellaneous Notes, SFA. Other interests include 'circumstantial evidence in criminal trials', John Adams' *History of the Republics of the World* and a 1785 *History of the Mogul Empire*. He quotes Helvetius in his journal for 24 February 1869.
82. Miscellaneous Notes, dated 25 February, 1, 3, March 1869, SFA.
83. *Autobiography*, pp. 237–8.
84. Journal, 5 January 1869.
85. Journal, 7 January.
86. *Autobiography*, p. 238.
87. Journal, 6 February.
88. Journal, 9 February.
89. Journal, 14 February.
90. Journal, 16 February.
91. Journal, 17–18 February.
92. Journal, 19 February.
93. Journal, 21 February.
94. Journal, 22 February.
95. Journal, 27 February.
96. Journal, 2 March.
97. *Autobiography*, p. 240.
98. Cadwalader Rowlands, p. 52.
99. *Saturday Review*, 5 July 1890.
100. *Autobiography*, p. 239.

Chapter five

1. RGS 13/1.
2. Journal, 3 March 1869.

3. Journal, 6 March.
4. Commonplace book (SFA), 1, 5, 8, 12, 13 March 1869.
5. Commonplace book, 19, 24, 28 March.
6. Journal, 9 March.
7. What wives were supposed to be, according to Elizabeth Parry, was summed up in a couplet she quoted to her son:
   The wife that expects to have a good name
   Is always at home as though she were lame. (Ibid.)
8. Journal, 10–11 March.
9. Journal, 17 March.
10. Katie Bradshaw (née Gough-Roberts) to Wellcome, 20 November 1907, RGS 13/2.
11. Jones, *H. M. Stanley and Wales*, pp. 21–3.
12. Stanley to Katie Gough-Roberts, 22 March 1869, SFA.
13. Journal, 25 March 1869.
14. Journal, 27 October 1869. In *How I Found Livingstone* xv-xvi Stanley completely rewrites this incident. He claims that he received Bennett's cable in Madrid at 10 a.m. on 16 October, was on the Hendaye express at 3 p.m. and arrived in Paris on the evening of the 17th! Obviously this makes better reading than the prosaic facts. There is more to this than the journalistic 'Never let the facts interfere with a good story.' It suggests a compulsion to lie even when there is no need.
15. HIFL, xvii-xviii. Bennett's hotel was the Grand, in Place de l'Opera.
16. The two best biographies of Livingstone are Tim Jeal, *Livingstone* (1973) and Oliver Ransford, *David Livingstone, the Dark Interior* (1978).
17. For this period of Livingstone's life see *Missionary Travels and Researches in South Africa* (1857); I. Schapera, ed., *David Livingstone: Family Letters 1841–1856*, 2 vols (1959); *Livingstone's African Journal 1853–56*, 2 vols (1963); *Livingstone's Missionary Correspondence 1841–1856* (1961); *Livingstone's Private Journals 1851–1852* (1960).
18. For the Zambezi expedition see David and Charles Livingstone, *Narrative of an Expedition to the Zambezi* (New York, 1866); J. P. R. Wallis, ed., *The Zambezi Expedition of David Livingstone 1858–1863*, 2 vols (1956); George Shepperson, ed., *David Livingstone and Rovuma* (Edinburgh 1965); Reginald Foskett, ed., *The Zambezi Journals and Letters of Dr John Kirk 1858–63*, 2 vols (Edinburgh 1965).
19. For Livingstone's final expedition see Horace Waller, ed., *The Last Journals of David Livingstone*, 2 vols (1874); Reginald Coupland, *Livingstone's Last Journey* (1945).
20. See Charles L. Robertson, *The International Herald Tribune: The First Hundred Years* (New York 1987); Douglas Fenner, *James Gordon Bennett and the New York Herald* (1986).

21. See in general Don C. Seitz, *The James Gordon Bennetts* (Indianapolis 1928); Oliver Carlson, *The Man Who Made News* (New York 1942).
22. *New York Herald*, 2 January 1870.
23. *The Times*, 20 January, 19, 20 April, 16 July, 6, 7, 15 September, 1 October 1869.
24. There was nothing doing in the world. Europe was taking breath between two wars. Asia seemed more than usually lethargic except for some civil strife in Japan. And from Africa, despite the cliché, came nothing new, nothing at any rate on the Abyssinian scale, nothing but a rumour that the lost Livingstone had found the source of the Nile and was on his way down the river. Something, perhaps, might be made of that.' (Coupland, *Livingstone's Last Journey* p. 137.)
25. Seitz, *The James Gordon Bennetts*, p. 303.
26. Hall, *Stanley*, p. 381. Interestingly, Keim later went on to tread in Stanley's footsteps in the American West. See Randolph de B. Keim, *Sheridan's Troopers on the Border* (Philadelphia 1885).
27. Quoted in Ian Anstruther, *I Presume*, p. 167. According to Minister Edward Jay Morris, who met Stanley in Constantinople in 1870, Stanley himself was going to fulfil the prophecy by travelling to Tibet to interview the Grand Lama (Bennett, p. 439).
28. See Journal, 10 July 1872, after the finding of Livingstone: 'Cabled immediately on arrival (Aden) this morning to London to Hosmer. *Am I to continue journey to China as ordered in Paris* (italics mine) or return?'
29. *New York Herald*, 9 August 1869.
30. Levien to Stanley, 29 November 1869, included in Journal, 14 February 1872.
31. RGS 13/1.
32. Stanley recapitulated the one-hour interview in Stanley to Gough-Roberts, 1 December 1869 (SFA), written on board the steamer *Pelusi* on the Nile. He complained of her coldness and her 'profound ignorance . . . concerning upper Egypt'.
33. Stanley to Katie Gough-Roberts, 3, 12 April 1870 (SFA).
34. RGS 14/2.
35. RGS 13/2.
36. Wellcome to Katie Bradshaw, August 1904, RGS 13/1.
37. Edwin Swift Balch, 'American Explorers of Africa', *Geographical Review* 5 (1918), pp. 274–81.
38. Edward King, 'H. M. Stanley in Spain', *Scribner's Monthly* 5 (1872), pp. 105–12.
39. For these travels see Volume 2 of *My Early Life and Adventures* (1895).
40. Journal, 1 August 1870.

1. *Autobiography*, p. 256.
2. Stanley, *My African Travels* (1886), p. 3.
3. Journal, 8, 12, 13 October 1870.
4. Journal, 23, 30 October, 3 November.
5. Journal, 24 October.
6. Journal, 1 November.
7. There are a number of early entries in *How I Found Livingstone* which establish this: his contempt for half-castes: 'this syphilitic, blear-eyed, pallid-skinned abortion of an Africanised Arab' (HIFL p. 6); for Maganga, chief of his fourth caravan: 'it was Maganga, composed of greed and laziness, and his weakly-bodies syphilitic tribe, who were ever falling sick' (HIFL p. 122); and for his men in general: 'the soldiers and *pagazis* employed the interval in visiting their female friends; but I forbear the *chronique scandaleuse*' (HIFL p. 75).
8. Journal, 18–21 November.
9. Journal, 2 December.
10. Journal, 28 November.
11. Journal, 7–9 December.
12. Journal, 11–12 December.
13. Journal, 14–19 December.
14. Journal, 23 December. For this practice of 'gamming', where sea-captains visited each other's ships, see Herman Meville, *Moby-Dick*, Chapter 52.
15. 'The boats lowered after a school but returned unsuccessful.' (Journal, 25 December 1870.)
16. Journal, 22 December.
17. Journal, 28 December.
18. Journal, 2 January 1871.
19. Journal, 4 January.
20. Journal, 6 January.
21. *New York Herald*, 26 December 1874.
22. Oscar Baumann, *Der Sansibar-Archipel*, Vol. 2. *Die Insel Sansibar und ihre Kleineren Nachbarinseln* (Leipzig 1897).
23. R. F. Burton, *Zanzibar*, 2 vols (1872).
24. HIFL, p. 11.
25. For details see Norman R. Bennett and George E. Brooks, eds, *New England Merchants in Africa* (Boston 1965); cf. also George Granville Putnam, 'Salem Vessels and their Voyages', *Essex Institute Historical Collections* 60 (1924), pp. 17–45.
26. For Webb see Norman R. Bennett, 'Americans in Zanzibar 1865–1915', *TNR* 60 (1963), pp. 49–66; cf. also Bennett, *Studies in East African History* (Boston 1963), pp. 31–53.

27. See Reginald Foskett, ed., *The Zambezi Doctors: David Livingstone's Letters to John Kirk 1858; 1872* (Edinburgh 1964).

28. *Autobiography*, p. 251.

29. For Webb's assistance see Stanley, *My African Travels*, p. 5; cf. Webb's despatch to Washington, 6 February 1871 reproduced in Peggy H. Jackson, *Meteor out of Africa*, p. 16. For Webb's motivation see Bennett, 'Stanley and the American Consuls at Zanzibar', *Essex Institute Historical Collections* 100 (1964), pp. 41–58.

30. Journal, 8 January 1871. For Sultan Barghash see Reginald Coupland, *The Exploitation of East African 1856–1890* (1939).

31. See Speke, *Journal of the Discovery of the Source of the Nile* (1863), p. 99.

32. Later allegedly poisoned by Barghash. Paul Reichard, *Deutsch Ostafrika* (Leipzig 1892), p. 101.

33. *New York Herald*, 22 December 1871.

34. For Shaw see Kirk to F.O. 10 April 1872, F.O. 84/1357; Jackson, *Meteor out of Africa*, pp. 134, 181–3, 351–3.

35. For the key role of these men in European exploration of Africa see Donald Simpson, *Dark Companions* (1975).

36. Stanley's later verdict on these two men was as follows: 'Bombay was neither very honest nor very dishonest – that is he did not venture to steal much . . . he was greedy and tried to get bigger meals than his fellows . . . as a servant he would have been excellent – as a superintendent . . . he was out of his place.' On Mabruki: 'My policeman, my porter and as such he was invaluable, always faithful at his post. He saw to feeding the donkeys, bringing up the stragglers. No one could have been better.' (Miscellaneous notes, SFA.) For Bombay's service with Burton and Speke see Speke, *What Led to the Discovery of the Source of the Nile* (Edinburgh 1864), pp. 186, 210–12, 264–5.

37. Allington to Jones, 16 January 1873, A.1.111. UMCA Archives, SOAS. For Stanley's critical remarks on Tozer see HIFL pp. 19–20. For Tozer see Gertrude Ward, ed., *Letters of Bishop Tozer* (1902); Owen Chadwick, *Mackenzie's Grave* (1959).

38. For favourable views of Kirk see James B. Thomson, *Joseph Thomson, African Explorer* (1896), pp. 51–2; Frederick Jackson, *Early Days in East Africa* (1930), pp. 60–65. But many other observers found Kirk overbearing and arrogant. Bishop Tozer recorded: 'He is a great hand at contradicting you flat, and aims at being *the* authority on all points under debate.' (Bennett, *Stanley's Despatches*, p. 29.)

39. Journal, 9 January 1871.

40. Journal, 17 January.

41. Journal, 9, 14 January; HIFL, pp. 22–5, 36–8. For Ladha Damji see David Chamberlin, ed., *Some Letters from Livingstone 1840–1872* (1940). For Sewa Haji Paru, eventually one of the wealthiest of East Africa's Indians,

see Lucien Heudebert, *Vers les Grands Lacs de l'Afrique Orientale* (Paris 1900), p. 86; David F. Clyde, *History of the Medical Services of Tanganyika* (Dar-es-Salaam 1962), pp. 5–11; A. T. Matson, 'Sewa Haj: a note', TNR 65 (1966), pp. 91–4.

42. HIFL, pp. 35, 39; Jackson, *Meteor out of Africa*, pp. 353–4.

43. HIFL, pp. 39–40.

44. *New York Herald*, 22 December 1871.

45. Bennett, *Studies in East African History*, pp. 54–75.

46. For Horner see *Bulletin Général de la Congrégation du St Esprit et de l'Immaculé Coeur de Marie* 11, pp. 76–808; cf. also L. A. Ricklin, *La Mission Catholique du Zanguebar, Travaux et Voyages de R. P. Horner* (Paris 1880); For Tucker see Clowes, *Royal Navy*, vii, p. 234. For the missionaries' version of the dinner see *Annales de la Propagation de la Foi* 56 (1884), p. 58.

47. For Charles de Vienne see Vienne, 'De Zanzibar à l'Oukami', *Bulletin de la Société de Geographie* 14 (1872), pp. 356–99; Bennett, 'Charles de Vienne and the Frère mission to Zanzibar', *Boston University Papers on Africa* 2 (1966), pp. 109–221.

48. HIFL, p. 44; *New York Herald*, 9 August 1872.

49. Livingstone to Agnes Livingstone, 18 November 1871, 16 December 1871, February 1872, Add. MSS. 50, 184 ff. 175–82.

50. HIFL, pp. 64–6. In a later despatch (*New York Herald*, 9 August 1872) Stanley contemptuously pointed out that in five days' shooting with Vienne, Kirk 'bagged' just one hartebeeste and one giraffe.

51. This is essentially the 'defence' of Kirk attempted by Coupland in *Livingstone's Last Journey*.

52. Oliver Ransford, *Livingstone*, pp. 142, 164, 206, 211.

53. See James Christie, *Cholera Epidemics in East Africa* (1875).

54. *New York Herald*, 22 December 1871.

55. For the crucial role of porters see Edmund Dahl, *Nyamwezi-Wörterbuch* (Hamburg 1915); S. C. Lamden, 'Some Aspects of Porterage in East Africa', *TNR* 61 (1963), pp. 155–64.

56. See the fundamental work by R. G. Abrahams, *The Political Organisation of Unyamwezi* (Cambridge 1967); *The Peoples of Greater Unyamwezi, Tanzania* (1967).

57. HIFL, p. 46.

58. *New York Herald*, 22 December 1871. For Stanley's impatience with Sewa see HIFL, pp. 59–60.

59. Here as elsewhere on the Livingstone expedition all dates are rough estimates. There are discrepancies both *within* Stanley's own accounts and between his accounts and those of others. According to the *New York Herald*, 22 December 1871, Stanley left Bagamoyo on 1 April, *eighty-three* days after arriving from Zanzibar. In HIFL, p. 70, Stanley says the date was 21 March, seventy-three days later. Stanley's journal confirms the HIFL

dating. His entries for the despatch of previous caravans are 18 February (first), 21 February (second), 25 February (third). HIFL, p. 68, adds 11 March for the fourth, but there is no mention of this in the diary.

60. *New York Herald*, 22 December 1871. Stanley recommended the twelve-bore as a fowling-piece, the English O'Reilly rifle for big-game hunting, but said that the best 'human fighting rifle' was the American Winchester (HIFL, p. 62).

61. See Jackson, *Early Days in East Africa* (1930), pp. 142–3; Emil Ludwig, *Genius and Character* (1927), pp. 69–70; Isabel Burton, *The Life of Captain Sir Richard F. Burton*, 2 vols (1893), i, p. 304.

62. Eric Halladay, 'Henry Morton Stanley. The Opening up of the Congo Basin', in R. I. Rotberg, *Africa and its Explorers* (Harvard 1970), pp. 229–30.

63. HIFL, p. 76.

64. HIFL, pp. 80–82.

65. Journal, 24–28 March 1871; HIFL, pp. 94, 101.

66. HIFL, p. 88.

67. There is a large and expanding literature on African diseases. See Oliver Ransford, *Let the Sickness Cease* (1983); G. W. Hartwig and K. D. Paterson, *Disease in African History: an Introductory Survey and Case Studies* (Durham, N. C. 1978); John Ford, *The Role of Trypanosomiasis in African Ecology: A Study of the Tsetse Fly Problem* (Oxford 1971); Michael Colbourne, *Malaria in Africa* (1966); Paul F. Russell, *Man's Mastery of Malaria* (1955); Jaime Jaramillo Arango, *The Conquest of Malaria* (1950).

68. HIFL, pp. 96, 99. See also Brom, *Sur les traces*, p. 44.

69. Journal, 28 March 1871.

70. It particularly irked Stanley that Kirk had predicted the early demise of his two horses (HIFL, p. 99).

71. HIFL, p. 92.

72. For Shaw's promiscuity see Byron Farwell, *The Man who Presumed*, pp. 67–8.

73. HIFL, p. 67.

74. Journal, 6–8 April.

75. HIFL, p. 103.

76. Ibid., p. 101.

77. Ibid., p. 103.

78. Ibid., p. 108.

79. Journal, 11 April.

80. For the Wakwere, Wakami (now considered to be a branch of the Luguru and not a separate people) and other peoples met by Stanley so far on this expedition see Thomas O. Beidelman, *The Matrilineal Peoples of Eastern Tanzania* (1967), pp. 22–6. The Doe, who lived near Bagamoyo, had the reputation of being East Africa's only cannibals (Père Schynse, *A Travers l'Afrique avec Stanley et Emin-Pacha* (Paris 1890), p. 290; Edmund A.

Bojarksi, 'The Last Years of the Cannibals in Tanganyika', *TNR* 51 (1958), pp. 227–31. Cf. also H. Baumann and D. Westermann, *Les Peuplades et les Civilisations de l'Afrique* (Paris 1948)). For the impact of the slave trade on the Luguru/Wakami see L. A. Ricklin, *La Mission Catholique du Zanguebar. Travaux et Voyages de R. P. Horner* (1880), p. 160.

81. HIFL, pp. 111–14.
82. Burton, 'The Lake Regions of Central Equatorial Africa', *JRGS* 29 (1859), pp. 260, 270, 275, 346.
83. HIFL, p. 118.
84. Journal, 19 April.
85. For Kisabengo and Simbawenni see Lucien Heudebert, *Vers les grands lacs*, pp. 150–60; Burton, 'Lake Regions', pp. 45, 76. For Simbawenni as the site of modern Morogoro see Jackson, *Meteor*, pp. 89–110. The missionary Dodgshun later facetiously referred to the Sultana as 'Stanley's friend' (Norman R. Bennett, ed., *From Zanzibar to Ujiji. The Journal of Arthur W. Dodgshun 1877–79* (Boston 1969) – hereinafter Dodgshun Journal – 27 December 1877, p. 51).
86. Journal, 18 April; HIFL, pp. 117, 120.
87. HIFL, p. 124.
88. Journal, 20–21 April.
89. HIFL, p. 124.
90. Journal, 23 April; HIFL, pp. 124–6.
91. *New York Herald*, 22 December 1871. There is a certain confusion over this episode. Stanley says in HIFL (pp. 129–32) that he ordered the cook to leave the expedition but did not mean it; unfortunately the cook took him literally.
92. For the very real horrors of this see Dodgshun Journal, 7 September 1878, p. 81 (Dodgshun crossed it on a tree bridge).
93. See the discussion in Jackson, *Meteor*, pp. 112–16.
94. *New York Herald*, 22 December 1871.
95. HIFL, p. 212.
96. Ibid., p. 135.
97. Ibid., pp. 139–40.
98. Ibid., pp. 145–7.
99. To run down Shaw only to set up the even more egregious 'incompetence' of Farquahar is a technique that recalls a favourite ploy of Stanley's friend Mark Twain, who stated that he would rather be damned to John Bunyan's heaven than read Henry James's *The Bostonians*.
100. *New York Herald*, 22 December 1871.
101. HIFL, p. 147.
102. Ibid., p. 150.
103. *Autobiography*, p. 256.
104. HIFL, pp. 151–2.
105. Journal, 12 May 1871.

106. HIFL, p. 153.
107. For an assessment of Stanley at Lake Gombo see Dodgshun Journal, 9–10 May 1878, p. 65.
108. HIFL, pp. 156–8.
109. Ibid., p. 159.
110. Ibid., p. 160.
111. Journal, 14–16 May.
112. HIFL, p. 161.
113. Journal, 17 May. For Mpapwa see T. O. Beidelman, 'A History of Ukaguru 1857–1916', *TNR* 58–59 (1962), pp. 10–39.
114. HIFL, p. 163.
115. For Nasibu see Bennett, *Studies in East African History* (Boston 1963), pp. 5–15; Paul Reichard, *Deutsch Ostafrika* (Leipzig 1892), pp. 93–6; Jerome Becker, *La Troisième Expédition Belge* (Brussels 1891), p. 89.
116. Journal, 21–22 May.
117. HIFL, p. 169.
118. Journal, 30 May.
119. HIFL, pp. 164–5.
120. *New York Herald*, 1 March 1875; HIFL, pp. 291, 293; T. Griffith Jones, 'Stanley's first and second expeditions through Mpapwa and W. L. Farquahar's grave', *TNC* 25 (1948), pp. 28–33.
121. There is a long, self-justifying and disingenuous account of Farquahar's service on the expedition – 'inebriated . . . inveterately lazy and insolent' – in Stanley's diary entry for 20 May (Journal, 20 May 1871, SFA).

Chapter seven

1. For German reactions see Joachim Graf von Pfeil, *Die Erwerbung von Deutsch Ostafrika* (Berlin n.d.), pp. 56–7; Carl Peters, *Wie Deutsch-Ostafrika enstandt* (Leipzig 1940), p. 25. For the Sagara peoples see Beidelman, *Matrilinear Peoples*.
2. Bennett, *Stanley's Despatches*, p. 20.
3. For the Wagogo see Heinrich Claus, *Die Wagogo* (Leipzig 1911); Hermann Graf von Schweinitz, *Deutsch Ost-Afrika in Krieg und Frieden* (Berlin 1894). For the Hehe see E. Nigmann, *Die Wahehe* (Berlin 1908).
4. Journal, 31 May 1871.
5. The Wagogo tried the patience of most European travellers. The following entries from the missionary Dodgshun to his correspondent Mullen (Dodgshun Journal) give some idea of the hatred entertained for them: 'bloodthirsty wild beasts, and if I shoot it will be as against wolves' (25 November 1878); someone 'ought to come and scour Ugogo from end to end with bullets. The insolence and extortion of the whole lot need

punishment' (ibid.); 'such wretches cannot claim the rights of men. They are wild beasts, only to be kept in their place by superior force' (28 December 1878).

6. HIFL, p. 173.
7. Ibid., pp. 174–6.
8. Journal, 1 June.
9. Journal, 3 June.
10. Journal, 4 June.
11. HIFL, p. 184.
12. Ibid., pp. 186–7, 196–7.
13. Ibid., p. 184.
14. Ibid., pp. 191–2.
15. HIFL, p. 188.
16. Ibid., pp. 189–91.
17. Ibid., pp. 199–203.
18. Journal, 7 June.
19. HIFL, p. 203.
20. Ibid., pp. 205–6.
21. Journal, 10–11 June.
22. HIFL, pp. 211–15.
23. HIFL, p. 217.
24. Journal, 19 June.
25. HIFL, p. 218.
26. Journal, 14–16 June.
27. Journal, 13, 20 June.
28. On this part of the expedition Stanley was most definitely in Burton's footsteps. For Tura, Rubuga and Kigwa see Burton, 'Lake Regions', pp. 159, 164, 178–9. For a later view of Rubuga see Franz Stuhlmann, *Mit Emin Pascha ins Herz von Afrika* (Berlin 1894), p. 57.
29. HIFL, pp. 219–21. 'Music and dancing from the girls and a wandering minstrel from Uganda with a harp not unlike that pictured in the . . . trunk discovered by Belzoni at Thebes . . .' (The local beer was) 'a poor kind of Burton ale in taste.' (Journal, 22 June.)
30. For Mirambo see Norman Bennett, *Mirambo* (New York 1971); John B. Kabeya, *Ntembi Mirambo* (Dar-es-Salaam 1966); R. P. Fouquer, *Mirambo* (Paris 1966).
31. Speke, *What Led to the Discovery of the Source of the Nile*, pp. 264–5; Charles New, 'Journal from the Pangani via Usambara to Mombasa', *JRGS* 45 (1875), pp. 414–20; John M. Gray, 'Livingstone's Muganda servant', *UJ* 13 (1949), pp. 119–29.
32. Jackson, *Meteor*, p. 286. Of these, twenty-two are venomous, including some of the deadliest serpents in the world: the black mamba, green mamba, cobra, puff-adder and night-adder. For the ferocity of the black

mamba in Tanzania see Horace Waller, ed., *The Last Journals of David Livingstone* (hereinafter LLJ), ii, pp. 343–44.

33. HIFL, pp. 263–4.
34. For Said bin Majid and his son see LLJ, ii, pp. 155, 176; Burton, *The Lake Regions of Central Africa*, 2 vols (1860), i, p. 323. At Tabora Salim contacted Stanley and talked over his days with Burton (Journal, 24 June).
35. See Bennett, *Mirambo*, passim.
36. Stanley recovered from the first bout on 14 July, then relapsed until 25 July (Journal, SFA). Cf. also HIFL, p. 274.
37. Journal, 29–31 July.
38. *New York Herald*, 9 August 1872.
39. Kirk to F.O., 10 April 1872, F.O. 84/1357. In Vienne to French Ministry, 20 October 1871, AECC, Zanzibar, Vienne reports the mendacious Arab story, put out to cover their own incompetence, that the ambush took place at night.
40. For Khamis see Speke, *Journal of the Discovery of the Nile*, p. 107; Heinrich Brode, *Tippoo Tib* (1907), p. 136.
41. *New York Herald*, 9 August 1872.
42. For Uledi see Herbert Ward, *A Voice from the Congo* (New York 1910), pp. 193–200. For Sarmean (who served with Stanley in 1874–7) see also Joseph Thomson, *Through Masailand* (1885), p. 21; Mary Yule, *Mackay of Uganda* (1890), p. 127.
43. *New York Herald*, 5 July 1872.
44. For the Ngoni see G. W. Hatchell, 'The Ngoni of Tanganyika Territory', *Man* 35 (1935), pp. 69–71; J. A. Barnes, *Politics in a Changing Society. A Political History of the Fort Jameson Ngoni* (1954). For the 'Ruga-Ruga' see Aylward Shorter, 'Nyung-ya-Mawe and the Empire of the Ruga-Rugas', *Journal of African Studies* (1968), pp. 248–51; Paul Reichard, 'Die Wanjamuesi', *Zeitschrift der Gesellschaft für Erdkunde zu Berlin* 24 (1889), pp. 304–31.
45. For the important Arabs of Tabora see LLJ, ii, p. 194; Brode, *Tippoo-Tib*, p. 29; Frere to Granville, 7 May 1873, F.O. 84/1391. For Masudi's later years see Last to Wigram, 20 June 1879, CA 6/0104, CMS archives.
46. *New York Herald*, 9 August 1872.
47. *New York Herald*, 15 July 1872.
48. 'As soon as they were dead, they were mutilated in the manner of medicine-making Africans. The skin of forehead, the beard and skin, the forepart of the nose, the fat over the stomach and abdomen, the genital organs and lastly a bit from each heel . . .' (Journal, 24 August).
49. Journal, 23 August.
50. Bennett, *Mirambo*, pp. 55–6.
51. Journal, 25–7 August.
52. Journal, 28 August.

53. Bennett, *Mirambo*, p. 68.
54. Kirk to F.O., 22 September 1871, F.O. 84/1344; cf. also Kirk to Merchison, 25 September 1871, *PRGS* 16 (1871–2), pp. 102–3: 'His prospect of getting on is at present small, but I really cannot say where he desires to go to; he never disclosed his plans here . . . I fancy he will make a point of meeting Livingstone first; but whether, having seen what is best to do, he will push on or come back, I cannot say.'
55. Kirk to Rawlinson, 15 January 1872, *PRGS* 16 (1871–2), p. 226 pointed out that the Lufiji exploration idea was an obvious blind; the only way a commercial newspaper could get its money back was if Stanley found Livingstone. Sir Clements Markham, the secretary of the RGS, thought the fact that Stanley had been stopped by the Mirambo war was a cogent argument for the RGS to send a proper expedition (ibid., pp. 159–60).
56. HIFL, pp. 303, 352.
57. *New York Herald*, 9 August 1872.
58. Journal, 1 June.
59. Journal, 2 June.
60. 'In relating the tale of Lady Flora Hastings and the Lady of Bute, the poor fellow silently dropped tears for her sad state as if she had been his sister.' (Journal, 1 July.)
61. Journal, 29–31 August.
62. HIFL, p. 305.
63. Ibid., p. 301.
64. Journal, 30 August.
65. 'Shaw is sick, stubbornly so, he is a spiritless man totally devoid of the commendable ambition to do a good thing of whatever nature it may be. By disclosing to him the purpose of the expedition, I thought to interest him, to stir him into action but no, he seems to be played into apathy . . . Shaw is "self-absorbed". Instead of looking towards the farthest distance, he regards the ground at his feet with a look which seems to say – there is something wrong somewhere and I am trying to find out where it can be and how to rectify it.' (Journal, 13 September.)
66. HIFL, p. 293.
67. Ibid., p. 300.
68. *New York Herald*, 9 August 1872.
69. *My African Travels*, p. 15.
70. *Autobiography*, pp. 256–7.
71. *Coomassie and Magdala*, p. 11.
72. *New York Herald*, 9 August 1872.
73. *New York Herald*, 5 July 1872.
74. Journal, 1 September.
75. Journal, 2 September.
76. Ibid.

77. The Bende lived along the shores of Lake Tanganyika from Karema to the Malagarazi in the area known as Ukawendi (Edward Coode Hore, 'On the Twelve Tribes of Tanganyika', *Journal of the Royal Anthropological Institute* 12 (1882), pp. 2–21.

78. Journal, 8–9 September.

79. Journal, 4, 6 September.

80. Journal, 4, 9, 10, 11, 14 September.

81. Journal, 12 September.

82. *New York Herald*, 5 July 1872.

83. Journal, 15 September.

84. Journal, 17 September.

85. HIFL, p. 307.

86. Ibid., p. 315.

87. Ibid., pp. 320–21.

88. Journal, 26 September.

89. *New York Herald*, 10 August 1872.

90. See Webb to Assistant Secretary of State, 10 October 1871, reproduced in Jackson, *Meteor*, p. 270. One of the explorer Philippe Bronyon's children was later given a grave right next to Shaw's (Dodgshun Journal, 24 January 1879, p. 101).

91. Journal, 24 September. Chowpereh later remained with Livingstone when Stanley returned to the coast (LLJ, ii, pp. 299 *et seq.*). He also served with Stanley in 1874–7 and in the Congo in 1879.

92. Exeter Hall in London was where humanitarian and aboriginal protection societies held their meetings.

93. *New York Herald*, 10 August 1872.

94. Bennett, *Stanley's Despatches*, p. 64.

95. See Wilhelm Blohm, *Die Nyamwezi, Land und Wirtschaft* (Hamburg 1931), p. 3; Richard Böhm, *Von Sansibar zum Tanganjika* (Leipzig 1888), p. 33.

96. Journal, 27–8 September.

97. Journal, 1–4 October.

98. HIFL, p. 329.

99. Ibid., p. 330.

100. Journal, 5 October.

101. Bennett, *Stanley's Despatches*, p. 68.

102. HIFL, p. 338.

103. Ibid., p. 339.

104. New travellers in Africa narrowly escaping death at the jaws of a crocodile were a staple of 'Africa lore' which the Victorian reading public expected. See James B. Thomson, *Joseph Thomson, African Explorer* (1896). Cf. also Livingstone's story of his friend Murray, a Scottish traveller who lost his zest for Africa for good after narrowly escaping being taken by a crocodile (Journal, 28 December 1871).

105. HIFL, pp. 343–5.
106. *New York Herald*, 9 August 1872.
107. Bennett, *Stanley's Despatches*, p. 71.
108. Journal, 8 October.
109. Journal, 8 October. For the greater honey guide (*indicator indicator*) see John G. Williams, *A Field Guide to the Birds of East and Central Africa* (1963), p. 170.
110. See Aylward Shorter, 'Nyungu-ya-Mawe', loc. cit.
111. This war involved Mkasiwa's son Simba, who was later an important figure in East African history (see Jerome Becker, *La Vie en Afrique* (Brussels 1887), 2 vols; Adolpe Burdo, *Les Belges dans l'Afrique Centrale: De Zanzibar au Lac Tanganika* (Brussels 1886), pp. 53–5; *Association Internationale Africaine. Rapports sur les marches de la première expédition* (Brussels 1879), pp. 67–9.
112. HIFL, p. 356.
113. Journal, 11 October.
114. Journal, 18 October. Cf. also Burton, 'Lake Regions', pp. 63–4, 143; Ivan R. Dale and P. J. Greenway, *Kenya Trees and Shrubs* (Nairobi 1961), pp. 109, 256.
115. Bennett, *Stanley's Despatches*, p. 75. 'Selim is ill, seems to be affected with the same disease as Shaw, has a weakness in the legs and sprawls and trembles most painfully when walking.' (Journal, 11 October.)
116. Journal, 9 October.
117. Journal, 12 October.
118. HIFL, p. 358.
119. Journal, 14 October; HIFL, p. 358.
120. Journal, 15–16 October.
121. Journal, 19–21 October.
122. HIFL, p. 365.
123. Journal, 19 October.
124. Journal, 21 October.
125. Journal, 22 October; HIFL, pp. 368–9.
126. HIFL, pp. 370–71.
127. Jackson, *Meteor*, p. 317.
128. HIFL, pp. 370–71.
129. Journal, 26 October.
130. Monkeys, lions, leopards and buffalo are mentioned during this period (Journal, 26–7 October; HIFL, p. 374).
131. Journal, 28 October; HIFL, p. 376.
132. *New York Herald*, 10 August 1872.
133. HIFL, pp. 377–81.
134. Journal, 29–30 October.
135. Bennett, *Stanley's Despatches*, p. 79.

136. *New York Herald*, 10 August 1872.

137. The *sami-sami* bead was a small coral bead, scarlet enamelled on white ground. See Burton, 'Lake Regions', p. 425; François Coulbois, *Dix Années en Tanganyika* (Limoges 1901), pp. 79–80; J. R. Harding, 'Nineteenth-Century Trade Beads in Tanganyika', *Man* 62 (1962), pp. 104–6.

138. *New York Herald*, 10 August 1872.

139. Journal, 2 November. The explanation that it was a number of crocodiles that dragged the donkey under was repeated in Stanley's talk with Livingstone on the subject (Journal, 21 December 1871). HIFL, p. 383 and *New York Herald*, 10 August 1872 speak merely of a single crocodile, which is implausible from a mechanical point of view.

140. Bennett, *Stanley's Despatches*, p. 82.

141. HIFL, p. 384.

142. As early as 5 June he had noted in his diary that the Ha were the 'Romans' of East Africa (Journal, 5 June).

143. See J. H. Scherer, 'The Ha of Tanganyika', *Anthropos* 54 (1959), pp. 841–904.

144. Journal, 4–6 November.

145. HIFL, pp. 387–94.

146. *New York Herald*, 10 August 1872.

147. *New York Herald*, 15 July 1872.

148. HIFL, pp. 395–6.

149. Bennett, *Stanley's Despatches*, pp. 51, 86.

150. HIFL, pp. 398–9.

151. Journal, 7 November. The Jacksons (*Meteor*, p. 332) later found that this was really a depression of the Sabaga swamp which was seasonally filled with water.

152. HIFL, p. 402.

153. Journal, 8–9 November. For the Bende people they now came to see R. P. Avon, 'Vie sociale des Wabende au Tanganika', *Anthropos* 10–11 (1915–16), pp. 98–113; Burton, 'Lake Regions', pp. 213–18.

154. For Ukaranga in 1874 see V. L. Cameron, *Across Africa*, 2 vols (1877), i, p. 236.

155. *New York Herald*, 10 August 1872.

156. *New York Herald*, 15 July 1872. Ludwig, *Genius and Character*, p. 73, particularly remarked on the poetic response of Stanley's first view of Lake Tanganyika.

157. HIFL, p. 412.

158. *New York Herald*, 10, 15 August 1872.

Chapter eight

1. There is considerable scholarly debate about the exact date of the meeting. Stanley's own journal gives the date as 10 November, but he admits himself he 'lost' a week through fever at Tabora, and in his *New York Herald* despatches he gives the date as 3 November. However, it is likely that further chronological 'slippage' took place during the expedition. The most careful recent estimate fixes on Friday 27 October as the most likely date (see François Bontinck, 'La date de la rencontre Stanley-Livingstone', *Africa, Rivista trimestrale di studi e documentazione dell'Istituto Italo-Africano* 24 (1979), pp. 225–41.

2. Mary Grierson, *Donald Francis Tovey* (Oxford 1951), p. 2.

3. Stanley, *In Darkest Africa*, 2 vols (1890), ii, pp. 208–9; cf. HIFL, pp. 558–9.

4. 'He may be a very cranky fellow after all. If he gets into any tantrums, off I go.' (Journal, 11 November.)

5. Stanley recorded that he was wary of Englishmen ever since he said good morning to one in a foreign land where they were the only white men in a hundred miles. The Englishman 'would not answer me but screwed on a large eye-glass in a manner which must have been as painful to him as it was to me, and then deliberately viewed my horse and myself for the space of thirty seconds, and passed on his way with as much insouciance as if he had seen me a thousand times and there was nothing at all in the meeting to justify him coming out of that shell of imperturbability in which he had covered himself.' (*New York Herald*, 15 August 1872.)

6. *New York Herald*, 15 July 1872. Cf. also Alan C. Cairns, *Prelude to Imperialism. British Reactions to Central African Society, 1840–1890* (1965), p. 38.

7. Even explorers treated Stanley's famous four words as a joke. The explorer Joseph Thomson was greeted by a compatriot in Africa with the words: 'Mr Thomson, I presume.' (Joseph Thomson, *To the Central African Lakes and Back* (1881), ii, p. 4.) For the Arab reaction see the remarks of Richard Burton, who knew Arab culture through and through: 'Had the travellers fallen upon one another's bosoms and embraced, they would have acted like Arabs from the days of Esau and Jacob until AD 1873. Walking deliberately up to each other, taking off hats and addressing a few ceremonious words, so far from impressing the Arabs with a sense of dignity would only draw forth such comments (to put it in a complimentary form) as "Wallah, what sort of meeting is this? Verily they are wonderful things, these Franks."' (R. F. Burton, 'Notes on Mr Stanley's Work', *Ocean Highways*, May 1873, pp. 52–9.)

8. Anstruther, *I Presume*, pp. 189–90.

9. Journal, 10 November 1871.

10. For an extended analysis see Hellinga, *Een Individualpsychologische Interpretatie*, pp. 107–15.

11. HIFL, pp. 413–14.
12. *New York Herald*, 15 August 1872.
13. HIFL, pp. 415–19; Bennett, *Stanley's Despatches*, pp. 95–7.
14. Coupland, *Livingstone's Last Journey*, pp. 97–9, 130–33.
15. HIFL, pp. 418–19.
16. Journal, 12 November.
17. Journal, 11 November.
18. HIFL, p. 422.
19. Journal, 11 November.
20. This is confirmed in Livingstone's own journals where he says that instead of four sparse meals he now eats four hearty ones: 'Bales of goods, baths of tin, huge kettles, cooking pots, tents etc. made me think "this must be a luxurious traveller and not one at his wits' ends like me" . . . I am not of a demonstrative turn; as cold, indeed, as we islanders are usually reputed to be, but this disinterested kindness of Mr Bennett, so nobly carried into effect by Mr Stanley, was simply overwhelming. I really do feel extremely grateful and at the same time I am a little ashamed at not being more worthy of the generosity. Mr Stanley has done his part with untiring energy: good judgement in the teeth of very serious obstacles.' (LLJ, ii, p. 156.)
21. HIFL, p. 426.
22. Livingstone to Mr and Mrs Livingstone, 26 September 1852.
23. Jeal, *Livingstone*, p. 289.
24. David and Charles Livingstone, *Narrative of an Expedition to the Zambezi*, p. 579.
25. Ransford, *Livingstone*, p. 141.
26. For the contributions of these men see Judith Listowel, *The Other Livingstone* (Lewes 1974).
27. Jeal, *Livingstone*, p. 184; Ransford, *Livingstone*, p. 172.
28. Ransford, p. 164.
29. For Livingstone's shortness of stature see Ransford, pp. 16, 241.
30. RGS 16/26.
31. See Ransford, *passim*.
32. For Robert Livingstone see Jeal, pp. 279–81; Ransford, pp. 225–7.
33. Journal, 8 January 1872.
34. Ward, *A Voice from the Congo*, p. 172.
35. Journal, 3 December.
36. Journal, 16 December.
37. Journal, 12 November.
38. Stanley suggested to Livingstone several times that he should return home to rebuild his strength.
    'No, no, no!'
    'See home, friends, country?'
    'No, no, no!'

'To be knighted by the queen and welcomed by thousands of admirers!'
'Yes but impossible! Must not, will not, cannot!' (*New York Herald*, 10
October 1877.)

39. HIFL, pp. 436–7.
40. Journal, 12–13 November.
41. Journal, 14 November.
42. Ibid.
43. 'I do not think I was made for an African explorer for I detest the land
    most heartily and I doubt whether he [Livingstone] could have a worse
    companion.' (Journal, 14 November.)
44. Journal, 14 November.
45. LLJ, ii, p. 157.
46. Livingstone to Agnes Livingstone, 18 November 1871, Add. MSS. 50, 184
    f. 174: 'He came with the American characteristic generosity. The tears
    often started into my eyes on every fresh proof of kindness.'
47. Journal, 15 November.
48. Mukamba of Usige in Burundi had earlier defeated the Arabs (LLJ, ii,
    pp. 13–16).
49. Journal, 16 November.
50. HIFL, pp. 479–80.
51. Journal, 16 November; HIFL, p. 482–3.
52. HIFL, pp. 483–5.
53. 'The Wajiji inhale tobacco through their nose. Only occasionally is a pipe
    seen. A treatise could be written on African pipe smoking. As far as
    Unyanyembe the people use a pipe similar to the Cheyenne pipe. In
    Ukorongo they use a pipe that may be said to resemble the funnel of a
    miniature steamer. In Uriri we begin to see people holding their fingers to
    their noses as if they were an abomination to be near us.' (Journal, 19
    November). The modern research on the topic is provided in John Edward
    Philips, 'African Smoking and Pipes', *Journal of African History* 24 (1983),
    pp. 303–19.
54. Journal, 20 November.
55. HIFL, p. 487.
56. LLJ, ii, p. 158.
57. Journal, 21 November.
58. LLJ, ii, p. 158; HIFL, pp. 491–3.
59. HIFL, p. 494.
60. Journal, 23–6 November; LLJ, ii, p. 158; HIFL, pp. 494–7.
61. Journal, 26 November; HIFL, p. 498.
62. Mukamba's successor Mvurumba was for this reason hostile to later
    European visitors (Huntley to LMS, 19 October 1879, LMS archives; cf.
    also Pierre Leroy, 'Stanley et Livingstone en Urundi', *Lovania* 43 (1957),
    pp. 23–44).

63. *New York Herald*, 15 July 1872.
64. Journal, 27–8 November.
65. See Burton, 'Lake Regions', pp. 17, 254; Speke, *What Led*, pp. 246–7.
66. LLJ, ii, p. 159; HIFL, pp. 503–4.
67. HIFL, pp. 501–3, 506.
68. Journal, 29–30 November.
69. Journal, 1–4 December.
70. LLJ, ii, p. 159; Journal, 3, 5 December.
71. Journal, 29 November.
72. Journal, 8 December.
73. Journal, 3 December.
74. 'There. We have a proof of the way servants behave when their masters are absent. I should never have believed had I not seen it that Selim would have behaved in that way. Clearly the Christian religion has not had much effect on him.' (Journal, 2 December.)
75. See R. Bourgeois, *Banyarwanda et Burundi*, 2 vols (Brussels 1957); William Roger Louis, *Ruanda-Urundi* (Oxford 1963); Jan Vansina, 'Notes sur l'histoire du Burundi', *Aequatoria* 24 (1961), pp. 1–10.
76. HIFL, p. 507.
77. LLJ, ii, p. 160.
78. For the Wasansi see Edward Coole Hore, 'On the Twelve Tribes of Tanganyika', *JRAI* 12, pp. 2–21; Vansina, *Introduction à l'Ethnographie du Congo*, Chapter 7.
79. HIFL, pp. 511–13.
80. LLJ, ii, p. 161; Journal, 12 December.
81. LLJ, ii, p. 154.
82. Journal, 13–14 December.
83. 'I had gone over battlefields, witnessed revolutions, civil wars, rebellions, *émeutes* and massacres, stood close to the condemned murderer to record his last struggles and last signs; but never had I been called to record anything that moved me so much as this man's woes and sufferings, his privations and disappointments, which now were poured into my ear.' (HIFL, p. 425.)
84. *New York Herald*, 14 October 1877.
85. 'From being hated and thwarted in every possible way by Arabs and half-castes upon first arrival in Ujiji, through his uniform kindness and mild pleasant temper he has now won all hearts. I perceived that universal respect was paid to him by all.' (Bennett, *Stanley's Despatches*, p. 98.)
86. HIFL, p. 515.
87. Stanley, 'Twenty-Five Years Progress in Equatorial Africa', *Atlantic Monthly* 80 (1897), pp. 471–84 (at p. 472). Interestingly, Kirk shared Stanley's horror of miscegenation and castigated the Swiss trader Philippe

Broyon for taking an African 'wife' and thus producing half-caste children (Kirk to Salisbury, 5 March 1879, F.O. 84/1547).

88. Journal, 14 December; HIFL, pp. 477–8.
89. *New York Herald*, 15 July 1872.
90. Journal, 15 December.
91. Journal, 17 December.
92. Journal, 16 December.
93. Journal, 17, 18, 20 December.
94. Journal, 18 December.
95. Journal, 12 February 1872.
96. See Livingstone, *Missionary Travels*.
97. Journal, 21 December.
98. Stanley's repelled fascination with crocodiles continued. In the Stanley papers is an unpublished five-page 'monograph' on the reptiles. His and Livingstone's revulsion was shared by other eminent Victorians. 'Crocodiles and rattlesnakes and pythons are at this moment vessels of life as real as we are; their loathsome existence fills every minute of every day that drags its length along; and whenever they or other wild beasts clutch their living prey, the deadly horror which an agitated melancholic feels is literally right reaction on the situation. It may indeed be that no religious reconciliation with the absolute totality of things is possible. Some evils, indeed, are ministerial to higher forms of good but it may be that there are forms of evil so extreme as to enter into no good system whatsoever, and that in respect of such evil, dumb submission or neglect to notice is the only practical recourse.' (William James, *Varieties of Religious Experience* (1935), p. 199.)
99. The daily shaving appealed to Stanley with his mania for neatness. In his later career, Stanley reproved Herbert Ward for his failure to adhere to the custom. Looking meaningfully at Ward's bristly chin, he said: 'Dr Livingstone, you know, used to shave *every* morning.' (Ward, *A Voice from the Congo*, p. 164.)
100. *New York Herald*, 15 August 1872.
101. See Stanley's letter to Harry Johnston, 15 February 1885, when he says that Livingstone 'died before he was able to lend ear and be drawn to say unjust things. (Roland Oliver, *Six Unpublished Letters of H. M. Stanley*.) (Brussels 1957).
102. Journal, 8 December.
103. *Autobiography*, p. 295.

Chapter nine

1. Journal, 25 December; HIFL, p. 565; cf. LLJ, ii, p. 161: 'Had but a sorry Christmas yesterday.'

2. Journal, 27–8 December; HIFL, p. 568.
3. Journal, 28–9 December; HIFL, pp. 569–70.
4. Journal, 30–31 December.
5. Journal, 1–3 January 1872; HIFL, pp. 575–6; cf. LLJ, ii, p. 162: 'Mr Stanley shot a fat zebra, its meat was very good.'
6. Journal, 7 January; LLJ, ii, p. 163; HIFL, pp. 567–78.
7. Journal, 9–11 January; HIFL, pp. 578–9.
8. Journal, 6–8 January.
9. Journal, 6 January.
10. Ibid.
11. HIFL, pp. 580–81.
12. Journal, 12–13 January; HIFL, pp. 581–2.
13. Journal, 14–16 January.
14. HIFL, p. 586.
15. Journal, 17 January.
16. HIFL, p. 587.
17. Ibid., p. 588.
18. Journal, 19 January.
19. LLJ, ii, p. 165; Journal, 21 January.
20. HIFL, pp. 590–91.
21. Ibid., pp. 593–4; Journal, 22 January.
22. LLJ, ii, p. 165. For the 'Livingstone pills' see LLJ, i, p. 177.
23. HIFL, p. 595.
24. LLJ, ii, p. 165.
25. Journal, 27 January.
26. Journal, 28–31 January; LLJ, ii, p. 166.
27. Journal, 1 February.
28. Journal, 1–2 February.
29. HIFL, p. 601.
30. LLJ, ii, pp. 166–7; HIFL, p. 598.
31. Journal, 7 February; HIFL, p. 602.
32. LLJ, ii, p. 167; HIFL, p. 603; Journal, 8–9 February.
33. Journal, 9 February.
34. Bennett, *Mirambo*, pp. 57–8.
35. Journal, 12 February.
36. Journal, 11 February.
37. Journal, 13 February.
38. HIFL, p. 606.
39. Journal, 14 February.
40. Ibid. Cf. also Olivier de Bouveignes, 'Deux lettres inédites de Stanley sur le façon dont il découvert Livingstone dans "Afrique Centrale"', *Brousse* 1–2 (1947), pp. 9–40.
41. Journal, 14 February.

42. *New York Herald*, 15 July 1872.
43. HIFL, p. 612.
44. LLJ, ii, pp. 171–2.
45. See Thomson, *To the Central African Lakes and Back*, ii, pp. 249–51. Cf. also F. Longland, 'A Note on the *tembe* at Kwihara', *TNR* (1936), pp. 84–6; R. B. Richardson, 'Livingstone's *tembe* at Kwihara, Tabora', *TNR* 9 (1940). The *tembe* later became a favourite sightseeing spot for European travellers. See Michael Davie, ed., *The Diaries of Evelyn Waugh* (1976), p. 349: '30 January 1931. Drove to ruined house where Stanley and Livingstone lived.'
46. Journal, 19 February; HIFL, p. 612.
47. Add. MSS. 50, 184 f. 184.
48. 'Though I have hung my balance scales temptingly before his eyes, I have never been able to get him to weigh himself.' (*New York Herald*, 15 July 1872.)
49. Journal, 20 February.
50. Journal, 21 February.
51. Journal, 8 March; cf. also *PRGS* 12 (1890), p. 331.
52. Journal, 4 March.
53. *Autobiography*, p. 274.
54. Journal, 3 March.
55. *Autobiography*, p. 276.
56. There is a long series of letters in the Zanzibar archives (copies at RCS) laying out the basis of Livingstone's complaints.
57. Livingstone to Agnes Livingstone, 18 November 1871, Add. MSS. 50, 184 f. 175. The letter to Lord Granville (14 November 1871) merely treats of Granville's succession on the death of Lord Clarendon (F.O. 2/49B ff. 76–83).
58. Livingstone to Stanley, 1 January 1873, in *The Times*, 7 April 1874.
59. Add. MSS. 50, 184 f. 182.
60. HIFL, p. 562.
61. Livingstone to Waller, November 1871, February 1872. Waller Papers, Rhodes House, Oxford (hereinafter W.P.), i, ff. 174–5.
62. Livingstone to Waller, 7 November 1871, 8 March 1872, W. P. ibid.
63. Livingstone to Lord Granville, 20 February 1872, F.O. 2/49B ff. 89–98.
64. HIFL, pp. 707–8.
65. Livingstone to Gordon Bennett, 9 April 1872 in *The Times*, 10 April 1874.
66. Journal, 26 February.
67. 'Doctor said he often wished to be buried in the depths of the still forests of Africa – in England there was no elbow room.' (Journal, 31 February.)
68. Journal, 24 February.
69. Journal, 2 March.
70. Miscellaneous notes, SFA.
71. Journal, 5–6 March.

72. Livingstone to Stanley, 15, 16 March, SFA.
73. *Autobiography*, p. 284.
74. Journal, 11 March.
75. *Autobiography*, p. 279.
76. Journal, 13 March.
77. *Autobiography*, p. 280.
78. Journal, 14 March.
79. Livingstone to Rev. W. Thompson, November 1872, LMS Archives.
80. Add. MSS. 50, 184 f. 188; W.P. i. f. 180.
81. Livingstone to Agnes Livingstone, 2 June 1872, Add. MSS. 50, 184 f. 186.
82. Livingstone to Waller, 2 September 1872, W.P. ii. f. 180.
83. Miscellaneous notes, SFA.
84. Journal, 14 March.
85. Stanley to Livingstone, 15 March 1872, SFA. There is a heavily edited (by Dorothy Stanley) copy in RGS 16/9.

Chapter ten

1. Journal, 15–18 March.
2. Journal, 20–24 March.
3. 'On the road the women exhibited the most profound emotion when after running perhaps half a mile or so to gain sight of the wonderful white man they uttered just such a sound as I have heard some ladies in America when they for the first time saw a magnificent painting. Phonetically the sound is spelt "Augh".' (Miscellaneous notes, SFA.)
4. HIFL, pp. 631–2.
5. Ibid., pp. 633–4.
6. Journal, 2 April.
7. HIFL, pp. 637–8.
8. Journal, 3–5 April.
9. HIFL, pp. 639–40. 'Poor Farquahar. A sad fate was his, and all for his lust for brandy.' (Journal, 7 April.)
10. Journal, 10–11 April.
11. HIFL, p. 641.
12. Journal, 12 April.
13. HIFL, p. 642.
14. Ibid., p. 643.
15. Ibid., p. 644.
16. Journal, 14–21 April.
17. HIFL, p. 645.
18. Journal, 23 April.
19. Journal, 25 April. For Simbawenni a few years after its destruction see Dodgshun Journal, 4 September 1878, pp. 80–81.

20. HIFL, pp. 648–9.
21. Bennett, *Stanley Despatches*, p. 124.
22. Ibid.
23. New to New, 22 April 1872, ZA (RCS); Stanley to Livingstone, 25 May 1872, NLS 10705 ff. 7–12.
24. HIFL, p. 653.
25. Rawlinson to Kirk, 15 December 1871; Kirk to Murchison, 25 September 1871, ZA (RCS); cf. also *PRGS* (1871–2), pp. 102–3, 159–60, 226. The request from Stanley for medical supplies (Stanley to Dr Christie, 14 August 1871 (ZA)) seemed merely to underline the hopelessness of his position.
26. But New alleged that Dawson was unfit to head a relief expedition for Livingstone as he was interested only in hunting buffalo and elephants (New to Stanley, n.d. ZA (RCS)).
27. Charles New, *Life, Wanderings and Labours in Eastern Africa* (1873, new ed. 1971, ed. Alison Smith), p. 511.
28. HIFL, p. 654.
29. New, *Life and Wanderings*, p. 515.
30. 'This is quite extraordinary,' Stanley said of Oswell Livingstone's decision (Journal, 19 May); cf. HIFL, p. 673.
31. HIFL, p. 663. For an analysis of Fraser see Coupland, *Livingstone's Last Journey*, pp. 151–2.
32. Journal, 8 May.
33. Journal, 21, 23, 27 May.
34. HIFL, p. 707.
35. Ibid., p. 675.
36. Kirk to Granville, 9, 18 May, HIFL, pp. 708–10.
37. New, *Life and Wanderings*, p. 518.
38. Stanley to Livingstone, 25 May 1872, NLS 10705 ff. 7–12.
39. Journal, 25, 28 May.
40. Journal, 29 May.
41. New, *Life and Wanderings*, pp. 519–22. Henn put up in a hotel (HIFL, p. 678).
42. Journal, 12, 14 June.
43. Journal, 2 July.
44. Journal, 9 July.
45. Journal, 10 July.
46. HIFL, p. 669.
47. The porters' loads could be as much as 70 pounds, a staggering weight in itself, quite apart from its bulk and awkwardness. The highest recorded weight for a single porter was 80 pounds (W. A. Chanler, *Through Jungle and Desert* (1896), p. 33).
48. See also Clark to Wright, 27 September 1876, C.A. 6/07, LMS Archives.
49. There is a good example in Jackson, *Meteor*, p. 71.

50. The 'pond' described by Stanley in western Tura (HIFL, p. 215) is in fact a swamp (see *Meteor*, pp. 248–9).
51. *PRGS* 18 (1873–4), p. 178.
52. *New York Herald*, 10 August 1872.
53. Thomson, *To the Central African Lakes and Back*, ii, p. 281.
54. *PRGS* 18 (1873–4), p. 70.
55. Edward C. Hore, *Tanganyika* (1892), p. 58.
56. Jackson, *Meteor*, pp. 63–4.
57. Ibid., p. 242.
58. Ibid., p. 187.
59. See Wilhelm Blohm, *Die Nyamwezi. Land und Wirtschaft*, pp. 8–10; Fr. Bösch, *Les Banyamwezi* (Munster 1930), pp. 3–9.
60. For Stanley's general accuracy on place names and the marginal corrections needed see Aylward Shorter, *Chiefship in Western Tanzania: A Political History of the Kimbu* (Oxford 1972), pp. 168, 264.
61. Stanley's 'Southern Gombe' was later modified to Iragalla and the Gombe proper assigned to what he called 'Northern Gombe' (Richard Böhm, *Von Sansibar zum Tanganyika* (Leipzig 1888), pp. 56, 63).
62. For example, Stanley makes one brief passing reference to the Wasegura or Zigula, the people living between the Iruvu and Wami Rivers (see Oscar Baumann, *Der Sansibar Archipel. Vol. 3 Die Insel Pemba un ihre Kleineren Nachbarinseln* (Leipzig 1897), p. 97; Beidelman, *Matrilineal Peoples of Eastern Tanzania* pp. 66–72).
63. HIFL, p. 257. For the Kimbu see Aylward Shorter, *Chiefship in Western Tanzania*; cf. also J. P. Moffet, ed., *Handbook of Tanganyika*, 2nd ed. (1958); Burton 'Lake Regions'; Cameron, *Across Africa*, i, pp. 127–8, ii, pp. 295–6; Roland Oliver, 'Discernible Developments in the Interior c. 1500–1840', in R. Oliver and G. Mathew, eds, *History of East Africa*, Vol. 1 (Oxford 1963).
64. As an example of this among the Nyamwezi see 'Isike, *Ntemi* of Unyanyembe', in Mark Karp, ed., *African Dimensions: Essays in Honor of William O. Brown* (Boston 1975).
65. Shorter, *Chiefship in Western Tanzania*, pp. 269–82.
66. 'I was thus prepared to admit any black man, possessing the attributes of pure manhood or any good qualities, to my friendship, even to a brotherhood with myself, and to respect him for such, as much as if he were my own colour and race.' (HIFL, p. 10.) For Stanley's sympathy for blacks see also Brom, *Sur les traces*, pp. 289–91.
67. Congo Journal, 25 October 1883, SFA.
68. For this general theme see Howard Lamar and Leonard Thompson, *The Frontier in History; North America and Southern Africa compared* (Yale 1981). Stanley said that if Malthus had ever seen Africa's vast open spaces 'he would never have penned that foolish pamphlet of his about legislating for the prevention of early marriages and raved like "Adversity Hume" about

overcrowded populations and certain ruin to England. If there are too many English-speaking people in any one place I . . . know that stout elbows will make room elsewhere, let the weal or woe of those who withstand them light where it may. There are plenty of Hengists and Horsas, Captain John Smiths and Pilgrim Fathers among the Anglo-Saxon race yet, and when America is filled up with their descendants, who shall say that Africa, and especially this glorious part of it, shall not be their next resting place.' (HIFL, pp. 112–13.)

69. HIFL, p. 61.
70. For other early reports of the tsetse fly (apart from HIFL, pp. 87–91) see Speke, *Journal of the Discovery of the Source of the Nile*, p. 41; Isabel Burton, *Life of Captain Sir Richard Burton* (1893), i, pp. 285–6.
71. Kirk to Mackinnon, 29 July 1876, Mackinnon Papers Box 22.
72. Kirk to F.O., 28 March 1878, F.O. 84/1514. For the debate on the tsetse fly (and the difficulties in identifying it) see Edwin W. Smith, *Great Lion of Bechuanaland: the life and times of Roger Price, missionary* (1957), pp. 251–5.
73. I. Schapera, *Livingstone's Private Journals 1851–53*, p. 64; H. H. Johnston, *Livingstone and the Exploration of Central Africa* (1891), pp. 47, 107.
74. Jackson, *Meteor*, pp. 244–5.
75. See e.g. HIFL, p. 259.
76. Later he made a point of twitting E. J. Glave on his mania for big game (Ward, *A Voice from the Congo*, p. 168).
77. *New York Herald*, 9 August 1872.
78. Alan C. Cairns, *Prelude to Imperialism*, p. 44.
79. Wassermann, *Bula Matari*, pp. 216–17.
80. 'His intercourse with the females of Unyanyembe put the last finishing touch to his enfeebled frame.' (*New York Herald*, 9 August 1872.)
81. *Autobiography*, p. 351.
82. Stanley to H. H. Johnston, 15 February 1885, Oliver, *Six Unpublished Letters*; cf. Ward, *A Voice from the Congo*, p. 157: 'He appeared to take it as an accepted fact that every man's hand was against him.'

Chapter eleven

1. Journal, 15 July 1872.
2. Journal, 18 July.
3. New, *Life and Wanderings*, p. 522.
4. *Daily Telegraph*, 25, 27 July; John Camden Hotten (officially Anon), *Life and Finding of Dr Livingstone* (1874), p. 147.
5. Journal, 24 July.
6. Journal, 27 July.
7. Cadwalader Rowlands, pp. 155–6.
8. Journal, 28–30 July.

9. Journal, 29 July.
10. Ibid.
11. Journal, 31 July.
12. Camden Hotten, *Life and Finding*, p. 168.
13. See the remarks of Sir Henry Rawlinson: 'Those who know Mr Stanley personally are much impressed with his determined character and his aptitude for African travel . . . I need hardly add that if he succeeds in restoring Livingstone to us, or in assisting him to solve the great problem of the upper drainage into the Nile and Congo, he will be welcomed by this society as heartily and warmly as if he were an English explorer acting under our own immediate auspices.' (*PRGS* 16 (1871–2), p. 88).
14. 'I put considerable faith in the little American Stanley. I had spoken to him during the Abyssinian war and he has a very sharp fellow "Bombay" – Speke's factotum – along with him. Bombay is a man of great influence with the natives and I do hope he will carry Stanley through to Livingstone.' (Grant to Rawlinson, 14 December 1871, RGS.)
15. *PRGS* 16 (1871–2), p. 421.
16. 'I see by the Times that Stanley has arrived with Livingstone's son at Aden in Suez [*sic*] – and feel much disappointed that young Livingstone should have left his father to his fate . . . no one believes that Stanley has found Livingstone.' (Grant to Bates, 12 July 1872, RGS). Cf. also Grant to Bates, 25 July 1872, RGS: 'You will have a difficult part to play with Stanley but if I were you, I would recommend that the RGS have nothing to say to him unless he produces letters written by Livingstone himself.'
17. *PRGS* 16 (1871–2), pp. 241, 370; *Standard*, 27 July 1872; *Echo*, 26 July 1872.
18. Journal, 1 August.
19. These letters were published in *Parliamentary Papers*, Session 1872, vol. lxx (C. 598), pp. 10–24.
20. Journal, 2 August.
21. *PRGS* 16 (1871–2), pp. 433–6.
22. Kirk to Granville, 28 May 1872, *PRGS* 16 (1871–2), pp. 436–7.
23. Livingstone to Granville, 1 July 1872, ibid., pp. 437–40; Livingstone to Bartle Frere, ibid., p. 440. For other Livingstone letters to Bartle Frere see *The Times*, 9 August 1872.
24. *Correspondence concerning Sir Bartle Frere's Mission 1873* (C. 820), p. 49–51.
25. Coupland, *Livingstone's Last Journey*, pp. 212–14.
26. W.P. i. ff. 174–81.
27. Ibid. ff. 227–8.
28. Journal, 1 August. American editors burlesqued this piece of vainglory by changing 'steel head' to 'brass head'.
29. Waller to Livingstone, 12 August 1872, W.P. i. ff. 233–4.
30. Ibid. ff. 235–9. There is a sameness about the sanctimonious way in which

Kirk's supporters endorsed the theory of his infallibility that smacks of protesting too much. Cf. Dawson's report to the RGS: 'If in Mr Stanley he [Livingstone] has found a firmer or more trusty friend than in Dr Kirk, Mr Stanley must be a friend indeed.' (*PRGS* 16 (1871–2), p. 420.)

31. Waller to Bates, August 1872, RGS: 'We may, I think, make our minds quite easy and not encourage any doubts.'
32. Journal, 2, 6, 7 August.
33. Journal, 7 August; Edward Marston, *After Work* (1904), pp. 204–9. Mr Robert Cooke of Murray's eventually replied and said he regretted Stanley had not been able to postpone a decision until 20 August. 'And I in want of money to appease the demands of living in London, in a whirl of cabs, soirees, dinners, dress clothes and gloves!' (Journal, 10 August.)
34. Journal, 7 August; for progress on Hotten's book see *The Times*, 12 November 1872.
35. Journal, 7 August.
36. Journal, 12 August.
37. Journal, 7 August.
38. Emin Pasha Journal, January 1890, SFA.
39. Journal, 7, 10 August.
40. Rawlinson to Stanley, 2 August 1872, SFA.
41. Others present were (naturally) all the luminaries of the RGS (Galton, Rawlinson, Markham, Beke), Johnston of the Johnston's Atlas, Admiral Ammany of the Franklin Search Expedition and Petherick of the Nile (Journal, 16 August).
42. *The Times*, 17 August 1872.
43. Francis Galton, *Memories of My Life* (1908), pp. 206–7.
44. *Brighton Daily News*, 17 August 1872.
45. *Glasgow Herald*, 17 August 1872.
46. *The Scotsman*, 17 August 1872.
47. *The Times*, 17 August 1872.
48. Journal, 18 August.
49. Journal, 17 August.
50. *Brighton Daily News*, 22 August 1872.
51. Journal, 18 August.
52. Grant to Bates, 21 August 1872, RGS.
53. HIFL, pp. 688–9; *The Times*, 21, 22, 23 August 1872.
54. *The Times*, 3, 4 September 1872.
55. *Daily Telegraph*, 27 August 1872.
56. Journal, 18 August.
57. Journal, 26 October.
58. *New York Herald*, 6, 25 July 1872.
59. *The Graphic*, 17 August 1872; *Hamilton Advertiser*, 26 October 1872.
60. *Glasgow Herald*, 5 August 1872.

61. *The Times*, 7 November 1872.
62. *Manchester Examiner*, 27 August 1872.
63. W. R. Carpenter to Galton, 8 September 1872 in D. W. Forrest, *Francis Galton, the Life and Work of a Victorian Genius* (1974), pp. 118–19.
64. 'A medaller of the RGS is expected to be able to fix his latitudes, longitudes, heights above the sea etc, etc. with scientific precision, by observing meridian altitudes, lunar distances, etc, etc.'
65. Stanley to Markham, 5 September 1872 in Forrest, *Galton*, p. 118.
66. Markham to Stanley, 5 September 1872, SFA.
67. Markham to Stanley, September 1872, SFA; cf. also Journal, 13 September.
68. *Manchester Examiner*, 2 September 1872.
69. *New York Herald*, 19 September, 11 December 1871.
70. *New York Herald*, 23 December 1871.
71. *New York Herald*, 13 February 1872.
72. For Southworth see Alvan S. Southworth, *Four Thousand Miles of African Travel* (New York 1875). For his quest for Baker see *New York Herald*, 19, 30, January 1872, 26 March 1873. The mirror image of Waller's 'steel head' speech is the following: 'I am of the opinion that twelve energetic, live, I might say reckless Americans, each with his special mental and physical gifts, could bare this whole continent to the view of an anxious mankind.' (*New York Herald*, 28 December 1871.)
73. *New York Herald*, 7 January, 14, 17 February, 5 May 1872.
74. *New York Herald*, 29 August 1872. For Dana see James H. Wilson, *The Life of Charles A. Dana* (New York 1907), p. 380.
75. *New York Herald*, 27 August 1872.
76. *New York Herald*, 2, 3, 5 July, 4, 5, 10, 16, 18, 19, 23, 27 August 1872.
77. Journal, 25 August.
78. Journal, 8 September.
79. Journal, 27 August.
80. Rawlinson to Stanley, 4 September 1872, SFA.
81. Carpenter to Galton, 12 September 1872, in Forrest, *Francis Galton*, p. 119.
82. Journal, 8, 13 September.
83. Journal, 9 September.
84. Journal, 10 September; see also *Autobiography*, pp. 289–91.
85. Journal, 11 September.
86. Ponsonby to Mrs Ponsonby, 10 September 1872, RA, Add. A/36.
87. RA U/32.
88. Queen Victoria's Journals, 1872, p. 272 (RA).
89. Journal, 12 September.
90. Journal, 22 September.
91. Journal, 27 September.

92. Clements Markham, unpublished history of the RGS (RGS).
93. Beke to Bates, 19 October 1872, RGS.
94. Grant to Rawlinson, 15 October 1872, RGS.
95. Journal, 1 October.
96. *The Times*, 30 September 1872.
97. Stanley to Markham, 5 October 1872, RGS.
98. *The Times*, 22 October 1872.
99. *PRGS* 17 (1872–3), pp. 9, 229.
100. Fredk Anderson, M. S. Frank and K. M. Sanderson, eds, *Mark Twain's Notebooks and Journals*, Vol. 1 (1855–1873), (1975), p. 542.
101. Only in HIFL does Stanley relent a little and concede that the RGS had to move with caution (HIFL, pp. 691–2).
102. *The Times*, 19 October 1872; Journal, 18 October.
103. Waller to Bates, 25 October 1872, RGS.
104. Journal, 23 October.
105. Journal, 24 October.
106. Journal, 8 September.
107. For copious details see *Glasgow Herald*, 24, 25 October 1872; *Hamilton Advertiser*, 26 October 1872; *Evening Citizen*, 24 October, 2 November 1872; *The Scotsman*, 1 November 1872.
108. Journal, 4 November.
109. See the report of Stanley's speech in St James's Hall in *The Times*, 7 November 1872.
110. Journal, 4 November.
111. Quoted in Anstruther, *I Presume*, p. 161.
112. However, in the third edition Stanley excised most of his derogatory references to Kirk.
113. *The Times*, 16 August 1872; *Glasgow Herald*, 5 August 1872.
114. *Saturday Review*, 5 July 1890.
115. Dorothy Stanley to Scott Keltie, 19 January 1914, RGS.
116. Journal, 25 August.
117. Journal, 8 September.
118. Journal, 25 August.
119. Journal, 12 August.
120. Ibid.
121. Ibid.
122. 'My return from the finding of Livingstone introduced me (in 1872) to the larger world by name, a thing I had dreaded . . . I had no right to thrust myself before society, though it called for me loudly enough, for however kind it might wish to be to me, my name, birth, kindred, nationality debarred me from accepting its attention with that graceful elegance it would naturally expect.' (Emin Pasha Journal, January 1890, SFA.).
123. Journal, 1 October.

124. Frank Harris, *My Life and Loves*, p. 742.
125. Emin Pasha Journal, January 1890, SFA.
126. Ibid.
127. *The Times*, 15 November 1872.
128. *Saturday Review*, 26 October 1872.
129. W.P. i. ff. 247–8. For the *Herald*'s 'appropriation' of the Bartle Frere mission and its successful conclusion see *New York Herald*, 13 April, 13 August, 5 November 1872, 2 January, 18 June 1873.
130. *The Times*, 4 July 1861.
131. A. Z. Fraser, *Livingstone and Newstead* (1913), p. 196.
132. Ibid. pp. 192–8.
133. Hall, *Stanley*, p. 229.

Chapter twelve

1. *Autobiography*, p. 289.
2. Anstruther, *I Presume*, p. 146.
3. RGS 13/2.
4. Journal, 14 November.
5. Thomas Stevens, *Scouting for Stanley in East Africa* (1890), p. 262.
6. Ibid., p. 263.
7. Journal, 21–2 November.
8. Journal, 21 November.
9. Don C. Seitz, *The James Gordon Bennetts*, p. 300.
10. *New York Herald*, 29 July, 6 October 1872.
11. *New York Herald*, 21 November 1872.
12. For details see *New York Herald*, 23, 25, 27, 28 November 1872.
13. *New York Herald*, 22 November 1872; for Kalulu's earlier wrestling with English clothes see *Glasgow Herald*, 5 August 1872.
14. Stanley to Wallace, 27 November, SFA.
15. *Nonconformist*, 4 August 1872.
16. *Evening Citizen*, 1 November 1872.
17. *New York Evening Mail*, 4 December 1872.
18. *New York Tribune*, 4 December 1872.
19. *New York Times*, 4 December 1872.
20. Anstruther, p. 176.
21. *New York Herald*, 4 December 1872.
22. Anon, *Henry M. Stanley's American Lectures on the Discovery of Dr Livingstone* (New York 1872).
23. *New York Times*, 5 December 1872; *New York Herald*, 5 December 1872.
24. *New York Sun*, 7 December; *New York Evening Mail*, 7 December.
25. *Sunday Mercury*, 8 December 1872.

26. Anstruther, p. 174.
27. *New York Evening Mail*, 6 December 1872.
28. Journal, 1 January 1873.
29. *New York Herald*, 17, 18 December 1872.
30. *New York Herald*, 14, 15 January 1873; Anstruther, pp. 178–81.
31. *My Kalulu, King and Slave* (1873).
32. Journal, April 1873.
33. Journal, 8 April 1873.
34. Fraser, *Livingstone and Newstead*, pp. 199–201.
35. Journal, 12 May 1873.
36. Journal, 2 May 1873.
37. Journal, 25 February 1874.
38. *New York Herald*, 27 January 1874.
39. Coupland, *Livingstone's Last Journey*, pp. 247–53.
40. Journal, 9–10 March 1874.
41. Stanley to Agnes Livingstone, 18 March 1874, NLS 10705 f. 15.
42. *New York Herald*, 7 April 1874.
43. Journal, 11 April.
44. *New York Herald*, 16, 19 April 1874.
45. For Moffatt see Cecil Northcott, *Robert Moffatt, Pioneer in Africa 1817–1870* (1961).
46. *New York Herald*, 20, 29, 30 April, 1 May 1874. Stanley was very low in spirits at this time and was encouraged to be positive by Vincent Roys of the Savage Club (RGS 16/17). For correspondence on RGS on being a pall-bearer at the state funeral of Livingstone see Stanley to Bates, 6 April 1874, RGS. Incidentally, there was considerable irony in Livingstone's being placed next to Marshal Wade, since his great-grandfather had been 'out' with Prince Charlie in the '45.
47. At the funeral Sir Edwin Arnold remarked: 'This passing crowd thinks that Livingstone's work is done, that it lies beneath the flowers which we have placed on his grave. No, my son, it has only just begun, and there is one man who is capable of finishing that for which Livingstone strove. To that great task I will persuade him.' (Julian B. Arnold, *Giants in a Dressing Gown* (1942) p. 74.
48. For Arnold see Brooks Wright, *Interpreter of Buddhism to the West: Sir Edwin Arnold* (New York 1957).
49. Arnold, *Giants*, p. 74.
50. *Autobiography*, pp. 297–8.
51. *New York Herald*, 26 July 1874.
52. See Clara Burdett Patterson, *Angela Burdett-Coutts and the Victorians* (1953).
53. For Mackinnon see J. S. Galbraith, *Mackinnon and East Africa, 1878–1895* (Cambridge 1972); also *Biographie Coloniale Belge*, 5 vols (Brussels 1948–58), i, pp. 627–30; Maria J. Kiewet, 'History of the Imperial British East

African Company 1876–1895', unpublished PhD thesis, University of London 1955.

54. Boyd Cable, *A Hundred Year History of the P & O* (1937), pp. 170, 175.
55. *New York Herald*, 24 December 1874.
56. Ibid.
57. *Through the Dark Continent* (1899 edition, hereinafter TDC), 2 vols, i, p. 5.
58. Arnold, *Giants*, p. 75; TDC i, p. 4.
59. Stanley to Virginia Ambella, May 1874, SFA.
60. *Saturday Review*, 5 July 1890.
61. Journal, 13 May.
62. Journal, May 1874.
63. Ibid.
64. Journal, 13 June.
65. Journal, 16, 19, 25 June, 4 July.
66. Journal, 8 July.
67. Journal, 11 July.
68. Journal, 17 July.
69. Ibid.
70. Journal, 18 July.

Chapter thirteen

1. TDC, i, p. 6.
2. Journal, 4–5 August; Edward Pocock Diary (Rhodes House, MSS. Afr. 1522), ii, Frank Pocock Diary (ibid., hereinafter PD), p. 1. For the Pococks and Barker in general see *Biographie Coloniale Belge*, ii, pp. 775–8, iii, pp. 30–31.
3. Stanley to Mackinnon, 14 August 1874, MP/55.
4. TDC, i, p. 48.
5. For the Bartle Frere mission see John Martineau, *The Life and Correspondence of Sir Bartle Frere*, 2 vols (1895); R. J. Gavin, 'The Bartle Frere mission to Zanzibar', *Historical Journal* 5 (1962), pp. 122–48; N. R. Bennett, 'Charles de Vienne and the Frere mission to Zanzibar', *Boston University Papers on Africa* 2 (1966), pp. 109–221.
6. For Steere's popularity see Kirk to Hill, 29 August 1883, F.O. 84/1619.
7. TDC, i, p. 29.
8. *New York Herald*, 24 December 1874. For the district of Shangani see Thomson, *African Lakes*, i, p. 18.
9. 'It is to the *wangwana* that Livingstone, Burton, Speke and Grant owe, in great part, the accomplishments of their objectives.' (TDC i, p. 41.) Stanley adds that if the *wangwana* were superior as escorts the Wanyamwezi were better as porters since they were stronger and more resistant to disease.

10. And was later to serve with the Church Missionary Society (Smith to Wright, 22 August 1876, CA 6/M2, CMS Archives).

11. *New York Herald*, 24 December 1874.

12. TDC, i, pp. 25–9.

13. For this expedition see Journal, 23, 24, 30 September, 2 October; Edward Pocock Journal, ii-iii; PD, p. 2; *New York Herald*, 17 November 2, 3, 4 December 1874, 7 January 1875. For the Rufiji see Kirk to Derby, 20 April 1876, F.O. 84/1453; R. F. Burton, *Lake Regions*; R de la B. Barker, 'The Rufiji river', *TNR* 4 (1937), pp. 10–16.

14. H. Depage, 'Note au sujet de documents inédits relatifs à deux expéditions de H. M. Stanley en Afrique Centrale (1874–77)', *Bulletin de l'Institut Royale Coloniale Belge* 25 (1954), i, pp. 129–52.

15. TDC, i, pp. 49–52.

16. '29 October. In evening went on board *Thetis* to see a performance called Merchant of Venice.' (PD, p. 3.)

17. TDC, i, pp. 53–9, 64.

18. Ibid., pp. 59–63.

19. Bennett, *Stanley's Despatches*, p. 33.

20. Journal, 17 November 1874.

21. Stanley to Robinson, 11 November 1874, BL, RP 1100.

22. Alice Pike to Stanley, 13 October 1874, SFA.

23. Alice Pike to Stanley, 29 October 1874.

24. Alice Pike to Stanley, 2 December 1874.

25. 'Two years is such a long time to wait and I have so much to do, such a weary, weary journey to make before I can return.' (Journal, 17 July 1874.)

26. Hall, *Stanley*, pp. 93, 360–61.

27. Alice Pike to Stanley, 17 November 1877, SFA.

28. In a speech to the RGS on 27 March 1878 Stanley promoted the image of the Masai as 'a tribe that specially delights in blood' and compared them to the Apache or Comanche. 'If there are any ladies or gentlemen in the Society this evening who are specially ambitious of becoming martyrs. I do not know in all my lists of travels where you could become martyrs so quickly as in Masai.' (*PRGS* 22 (1878) p. 149.) Stanley was not alone in his fearful feelings about the Masai. His old enemy Kirk called for the ending of Masai raids by a war of annihilation (Alan C. Cairns, *Prelude to Imperialism*, p. 121). The myth of the especial ferocity of the Masai was finally demolished by Joseph Thomson in his *Through Masailand* (1883).

29. For Baker's views see *Ismailia*, 2 vols (1874), ii, p. 263; for Burton's J. N. C. Baker, 'Sir Richard Burton and the Nile Sources', *EHR* 59 (1944), pp. 49–61.

30. G. Birkbeck Hill, ed., *General Gordon in Central Africa 1874–79* (1881), pp. 47–8.

31. *New York Herald*, 24 December 1874.

32. Stanley to Alice Pike, 3 January 1875, SFA; TDC, i, pp. 79–80. For the early stages of the expedition see Richard Hall and Alan Neame, *Expedition Diaries* (1961 – the bulk of Stanley's journals for 1874–7 in published form, hereinafter ED) pp. 25–61; PD, pp. 4–6; TDC, i, pp. 66–110.
33. For this battle see Stanley to Alice Pike, 4 March 1875, SFA; *Daily Telegraph*, 15 November 1875; *New York Herald*, 11 October 1875; ED, pp. 49–50; TDC, i, pp. 97–101.
34. ED, pp. 42–3, 46; TDC, i, pp. 82–3, 86–7, 90, 93–5.
35. *New York Herald*, 14 August 1876.
36. ED, pp. 60–62.
37. *New York Herald*, 14 August 1875.
38. Stanley to Alice Pike, 4 March 1875, SFA.

Chapter fourteen

1. TDC, i, p. 118.
2. Stanley to Edward King, 19 May 1875; *New York Herald*, 12 August 1876. Pocock in a letter to his brother paid tribute to the courage and fighting qualities of the Ituru people (*New York Herald*, 7 May 1877).
3. ED, p. 63.
4. *Autobiography*, pp. 306–7.
5. TDC, i, p. 124.
6. Ibid., pp. 127–33. In his despatch to the *New York Herald* Stanley oddly felt it necessary to defend himself against imagined charges of cowardice in not tangling with the hippos: 'The *Lady Alice*, if I can help it, with her delicate skin of cedar and ribs of slender hickory, shall never come in close contact with the iron-hard ivory of the hippopotamus, for she would be splintered into matches and crushed like an egg before one could say "Jack Robinson" and then the hungry crocodiles would leisurely digest us.' (*New York Herald*, 12 October 1875.)
7. C. T. Wilson and R. W. Felkin, *Uganda and the Egyptian Sudan*, 2 vols (1882), i, p. 189; Oscar Baumann, *Durch Masailand* (1894), pp. 47–50; H. von Schweinitz, *Deutsch Ost-Afrika in Krieg und Frieden*, pp. 168–71.
8. For the mixed population of Ututwa see Carl Peters, *Das Deutsch Ostafrikanische Schutzgebeit* (1895), pp. 179–81. For the Sukuma see Hans Cory, *Sukuma Law and Customs* (1953).
9. For the Speke thesis see Speke, *What Led*, esp. pp. 306, 310. For Baringo see Thomson, *Masailand*, pp. 529–36. For the Kavirondo Gulf see Thomson, p. 484.
10. For the Bantu Kavirondo see Gunter Wagner, *The Bantu of North Kavirondo*, 2 vols (1949–56).
11. ED, pp. 67–8; TDC, i, pp. 134–7.

12. ED, p. 69; TDC, i, pp. 139–42, *New York Herald*, 29 November 1875.
13. See J. F. Cunningham, *Uganda and its Peoples* (1905), pp. 129–41.
14. See the references in Speke, *Journal of the Discovery of the Source of the Nile*, pp. 459, 469, 472.
15. TDC, i, pp. 143–5.
16. ED, pp. 69–70.
17. *New York Herald*, 29 November 1875.
18. *Daily Telegraph*, 15 November 1875.
19. ED, pp. 70–71.
20. ED, p. 72; TDC, i, p. 155.
21. TDC, i, p. 153.
22. *New York Herald*, 29 November 1875.
23. Samuel Baker, whose one excursion into Bunyoro territory had been so disastrous, had the effrontery to claim that Mutesa treated Stanley in such a friendly way because he, Baker, had sent orders *requiring* the Kabaka to afford such treatment to white men (*PRG* 20 (1875–6), pp. 48–9).
24. Bellefonds Journal, 13 April 1875, SFA; cf. also Brom, *Sur les traces*, p. 144.
25. *Daily Telegraph*, 15 November 1875.
26. For the consequences of Stanley's call see R. Oliver, *The Missionary Factor in East Africa* (1965); D. A. Low, *Religion and Society in Buganda 1875–1900* (*East African Studies* 8, Kampala, n.d.). For the arrival of CMS missionaries in Uganda and their difficult time following Stanley's 1875 call see Holger Bernt Hansenn, *Mission, Church and State in a Colonial Setting* (1984), pp. 12–20. For Stanley as Mutesa's dupe see Chaillé-Long, *Central Africa* (1876), p. 310: 'Stanley has been the dupe of the artful savage.' But according to Giegler, Chaillé-Long suffered an attack of megalomania after his visit to Mutesa's court: 'He travelled to Uganda and thereby became a nine-day wonder.' (Richard Hill, ed., *The Sudan Memoirs of Carl Christian Giegler Pasha 1873–1883* (1982).) Cf. also Alan Moorehead, *The White Nile* (1964 ed., p. 140): 'There is something naive about all Stanley's dealings with Mtesa and one pauses here to wonder why it was that he got so heavily involved with a man who was at once so savage and so cynical.'
27. In *Through the Dark Continent* Stanley admitted that Mutesa's conversion had been purely nominal but refused to accept that he had been duped.
28. John Milner Gray, 'Ernest Linant de Bellefonds', *UJ* 28 (1964), p. 31–54.
29. See Margaret Chase Fullers, *The Eastern Lacustrine Bantu* (1960); Lloyd A. Fullers, ed., *The King's Men* (1964).
30. See J. M. Beattie, *Bunyoro: An African Kingdom* (New York 1960); Brian K. Taylor, *The Western Lacustrine Bantu* (1962), pp. 17–41.
31. See Gaetano Casati, *Ten Years in Equatoria and the Return with Emin Pasha*, 2 vols (1891), ii, p. 218.
32. G. Birkbeck Hill, *Gordon in Central Africa*, pp. 65, 68, 183, 192.

33. Chaillé-Long, *My Life in Four Continents*, 2 vols (1912), i, pp. 67–8; cf. also B. M. Allen, *Gordon and the Sudan* (1931), p. 93.
34. Birbeck Hill, pp. 106, 148, 150, 159, 185.
35. M. F. Shukry, ed., *Equatoria under Egyptian Rule. The Unpublished Correspondence of Colonel (later Major-General) C. G. Gordon with Ismail Khedive of Egypt and the Sudan 1874–76* (1953), pp. 281, 317.
36. TDC, i, p. 161; ED, pp. 73–4.
37. Bellefonds Journal, 13 April 1875, SFA.
38. *New York Herald*, 29 November 1875.
39. There is an impressive literature on Bellefonds in 1875. Ernest Linant de Bellefonds, 'Itinéraire et Notes. Voyage de service fait entre le poste militaire de Fasiko et la capitale de Mtesa roi d'Uganda, février-juin 1875', *Bulletin Trimestriel de la Société Khediviale de Géographie du Caire* 1 (1875–6), pp. 1–104; Linant de Bellefonds, 'Account of Stanley's visit to King Mtesa's capital', *Journal of the American Geographical Society* 7 (1876), pp. 283–9; H. B. Thomas, 'Ernest Linant de Bellefonds and Stanley's letter to the Daily Telegraph', *UJ* 2 (1934–5), pp. 7–13.
40. Bellefonds to Gordon, 25 April, 8 June 1875, Shukry, *Equatoria under Egyptian Rule*, pp. 256–7, 272.
41. For estimates of Mutesa see John Allen Rowe, 'Revolution in Buganda 1856. Part One: The Reign of Kabaka Mutesa 1856–1884', (Ph.D. dissertation, University of Wisconsin 1966); J. M. Gray, 'Mutesa of Uganda', *UJ* 1 (1934), pp. 22–50. For an overview of Stanley's visit from the African standpoint see Frederick B. Welbourne, 'Speke and Stanley at the court of Mutesa', *UJ* 25 (1961), pp. 220–23, which incorporates oral testimony taken in 1934 from a man who was then a pageboy at the court.
42. TDC, i, pp. 163–8.
43. For the Sesse see John Roscoe, *The Baganda* (1911), pp. 383–91.
44. TDC, i, pp. 170–77.
45. Ibid., pp. 178–80.
46. *New York Herald*, 9 August 1876.
47. ED, pp. 75–6.
48. *New York Herald*, 9 August 1876.
49. Ibid.
50. Ibid.
51. TDC, i, p. 185.
52. Emin Pasha Journal, 9 October 1887, SFA.
53. TDC i, p. 187.
54. ED, p. 7.
55. PD, pp. 8–11; *New York Herald*, 11 October 1875.
56. PD, pp. 8–9.
57. ED, p. 78; TDC, i, p. 191.
58. For an analysis of Kaduma see Wilson and Felkin, *Uganda*, i, pp. 81–5.

59. *New York Herald*, 15 August 1876.
60. PD, p. 12.
61. Schweinitz, *Deutsch OstAfrika*, pp. 154–61; Wilhelm Langheld, *Zwanzig Jahre in deutschen Kolonien* (Berlin 1909), p. 101.
62. After Lukongeh had destroyed a White Fathers' mission station. See Paul Kollmann, *Auf Deutschen Boden in Afrika* (Berlin n.d.), pp. 240–41, 273–6; Schweinitz, *Deutsche OstAfrika*, pp. 162–3.
63. PD, pp. 12–15.
64. ED, p. 81.
65. Wilson to Wigram, 22 February 1877, C.A. 6/025, CMS archives.
66. For the people ruled by Lukongeh see Brian K. Taylor, *The Western Lacustrine Bantu* (1962), pp. 132–48.
67. TDC, i, pp. 195–7.
68. ED, p. 82; TDC, i, p. 201.
69. *New York Herald*, 10 August 1876.
70. TDC, i, p. 203.
71. Ibid., pp. 203–4.
72. ED, p. 84.
73. ED, p. 85; TDC, 1, pp. 205–6.
74. TDC, i, p. 207.
75. PD, pp. 18–19.
76. TDC, i, pp. 208–9.
77. ED, p. 87.
78. *New York Herald*, 10 August 1876.
79. For Kijaju see Peters, *Deutsch Ostafrikanische Schutzgebeit*, p. 186.
80. PD, p. 20; TDC, i, pp. 210–11.
81. TDC, i, pp. 211–13.
82. Ibid., pp. 215–16.
83. ED, pp. 88–90.
84. For Sabadu, killed in the Ganda troubles of 1888, see R. P. Ashe, *Chronicles of Uganda* (1894); Ashe, *Two Kings of Uganda* (1889), p. 136; cf. also J. F. Faupel, *African Holocaust* (New York 1962), p. 69.
85. ED, p. 91; TDC, i, pp. 218–221.
86. ED, p. 92; TDC, i, pp. 222–6, which contains a highly tendentious account of Stanley's motives for the attack. According to this, he agreed at the Ganda chiefs' insistence; they made it a test of his friendship for Mutesa.
87. *Daily Telegraph*, 10 August 1876.
88. ED, pp. 94–5.
89. TDC, i, pp. 227–9.
90. PD, pp. 23–4.
91. *New York Herald*, 10 August 1876.
92. ED, p. 96.
93. ED, p. 97; TDC, i, p. 231.

94. Stanley to Pocock, 18 August 1875, MSS. Afr. 1522 (s), Rhodes House, ff. 12–13.
95. PD, pp. 26–49.
96. TDC, i, pp. 232–7.
97. ED, p. 99.
98. TDC, i, p. 238, 251–5.
99. PD, pp. 43–4.
100. ED, pp. 100–101.
101. Ibid., p. 103.
102. TDC, i, pp. 264–7.
103. Stanley to Pocock, 8 October 1875, MSS. Afr. 1522 (s) f. 14.
104. ED, p. 106.
105. ED, p. 105; TDC, i, pp. 268–9.
106. PD, p. 49.

Chapter fifteen

1. Walter Rusch, *Klasser und Staat in Buganda von der Kolonialzeit* (Berlin 1975), p. 37; Frederick Lugard, *The Rise of our East African Empire*, 2 vols (1893), ii, p. 3.
2. PD, pp. 50–51.
3. For Sembuzi see Wilson and Felkin, *Uganda*, i, pp. 103, 258; John Taylor, *The Growth of the Church in Buganda* (1958), pp. 34, 36, 50. Cf. also J. F. Faupel, *African Holocaust* (New York 1962).
4. TDC, i, p. 331.
5. *New York Herald*, 14 August 1876.
6. *New York Herald*, 27 March 1877.
7. Pocock to his parents, 14 August 1875, 18 April 1876 in *New York Herald*, 14 August 1876.
8. PD, p. 51; ED, p. 107.
9. TDC, i, pp. 333–4. There were also 500 women and children.
10. Ibid., pp. 337–8.
11. PD, pp. 54–5.
12. *New York Herald*, 7 May 1877.
13. For Stanley's twenty-four hours in Ankole see Sir John Gray, 'Unpublished history of Ankole', (RCS), pp. 45–6. For the people of this area see Brian K. Taylor, *The Western Lacustrine Bantu* (1962), p. 95–114; for Mutambukwa, ruler of Ankole until 1878, see H. F. Morris, 'The Making of Ankole', *UJ* 21 (1957), pp. 1–15.
14. TDC, i, pp. 340–42.
15. B. W. Langlands, 'Early Travellers in Uganda 1860–1914', *UJ* 26 (1962), pp. 55–71.

16. ED, pp. 109–110.
17. *New York Herald*, 11 August 1876.
18. J. W. Nyakatura, *Abakamaba Bunyoro-Kitara* (St Justin PQ Canada 1947), p. 154; for Kabba Rega and his policies see A. R. Dunbar, *A History of Bunyoro Kitara* (Nairobi 1965), pp. 58 *et seq.*
19. TDC, i, pp. 344–5.
20. Emin Pasha Journal, 1 July 1889, SFA (when Stanley revisited the spot).
21. ED, pp. 110–13.
22. *New York Herald*, 11 August 1876. But Stanley had gained valuable information which he put to good use when he revisited the area in 1889 (*In Darkest Africa*, ii, pp. 193–4, 319, 325).
23. For later confirmation of Stanley's discoveries see Franz Stuhlmann, *Mit Emin Pascha ins Herz von Afrika* (Berlin 1894); H. F. Morris, *A History of Ankole* (Nairobi 1962); John Roscoe, *The Bagesu* (Cambridge 1924).
24. PD, pp. 57–9.
25. *New York Herald*, 11 August 1876; PD, p. 60; TDC, i, pp. 352–3. For Uganda's complex politics and feudal organisation see Roscoe, *The Baganda*; Wilson and Felkin, *Uganda*, Vol. 1; Speke, *Journal of the Discovery of the Source of the Nile*.
26. PD, pp. 62–4.
27. Brian K. Taylor, *The Western Lacustrine Bantu*, pp. 132–44; Hans Cory, *A History of the Bukoba District* (Mwanza, n.d.), pp. 17–34.
28. J. M. Gray, 'Ahmed bin-Ibrahim – the first Arab to reach Buganda', UJ 11 (1947), pp. 80–97; cf. also Gray, 'Trading expeditions from the coast to Lakes Tanganyika and Victoria before 1857', TNR 49 (1957), pp. 226–46.
29. For another portrait of Rumanika see Wilson to Wigram, 23 May 1878, CA6/0205, CMS archives.
30. TDC, i, pp. 358–61.
31. For this lake see Speke, *Journal of the Discovery*, p. 220; Stuhlmann, *Mit Emin Pascha*, p. 228.
32. TDC, i, pp. 361–3.
33. ED, p. 115.
34. See *Historique et chronique du Ruanda* (Astrida 1955), pp. 12–13; R. Bourgeois, *Banyarwanda et Burundi*, 2 vols (Brussels 1957), p. 167; Hans Meyer, *Die Barundi* (Leipzig 1916), p. 41; R. P. Pages, *Un royaume hamite au centre de l'Afrique* (Brussels 1933), pp. 161–4.
35. TDC, i, p. 365.
36. *New York Herald*, 11 August 1876.
37. For the Mtagata springs see Paul Kollmann, *The Victoria Nyanza* (1899), pp. 62–3.
38. See Israel K. Katoke, *The Karagwe Kingdom* (Nairobi 1975), pp. 94–8.
39. ED, p. 116.

40. TDC, i, pp. 372–5.
41. Shorter, *Chiefship in Western Tanzania*, pp. 282–3.
42. PD, p. 72.
43. Ibid., pp. 73–4.
44. TDC, i, pp. 376–81.
45. *Daily Telegraph*, 7 August 1876.
46. TDC, i, p. 386.
47. ED, p. 118.
48. TDC, i, pp. 386–7; cf. also Bennett, *Mirambo*, pp. 43, 68.
49. Stanley to Alice Pike, 2 June 1876, SFA.
50. TDC, i, pp. 388–90.
51. PD, pp. 77–80.
52. TDC, i, pp. 395–8.
53. Ibid., p. 398.
54. PD, pp. 80–82.
55. ED, p. 120.
56. TDC, ii, pp. 1–8.
57. Stanley to Alice Pike, 2 June 1876, SFA.
58. ED, p. 121.
59. Ibid., p. 122.
60. *Daily Telegraph*, 24 December 1874; *PRGS* 19 (1874–5), pp. 75–7.
61. *New York Herald*, 26 March 1877.
62. For the Lukuga see E. C. Hore, 'Lake Tanganyika', *PRGS* 4 (1882), pp. 1–28; Thomson, *To the Central African Lakes*, ii, pp. 55 *et seq*; Alex Delcommune, *Vingt Années de Vie Africaine*, 2 vols (Brussels 1922), i, pp. 504 *et seq*.
63. ED, pp. 123–5.
64. Ibid., p. 125.
65. Until 1894 when von Gotzen visited it (G. A. Graf von Gotzen, *Durch Afrika von Ost nach West* (Berlin 1895), p. 218).
66. PD, pp. 86–90.
67. *New York Herald*, 27 March 1877.
68. Stanley to Marston, 14 August 1876, SFA.
69. 'You would wonder to see how tall he is grown, he has shot up like a palm tree, and his strides would make tolerably fair yards in the absence of a yard measure.' (Stanley to Alice Pike, 14 August 1876, SFA.)
70. Stanley to Alice Pike, 14 August 1876, SFA.
71. TDC, ii, pp. 50–51.
72. ED, pp. 129–30.
73. PD, pp. 93–4.
74. TDC, ii, pp. 54–6; PD, pp. 95–7.
75. *New York Herald*, 10 October 1877.
76. See LLJ, ii, pp. 26–7, 70, 73.

77. For the Bangobano or Hombo peoples see J. Maes and O. Boone, *Les Peuplades du Congo Belge* (Brussels 1935), pp. 136–7, 369.

78. For the chimpanzees of Manyema see Georg Schweinfurth, *The Heart of Africa*, 2 vols (New York 1874), i, pp. 479, 518–22; Robert Schmidtz, *Les Bahololo* (Brussels 1912), p. 18.

79. ED, p. 131.

80. Livingstone met Tippu Tip on 29 July and 30 August 1867 (LLJ, i, pp. 222–3).

81. Heinrich Brode, *Tippoo Tib* (1907); F. Bontinck, ed., *L'Autobiographie de Hamed ben Mohammed el Murjebi* (Brussels 1974 – hereinafter Tippu Tip, *Autobiography*).

82. For the Luba see Thomas O. Reefe, *The Rainbow and the Kings: A History of the Luba Empire to 1891* (Berkeley 1981); cf. also Maes and Boone, *Les Peuplades du Congo Belge*, pp. 107–13, 347–8; Edmund Verhulpen, *Baluba et Balubaises du Katanga* (Brussels 1936); Jan Vansina, *Kingdoms of the Savanna* (Madison 1966), pp. 70 *et seq.*; Vansina, *Introduction à l'Ethnographie du Congo*, Chapter 11.

83. Brode, *Tippoo Tib*, p. 129.

84. Beverley Brown, 'Muslim Influences on Trade and Politics in the Lake Tanganyika Region', *African Historical Studies* 4 (1971), pp. 617–29. For Stanley's comments on the Manyema currency economy see TDC, ii, pp. 68–9.

85. Melvin E. Page, 'The Manyema Hordes of Tippu Tip: A Case Study in Social Stratification and the Slave Trade in Eastern Africa', *International Journal of African Studies* 7 (1974), pp. 69–84.

86. Oskar Lenz, *Wanderungen in Afrika* (Vienna 1895), p. 105; Speke, *Journal of the Discovery*, p. 11.

87. R. J. Cornet, *Maniema: Le pays des mangeurs d'hommes* (Brussels 1952), pp. 203–6.

88. Tippu Tip, *Autobiography*, p. 104.

89. V. L. Cameron, *Across Africa*, 2 vols (1877), i, pp. 147–8.

90. Tippu Tip, *Autobiography*, p. 100; Cameron, *Across Africa*, ii, pp. 1–28.

91. Otherwise he would have had to lament as did Baker of Speke: 'Why was this laurel wreath not left for me to pluck?' (Stanley to Edward King, 31 October 1876, *New York Herald*, 14 October 1877.)

92. Tippu Tip, *Autobiography*, pp. 104–5.

93. For Munza see W. Junker, *Travels in Africa during the years 1882–1886*, 3 vols (1892), iii, pp. 129–180. For the Mangbetu see Maes and Boone, pp. 270–75; P. Denis, *Histoire des Mangbetu et des Matihaga jusqu'a l'arrivée des Belges* (Tervuren 1970), pp. 63–109.

94. Jameson, *Story of the Rear Column*, p. 299.

95. TDC, ii, pp. 83–4.

96. ED, p. 135.

97. TDC, ii, pp. 85–8.
98. Ibid., pp. 89–90. For a modern journey covering exactly this terrain see John Blashford-Snell, *In the Steps of Stanley* (1975), pp. 43–5.
99. For Myinyi Dugambi of Nyangwe see R. Foskett, ed., *The Zambezi Doctors*, p. 154; Hermann von Wissmann, *Unter deutscher Flagge quer durch Afrika von West nach Ost* (Berlin 1889), p. 177. He died fighting the Belgians in 1893 (P. Ceulemans, *La question arabe et le Congo 1883–1892* (Brussels 1959), p. 177; Stuhlmann, *Mit Emin Pascha*, p. 599). For Mohammed bin Nassur of Kassessa see LLJ, ii, pp. 45, 178. For Muhammed bin Said of Mamba Mamba see Brode, *Tippoo Tib*, p. 102; Camille Coquilhat, *Sur le haut Congo* (Paris 1888), p. 429.
100. *New York Herald*, 10 October 1877.
101. For his later life see Wissmann, *Unter deutscher Flagge*, pp. 177–82; cf. also Wissmann, *My Second Journey through Equatorial Africa* (1891), p. 224.
102. Tippu Tip, *Autobiography*, p. 231; cf. also Cameron, *Across Africa*, i, p. 378, ii, pp. 2–3; LLJ, ii, p. 111; Stanley, *Autobiography*, p. 320.
103. Maes and Boone, pp. 328–31; F. M. de Thier, *Singhitini, la Stanleyville Musulmane* (Brussels 1963).
104. Emin Pasha Journal, 1 June 1887, SFA. For Stanley's various ditherings before, at, and after Nyangwe see F. Bontinck, 'Une lecture critique de Stanley', *Etudes Congolaises* 1 (1968), pp. 38–55.
105. Stanley to Edward King, 31 October 1876, *New York Herald*, 14 October 1877.
106. ED, p. 134; TDC, ii, p. 97.
107. W. Holman Bentley, *Pioneering on the Congo*, 2 vols (1900), i, pp. 115–17.
108. *New York Herald*, 9 October 1877.
109. Seven years later Stanley confessed that he was so uncertain of ultimate success that, thinking he might have to return to Lake Tanganyika, he buried twelve bottles of old brandy in Abed's courtyard (Congo Journal, 27 November 1883, SFA).

Chapter sixteen

1. It seems from internal evidence that among the men who followed Stanley down the Lualaba and on to the Congo was a handful of Ganda. See Stanley, *Tales from Africa* (1985) – originally published in 1893 as *My Dark Companions and their Strange Stories* – p. 64. For the forests through which Stanley now marched see Cameron, *Across Africa*, i, pp. 347–8; for the peoples, Maes and Boone, pp. 351–2.
2. *New York Herald*, 14 November 1877. For the unconscious's ignorance of death see Freud, S. E. 14, pp. 296.
3. TDC, ii, pp. 98–101.

4. Ibid., pp. 101–2.
5. PD, p. 101.
6. ED, p. 134.
7. ED, p. 135; TDC, ii, p. 103; cf. also Blashford-Snell, *In the Steps*, pp. 52–3.
8. ED, pp. 136–7. For the Regga see Van Overbergh and Delhaise, *Les Warega* (Brussels 1909); Maes and Boone, pp. 341–3; Vansina, *Introduction à l'Ethnographie du Congo*, Chapter 7.
9. ED, p. 136; TDC, ii, p. 106.
10. TDC, ii, pp. 107–8.
11. ED, p. 137; PD, p. 102; TDC, ii, pp. 108–9.
12. For the Songola see Maes and Boone, pp. 348–50. For the Kusu see ibid., pp. 87–90, 157–49, 185–8; Vansina, *Introduction*, Chapter 5; Edmund Verhulpen, *Baluba et Balubaises*, p. 65.
13. TDC, ii, p. 111; for the terrain between here and Vinya-Njara see Blashford-Snell, pp. 57–63.
14. TDC, ii, pp. 114–17.
15. ED, p. 138.
16. Ibid., p. 139; TDC, ii, pp. 120–21.
17. ED, p. 140; TDC, ii, pp. 122–3.
18. TDC, ii, pp. 124–5.
19. ED, p. 141; TDC, ii, p. 126.
20. TDC, ii, p. 127.
21. ED, p. 142.
22. TDC, ii, pp. 127–8.
23. Ibid., pp. 128–32.
24. ED, p. 143.
25. For Tippu Tip's experiences up to this point see Tippu Tip, *Autobiography*, pp. 105–7.
26. TDC, ii, pp. 133–4.
27. Ibid., pp. 135–6.
28. Ibid., pp. 137–8.
29. ED, p. 143.
30. TDC, ii, p. 139.
31. Ibid., pp. 140–41.
32. *Daily Telegraph*, 12 November 1877.
33. *New York Herald*, 24 November 1877.
34. TDC, ii, pp. 142–3; PD, pp. 103–4.
35. TDC, ii, p. 144.
36. *New York Herald*, 24 November 1877. For a modern view of the period 12 November–20 December 1876 see Blashford-Snell, pp. 57–63.
37. TDC, ii, pp. 145–7.
38. PD, p. 105.
39. Jameson, *Rear Column*, p. 300.

40. Tippu Tip, *Autobiography*, p. 108.
41. Ibid., p. 109.
42. Emin Pasha Journal, 1888–9. Tippu Tip (in his autobiography) claims that he sustained Stanley through periods of black despair. Stanley said, 'What do you think? How many days to the Congo?' Tippu Tip: 'Very near as the crow flies but it will take seven days to get there.' (Tippu Tip, *Autobiography*, p. 105.)
43. Journal, 27 December 1876, SFA.
44. Jameson, *Rear Column*, p. 308.
45. Jerome Becker, *La Vie en Afrique*, 2 vols (Paris 1887), ii, p. 37.
46. TDC, ii, pp. 148–51, p. 145.

Chapter seventeen

1. *Daily Telegraph*, 12 November 1877.
2. TDC, ii, pp. 155–6.
3. E. J. Glave, *Six Years of Adventure in Congoland*, pp. 35–6, 39.
4. Later, in the Belgian Congo period, the efficacy of the drums was clearly established. If a white man set out from Stanleyville for Kasongo (400 miles as the crow flies, the fact was known in Kasongo the same day by 'bush telegraph' (V. Roelens, *Notre Vieux Congo 1891–1917*, 2 vols (Namur 1948), i, pp. 118–19; cf. J. F. Carrington, *A Comparative Study of some Central African Gong Languages* (Brussels 1949).
5. ED, p. 146.
6. *Autobiography*, p. 325; for this stretch of river see Blashford-Snell, pp. 73–6.
7. ED, p. 147.
8. ED, pp. 148–9; TDC, ii, pp. 164–5.
9. TDC, ii, pp. 166–72; PD, pp. 105–6.
10. Stanley, *Congo*, ii, pp. 155–6. For the passage through Stanley Falls see also Blashford-Snell, pp. 80–91.
11. TDC, ii, pp. 172–3.
12. Ibid., p. 174.
13. ED, p. 150; TDC, ii, pp. 175–6.
14. TDC, ii, p. 177.
15. Ibid., p. 179.
16. ED, p. 151.
17. Ibid., pp. 152–4.
18. TDC, ii, pp. 181–3.
19. ED, p. 155.
20. TDC, ii, pp. 184–5.
21. Ibid., pp. 186–8.
22. Ibid., pp. 191–2.

23. ED, pp. 156–7.
24. TDC, ii, p. 195.
25. Ibid., ii, pp. 198–203.
26. Ibid., ii, pp. 204–5.
27. Ibid., pp. 207–9; cf. also Blashford-Snell, pp. 109–10.
28. ED, pp. 158–9.
29. *New York Herald*, 24 November 1877.
30. *Daily Telegraph*, 12 November 1877.
31. *Autobiography*, p. 327.
32. Congo Journal, 15 November 1883, SFA.
33. Most of this booty was lost before the expedition was over (ED, pp. 199–200).
34. TDC, ii, p. 217.
35. *New York Herald*, 24 November 1877.
36. This raises the entire vexed question of the extent and reality of cannibalism. William Arens, *The Man Eating Myth* (1979), contends that cannibalism is a myth erected on a misunderstanding of primitive witchcraft. But there are just too many well-authenticated accounts from unimpeachable sources in the Congo to make this a plausible thesis. See Coquilhat, *Sur le haut Congo*, pp. 270–74; John Weeks, *Among Congo Cannibals* (1913), pp. 69–70, 226; Ward, *A Voice from the Congo*, pp. 275–85; Jean Dybowski, *La route du Tchad* (Paris 1913), p. 102; Brom, *Sur les traces*, p. 207.
37. For the Soko see Maes and Boone, pp. 168–70; Stanley, *Congo*, ii, pp. 114–33. The explanation given by the Soko in 1883 for their belligerency is at *Congo*, ii, p. 120.
38. Ward, *A Voice from the Congo*, pp. 109–13.
39. TDC, ii, pp. 217–19.
40. ED, pp. 159–60.
41. For Rubunga's village see H. H. Johnston, *Grenfell and the Congo*, i, p. 283. For the Poto see Maes and Boone, pp. 157–9; Vansina, *Introduction*, Chapter 4.
42. ED, p. 161.
43. PD, pp. 108–9; ED, pp. 162–3.
44. TDC, ii, pp. 228–9.
45. Ibid., pp. 230–31; PD, p. 109.
46. ED, p. 164; TDC, ii, p. 232–4.
47. Stanley, *Congo*, ii, p. 82.
48. *Daily Telegraph*, 12 November 1877.
49. Brom, *Sur les traces*, pp. 259–60; Glave in 1885 found some of the Bangala still with scars and bullet wounds from this encounter (Glave, *Six Years*, pp. 165–6).
50. Congo Journal, 21 October 1883.
51. *New York Herald*, 24 November 1877.

52. Coquilhat, *Sur le haut Congo*, pp. 184–5.
53. W. Holman Bentley, *Pioneering on the Congo*, 2 vols (Oxford 1900), i, p. 64.
54. For the Bangala see H. Burssens, *Les Peuplades de l'Entre Congo-Ubangi* (1958), pp. 36–8. There is an academic controversy over the reality of the Bangala. Some deny that there is or was any such tribe, and others prefer to regard them as an example of 'super-tribalism' (Crawford Young, *Politics in the Congo: Decolonisation and Independence* (Princeton 1965), p. 242). But surely this is something of an argument *ex nihilo*. Since the people with whom Stanley fought and Coquilhat later lived were recruited into the *force publique* under the Belgian Congo, they suffered a diaspora and were probably no longer identifiable as a tribe by the time modern anthropology got to them. It was established that the people themselves never used the name 'Bangala' and that the 'Lingala' language was merely a pidgin lingua franca (John H. Weeks, *Among Congo Cannibals*, pp. 48–9, 161, 165). Confusion was probably caused by Coquilhat, who estimated a huge population of 110,000 and a vast area for the people originally identified by Stanley as living in a 10-mile string of villages. For the reality of the Bangala see Jan Vansina, *The Tio Kingdom* (1973), pp. 137, 421.
55. ED, p. 165.
56. For the Ruiki see Stanley, *Congo*, ii, pp. 31–8; H. H. Johnston, *George Grenfell and the Congo*, 2 vols (1908), i, pp. 139–45.
57. TDC, ii, pp. 240–42.
58. For the Wangata or Bolumba see Maes and Boone, pp. 338–9.
59. ED, p. 166; cf. PD, 25 February 1877, p. 111: 'Four canoes was [*sic*] sent to cut grass for the cattle and they were attacked by some ten or twelve hippopotamuses. One lifted two canoes lashed together above water, had the canoes been single it would have turned over him. Failing to capsize the two, he caught hold of the oar and crushed it in his mouth.'
60. ED, p. 167.
61. Ibid., p. 168.
62. Ibid., p. 169; PD, p. 113.
63. TDC, ii, pp. 250–51.
64. Probably by Ngobila of the Boloba (Vansina, *Tio Kingdom*, p. 409). For this stretch of river see Blashford-Snell, pp. 122–3.
65. Bentley, *Pioneering on the Congo*, i, p. 65.
66. TDC, ii, pp. 253–6.
67. *Daily Telegraph*, 12 November 1877.
68. ED, pp. 173–7; TDC, ii, pp. 263–6.
69. PD, pp. 114–18.
70. ED, p. 180.
71. Ibid.
72. TDC, ii, p. 285. For the Lower Congo see Blashford-Snell, pp. 134–53.
73. *New York Herald*, 24 November 1877.

74. PD, p. 126.
75. Ibid., pp. 114, 116, 120–21, 124.
76. TDC, ii, pp. 293–7.
77. *Daily Telegraph*, 12 November 1877.
78. ED, pp. 187–8.
79. PD, pp. 127–8.
80. TDC, ii, pp. 308–13.
81. ED, p. 189.
82. Ibid., p. 193.
83. Ward, *A Voice from the Congo*, p. 175.
84. *New York Herald*, 29 November 1877; *Daily Telegraph*, 28 November 1877.
85. Stanley to Edward Pocock, 2 September 1877, Rhodes Hse, MSS. Afr. 1522 (5) ff. 18–20.
86. ED, p. 194.
87. TDC, ii, pp. 323–4; ED, pp. 196–7.
88. ED, pp. 200–1; TDC, ii, pp. 333–4.
89. TDC, ii, p. 347.
90. ED, pp. 202–3. Cf. Stanley to Motta Veiga and Harrison, 8 August 1877: 'I am unable to express, just at present, how grateful I feel. We are so overjoyed and confused at our emotions at the sight of the stores exposed to our hungry eyes, at the sight of the rice, the fish, the rum, and for me wheat bread, butter, sardines, jam, peaches and beer. Ye Gods! Just think. Three bottles of pale ale, besides, tea and sugar.' (*New York Herald*, 12 October 1877.)

· BIBLIOGRAPHY ·

This is not a complete bibliography for Stanley's life but lists the most important sources for the years 1841–77 only.

1. Manuscript sources
Stanley Family Archives (originals at Musee Royal de l'Afrique Centrale, Tervuren, copies in British Library)
Royal Geographical Society Archives
Royal Archives, Windsor Castle
Mackinnon Papers, SOAS
Foreign Office Reports, Public Record Office
British Library, Add. MSS, RP etc.
Rhodes House, Oxford, African MSS, Waller Papers, etc.
National Library of Scotland
Royal Commonwealth Society (copies from the Zanzibar Archives)
French Foreign Office Reports, Quai d'Orsay
Church Missionary Society Archives, University of Birmingham
LMS and UCA Mission Archives, SOAS

2. Stanley's own writings
The Congo and the Founding of its Free State, 2 vols (1895)
Coomassie and Magdala (1874)
How I Found Livingstone in Central Africa (1872)
In Darkest Africa, 2 vols (1890)
My African Travels (1886)
My Dark Companions and their Strange Stories (1893)
My Early Travels in America and Asia, 2 vols (1895)
My Kalulu, King and Slave (1873)
Through the Dark Continent, 2 vols (1878)

3. Published collections of primary sources, eyewitness reports, memoirs, correspondence, etc.

Anderson, Fredk, Frank, M. S. and Sanderson, K. M., eds, *Mark Twain's Notebooks and Journals*, Vol. 1 1855–1873 (1975)

Anon, *Henry M. Stanley's American Lectures on the Discovery of Dr Livingstone* (New York 1872)

Arnold, Julian B., *Giants in a Dressing Gown* (Chicago 1942)

Baker, Samuel White, *The Albert Nyanza*, 2 vols (1866)

Baker, Samuel White, *Ismailia*, 2 vols (1874)

Barttelot, W. G., *The Life of Edmund Musgrave Barttelot* (1890)

Baumann, Oscar, *Der Sansibar Archipel*, Vol. 1. *Die Insel Mafia und ihre Kleineren Nachbainseln*; Vol. 2. *Die Insel Sansibar und ihre Kleineren Nach-barinseln*; Vol. 3. *Die Insel Pemba und ihre Kleineren Nachbarinseln* (Leipzig 1897–8)

Becker, Jerome, *La Troisième Expédition Belge au pays noir* (Brussels 1891)

Becker, Jerome, *La Vie en Afrique*, 2 vols (Brussels 1887)

Bennett, Norman R., ed., *Stanley's Despatches to the New York Herald 1871–77* (Boston 1970)

Bennett, Norman R., ed., *From Zanzibar to Ujiji. The Journal of Arthur W. Dodgshun 1877–79* (Boston 1969)

Bennett, Norman R. and Brooks, George E., eds, *New England Merchants in Africa* (Boston 1965)

Bentley, W. Holman, *Pioneering on the Congo*, 2 vols (Oxford 1900)

Böhm, Richard, *Von Sansibar zum Tanganjika* (Leipzig 1888)

Bontinck, François, ed. *L'Autobiographie de Hamed ben Mohammed el-Murjebi Tippu Tip* (Brussels 1974)

Burdo, Adolphe, *Les Arabes dans l'Afrique Centrale* (Paris 1885)

Burdo, Adolphe, *Les Belges dans l'Afrique Centrale: de Zanzibar au Lac Tanganika* (Brussels 1886)

Burton, Isabel, *The Life of Captain Sir Richard F. Burton*, 2 vols (1893)

Burton, Richard F., *The Lake Regions of Central Africa*, 2 vols (1860)

Cameron, Verney Lovett, *Across Africa*, 2 vols (1877)

Casati, Gaetano, *Ten Years in Equatoria and the Return with Emin Pasha*, 2 vols (1891)

Chaillé-Long, C., *Central Africa* (1876)

Chaillé-Long, C., *My Life in Four Continents*, 2 vols (1912)

Chamberlin, David, ed., *Some Letters from Livingstone 1840–1872* (1940)

Chanler, W. A., *Through Jungle and Desert* (1896)

Christie, James, *Cholera Epidemics in East Africa* (1875)

Coquilhat, Camille, *Sur le haut Congo* (Paris 1888)

Coulbois, François, *Dix Années en Tanganyika* (Limoges 1901)

Delcommune, Alex, *Vingt Années de Vie Africaine*, 2 vols (Brussels 1922)

Feather, A. G., *Stanley's Story* (1890, reprinted Chicago 1969)

Foskett, Reginald, ed., *The Zambezi Journals and Letters of Dr John Kirk 1858–63*, 2 vols (Edinburgh 1965)

Foskett, Reginald, ed., *The Zambezi Doctors. David Livingstone's Letters to John Kirk 1858–1872* (Edinburgh 1964)

Galton, Francis, *Memories of My Life* (1908)

George, Thomas, *The Birth, Boyhood and Younger Days of Henry Stanley* (1895)

Glave, E. J., *Six Years of Adventure in Congoland* (1893)

Gotzen, G. A. Graf von, *Durch Afrika von Ost nach West* (Berlin 1895)

Grant, Ulysses, S., *Personal Memoirs*, 2 vols (New York 1885–6)

Hall, Richard and Neame, Alan, *Expedition Diaries* (1961)

Harris, Frank, *My Life and Loves* (1964)

Heudebert, Lucien, *Vers les Grands Lacs de l'Afrique Orientale* (Paris 1900)

Heudebert, Lucien, *La Découverte du Congo* (Paris n.d.)

Hill, George Birkbeck, ed., *General Gordon in Central Africa, 1874–1879* (1881)

Hill, Richard, ed., *The Sudan Memoirs of Carl Christian Giegler Pasha 1873–1883* (1982)

Hoffman, William, *With Stanley in Africa* (1938)

Hore, Edward Coode, *Tanganyika* (1892)

Hotten, John Camden, *Life and Finding of Dr Livingstone* (1874)

Jackson, Frederick, *Early Days in East Africa* (1930)

Jameson, James S., *The Story of the Rear Column* (1890)

Johnston, H. H., *George Grenfell and the Congo*, 2 vols (1908)

Johnston, H. H., *Livingstone and the Exploration of Central Africa* (1891)

Johnston, H. H., *The River Congo* (1884)

Johnston, H. H., *The Nile Quest* (New York 1903)

Junker, W., *Travels in Africa during the years 1882–1886*, 3 vols (1892)

Keim, Randolph B., *Sheridan's Troopers on the Border* (Philadelphia 1885)

Keltie, J. Scott, *The Story of Emin's Rescue as Told in Stanley's Letters* (Boston 1890)

Kerfyser, E., ed., *Henry M. Stanley* (Brussels 1890)

Kollmann Paul, *The Victoria Nyanza* (1899)

Lenz, Oskar, *Wanderung in Afrika* (Vienna 1895)

Livingstone, David, *Missionary Travels and Researches in South Africa* (1857)

Livingstone, David and Charles, *Narrative of an Expedition to the Zambezi* (NY 1866)

Ludwig, Emil, *Genius and Character* (1927)

Lugard, F. D., *The Rise of our East African Empire*, 2 vols (Edinburgh 1893)

MacGregor, R., *The Rob Roy on the Jordan* (1869)

Martineau, John, *The Life and Correspondence of Sir Bartle Frere*, 2 vols (1895)

Marston, Edward, *After Work* (1904)

Middleton Dorothy, ed., *The Diary of A. J. Mounteney-Jephson* (Cambridge 1969)

New, Charles, *Life. Wanderings and Labours in Eastern Africa* (1873)

Oliver, Roland, ed., *Six Unpublished Letters of H. M. Stanley* (Brussels 1957)

Perham, Margery, ed., *The Diaries of Lord Lugard*, 4 vols (1959–63)

Peters, Carl, *Das Deutsch Ostafrikanische Schutzgebeit* (Leipzig 1895)

Peters, Carl, *Wie Deutsch-Ostafrika Enstandt* (Leipzig 1940)

Reichard, Paul, *Deutsch Ostafrika* (Leipzig 1892)

Reichard, Paul, *Stanley* (Berlin 1897)

Ricklin, L. A., *La Mission Catholique du Zanguebar. Travaux et Voyages de R. P. Horner* (Paris 1880)

Rowlands, Cadwalader, *H. M. Stanley, the Story of his Life* (1872)

Schapera, I., ed., *David Livingstone. Family Letters 1841–1856*, 2 vols (1959)

Schapera, I., ed., *Livingstone's African Journal 1853–56*, 2 vols (1963)

Schapera, I., ed., *Livingstone's Missionary Correspondence 1841–1856* (1961)

Schapera, I., ed., *Livingstone's Private Journals 1851–1853* (1960)

Schweinfurth, Georg, *The Heart of Africa*, 2 vols (New York 1874)

Schweinitz, H. Hermann Graf von, *Deutsch Ost-Afrika in Krieg und Frieden* (Berlin 1894)

Schynse, Père, *A Travers l'Afrique avec Stanley et Emin-Pacha* (Paris 1890)

Schepperson, George, ed., *David Livingstone and Rovuma* (Edinburgh 1965)

Shukry, M. F., ed., *Equatoria under Egyptian Rule. The Unpublished Correspondence of Colonel (later Major-General) C. G. Gordon with Ismail Khedive of Egypt and the Sudan 1874–76* (1953)

Southworth, Alvan S., *Four Thousand Miles of African Travel* (New York 1875)

Speke, John Hanning, *Journal of the Discovery of the Source of the Nile* (1863)

Speke, John Hanning, *What Led to the Discovery of the Source of the Nile* (Edinburgh 1864)

Stanley, Richard and Neame, Alan, eds, *The Exploration Diaries of H. M. Stanley* (1961)

Stevens, Thomas, *Scouting for Stanley in East Africa* (1890)

Thomson, James B., *Joseph Thomson, African Explorer* (1896)

Thomson, Joseph, *To the Central African Lakes and Back*, 2 vols (1881)

Thomson, Joseph, *Through Masailand* (1885)

Wallis, J. P. R., *The Zambezi Expedition of David Livingstone 1858–1863*, 2 vols (1956)

Ward, Gertrude, ed., *Letters of Bishop Tozer* (1902)

Ward, Herbert, *A Voice from the Congo* (1910)

Weeks, John, *Among Congo Cannibals* (1913)

Wilson, C. T. and Felkin, R. W., *Uganda and the Egyptian Sudan*, 2 vols (1882)

Wissmann, Hermann von, *My Second Journey through Equatorial Africa* (1891)

Wissmann, Hermann von, *Unter deutscher Flagge quer durch Afrika von West nach Ost* (Berlin 1891)

Yule, Mary, *Mackay of Uganda* (1890)

Secondary sources: books (articles in learned journals are
cited in the notes)

Abrahams, R. G., *The Peoples of Greater Unyamwezi, Tanzania (Nyamwezi, Sukuma, Sumbwa, Kimbu, Konongo)* (1967)

Abrahams, R. G., *The Political Organisation of Unyamwezi* (1967)

Adler, Alfred, *Superiority and Social Interest* (New York 1973)

Aimot, J. M., *Stanley, le dernier conquistador* (Paris 1951)

Allen, B. M., *Gordon and the Sudan* (1931)

Anstruther, Ian, *I Presume, Stanley's Triumph and Disaster* (1956)

Arango, Jaime Jaramillo, *The Conquest of Malaria* (1950)

Arens, William, *The Man Eating Myth* (1979)

Barnes, J. A., *Politics in a Changing Society. A Political History of the Fort Jameson Ngoni* (1954)

Beachey, R. W., *The Slave Trade of Eastern Africa* (1976)

Beattie, J. H. M., *Bunyoro: An African Kingdom* (1960)

Bennett, Norman R., *Studies in East African History* (Boston 1963)

Bennett, Norman R., *Mirambo of Tanzania* (1971)

Bennett, Norman R., *The Arab State of Zanzibar* (1984)

Bennett, Norman R., *A History of the Arab State of Zanzibar* (1978)

Bennett, Norman R., *Arab versus European* (1986)

Biographie Coloniale Belge, 5 vols (Brussels 1948–58)

Blashford-Snell, John, *In the Steps of Stanley* (1975)

Blohm, Wilhelm, *Die Nyamwezi. Gesellschaft und Weltbild* (Hamburg 1933)

Blohm, Wilhelm, *Die Nyamwezi, Land und Wirtschaft* (Hamburg 1931)

Bösch, Fr., *Les Banyamwezi* (Munster 1930)

Bourgeois, R., *Banyarwanda et Burundi*, 2 vols (Brussels 1957)

Brode, Heinrich, *Tippoo Tib* (1907)

Brom, John L., *Sur les traces de Stanley* (Paris 1958)

Burssens, H., *Les Peuplades de l'Entre Congo-Ubangi* (1958)

Cable, Boyd, *A Hundred Year History of the P & O* (1937)

Cairns, Alan C., *Prelude to Imperialism. British Reactions to Central African Society 1840–1890* (1965)

Carlson, Oliver, *The Man Who Made News* (New York 1942)

Carrington, J. F., *A Comparative Study of some Central African Gong Languages* (Brussels 1949)

Casada, James A., *Dr David Livingstone and Sir Henry Morton Stanley* (1976)

Ceulemans, P., *La question arabe et le Congo 1883–1892* (Brussels 1959)

Chadwick, Owen, *Mackenzie's Grave* (1959)

Claus, Heinrich, *Die Wagogo* (Leipzig 1911)

Clowes, William Laird, *The Royal Navy*, 7 vols (1897–1903)

Clyde, David C., *History of the Medical Services of Tanganyika* (Dar-es-Salaam 1962)

Colbourne, Michael, *Malaria in Africa* (1966)

Colle, Le R. P., *Les Baluba*, 2 vols (Brussels 1913)
Cornet, René J., *Maniema; Le pays des mangeurs d'hommes* (Brussels 1952)
Cory, Hans, *History of the Bukoba District* (Mwanza, n.d.)
Cory, Hans, *Sukuma Law and Custom* (1953)
Coupland, Reginald, *The Exploitation of East Africa 1856–1890* (1939)
Coupland, Reginald, *Livingstone's Last Journey* (1945)
Cunningham, J. F., *Uganda and its Peoples* (1905)
Dahl, Edmund, *Nyamwezi-Wurterbuch* (Hamburg 1915)
Dakin, Douglas, *The Unification of Greece 1770–1923* (1972)
Dale, Ivan R. and Greenway, P. J., *Kenya Trees and Shrubs* (Nairobi 1961)
Debenham, Frank, *The Way to Ilala* (1955)
Delhaise, Commandant, *Les Warega* (Brussels 1909)
Denis, P., *Histoire des Mangbetu et des Matihaga jusqu'à l'arrivée des Belges* (Tervuren 1970)
Driault, Edouard and Lheritier, Michel, *Histoire Diplomatique de la Grèce de 1821 à nos jours* (Paris 1925)
Dunbar, A. R., *A History of Bunyoro Kitara* (Nairobi 1965)
Fallers, Lloyd A., *Bantu Bureaucracy* (Cambridge 1956)
Fallers, Lloyd A., *The King's Men* (1964)
Fallers, Margaret Chase, *The Eastern Lacustrine Bantu (Ganda and Soga)* (1960)
Farwell, Byron, *The Man Who Presumed. A Biography of Henry M. Stanley* (1957)
Faupel, J. F., *African Holocaust* (New York 1962)
Fenner, Douglas, *James Gordon Bennett and the New York Herald* (1986)
Ford, John, *The Role of Trypanosomiasis in African Ecology: A Study of the Tsetse Fly Problem* (Oxford 1971)
Forrest, D. W., *Francis Galton, the Life and Work of a Victorian Genius* (1974)
Fouquer, R. P., *Mirambo* (Paris 1966)
Fraser, A. Z., *Livingstone and Newstead* (1913)
Freud, Sigmund, *Standard Edition of the Complete Psychological Works of*, ed. James Strachey (1953–74)
Galbraith, J. S., *Mackinnon and East Africa, 1878–1895* (Cambridge 1972)
Hall, Richard, *Stanley. An Adventurer Explored* (1974)
Hansenn, Holger Bernt, *Mission, Church and State in a Colonial Setting: Uganda 1890–1925* (New York 1984)
Hartwig, G. W. and Paterson, K. D., *Disease in African History: an Introductory Survey and Case Studies* (Durham, N.C. 1978)
Hellinga, Gerben, *Henry Morton Stanley. Een Individualpsychologische Interpretatie* (1978)
Helly, Dorothy O., *Livingstone's Legacy* (Athens, Ohio, 1987)
Hird, Frank, *H. M. Stanley. The Authorised Life* (1935)
Jackson, Peggy Hervey, *Meteor Out of Africa* (1962)
James, William, *The Varieties of Religious Experience* (1935)
Jeal, Tim, *Livingstone* (1973)

Jones, Lucy, M. & Ivor Wynne, *H. M. Stanley and Wales* (St Asaph 1972)

Kabeya, John B., *Ntembi Mirambo* (Dar es Salaam 1966)

Karp, Mark, ed., *African Dimensions: Essays in Honor of William O. Brown* (Boston 1975)

Katoke, Israel K., *The Karagwe Kingdom* (Nairobi 1975)

Lamar, Howard and Thompson, Leonard, *The Frontier in History: North America and Southern Africa compared* (Yale 1981)

Lewis, David Levering, *The Race to Fashoda* (1988)

Listowel, Judith, *The Other Livingstone* (Lewes 1974)

Louis, William Roger, *Ruanda-Urundi* (Oxford 1963)

Luwel, Marcel, *Stanley* (Brussels 1959)

Maes, J. and Boone, O., *Les Peuplades du Congo Belge* (Brussels 1935)

Malcolm, D. W., *Sukumaland* (1953)

Meyer, Bernard C., *Joseph Conrad. A Psychoanalytic Biography* (Princeton 1967)

Meyer, Hans, *Die Barundi* (Leipzig 1916)

Moorehead, Alan, *The White Nile* (1964)

Morris, H. F., *A History of Ankole* (Nairobi 1962)

Nigmann, E., *Die Wahehe* (Berlin 1908)

Northcott, Cecil, *Robert Moffat: Pioneer in Africa 1817–1870* (1961)

Nyakatura, J. W., *Abakamaba Bunyoro-Kitara* (St Justin PQ, Canada 1947)

Oliver, Roland, *The Missionary Factor in East Africa* (1965)

Pages, R. P., *Un royaume hamite au centre de l'Afrique* (Brussels 1933)

Patterson, Clara Burdett, *Angela Burdett-Coutts and the Victorians* (1953)

Ransford, Oliver, *David Livingstone. The Dark Interior* (1978)

Ransford, Oliver, *Let the Sickness Cease* (1983)

Reefe, Thomas O., *The Rainbow and the Kings: A History of the Luba Empire to 1891* (Berkeley 1981)

Renault, François, *Tippo Tip: un potentat arabe en Afrique centrale aux XIXe siècle* (Paris 1987)

Robertson, Charles L., *The International Herald Tribune. The First Hundred Years* (New York 1987)

Roelens, V., *Notre Vieux Congo 1891–1917*, 2 vols (Namur 1948)

Roscoe, John, *The Baganda* (1911)

Roscoe, John, *The Bagesu* (Cambridge 1924)

Rusch, Walter, *Klasser und Staat in Buganda von der Kolonialzeit* (Berlin 1975)

Russell, Paul F., *Man's Mastery of Malaria* (1955)

Seitz, Don C., *The James Gordon Bennetts* (Indianapolis 1928)

Shorter, Aylward, *Chiefship in Western Tanzania: A Political History of the Kimbu* (Oxford 1972)

Simpson, Donald, *Dark Companions* (1975)

Smith, Edwin W., *Great Lion of Bechuanaland: the life and times of Roger Price, missionary* (1957)

Taylor, Brian K., *The Western Lacustrine Bantu* (1962)

Taylor, John, *The Growth of the Church in Buganda* (1958)

Thier, de, F. M., *Singhitini, la Stanleyville Musulmane* (Brussels 1963)

Vansina, Jan, *The Tio Kingdom of the Middle Congo 1880–1892* (1973)

Vansina, Jan, *Kingdoms of the Savanna* (Madison 1966)

Vansina, Jan, *Introduction à l'Ethnographie du Congo* (Brussels 1966)

Verhulpen, Edmund, *Baluba et Balubaises du Katanga* (Brussels 1936)

Wagner, Gunter, *The Bantu of North Kavirondo*, 2 vols (1949–56)

Wassermann, Jakob, *Bula Matari* (1932)

Williams, John G., *A Field Guide to the Birds of East and Central Africa* (1963)

Wilson, James Harrison, *The Life of Charles A. Dana* (New York 1907)

Wright, Brooks, *Interpreter of Buddhism to the West, Sir Edwin Arnold* (New York 1957)

Young, Crawford, *Politics in the Congo. Decolonisation and Independence* (Princeton 1965)

· INDEX ·

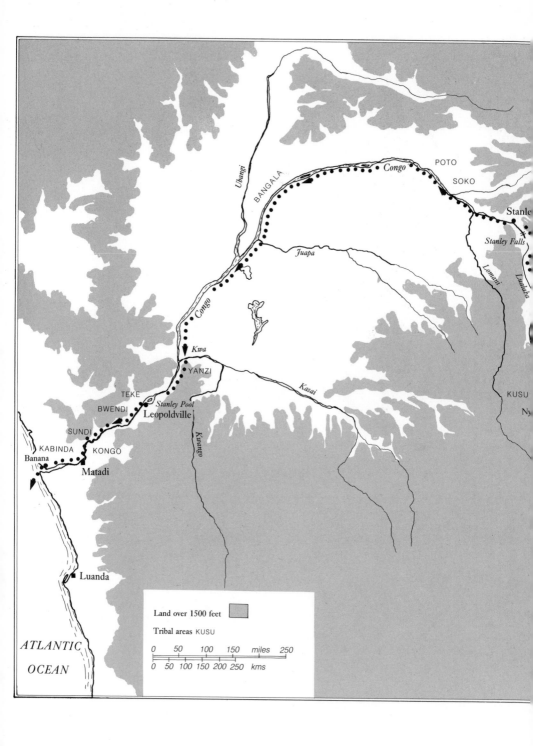

ATLANTIC
OCEAN

Land over 1500 feet
Tribal areas KUSU

0   50   100   150   miles   250
0   50 100 150 200 250   kms

Banana
KABINDA
KONGO
Matadi
SUNDI
BWENDI
TEKE
Stanley Pool
Leopoldville
YANZI
Kwa
Congo
Kwango
Kasai
KUSU
Ny
Juapa
Ubangi
BANGALA
Congo
POTO
SOKO
Stanle
Stanley Falls
Lomani
Lualaba
Luanda